High Performance Computing

High Performance Computing

Second Edition

Kevin Dowd & Charles R. Severance

O'REILLY™

Cambridge · Köln · Paris · Sebastopol · Tokyo

High Performance Computing, Second Edition
by Kevin Dowd and Charles R. Severance

Copyright © 1998, 1993 O'Reilly & Associates, Inc. All rights reserved.
Printed in the United States of America.

Published by O'Reilly & Associates, Inc., 101 Morris Street, Sebastopol, CA 95472.

Editor: Mike Loukides
Update Editor: Gigi Estabrook
Production Editor: Clairemarie Fisher O'Leary

Printing History:

June 1993:	First Edition.
November 1993:	Minor corrections.
July 1998:	Second Edition.

This book is printed on acid-free paper with 85% recycled content, 15% post-consumer waste. O'Reilly & Associates is committed to using paper with the highest recycled content available consistent with high quality.

ISBN: 1-56592-312-X

Table of Contents

Preface

It's hard to keep track of an industry that changes as quickly as ours. The super-computer market is being dissolved from below by a handful of microprocessor families. The processors in the typical home computer are faster than the super-computers of ten years ago. Parallel processing is increasingly coming to our inex-pensive computers. As our appetite for graphics and multimedia-oriented programs continues to increase, more and more computing is becoming "high performance computing."

On the other end of the spectrum, the fastest computers in the world are collections of hundreds or thousands of processing elements and are generally more difficult to program.

Where does the performance come from? Some of it comes from increased clock rates. But more significantly, microprocessor architectures are borrowing and innovating with techniques formerly unique to supercomputers and large mainframes. They can execute four or more instructions at a time and are being combined to form very powerful multiprocessors. A lot of this performance is available just for moving your code to a new machine. Sometimes though, these processors can be fickle performers and require your help.

Knowing how to judge the marketplace may be even more important than understanding how the new processors work. If you are faced with the task of interpreting benchmarks to support a purchase decision, it's good to feel confident about them. Industry benchmarks measure different things, some of which may apply to you and some of which may not. If you decide to run your own benchmarks, these will be your best barometer, provided that you administer them with care.

You can also tune your home-grown applications to squeeze more performance from the hardware you already own. But just as you can't tell what string to tune by banging all of a piano's keys at once, you can't tune a program based on a single performance measure. You need a profile that tells you how individual parts of your program behave. This will tell you where to focus your tuning efforts. Different flavors of applications exhibit characteristic execution profiles, revealing much about what can be done. For instance, simple source code transformations can make a big difference in numerically intensive applications. Ordering data access patterns or object files in the load module can ease troublesome cache behavior, and structuring critical branches correctly can lead to big performance gains.

Looking to the future, some applications will be good candidates for parallel computers. However, to run an application on a parallel machine, or to write code for a parallel machine, you need to think about how the program can be split into pieces. For some applications, parallel computers are a natural, but others will benefit very little.

Who Should Buy This Book?

This book is written for people who are interested in computer performance or who need to understand it for their job. Those faced with purchase decisions will find clear explanations of industry benchmarks and the benchmark process, as well as a few pointers on what to watch for. People writing or tuning code will learn techniques for getting the best performance from their workstations, plus an appreciation for how their programs play to the compiler and the hardware. And, for those who enjoy tracking computer-performance developments, this book can serve as a reference to answer some of the how and why questions as the statistics come in. This book could even be used by home computer users to better understand their own high performance personal computers.

What's in This Book

The book consists of 16 chapters and five appendixes, divided into six parts.

Part I, *Modern Computer Architecture*, describes the underlying hardware you will encounter in high performance computing.

Chapter 1, *What Is High Performance Computing?*, prepares the stage for the rest of the book.

Chapter 2, *High Performance Microprocessors*, briefly describes developments in computer architecture that led to the design of today's high performance processors and explains how they work.

Chapter 3, *Memory*, explains how computer memory systems are organized and why a good memory system is crucial for performance.

Chapter 4, *Floating-Point Numbers*, gives an overview of the field of numerical analysis and introduces the issues you must face when your results need to be fast *and* accurate.

Part II, *Programming and Tuning Software*, is a hands-on guide to the software you will encounter in your quest for high performance. We cover compilation, profiling, timing, and tuning, with some time out to consider what the compiler is looking for from the programmer.

Chapter 5, *What a Compiler Does*, gives a tour of an optimizing compiler and describes the techniques employed by most compilers.

Chapter 6, *Timing and Profiling*, tells you how you can measure the performance of a program, subroutine, or loop. This is important if you will be benchmarking or tuning your code.

Chapter 7, *Eliminating Clutter*, discusses optimization techniques for eliminating those parts of code that add to runtime but don't contribute to the answer.

Chapter 8, *Loop Optimizations*, explains how you can examine and improve the performance of the loops that generally take most of the time in a high performance application. This chapter also describes techniques for improving the way programs make use of the memory system.

Part III, *Shared-Memory Parallel Processors*, focuses on programming for symmetric parallel processors. We cover the fundamentals of parallelism and its effects on the compiler, parallel processing hardware, and programming techniques for these systems.

Chapter 9, *Understanding Parallelism*, takes a break from the hands-on to explain what parallelism is. This chapter is good background for the tuning tips in the following chapters, but it can also be read by itself or as a follow-up to Chapter 5.

Chapter 10, *Shared-Memory Multiprocessors*, describes shared-memory computers, such as the multiprocessing workstations being offered by several vendors. These are programmed differently from distributed-memory machines. Multiprocessing and multithreaded applications are discussed in this chapter.

Chapter 11, *Programming Shared-Memory Multiprocessors*, describes the techniques for using automatic parallelizing compilers and for parallelizing your applications by hand on these shared-memory multiprocessors.

Part IV, *Scalable Parallel Processing*, covers topics you will encounter when you begin to work with large-scale parallel processing systems.

Chapter 12, *Large-Scale Parallel Computing*, introduces the hardware architectures and concepts you will need to use large-scale parallel processors. It includes a survey of existing processor interconnects and scalable parallel processor architectures.

Chapter 13, *Language Support for Performance*, covers two data-parallel languages used on large-scale parallel processors. These languages are FORTRAN-90 and High Performance FORTRAN. An easily understandable heat-flow problem is used to provide complete working example programs in both languages.

Chapter 14, *Message Passing Environments*, covers the parallel virtual machine (PVM) and message-passing interface (MPI) environments. The heat-flow example is continued into this chapter with complete working example codes. This chapter also covers different models of scalable computing.

Part V, *Benchmarking*, describes published benchmarks and discusses benchmarking strategies when you are running your own.

Chapter 15, *Using Published Benchmarks*, describes the meaning of MIPs, megaflops, SPECMarks, LINPACK, and other commonly quoted measures of performance. This chapter can be read independently of the others.

Chapter 16, *Running Your Own Benchmarks*, discusses benchmarking strategies at a high level. This chapter is a good guide when you are planning a new system acquisition and want to be sure your benchmarks are comprehensive.

Part VI, *Appendixes*, offers additional information on architecture and languages as they relate to performance issues.

Appendix A, *Processor Architectures*, surveys a number of existing microprocessor designs and relates them to the concepts discussed in Chapter 2.

Appendix B, *Looking at Assembly Language*, looks at the effect of instruction set design and compiler technology on the ultimate machine language used on various architectures.

Appendix C, *Future Trends: Intel IA-64*, gives a very brief overview of the Intel IA-64 architecture. Not all of the details of this architecture are available at the time of the printing of this book, but this chapter gives some insight into how this processor will operate.

Appendix D, *How FORTRAN Manages Threads at Runtime*, looks at the FORTRAN runtime environment on a parallel processing system and examines the effect of having too many threads for the available processing resources.

Appendix E, *Memory Performance*, examines the performance of a simple two-dimensional array application on several architectures.

Most chapters are followed by a short set of exercises. Unlike the exercises in most engineering texts, these are mostly thought experiments, without well-defined answers. They are designed to get you thinking about the hardware on your desk. Most of the answers depend on the particular hardware you have, and will certainly change over time. We've written up some answers for a few common architectures; they are available via anonymous FTP. The example programs used throughout the book are also available via anonymous FTP.

Some related subjects fall outside the scope of this book, particularly algorithms, graphics, and I/O performance. However, this book gives you a good foundation for understanding these topics, as it will help you recognize the potential for performance in an algorithm or method.

Changes in the Second Edition

Certainly there have been many changes in this industry since the first edition of the book was printed. There has been a distinct shift from special purpose computers to more general purpose computers. The overall performance of microprocessors has increased so dramatically that "high performance computing" issues are important even in our desktop workstations.

To address these dramatic shifts in the industry, numerous areas have been brought up to date in this edition, including: processor architecture, memory architecture, symmetric multiprocessing, and scalable parallel processing architectures.

A number of new topics have been added to the book, including: floating-point numbers, High Performance Fortran (HPF), Parallel Virtual Machine (PVM), and Message Passing Interface (MPI).

When the first edition was published, FORTRAN-77 was the dominant language for high performance computing. While FORTRAN-77 is still the primary language for scientific computing, other languages are emerging in the high performance area including C, HPF, and FORTRAN-90. New high performance applications are generally coded in some combination of FORTRAN and C. All of the languages are featured in the examples throughout the book. We tend to use the best language for each particular example. For example, most of the loop examples are in FORTRAN while some of the operating system and communications examples are written in C. The question as to which language is better is visited several times throughout the book.

Conventions Used in This Book

The following conventions are used in this book:

`Constant Width`

>   is used for source code samples and for quotations from source code within the text, including variable and function names. Constant width is also used for output printed by a computer and for the contents of files.

`Constant Bold`

>   is used for commands typed verbatim by the user.

Italic

>   is used for command names, directory names, and filenames. It is also used for new terms when they are defined.

Bold

>   is used for vectors (in the mathematical sense) and for command options. I admit that the difference between a mathematical vector and an array in a program is miniscule.

Acknowledgments

First Edition

The key to writing is learning to organize thoughts, to tell a story, to see things the way others see them. I'd like to thank Mike Loukides, my editor, for helping me understand this. Mike has an unassuming manner that conceals a great talent for finding the simple truth in things and stating it plainly.

I'd also like to thank the staff at O'Reilly & Associates, particularly Leslie Chalmers, Stephen Spainhour, Clairemarie Fisher O'Leary, Chris Reilley, Edie Freedman, Ellie Cutler, Donna Woonteiler, Linda Walsh, Tim O'Reilly, and everyone whose behind-the-scenes efforts went into the finished product. A personal thanks to Leslie for copyediting the text several times, preening and polishing my English. Chris quickly and professionally created enough illustrations for a dozen books this size.

Thanks also to the reviewers, Philip Koopman Jr., Keith Bierman, Harold Dolan, Marshall Presser, Mike Frisch, Darryl Parsley, Andy Oram, and Eric Pearce for keeping me honest.

Thanks to my parents, Don and Carol, for making me what I am. And thanks to my wife Paula for making this possible, and for the time we sacrificed getting here.

Kevin Dowd

Second Edition

I would first like to thank Kevin Dowd for writing such a clear and direct book on my favorite topic. I also thank him for letting me take my own paintbrush in hand and try to improve on his work of art. I hope the resulting work is something that the reader will find useful.

I have many people to thank for their assistance in developing this book. The people who helped in the technical content of this book include: Richard Enbody, Bernie Weinberg, Barb Birchler, Mark Brehob, Katrina Brehob, William Kahan, Paul Petersen, Jose Alvarez, Colin Evans, Kelvin Yue, Bill Moore, Sherri Moore, Bill Rosenkrans, Greg Astfalk, John Mashey, John McCalpin, Ron Averill, Ron Sass, and Travis Doom.

I would like to thank the ever-efficient and helpful staff at O'Reilly & Associates, including Gigi Estabrook, Clairemarie Fisher O'Leary, Robert Romano, Lenny Muellner, and Mike Loukides.

And I certainly need to thank my parents Marcia and Russ for setting high goals and expectations. And thanks to my wife Teresa and children Brent and Amanda for their patience as I arrived home very late many times because of "the book."

I would like to thank Lewis Greenberg, Tony Wojcik, Anil Jain, and Ted Bickart for allowing me the time, opportunity, travel, and resources to spend the last 10 years playing with really fast computers and then write a book about it.

Chuck Severance

We'd Like to Hear from You

We have tested and verified all of the information in this book to the best of our ability, but you may find that features have changed (or even that we have made mistakes!). Please let us know about any errors you find, as well as your suggestions for future editions, by writing:

O'Reilly & Associates, Inc.
101 Morris Street
Sebastopol, CA 95472
1-800-998-9938 (in the U.S. or Canada)
1-707-829-0515 (international/local)
1-707-829-0104 (fax)

You can also send us messages electronically. To be put on the mailing list or request a catalog, send email to:

nuts@oreilly.com

To ask technical questions or comment on the book, send email to:

bookquestions@oreilly.com

I

Modern Computer Architectures

1

What Is High Performance Computing?

Why Worry About Performance?

Over the last decade, the definition of what is called *high performance computing* has changed dramatically. In 1988, an article appeared in the *Wall Street Journal* titled "Attack of the Killer Micros" that described how computing systems made up of many small inexpensive processors would soon make large supercomputers obsolete. At that time, a "personal computer" costing $3000 could perform 0.25 million floating-point operations per second, a "workstation" costing $20,000 could perform 3 million floating-point operations, and a supercomputer costing $3 million could perform 100 million floating-point operations per second. Therefore, why couldn't we simply connect 400 personal computers together to achieve the same performance of a supercomputer for $1.2 million?

This vision has come true in some ways, but not in the way the original proponents of the "killer micro" theory envisioned. Instead, the microprocessor performance has relentlessly gained on the supercomputer performance. This has occurred for two reasons. First, there was much more technology "headroom" for improving performance in the personal computer area, whereas the supercomputers of the late 1980s were pushing the performance envelope. Also, once the supercomputer companies broke through some technical barrier, the microprocessor companies could quickly adopt the successful elements of the supercomputer designs a few short years later. The second and perhaps more important factor was the emergence of a thriving personal and business computer market with ever-increasing performance demands. Computer usage such as 3D graphics, graphical user interfaces, multimedia, and games were the driving factors in this market. With such a large market, available research dollars poured into developing inexpensive high performance processors for the home market. The result of this trend toward faster smaller computers is directly evident as former supercomputer manufacturers are being purchased by workstation companies (Silicon Graphics purchased Cray, and Hewlett-Packard purchased Convex in 1996).

As a result nearly every person with computer access has some "high performance" processing. As the peak speeds of these new personal computers increase, these computers encounter all the performance challenges typically found on supercomputers.

While not all users of personal workstations need to know the intimate details of high performance computing, those who program these systems for maximum performance will benefit from an understanding of the strengths and weaknesses of these newest high performance systems.

Scope of High Performance Computing

High performance computing runs a broad range of systems, from our desktop computers through large parallel processing systems. Because most high performance systems are based on *reduced instruction set computer* (RISC) processors, many techniques learned on one type of system transfer to the other systems.

High performance RISC processors are designed to be easily inserted into a multiple-processor system with 2 to 64 CPUs accessing a single memory using *symmetric multi processing* (SMP). Programming multiple processors to solve a single problem adds its own set of additional challenges for the programmer. The programmer must be aware of how multiple processors operate together, and how work can be efficiently divided among those processors.

Even though each processor is very powerful, and small numbers of processors can be put into a single enclosure, often there will be applications that are so large they need to span multiple enclosures. In order to cooperate to solve the larger application, these enclosures are linked with a high-speed network to function as a *network of workstations* (NOW). A NOW can be used individually through a batch queuing system or can be used as a large multicomputer using a message passing tool such as *parallel virtual machine* (PVM) or *message-passing interface* (MPI).

For the largest problems with more data interactions and those users with compute budgets in the millions of dollars, there is still the top end of the high performance computing spectrum, the scalable parallel processing systems with hundreds to thousands of processors. These systems come in two flavors. One type is programmed using *message passing*. Instead of using a standard local area network, these systems are connected using a proprietary, scalable, high-bandwidth, low-latency interconnect (how is that for marketing speak?). Because of the high performance interconnect, these systems can scale to the thousands of processors while keeping the time spent (wasted) performing overhead communications to a minimum.

The second type of large parallel processing system is the *scalable non-uniform memory access* (NUMA) systems. These systems also use a high performance interconnect to connect the processors, but instead of exchanging messages, these systems use the interconnect to implement a distributed shared memory that can be accessed from any processor using a load/store paradigm. This is similar to programming SMP systems except that some areas of memory have slower access than others.

Studying High Performance Computing

The study of high performance computing is an excellent chance to revisit computer architecture. Once we set out on the quest to wring the last bit of performance from our computer systems, we become more motivated to fully understand the aspects of computer architecture that have a direct impact on the system's performance.

Throughout all of computer history, salespeople have told us that their compiler will solve all of our problems, and that the compiler writers can get the absolute best performance from their hardware. This claim has never been, and probably never will be, completely true. The ability of the compiler to deliver the peak performance available in the hardware improves with each succeeding generation of hardware and software. However, as we move up the hierarchy of high performance computing architectures we can depend on the compiler less and less, and programmers must take responsibility for the performance of their code.

In the single processor and SMP systems with few CPUs, one of our goals as programmers should be to stay out of the way of the compiler. Often constructs used to improve performance on a particular architecture limit our ability to achieve performance on another architecture. Further, these "brilliant" (read obtuse) hand optimizations often confuse a compiler, limiting its ability to automatically transform our code to take advantage of the particular strengths of the computer architecture.

As programmers, it is important to know how the compiler works so we can know when to help it out and when to leave it alone. We also must be aware that as compilers improve (never as much as salespeople claim) it's best to leave more and more to the compiler.

As we move up the hierarchy of high performance computers, we need to learn new techniques to map our programs onto these architectures, including language extensions, library calls, and compiler directives. As we use these features, our programs become less portable. Also, using these higher-level constructs, we must not make modifications that result in poor performance on the individual RISC microprocessors that often make up the parallel processing system.

Measuring Performance

When a computer is being purchased for computationally intensive applications, it is important to determine how well the system will actually perform this function. One way to choose among a set of competing systems is to have each vendor loan you a system for a period of time to test your applications. At the end of the evaluation period, you could send back the systems that did not make the grade and pay for your favorite system. Unfortunately, most vendors won't lend you a system for such an extended period of time unless there is some assurance you will eventually purchase the system.

More often we evaluate the system's potential performance using *benchmarks*. There are industry benchmarks and your own locally developed benchmarks. Both types of benchmarks require some careful thought and planning for them to be an effective tool in determining the best system for your application.

The Next Step

Quite aside from economics, computer performance is a fascinating and challenging subject. Computer architecture is interesting in its own right and a topic that any computer professional should be comfortable with. Getting the last bit of performance out of an important application can be a stimulating exercise, in addition to an economic necessity. There are probably a few people who simply enjoy matching wits with a clever computer architecture.

What do you need to get into the game?

- A basic understanding of modern computer architecture. You don't need an advanced degree in computer engineering, but you do need to understand the basic terminology.

- A basic understanding of benchmarking, or performance measurement, so you can quantify your own successes and failures and use that information to improve the performance of your application.

This book is intended to be an easily understood introduction and overview of high performance computing. It is an interesting field, and one that will become more important as we make even greater demands on our most common personal computers. In the high performance computer field, there is always a tradeoff between the single CPU performance and the performance of a multiple processor system. Multiple processor systems are generally more expensive and difficult to program (unless you have this book).

Some people claim we eventually will have single CPUs so fast we won't need to understand any type of advanced architectures that require some skill to program.

So far in this field of computing, even as performance of a single inexpensive microprocessor has increased over a thousandfold, there seems to be no less interest in lashing a thousand of these processors together to get a millionfold increase in power. The cheaper the building blocks of high performance computing become, the greater the benefit for using many processors. If at some point in the future, we have a single processor that is faster than any of the 512-processor scalable systems of today, think how much we could do when we connect 512 of those new processors together in a single system.

That's what this book is all about. If you're interested, read on.

2

High Performance
Microprocessors

It has been said that history is rewritten by the victors. It is clear that high performance RISC-based microprocessors are defining the current history of high performance computing. We begin our study with the basic building blocks of modern high performance computing: the high performance RISC microprocessors.

A *complex instruction set computer* (CISC) instruction set is made up of powerful primitives, close in functionality to the primitives of high-level languages like C or FORTRAN. It captures the sense of "don't do in software what you can do in hardware." RISC, on the other hand, emphasizes low-level primitives, far below the complexity of a high-level language. You can compute anything you want using either approach, though it will probably take more machine instructions if you're using RISC. The important difference is that with RISC you can trade instruction-set complexity for speed.

To be fair, RISC isn't really all that new. There were some important early machines that pioneered RISC philosophies, such as the CDC 6600 (1964) and the IBM 801 project (1975). It was in the mid-1980s, however, that RISC machines first posed a direct challenge to the CISC installed base. Heated debate broke out— RISC versus CISC—and even lingers today, though it is clear that the RISC* approach is in greatest favor; late-generation CISC machines are looking more

---

* One of the most interesting remaining topics is the definition of "RISC." Don't be fooled into thinking there is one definition of RISC. The best I have heard so far is from John Mashey: "RISC is a label most commonly used for a set of instruction set architecture characteristics chosen to ease the use of aggressive implementation techniques found in high performance processors (regardless of RISC, CISC, or irrelevant)."

RISC-like, and some very old families of CISC, such as the DEC VAX, are being retired.

This chapter is about CISC and RISC instruction set architectures and the differences between them. We also describe newer processors that can execute more than one instruction at a time and can execute instructions out of order.

Why CISC?

You might ask, "If RISC is faster, why did people bother with CISC designs in the first place?" The short answer is that in the beginning, CISC *was* the right way to go; RISC wasn't always both feasible and affordable. Every kind of design incorporates trade-offs, and over time, the best systems will make them differently. In the past, the design variables favored CISC.

Space and Time

To start, we'll ask you how well you know the assembly language for your workstation. The answer is probably that you haven't even seen it. Why bother? Compilers and development tools are very good, and if you have a problem, you can debug it at the source level. However, 30 years ago, "respectable" programmers understood the machine's instruction set. High-level language compilers were commonly available, but they didn't generate the fastest code, and they weren't terribly thrifty with memory. When programming, you needed to save both space and time, which meant you knew how to program in assembly language. Accordingly, you could develop an opinion about the machine's instruction set. A good instruction set was both easy to use and powerful. In many ways these qualities were the same: "powerful" instructions accomplished a lot, and saved the programmer from specifying many little steps—which, in turn, made them easy to use. But they had other, less apparent (though perhaps more important) features as well: powerful instructions saved memory and time.

Back then, computers had very little storage by today's standards. An instruction that could roll all the steps of a complex operation, such as a do-loop, into single opcode* was a plus, because memory was precious. To put some stakes in the ground, consider the last vacuum-tube computer that IBM built, the model 704 (1956). It had hardware floating-point, including a division operation, index registers, and instructions that could operate directly on memory locations. For instance, you could add two numbers together and store the result back into memory with a single command. The Philco 2000, an early transistorized machine (1959), had an operation that could repeat a sequence of instructions until the

---

* Opcode = operation code = instruction.

contents of a counter was decremented to zero—very much like a do-loop. These were complex operations, even by today's standards. However, both machines had a limited amount of memory—32-K words. The less memory your program took up, the more you had available for data, and the less likely that you would have to resort to overlaying portions of the program on top of one another.

Complex instructions saved time, too. Almost every large computer following the IBM 704 had a memory system that was slower than its central processing unit (CPU). When a single instruction can perform several operations, the overall number of instructions retrieved from memory can be reduced. Minimizing the number of instructions was particularly important because, with few exceptions, the machines of the late 1950s were very sequential; not until the current instruction was completed did the computer initiate the process of going out to memory to get the next instruction.* By contrast, modern machines form something of a bucket brigade—passing instructions in from memory and figuring out what they do on the way—so there are fewer gaps in processing.

If the designers of early machines had had very fast and abundant instruction memory, sophisticated compilers, and the wherewithal to build the instruction "bucket brigade"—cheaply—they might have chosen to create machines with simple instruction sets. At the time, however, technological choices indicated that instructions should be powerful and thrifty with memory.

Beliefs About Complex Instruction Sets

So, given that the lot was cast in favor of complex instruction sets, computer architects had license to experiment with matching them to the intended purposes of the machines. For instance, the do-loop instruction on the Philco 2000 looked like a good companion for procedural languages like FORTRAN. Machine designers assumed that compiler writers could generate object programs using these powerful machine instructions, or possibly that the compiler could be eliminated, and that the machine could execute source code directly in hardware.

You can imagine how these ideas set the tone for product marketing. Up until the early 1980s, it was common practice to equate a bigger instruction set with a more powerful computer. When clock speeds were increasing by multiples, no increase in instruction set complexity could fetter a new model of computer enough so that there wasn't still a tremendous net increase in speed. CISC machines kept getting faster, in spite of the increased operation complexity.

---

* In 1955, IBM began constructing a machine known as *Stretch*. It was the first computer to process several instructions at a time in stages, so that they streamed in, rather than being fetched in a piecemeal fashion. The goal was to make it 25 times faster than the then brand-new IBM 704. It was six years before the first Stretch was delivered to Los Alamos National Laboratory. It was indeed faster, but it was expensive to build. Eight were sold for a loss of $20 million.

As it turned out, assembly language programmers used the complicated machine instructions, but compilers generally did not. It was difficult enough to get a compiler to recognize when a complicated instruction could be used, but the real problem was one of optimizations: verbatim translation of source constructs isn't very efficient. An optimizing compiler works by simplifying and eliminating redundant computations. After a pass through an optimizing compiler, opportunities to use the complicated instructions tend to disappear.

Fundamentals of RISC

A RISC machine could have been built in 1960. (In fact, Seymour Cray built one in 1964—the CDC 6600.) However, given the same costs of components, technical barriers, and even expectations for how computers would be used, you would probably still have chosen a CISC design—even with the benefit of hindsight.

The exact inspiration that led to developing high performance RISC microprocessors in the 1980s is a subject of some debate. Regardless of the motivation of the RISC designers, there were several obvious pressures that affected the development of RISC:

- The number of transistors that could fit on a single chip was increasing. It was clear that one would eventually be able to fit all the components from a processor board onto a single chip.

- Techniques such as pipelining were being explored to improve performance. Variable-length instructions and variable-length instruction execution times (due to varying numbers of microcode steps) made implementing pipelines more difficult.

- As compilers improved, they found that well-optimized sequences of streamlined instructions often outperformed the equivalent complicated multi-cycle instructions. (See Appendix A, *Processor Architectures*, and Appendix B, *Looking at Assembly Language*.)

The RISC designers sought to create a high performance single-chip processor with a fast clock rate. When a CPU can fit on a single chip, its cost is decreased, its reliability is increased, and its clock speed can be increased. While not all RISC processors are single-chip implementation, most use a single chip.

To accomplish this task, it was necessary to discard the existing CISC instruction sets and develop a new minimal instruction set that could fit on a single chip. Hence the term *reduced instruction set computer*. In a sense reducing the instruction set was not an "end" but a means to an end.

For the first generation of RISC chips, the restrictions on the number of components that could be manufactured on a single chip were severe, forcing the designers to leave out hardware support for some instructions. The earliest RISC processors had no floating-point support in hardware, and some did not even support integer multiply in hardware. However, these instructions could be implemented using software routines that combined other instructions (a microcode of sorts).

These earliest RISC processors (most severely reduced) were not overwhelming successes for four reasons:

- It took time for compilers, operating systems, and user software to be retuned to take advantage of the new processors.

- If an application depended on the performance of one of the software-implemented instructions, its performance suffered dramatically.

- Because RISC instructions were simpler, more instructions were needed to accomplish the task.

- Because all the RISC instructions were 32 bits long, and commonly used CISC instructions were as short as 8 bits, RISC program executables were often larger.

As a result of these last two issues, a RISC program may have to fetch more memory for its instructions than a CISC program. This increased appetite for instructions actually clogged the memory bottleneck until sufficient caches were added to the RISC processors. In some sense, you could view the caches on RISC processors as the microcode store in a CISC processor. Both reduced the overall appetite for instructions that were loaded from memory.

While the RISC processor designers worked out these issues and the manufacturing capability improved, there was a battle between the existing (now called CISC) processors and the new RISC (not yet successful) processors. The CISC processor designers had mature designs and well-tuned popular software. They also kept adding performance tricks to their systems. By the time Motorola had evolved from the MC68000 in 1982 that was a CISC processor to the MC68040 in 1989, they referred to the MC68040 as a RISC processor.*

However, the RISC processors eventually became successful. As the amount of logic available on a single chip increased, floating-point operations were added back onto the chip. Some of the additional logic was used to add on-chip cache to solve some of the memory bottleneck problems due to the larger appetite for instruction memory. These and other changes moved the RISC architectures from the defensive to the offensive.

---

* And they did it without ever taking out a single instruction!

RISC processors quickly became known for their affordable high-speed floating-point capability compared to CISC processors.* This excellent performance on scientific and engineering applications effectively created a new type of computer system, the workstation. Workstations were more expensive than personal computers but their cost was sufficiently low that workstations were heavily used in the CAD, graphics, and design areas. The emerging workstation market effectively created three new computer companies in Apollo, Sun Microsystems, and Silicon Graphics.

Some of the existing companies have created competitive RISC processors in addition to their CISC designs. IBM developed its RS-6000 (RIOS) processor, which had excellent floating-point performance. The Alpha from DEC has excellent performance in a number of computing benchmarks. Hewlett-Packard has developed the PA-RISC series of processors with excellent performance. Motorola and IBM have teamed to develop the PowerPC series of RISC processors that are used in IBM and Apple systems.

By the end of the RISC revolution, the performance of RISC processors was so impressive that single and multiprocessor RISC-based server systems quickly took over the minicomputer market and are currently encroaching on the traditional mainframe market.

Characterizing RISC

RISC is more of a design philosophy than a set of goals. Of course every RISC processor has its own personality. However, there are a number of features commonly found in machines people consider to be RISC:

- Instruction pipelining
- Pipelining floating-point execution
- Uniform instruction length
- Delayed branching
- Load/store architecture
- Simple addressing modes

This list highlights the differences between RISC and CISC processors. Naturally, the two types of instruction-set architectures have much in common; each uses registers, memory, etc. And many of these techniques are used in CISC machines too, such as caches and instruction pipelines. It is the fundamental differences that

---

* The typical CISC microprocessor in the 1980s supported floating-point operations in a separate co-processor.

give RISC its speed advantage: focusing on a smaller set of less powerful instructions makes it possible to build a faster computer.

However, the notion that RISC machines are generally simpler than CISC machines isn't correct. Other features, such as functional pipelines, sophisticated memory systems, and the ability to issue two or more instructions per clock make the latest RISC processors the most complicated ever built. Furthermore, much of the complexity that has been lifted from the instruction set has been driven into the compilers, making a good optimizing compiler a prerequisite for machine performance.

Let's put ourselves in the role of computer architect again and look at each item in the list above to understand why it's important.

Pipelines

Everything within a digital computer (RISC or CISC) happens in step with a *clock:* a signal that paces the computer's circuitry. The rate of the clock, or *clock speed,* determines the overall speed of the processor. There is an upper limit to how fast you can clock a given computer.

A number of parameters place an upper limit on the clock speed, including the semiconductor technology, packaging, the length of wires tying the pieces together, and the longest path in the processor. Although it may be possible to reach blazing speed by optimizing all of the parameters, the cost can be prohibitive. Furthermore, exotic computers don't make good office mates; they can require too much power, produce too much noise and heat, or be too large. There is incentive for manufacturers to stick with manufacturable and marketable technologies.

Reducing the number of clock ticks it takes to execute an individual instruction is a good idea, though cost and practicality become issues beyond a certain point. A greater benefit comes from partially overlapping instructions so that more than one can be in progress simultaneously. For instance, if you have two additions to perform, it would be nice to execute them both at the same time. How do you do that? The first, and perhaps most obvious, approach, would be to start them simultaneously. Two additions would execute together and complete together in the amount of time it takes to perform one. As a result, the throughput would be effectively doubled. The downside is that you would need hardware for two adders in a situation where space is usually at a premium (especially for the early RISC processors).

Other approaches for overlapping execution are more cost-effective than side-by-side execution. Imagine what it would be like if, a moment after launching one operation, you could launch another without waiting for the first to complete.

Perhaps you could start another of the same type right behind the first one—like the two additions. This would give you nearly the performance of side-by-side execution without duplicated hardware. Such a mechanism does exist to varying degrees in all computers—CISC and RISC. It's called a *pipeline*. A pipeline takes advantage of the fact that many operations are divided into identifiable steps, each of which uses different resources on the processor.*

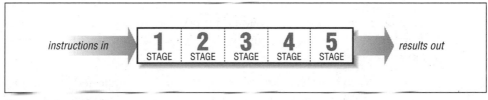

Figure 2-1· A pipeline

Figure 2-1 shows a conceptual diagram of a pipeline. An operation entering at the left proceeds on its own for five clock ticks before emerging at the right. Given that the pipeline stages are independent of one another, up to five operations can be in flight at a time as long as each instruction is delayed long enough for the previous instruction to clear the pipeline stage. Consider how powerful this mechanism is: where before it would have taken five clock ticks to get a single result, a pipeline produces as much as one result every clock tick.

Pipelining is useful when a procedure can be divided into stages. Instruction processing fits into that category. The job of retrieving an instruction from memory, figuring out what it does, and doing it are separate steps we usually lump together when we talk about executing an instruction. The number of steps varies, depending on whose processor you are using, but for illustration, let's say there are five:

Instruction fetch
    The processor fetches an instruction from memory.

Instruction decode
    The instruction is recognized or decoded.

Operand Fetch
    The processor fetches the operands the instruction needs. These operands may be in registers or in memory.

---

* Here is a simple analogy: imagine a line at a fast-food drive up window. If there is only one window, one customer orders and pays, and the food is bagged and delivered to the customer before the second customer orders. For busier restaurants, there are three windows. First you order, then you move ahead. Then at a second window, you pay and move ahead. At the third window you pull up, grab the food and roar off into the distance. While your wait at the three-window (pipelined) drive-up may have been slightly longer than your wait at the one-window (non-pipelined) restaurant, the pipeline solution is significantly better because multiple customers are being processed simultaneously.

Execute

    The instruction gets executed.

Writeback

    The processor *writes* the results *back* to wherever they are supposed to go—
    possibly registers, possibly memory.

Ideally, instruction 1 will be entering the operand fetch stage as instruction 2
enters instruction decode stage and instruction 3 starts instruction fetch, and so on.
Our pipeline is five stages deep, so it should be possible to get five instructions in
flight all at once. If we could keep it up, we would see one instruction complete
per clock cycle.

Simple as this illustration seems, instruction pipelining is complicated in real life.
Each step must be able to occur on different instructions simultaneously, and
delays in any stage have to be coordinated with all those that follow. In Figure 2-2
we see three instructions being executed simultaneously by the processor, with
each instruction in a different stage of execution.

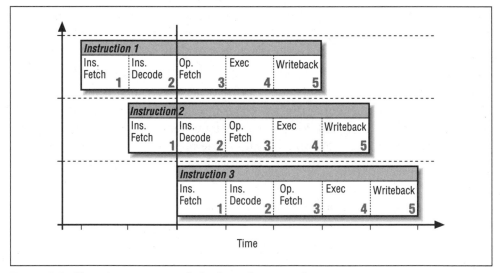

Figure 2-2: Three instructions in flight through one pipeline

For instance, if a complicated memory access occurs in stage three, the instruction
needs to be delayed before going on to stage four because it takes some time to
calculate the operand's address and retrieve it from memory. All the while, the rest
of the pipeline is stalled. A simpler instruction, sitting in one of the earlier stages,
can't continue until the traffic ahead clears up.

Now imagine how a jump to a new program address, perhaps caused by an if
statement, could disrupt the pipeline flow. The processor doesn't know an

instruction is a branch until the decode stage. It usually doesn't know whether a branch will be taken or not until the execute stage. As shown in Figure 2-3, during the four cycles after the branch instruction was fetched, the processor blindly fetches instructions sequentially and starts these instructions through the pipeline.

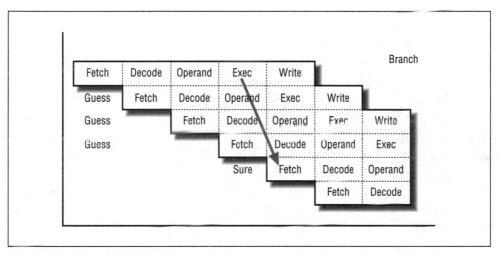

Figure 2-3: Detecting a branch

If the branch "falls through," then everything is in great shape; the pipeline simply executes the next instruction. It's as if the branch were a "no-op" instruction. However, if the branch jumps away, those three partially processed instructions never get executed. The first order of business is to discard these "in-flight" instructions from the pipeline. It turns out that because none of these instructions was actually going to *do* anything until its execute stage, we can throw them away without hurting anything (other than our efficiency). Somehow the processor has to be able to clear out the pipeline and restart the pipeline at the branch destination.

Unfortunately, branch instructions occur every five to ten instructions in many programs. If we executed a branch every fifth instruction and only half our branches fell through, the lost efficiency due to restarting the pipeline after the branches would be 20 percent.

You need optimal conditions to keep the pipeline moving. Even in less-than-optimal conditions, instruction pipelining is a big win—especially for RISC processors. Interestingly, the idea dates back to the late 1950s and early 1960s with the UNIVAC LARC and the IBM Stretch. Instruction pipelining became mainstreamed in 1964, when the CDC 6600 and the IBM S/360 families were introduced with pipelined instruction units—on machines that represented RISC-ish and CISC designs, respectively. To this day, ever more sophisticated techniques are being applied to instruction pipelining, as machines that can overlap instruction execution become commonplace.

Pipelined Floating-Point Operations

Because the execution stage for floating-point operations can take longer than the execution stage for fixed-point computations, these operations are typically pipelined, too. Generally, this includes floating-point addition, subtraction, multiplication, comparisons, and conversions, though it might not include square roots and division. Once a pipelined floating-point operation is started, calculations continue through the several stages without delaying the rest of the processor. The result appears in a register at some point in the future.

Some processors are limited in the amount of overlap their floating-point pipelines can support. Internal components of the pipelines may be shared (for adding, multiplying, normalizing, and rounding intermediate results), forcing restrictions on when and how often you can begin new operations. In other cases, floating-point operations can be started every cycle regardless of the previous floating-point operations. We say that such operations are *fully pipelined*.

The number of stages in floating-point pipelines for affordable computers has decreased over the last 10 years. More transistors and newer algorithms make it possible to perform a floating-point addition or multiplication in just one to three cycles. Generally the most difficult instruction to perform in a single cycle is the floating-point multiply. However, if you dedicate enough hardware to it, there are designs that can operate in a single cycle at a moderate clock rate.

Uniform Instruction Length

Our sample instruction pipeline had five stages: instruction fetch, instruction decode, operand fetch, execution, and writeback. We want this pipeline to be able to process five instructions in various stages without stalling. Decomposing each operation into five identifiable parts, each of which is roughly the same amount of time, is challenging enough for a RISC computer. For a designer working with a CISC instruction set, it's especially difficult because CISC instructions come in varying lengths. A simple "return from subroutine" instruction might be one byte long, for instance, whereas it would take a longer instruction to say "add register four to memory location 2005 and leave the result in register five." The number of bytes to be fetched must be known by the fetch stage of the pipeline as shown in Figure 2-4.

The processor has no way of knowing how long an instruction will be until it reaches the decode stage and determines what it is. If it turns out to be a long instruction, the processor may have to go back to memory and get the portion left

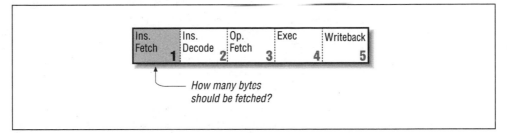

Figure 2-4: Variable length instructions make pipelining difficult

behind; this stalls the pipeline. We could eliminate the problem by requiring that all instructions be the same length, and that there be a limited number of instruction formats as shown in Figure 2-5. This way, every instruction entering the pipeline is known *a priori* to be complete—not needing another memory access. It would also be easier for the processor to locate the instruction fields that specify registers or constants. Altogether because RISC can assume a fixed instruction length, the pipeline flows much more smoothly.

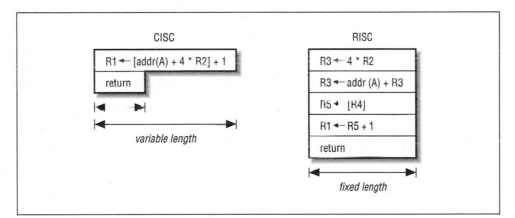

Figure 2-5: Variable-length CISC versus fixed-length RISC instructions

Delayed Branches

As described earlier, branches are a significant problem in a pipelined architecture. Rather than take a penalty for cleaning out the pipeline after a misguessed branch, many RISC designs require an instruction after the branch. This instruction, in what is called the *branch delay slot,* is executed no matter what way the branch goes. An instruction in this position should be useful, or at least harmless, whichever way the branch proceeds. That is, you expect the processor to execute the instruction following the branch in either case, and plan for it. In a pinch, a no-op can be used. A slight variation would be to give the processor the ability to *annul* (or

squash) the instruction appearing in the branch delay slot if it turns out that it
shouldn't have been issued after all:

```
ADD       R1,R2,R1          add r1 to r2 and store in r1
SUB       R3,R1,R3          subtract r1 from r3, store in r3
BRA       SOMEWHERE         branch somewhere else
LABEL1    ZERO R3           instruction in branch delay slot
          . . .
```

While branch delay slots appeared to be a very clever solution to eliminating
pipeline stalls associated with branch operations, as processors moved toward executing two and four instructions simultaneously, another approach was needed.*

A more robust way of eliminating pipeline stalls was to "predict" the direction of
the branch using a table stored in the decode unit. As part of the decode stage, the
CPU would notice that the instruction was a branch and consult a table that kept
the recent behavior of the branch; it would then make a guess. Based on the
guess, the CPU would immediately begin fetching at the predicted location. As
long as the guesses were correct, branches cost exactly the same as any other
instruction.

If the prediction was wrong, the instructions that were in process had to be can-
celled, resulting in wasted time and effort. A simple branch prediction scheme is
typically correct well over 90% of the time, significantly reducing the overall negative performance impact of pipeline stalls due to branches. All recent RISC designs
incorporate some type of branch prediction, making branch delay slots effectively
unnecessary.

Another mechanism for reducing branch penalties is *conditional execution*. These
are instructions that look like branches in source code, but turn out to be a special
type of instruction in the object code. They are very useful because they replace
test and branch sequences altogether. The following lines of code capture the
sense of a conditional branch:

```
IF ( B < C ) THEN
   A = D
ELSE
   A = E
ENDIF
```

Using branches, this would require at least two branches to ensure that the proper
value ended up in A. Using conditional execution, one might generate code that
looks as follows:

---

* Interestingly, while the delay slot is no longer critical in processors that execute four instructions
simultaneously, there is not yet a strong reason to remove the feature. Removing the delay slot would
be nonupwards-compatible, breaking many existing codes. To some degree, the branch delay slot has
become "baggage" on those "new" 10-year-old architectures that must continue to support it.

```
COMPARE  B < C
IF TRUE  A = D      conditional instruction
IF FALSE A = E      conditional instruction
```

This is a sequence of three instructions with *no branches*. One of the two assignments executes, and the other acts as a no-op. No branch prediction is needed, and the pipeline operates perfectly. There is a cost to taking this approach when there are a large number of instructions in one or the other branch paths that would seldom get executed using the traditional branch instruction model.

Load/Store Architecture

In a load/store instruction set architecture, memory references are limited to explicit load and store instructions. Each instruction may not make more than one memory reference per instruction. In a CISC processor, arithmetic and logical instructions can include embedded memory references. There are three reasons why limiting loads and stores to their own instructions is an improvement:

- First, we want all instructions to be the same length, for the reasons given above. However, fixed lengths impose a budget limit when it comes to describing what the operation does and which registers it uses. An instruction that both referenced memory and performed some calculation wouldn't fit within one instruction word.

- Second, giving every instruction the option to reference memory would complicate the pipeline because there would be two computations to perform—the address calculation plus whatever the instruction is supposed to do—but there is only one execution stage. We could throw more hardware at it, but by restricting memory references to explicit loads and stores, we can avoid the problem entirely. Any instruction can perform an address calculation or some other operation, but no instruction can do both.

- The third reason for limiting memory references to explicit loads and stores is that they can take more time than other instructions—sometimes two or three clock cycles more. A general instruction with an embedded memory reference would get hung up in the operand fetch stage for those extra cycles, waiting for the reference to complete. Again we would be faced with an instruction pipeline stall.

Explicit load and store instructions can kick off memory references in the pipeline's execute stage, to be completed at a later time (they might complete immediately; it depends on the processor and the cache). An operation downstream may require the result of the reference, but that's all right, as long as it is far enough downstream that the reference has had time to complete.

Simple Addressing Modes

Just as we want to simplify the instruction set, we also want a simple set of memory addressing modes. The reasons are the same: complicated address calculations, or those that require multiple memory references, will take too much time and stall the pipeline. This doesn't mean that your program can't use elegant data structures; the compiler explicitly generates the extra address arithmetic when it needs it, as long as it can count on a few fundamental addressing modes in hardware. In fact, the extra address arithmetic is often easier for the compiler to optimize into faster forms (see Appendix B, *Looking at Assembly Language*, and the section "Induction Variable Simplification" in Chapter 5, *What a Compiler Does*).

Of course, cutting back the number of addressing modes means that some memory references will take more real instructions than they might have taken on a CISC machine. However, because everything executes more quickly, it generally is still a performance win.

Second-Generation RISC Processors

The Holy Grail for early RISC machines was to achieve one instruction per clock. The idealized RISC computer running at, say, 50 MHz, would be able to issue 50 million instructions per second assuming perfect pipeline scheduling. As we have seen, a single instruction will take five or more clock ticks to get through the instruction pipeline, but if the pipeline can be kept full, the aggregate rate will, in fact, approach one instruction per clock. Once the basic pipelined RISC processor designs became successful, competition ensued to determine which company could build the best RISC processor.

Second-generation RISC designers used three basic methods to develop competitive RISC processors:

- Improve the manufacturing processes to simply make the clock rate faster. Take a simple design; make it smaller and faster. This approach was taken by the Alpha processors from DEC. Alpha processors typically have had clock rates double those of the closest competitor.

- Add duplicate compute elements on the space available as we can manufacture chips with more transistors. This could allow two instructions to be executed per cycle and could double performance without increasing clock rate. This technique is called *superscalar*.

- Increase the number of stages in the pipeline above five. If the instructions can truly be decomposed evenly into, say, ten stages, the clock rate could theoretically be doubled without requiring new manufacturing processes. This technique was called *superpipelining*. The MIPS processors used this technique with some success.

Superscalar Processors

The way you get two or more instructions per clock is by starting several operations side by side, possibly in separate pipelines. In Figure 2-6, if you have an integer addition and a multiplication to perform, it should be possible to begin them simultaneously, provided they are independent of each other (as long as the multiplication does not need the output of the addition as one of its operands or vice versa). You could also execute multiple fixed-point instructions—compares, integer additions, etc.—at the same time, provided that they, too, are independent. Another term used to describe superscalar processors is *multiple instruction issue* processors.

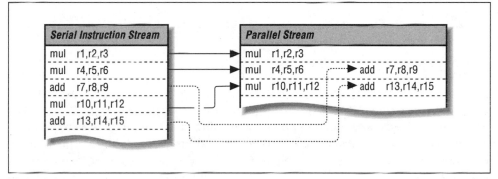

Figure 2-6: Decomposing a serial stream

The number and variety of operations that can be run in parallel depends on both the program and the processor. The program has to have enough usable parallelism so that there are multiple things to do, and the processor has to have an appropriate assortment of functional units and the ability to keep them busy. The idea is conceptually simple, but it can be a challenge for both hardware designers and compiler writers. Every opportunity to do several things in parallel exposes the danger of violating some precedence (i.e., performing computations in the wrong order).

Superpipelined Processors

Roughly stated, simpler circuitry can run at higher clock speeds. Put yourself in the role of a CPU designer again. Looking at the instruction pipeline of your processor, you might decide that the reason you can't get more speed out of it is that some of the stages are too complicated or have too much going on, and they are placing limits on how fast the whole pipeline can go. Because the stages are clocked in unison, the slowest of them forms a weak link in the chain.

If you divide the complicated stages into less complicated portions, you can increase the overall speed of the pipeline. This is called *superpipelining*. More instruction pipeline stages with less complexity per stage will do the same work as a pipelined processor, but with higher throughput due to increased clock speed. Figure 2-7 shows an eight-stage pipeline used in the MIPS R4000 processor.

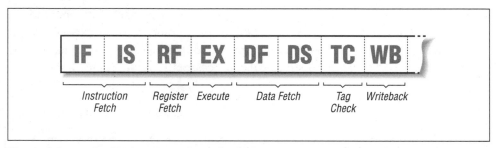

Figure 2-7: MIPS R4000 instruction pipeline

Theoretically, if the reduced complexity allows the processor to clock faster, you can achieve nearly the same performance as superscalar processors, yet without instruction mix preferences. For illustration, picture a superscalar processor with two units—fixed- and floating-point—executing a program that is composed solely of fixed-point calculations; the floating-point unit goes unused. This reduces the superscalar performance by one half compared to its theoretical maximum. A superpipelined processor, on the other hand, will be perfectly happy to handle an unbalanced instruction mix at full speed.

Superpipelines are not new; deep pipelines have been employed in the past, notably on the CDC 6600. The label is a marketing creation to draw contrast to superscalar processing, and other forms of efficient, high-speed computing.

Superpipelining can be combined with other approaches. You could have a super-scalar machine with deep pipelines (DEC AXP and MIPS R-8000 are examples). In fact, you should probably expect that faster pipelines with more stages will become so commonplace that nobody will remember to call them superpipelines after a while.

RISC Means Fast

We all know that the "R" in RISC means "reduced." Lately, as the number of components that can be manufactured on a chip has increased, CPU designers have been looking at ways to make their processors faster by adding features. We have already talked about many of the features such as on-chip multipliers, very fast floating-point, lots of registers, and on-chip caches. Even with all of these features, there seems to be space left over. Also, because much of the design of the control section of the processor is automated, it might not be so bad to add just a "few" new instructions here and there. Especially if simulations indicate a 10% overall increase in speed!

So, what does it mean when they add 15 instructions to a RISC instruction set architecture (ISA)? Would we call it "not-so-RISC"? A suggested term for this trend is FISC, or *fast instruction set computer.* The point is that reducing the number of instructions is not the goal. The goal is to build the fastest possible processor within the manufacturing and cost constraints.*

Some of the types of instructions that are being added into architectures include:

* More addressing modes

* Meta-instructions such as "decrement counter and branch if non-zero"

* Specialized graphics instructions such as the Sun VIS set, the HP graphics instructions, the MIPS Digital Media Extentions (MDMX), and the Intel MMX instructions

Interestingly, the reason that the first two are feasible is that adder units take up so little space, it is possible to put one adder into the decode unit and another into the load/store unit. Most visualization instruction sets take up very little chip area. They often provide "ganged" 8-bit computations to allow a 64-bit register to be used to perform eight 8-bit operations in a single instruction.

Out-of-Order Execution: The Post-RISC Architecture

We're never satisfied with the performance level of our computing equipment and neither are the processor designers. Two-way superscalar processors were very successful around 1994. Many designs were able to execute 1.6–1.8 instructions per cycle on average, using all of the tricks described so far. As we became able to manufacture chips with an ever-increasing transistor count, it seemed that we

---

* People will argue forever but, in a sense, reducing the instruction set was never an end in itself, it was a means to an end.

would naturally progress to four-way and then eight-way superscalar processors. The fundamental problem we face when trying to keep four functional units busy is that it's difficult to find contiguous sets of four (or eight) instructions that can be executed in parallel. It's an easy cop-out to say, "the compiler will solve it all."

The solution to these problems that will allow these processors to effectively use four functional units per cycle and hide memory latency is *out-of-order execution* and *speculative execution*. Out-of-order execution allows a later instruction to be processed before an earlier instruction is completed. The processor is "betting" that the instruction will execute, and the processor will have the precomputed "answer" the instruction needs. In some ways, portions of the RISC design philosophy are turned inside-out in these new processors.

Speculative Computation

To understand the post-RISC architecture, it is important to separate the concept of *computing* a value for an instruction and actually *executing* the instruction. Let's look at a simple example:

```
LD    R10,R2(R0)    Load into R10 from memory

...                 30 Instructions of various kinds (not FDIV)

FDIV  R4,R5,R6      R4 = R5 / R6
```

Assume that (1) we are executing the load instruction, (2) R5 and R6 are already loaded from earlier instructions, (3) it takes 30 cycles to do a floating-point divide, and (4) there are no instructions that need the divide unit between the LD and the FDIV. Why not start the divide unit *computing* the FDIV right now, storing the result in some temporary scratch area? It has nothing better to do. When or if we arrive at the FDIV, we will know the result of the calculation, copy the scratch area into R4, and the FDIV will appear to *execute* in one cycle. Sound far-fetched? Not for a post-RISC processor.

The post-RISC processor must be able to speculatively compute results before the processor knows whether or not an instruction will actually execute. It accomplishes this by allowing instructions to start that will never finish and allowing later instructions to start before earlier instructions finish.

To store these instructions that are in limbo between started and finished, the post-RISC processor needs some space on the processor. This space for instructions is called the *instruction reorder buffer* (IRB).

The Post-RISC Pipeline

The post-RISC processor pipeline in Figure 2-8 looks somewhat different from the RISC pipeline. The first two stages are still instruction fetch and decode. Decode includes branch prediction using a table that indicates the probable behavior of a branch. Once instructions are decoded and branches are predicted, the instructions are placed into the IRB to be computed as soon as possible.

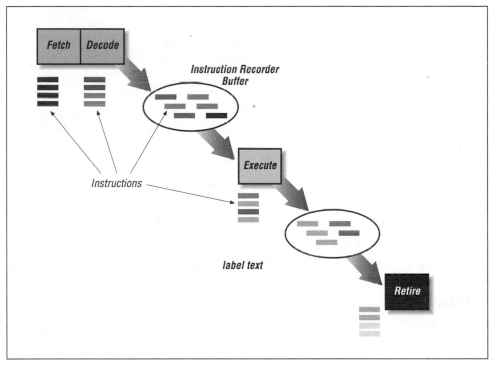

Figure 2-8: Post-RISC pipeline

The IRB holds up to 60 or so instructions that are waiting to execute for one reason or another. In a sense, the fetch and decode/predict phases operate until the buffer fills up. Each time the decode unit predicts a branch, the following instructions are marked with a different indicator so they can be found easily if the prediction turns out to be wrong. Within the buffer, instructions are allowed to go to the computational units when the instruction has all of its operand values. Because the instructions are computing results without being executed, any instruction that has its input values and an available computation unit can be computed. The results of these computations are stored in extra registers not visible to the programmer called *rename registers*. The processor allocates rename registers, as they are needed for instructions being computed.

The execution units may have one or more pipeline stages, depending on the type of the instruction. This part looks very much like traditional superscalar RISC processors. Typically up to four instructions can begin computation from the IRB in any cycle, provided four instructions are available with input operands and there are sufficient computational units for those instructions.

Once the results for the instruction have been computed and stored in a rename register, the instruction must wait until the preceding instructions finish so we know that the instruction actually executes. In addition to the computed results, each instruction has flags associated with it, such as exceptions. For example, you would not be happy if your program crashed with the following message: "Error, divide by zero. I was precomputing a divide in case you got to the instruction to save some time, but the branch was mispredicted and it turned out that you were never going to execute that divide anyway. I still had to blow you up though. No hard feelings? Signed, the post-RISC CPU." So when a speculatively computed instruction divides by zero, the CPU must simply store that fact until it knows the instruction will execute and at that moment, the program can be legitimately crashed.

If a branch does get mispredicted, a lot of bookkeeping must occur very quickly. A message is sent to all the units to discard instructions that are part of all control flow paths beyond the incorrect branch.

Instead of calling the last phase of the pipeline "writeback," it's called "retire." The retire phase is what "executes" the instructions that have already been computed. The retire phase keeps track of the instruction execution order and retires the instructions in program order, posting results from the rename registers to the actual registers and raising exceptions as necessary. Typically up to four instructions can be retired per cycle.

So the post-RISC pipeline is actually three pipelines connected by two buffers that allow instructions to be processed out of order. However, even with all of this speculative computation going on, the retire unit forces the processor to appear as a simple RISC processor with predictable execution and interrupts.

Future Trends: Intel IA-64 and EPIC

In many ways the balance between implementing features in hardware and/or software is a pendulum that swings back and forth. In the early days of CISC, many features were added to hardware. The very complexity of these fully developed CISC processors began to limit their overall performance. RISC decided to start over from scratch by implementing only the most basic functionality. However, almost as soon as the first RISC processors were on the market, RISC began to see continued creeping elegance. The current out-of-order post-RISC processors are very powerful processors that perform many runtime optimizations to achieve their very high performance.

The EPIC processor is a swing toward a more basic approach to out-of-order and speculative execution. Like the initial RISC revolution, this revolution will result in one or more new instruction set(s) such as the IA-64.

Unlike the post-RISC processors that use out-of-order execution and speculative execution to implement a traditional RISC instruction set, the IA-64 instruction set exposes speculative execution and out-of-order processing to the user. One of the fundamental problems that limits the post-RISC processor's ability to scale to 8 or 16 functional units is the complexity of maintaining the "image" that these are vanilla RISC processors. With the EPIC, the inner workings of the execution core are not hidden from the instruction set.

The IA-64 implements an explicitly parallel instruction set. Instead of having the processor determine the intra-instruction dependencies as part of the decode stage, in IA-64 the compiler must add dependency information to the instructions. By indicating which instructions do not depend on one another, the compiler is communicating which instructions can execute in parallel. This greatly simplifies the hardware needed in the processor for instruction scheduling.

The compiler also has added responsibility for memory operations using a pre-fetch style of memory accesses. To eliminate branches and their associated penalties, the IA-64 has extensive support for predicated execution. There can be a number of active logical predicates and instructions that are conditionally executing based on the evaluation of the predicates. From the processor perspective, this is much simpler than keeping track of the many control paths as the processor speculatively executes beyond uncomputed branches.

This new architecture is covered in more detail in Appendix C, *Future Trends: Intel IA-64*.

Closing Notes

Congratulations for reaching the end of a long chapter! We have talked a little bit about old computers, CISC, RISC, post-RISC, and EPIC, and mentioned supercomputers in passing. I think it's interesting to observe that RISC processors are a branch off a long-established tree. Many of the ideas that have gone into RISC designs are borrowed from other types of computers, but none of them evolved into RISC—RISC started at a discontinuity. There were hints of a RISC revolution (the CDC 6600 and the IBM 801 project) but it really was forced on the world (for its own good) by CPU designers at Berkeley and Stanford in the 1980s.

As RISC has matured, there have been many improvements. Each time it appears that we have reached the limit of the performance of our microprocessors there is a new architectural breakthrough improving our single CPU performance. How long can it continue? It is clear that as long as competition continues, there is significant performance headroom using the out-of-order execution as the clock rates move from a typical 200 MHz to 500+ MHz. DEC's Alpha 21264 is planned to have four-way out-of-order execution at 500 MHz by 1998. As of 1998, vendors are beginning to reveal their plans for processors clocked at 1000 MHz or 1 GHz.

Unfortunately, developing a new processor is a *very* expensive task. If enough companies merge and competition diminishes, the rate of innovation will slow. Hopefully we will be seeing four processors on a chip, each 16-way out-of-order superscalar, clocked at 1 GHz for $200 before we eliminate competition and let the CPU designers rest on their laurels. At that point, scalable parallel processing will suddenly become interesting again.

How will designers tackle some of the fundamental architectural problems, perhaps the largest being memory systems? Even though the post-RISC architecture and the EPIC alleviate the latency problems somewhat, the memory bottleneck will always be there. The good news is that even though memory performance improves more slowly than CPU performance, memory system performance does improve over time. We'll look next at techniques for building memory systems.

As discussed in the Preface, the exercises that come at the end of most chapters in this book are not like the exercises in most engineering texts. These exercises are mostly thought experiments, without well-defined answers, designed to get you thinking about the hardware on your desk.

Exercises

1. Speculative execution is safe for certain types of instructions; results can be discarded if it turns out that the instruction shouldn't have executed. Floating-point instructions and memory operations are two classes of instructions for which speculative execution is trickier, particularly because of the chance of generating exceptions. For instance, dividing by zero or taking the square root of a negative number causes an exception. Under what circumstances will a speculative memory reference cause an exception?

2. Picture a machine with floating-point pipelines that are 100 stages deep (that's ridiculously deep), each of which can deliver a new result every nanosecond. That would give each pipeline a peak throughput rate of 1 Gflop, and a worst-case throughput rate of 10 Mflops. What characteristics would a program need to have to take advantage of such a pipeline?

3

Memory

Let's say that you are fast asleep some night and begin dreaming. In your dream, you have a time machine and a few 500-MHz four-way superscalar processors. You turn the time machine back to 1981. Once you arrive back in time, you go out and purchase an IBM PC with an Intel 8088 microprocessor running at 4.77 MHz. For much of the rest of the night, you toss and turn as you try to adapt the 500-MHz processor to the Intel 8088 socket using a soldering iron and Swiss Army knife. Just before you wake up, the new computer finally works, and you turn it on to run the Linpack* benchmark and issue a press release. Would you expect this to turn out to be a dream or a nightmare? Chances are good that it would turn out to be a nightmare, just like the previous night where you went back to the Middle Ages and put a jet engine on a horse. (You have got to stop eating double pepperoni pizzas so late at night.)

Even if you can speed up the computational aspects of a processor infinitely fast, you still must load and store the data and instructions to and from a memory. Today's processors continue to creep ever closer to infinitely fast processing. Memory performance is increasing at a much slower rate (it will take longer for memory to become infinitely fast). Many of the interesting problems in high performance computing use a large amount of memory. As computers are getting faster, the size of problems they tend to operate on also goes up. The trouble is that when you want to solve these problems at high speeds, you need a memory system that is large, yet at the same time fast—a big challenge. Possible approaches include the following:

---

* See Chapter 15, *Using Published Benchmarks*, for details on the Linpack benchmark.

- Every memory system component can be made individually fast enough to respond to every memory access request.

- Slow memory can be accessed in a round-robin fashion (hopefully) to give the effect of a faster memory system.

- The memory system design can be made "wide" so that each transfer contains many bytes of information.

- The system can be divided into faster and slower portions and arranged so that the fast portion is used more often than the slow one.

Again, economics are the dominant force in the computer business. A cheap, statistically optimized memory system will be a better seller than a prohibitively expensive, blazingly fast one, so the first choice is not much of a choice at all. But these choices, used in combination, can attain a good fraction of the performance you would get if every component were fast. Chances are very good that your high performance workstation incorporates several or all of them.

Once the memory system has been decided upon, there are things we can do in software to see that it is used efficiently. A compiler that has some knowledge of the way memory is arranged and the details of the caches can optimize their use to some extent. The other place for optimizations is in user applications, as we'll see later in the book. A good pattern of memory access will work with, rather than against, the components of the system.

In this chapter we discuss how the pieces of a memory system work. We look at how patterns of data and instruction access factor into your overall runtime, especially as CPU speeds increase. We also talk a bit about the performance implications of running in a virtual memory environment.

Memory Technology

Almost all fast memories used today are semiconductor-based.* They come in two flavors: *dynamic random access memory* (DRAM) and *static random access memory* (SRAM). The term *random* means that you can address memory locations in any order. This is to distinguish random access from serial memories, where you have to step through all intervening locations to get to the particular one you are interested in. An example of a storage medium that is *not* random is magnetic tape. The terms dynamic and static have to do with the technology used in the design of the memory cells. DRAMs are charge-based devices, where each bit is represented by an electrical charge stored in a very small capacitor. The charge can leak away in a short amount of time, so the system has to be continually

---

* Magnetic core memory is still used in applications where radiation "hardness"—resistance to changes caused by ionizing radiation—is important.

refreshed to prevent data from being lost. The act of reading a bit in DRAM also discharges the bit, requiring that it be refreshed. It's not possible to read the memory bit in the DRAM while it's being refreshed.

SRAM is based on gates, and each bit is stored in four to six connected transistors. SRAM memories retain their data as long as they have power, without the need for any form of data refresh.

DRAM offers the best price/performance, as well as highest density of memory cells per chip. This means lower cost, less board space, less power, and less heat. On the other hand, some applications such as cache and video memory require higher speed, to which SRAM is better suited. Currently, you can choose between SRAM and DRAM at slower speeds—down to about 50 nanoseconds (ns). SRAM has access times down to about 7 ns at higher cost, heat, power, and board space.

In addition to the basic technology to store a single bit of data, memory performance is limited by the practical considerations of the on-chip wiring layout and the external pins on the chip that communicate the address and data information between the memory and the processor.

Access Time

The amount of time it takes to read or write a memory location is called the *memory access time*. A related quantity is the *memory cycle time*. Whereas the access time says how quickly you can reference a memory location, cycle time describes how often you can repeat references. They sound like the same thing, but they're not. For instance, if you ask for data from DRAM chips with a 50-ns access time, it may be 100 ns before you can ask for more data from the same chips. This is because the chips must internally recover from the previous access. Also, when you are retrieving data sequentially from DRAM chips, some technologies have improved performance. On these chips, data immediately following the previously accessed data may be accessed as quickly as 10 ns.

Access and cycle times for commodity DRAMs are shorter than they were just a few years ago, meaning that it is possible to build faster memory systems. But CPU clock speeds have increased too. The home computer market makes a good study. In the early 1980s, the access time of commodity DRAM (200 ns) was shorter than the clock cycle (4.77 MHz = 210 ns) of the IBM PC XT. This meant that DRAM could be connected directly to the CPU without worrying about over running the memory system. Faster XT and AT models were introduced in the mid-1980s with CPUs that clocked more quickly than the access times of available commodity memory. Faster memory was available for a price, but vendors punted by selling computers with *wait states* added to the memory access cycle. Wait states are artificial delays that slow down references so that memory appears to match the speed of a faster CPU—at a penalty. However, the technique of adding wait states begins to significantly impact performance around 25–33MHz. Today, CPU speeds are even farther ahead of DRAM speeds.

The clock time for commodity home computers has gone from 210 ns for the XT to around 3 ns for a 300-MHz Pentium-II, but the access time for commodity DRAM has decreased disproportionately less—from 200 ns to around 50 ns. Processor performance doubles every 18 months, while memory performance doubles roughly every seven years.

The CPU/memory speed gap is even larger in workstations. Some models clock at intervals as short as 1.6 ns. How do vendors make up the difference between CPU speeds and memory speeds? The memory in the Cray-1 supercomputer used SRAM that was capable of keeping up with the 12.5-ns clock cycle. Using SRAM for its main memory system was one of the reasons that most Cray systems needed liquid cooling.

Unfortunately, it's not practical for a moderately priced system to rely exclusively on SRAM for storage. It's also not practical to manufacture inexpensive systems with enough storage using exclusively SRAM.

The solution is a hierarchy of memories using processor registers, one to three levels of SRAM cache, DRAM main memory, and virtual memory stored on media such as disk. At each point in the memory hierarchy, tricks are employed to make the best use of the available technology. For the remainder of this chapter, we will examine the memory hierarchy and its impact on performance.

In a sense, with today's high performance microprocessor performing computations so quickly, the task of the high performance programmer becomes the careful management of the memory hierarchy. In some sense it's a useful intellectual exercise to view the simple computations such as addition and multiplication as "infinitely fast" in order to get the programmer to focus on the impact of memory operations on the overall performance of the program.

Registers

At least the top layer of the memory hierarchy, the CPU registers, operate as fast as the rest of the processor. The goal is to keep operands in the registers as much as possible. This is especially important for intermediate values used in a long computation such as:

```
X = G * 2.41 + A / W - W * M
```

While computing the value of A divided by W, we must store the result of multiplying G by 2.41. It would be a shame to have to store this intermediate result in memory and then reload it a few instructions later. On any modern processor with moderate optimization, the intermediate result is stored in a register. Also, the value W is used in two computations, and so it can be loaded once and used twice to eliminate a "wasted" load.

Compilers have been very good at detecting these types of optimizations and efficiently making use of the available registers since the 1970s. Adding more registers to the processor has some performance benefit. It's not practical to add enough registers to the processor to store the entire problem data. So we must still use the slower memory technology.

Caches

Once we go beyond the registers in the memory hierarchy, we encounter caches. Caches are small amounts of SRAM that store a subset of the contents of the memory. The hope is that the cache will have the right subset of main memory at the right time.

The actual cache architecture has had to change as the cycle time of the processors has improved. The processors are so fast that off-chip SRAM chips are not even fast enough. This has lead to a multilevel cache approach with one, or even two, levels of cache implemented as part of the processor. Table 3-1 shows the approximate speed of accessing the memory hierarchy on a 500-MHz DEC 21164 Alpha.

Table 3-1: Memory Access Speed on a DEC 21164 Alpha

Registers	2 ns
L1 On-Chip	4 ns
L2 On-Chip	5 ns
L3 Off-Chip	30 ns
Memory	220 ns

The off-chip and memory timings include more than just the access time for the SRAM and DRAM. There is overhead in moving the data between the chips and the cost of keeping the caches consistent with the main memory. When data is loaded from the memory, it's loaded into the caches as well, unless the cache is bypassed.

When every reference can be found in a cache, you say that you have a 100% hit rate. Generally, a hit rate of 90% or better is considered good for a level-one (L1) cache. In level-two (L2) cache, a hit rate of above 50% is considered acceptable. Below that, application performance can drop off steeply.

One can characterize the average read performance of the memory hierarchy by examining the probability that a particular load will be satisfied at a particular level of the hierarchy. For example, assume a memory architecture with an L1 cache speed of 10 ns, L2 speed of 30 ns, and memory speed of 300 ns. If a memory reference were satisfied from L1 cache 75% of the time, L2 cache 20% of the time, and main memory 5% of the time, the average memory performance would be:

```
(0.75 * 10 ) + ( 0.20 * 30 ) + ( 0.05 * 300 ) = 28.5 ns
```

You can easily see why it's important to have an L1 cache hit rate of 90% or higher.

Given that a cache holds only a subset of the main memory at any time, it's important to keep an index of which areas of the main memory are currently stored in the cache. To reduce the amount of space that must be dedicated to tracking which memory areas are in cache, the cache is divided into a number of equal sized slots known as *lines*. Each line contains some number of sequential main memory locations, generally four to sixteen integers or real numbers. Whereas the data within a line comes from the same part of memory, other lines can contain data that is far separated within your program, or perhaps data from somebody else's program, as in Figure 3-1. When you ask for something from memory, the computer checks to see if the data is available within one of these cache lines. If it is, the data is returned with a minimal delay. If it's not, your program may be delayed while a new line is fetched from main memory. Of course, if a new line is brought in, another has to be thrown out. If you're lucky, it won't be the one containing the data you are just about to need.

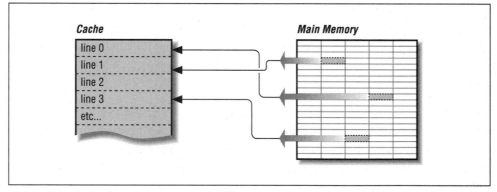

Figure 3-1: Cache lines can come from different parts of memory

When data is modified by storing a new value into a cache line, there must be some mechanism to update the data in main memory. When caches are involved, there are two approaches that are used when data is written back into main memory. When the cache operates as a writeback cache, data written into cache generally stays in the cache until the cache line is replaced, at which point it is written into main memory. This works well if the processor is storing into successive locations in the same line. In a "write-through" cache, data is immediately written into main memory and into the cache. Then when the cache line is needed for another area of memory, it can simply be discarded without any need for a write-back. Writeback is most common on single processors.

On multiprocessors (computers with several CPUs), written data must be returned to main memory so the rest of the processors can see it, or all other processors must be made aware of local cache activity. Perhaps they need to be told to invalidate old lines containing the previous value of the written variable so that they don't accidentally use stale data. This is known as maintaining *coherency* between the different caches. The problem can become very complex in a multiprocessor system.*

Caches are effective because programs often exhibit characteristics that help keep the hit rate high. These characteristics are called *spatial* and *temporal locality of reference*; programs often make use of instructions and data that are near to other instructions and data, both in space and time. When a cache line is retrieved from main memory, it contains not only the information that caused the cache miss, but also some neighboring information. Chances are good that the next time your program needs data, it will be in the cache line just fetched or another one recently fetched.

Caches work best when a program is reading sequentially through the memory. Assume a program is reading 32-bit integers with a cache line size of 256 bits. When the program references the first word in the cache line, it waits while the cache line is loaded from main memory. Then the next seven references to memory are satisfied quickly from the cache. This is called *unit stride* because the address of each successive data element is incremented by one and all the data retrieved into the cache is used. The following loop is a unit-stride loop:

```
DO I=1,1000000
  SUM = SUM + A(I)
END DO
```

When a program accesses a large data structure using "non-unit stride," performance suffers because data is loaded into cache that is not used. For example:

```
DO I=1,1000000,8
  SUM = SUM + A(I)
END DO
```

This code would experience the same number of cache misses as the previous loop, and the same amount of data would be loaded into the cache. However, the program needs only one of the eight 32-bit words loaded into cache. Even though

---

* Chapter 10, *Shared-Memory Multiprocessors*, describes cache coherency in more detail.

this program performs one-eighth the additions of the previous loop, its elapsed time is roughly the same as the previous loop because the memory operations dominate performance.

While this example may seem a bit contrived, there are several situations in which non-unit strides occur quite often. First, when a FORTRAN two-dimensional array is stored in memory, successive elements in the first column are stored sequentially followed by the elements of the second column. If the array is processed with the row iteration as the inner loop, it produces a unit-stride reference pattern as follows:

```
REAL*4 A(200,200)
DO J = 1,200
  DO I = 1,200
    SUM = SUM + A(I,J)
  END DO
END DO
```

Interestingly, a FORTRAN programmer would most likely write the loop (in alphabetical order) as follows, producing a non-unit stride of 800 bytes between successive load operations:

```
REAL*4 A(200,200)
DO I = 1,200
  DO J = 1,200
    SUM = SUM + A(I,J)
  END DO
END DO
```

Because of this, some compilers can detect this suboptimal loop order and reverse the order of the loops to make best use of the memory system. As we will see in Chapter 4, however, this code transformation may produce different results, and so you may have to give the compiler "permission" to interchange these loops in this particular example (or, after reading this book, you could just code it properly in the first place).

Another situation that typically results in non-unit stride is the traversal of a linked list:

```
while ( ptr != NULL ) ptr = ptr->next;
```

The next element that is retrieved is based on the contents of the current element. This type of loop bounces all around memory in no particular pattern. This is called *pointer chasing* and there are no good ways to improve the performance of this code.

A third pattern often found in certain types of codes is called *gather* (or *scatter*) and occurs in loops such as:

```
SUM = SUM + ARR ( IND(I) )
```

where the IND array contains offsets into the ARR array. Again, like the linked list, the exact pattern of memory references is known only at runtime when the values stored in the IND array are known. Some special-purpose systems have special hardware support to accelerate this particular operation.

Cache Organization

The process of pairing memory locations with cache lines is called *mapping*. Of course, given that a cache is smaller than main memory, you have to share the same cache lines for different memory locations. In caches, each cache line has a record of the memory address (called the *tag*) it represents and perhaps when it was last used. The tag is used to track which area of memory is stored in a particular cache line.

The way memory locations (tags) are mapped to cache lines can have a beneficial effect on the way your program runs, because if two heavily used memory locations map onto the same cache line, the miss rate will be higher than you would like it to be. Caches can be organized in one of several ways: direct mapped, fully associative, and set associative.

Direct-Mapped Cache

Direct mapping, as shown in Figure 3-2, is the simplest algorithm for deciding how memory maps onto the cache. Say, for example, that your computer has a 4-KB cache. In a direct mapped scheme, memory location 0 maps into cache location 0, as do memory locations 4K, 8K, 12K, etc. In other words, memory maps onto the cache size. Another way to think about it is to imagine a metal spring with a chalk line marked down the side. Every time around the spring, you encounter the chalk line at the same place modulo the circumference of the spring. If the spring is very long, the chalk line crosses many coils, the analog being a large memory with many locations mapping into the same cache line.

Problems occur when alternating runtime memory references in a direct-mapped cache point to the same cache line. Each reference causes a cache miss and replaces the entry just replaced, causing a lot of overhead. The popular word for this is *thrashing*. When there is lots of thrashing, a cache can be more of a liability than an asset because each cache miss requires that a cache line be refilled—an operation that moves more data than merely satisfying the reference directly from

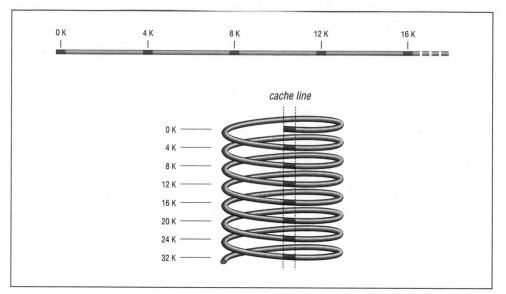

Figure 3-2: Many memory addresses map to the same cache line

main memory. It is easy to construct a pathological case that causes thrashing in a 4-KB direct-mapped cache:

```
REAL*4 A(1024), B(1024)
COMMON /STUFF/ A,B
DO I=1,1024
  A(I) = A(I) * B(I)
END DO
END
```

The arrays A and B both take up exactly 4 KB of storage, and their inclusion together in COMMON assures that the arrays start exactly 4 KB apart in memory. In a 4-KB direct mapped cache, the same line that is used for A(1) is used for B(1), and likewise for A(2) and B(2), etc., so alternating references cause repeated cache misses. To fix it, you could either adjust the size of the array A, or put some other variables into COMMON, between them. For this reason one should generally avoid array dimensions that are close to powers of two.

Fully Associative Cache

At the other extreme from a direct mapped cache is a *fully associative cache*, where any memory location can be mapped into any cache line, regardless of memory address. Fully associative caches get their name from the type of memory used to construct them—associative memory. Associative memory is like regular memory, except that each memory cell knows something about the data it contains.

When the processor goes looking for a piece of data, the cache lines are asked all at once whether any of them has it. The cache line containing the data holds up its hand and says "I have it"; if none of them do, there is a cache miss. It then becomes a question of which cache line will be replaced with the new data. Rather than map memory locations to cache lines via an algorithm, like a direct-mapped cache, the memory system can ask the fully associative cache lines to choose among themselves which memory locations they will represent. Usually the least recently used line is the one that gets overwritten with new data. The assumption is that if the data hasn't been used in quite a while, it is least likely to be used in the future.

Fully associative caches have superior utilization when compared to direct mapped caches. It's difficult to find real-world examples of programs that will cause thrashing in a fully associative cache. The expense of fully associative caches is very high, in terms of size, price, and speed. The associative caches that do exist tend to be small.

Set-Associative Cache

Now imagine that you have two direct mapped caches sitting side by side in a single cache unit as shown in Figure 3-3. Each memory location corresponds to a particular cache line in each of the two direct-mapped caches. The one you choose to replace during a cache miss is subject to a decision about whose line was used last—the same way the decision was made in a fully associative cache except that now there are only two choices. This is called a *set-associative cache*. Set-associative caches generally come in two and four separate banks of cache. These are called *two-way* and *four-way* set associative caches, respectively. Of course, there are benefits and drawbacks to each type of cache. A set-associative cache is more immune to cache thrashing than a direct-mapped cache of the same size, because for each mapping of a memory address into a cache line, there are two or more choices where it can go. The beauty of a direct-mapped cache, however, is that it's easy to implement and, if made large enough, will perform roughly as well as a set-associative design. Your machine may contain multiple caches for several different purposes. Here's a little program for causing thrashing in a 4-KB two-way set-associative cache:

```
REAL*4 A(1024), B(1024), C(1024)
COMMON /STUFF/ A,B,C
DO I=1,1024
  A(I) = A(I) * B(I) + C(I)
END DO
END
```

Like the previous cache thrasher program, this forces repeated accesses to the same cache lines, except that now there are three variables contending for the

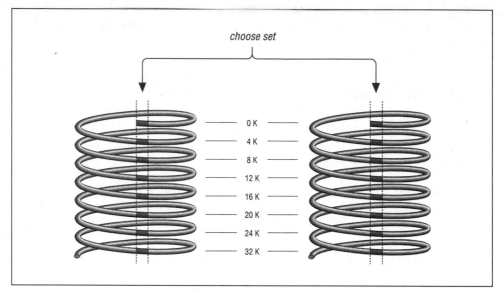

Figure 3-3: Two-way set-associative cache

same mapping instead of two. Again, the way to fix it would be to change the size of the arrays or insert something in between them, in COMMON. By the way, if you accidentally arranged a program to thrash like this, it would be hard for you to detect it—aside from a feeling that the program runs a little slow. Few vendors provide tools for measuring cache misses.

Instruction Cache

So far we have glossed over the two kinds of information you would expect to find in a cache between main memory and the CPU: instructions and data. But if you think about it, the demand for data is separate from the demand for instructions. In superscalar processors, for example, it's possible to execute an instruction that causes a data cache miss alongside other instructions that require no data from cache at all, i.e., they operate on registers. It doesn't seem fair that a cache miss on a data reference in one instruction should keep you from fetching other instructions because the cache is tied up. Furthermore, a cache depends on locality of reference between bits of data and other bits of data or instructions and other instructions, but what kind of interplay is there between instructions and data? It would seem possible for instructions to bump perfectly useful data from cache, or vice versa, with complete disregard for locality of reference.

Many designs from the 1980s used a single cache for both instructions and data. But newer designs are employing what is known as the *Harvard Memory Architecture*, where the demand for data is segregated from the demand for instructions.

Main memory is a still a single large pool, but these processors have separate data and instruction caches, possibly of different designs. By providing two independent sources for data and instructions, the aggregate rate of information coming from memory is increased, and interference between the two types of memory references is minimized. Also, instructions generally have an extremely high level of locality of reference because of the sequential nature of most programs. Because the instruction caches don't have to be particularly large to be effective, a typical architecture is to have separate L1 caches for instructions and data and to have a combined L2 cache. For example, the IBM/Motorola PowerPC 604e has separate 32-K four-way set-associative L1 caches for instruction and data and a combined L2 cache.

Virtual Memory

Virtual memory decouples the addresses used by the program (virtual addresses) from the actual addresses where the data is stored in memory (physical addresses). Your program sees its address space starting at 0 and working its way up to some large number, but the actual physical addresses assigned can be very different. It gives a degree of flexibility by allowing all processes to believe they have the entire memory system to themselves. Another trait of virtual memory systems is that they divide your program's memory up into *pages*—chunks. Page sizes vary from 512 bytes to 1 MB or larger, depending on the machine. Pages don't have to be allocated contiguously, though your program sees them that way. By being separated into pages, programs are easier to arrange in memory, or move portions out to disk.

Page Tables

Say that your program asks for a variable stored at location 1000. In a virtual memory machine, there is no direct correspondence between your program's idea of where location 1000 is and the physical memory systems' idea. To find where your variable is actually stored, the location has to be translated from a virtual to a physical address. The map containing such translations is called a *page table*. Each process has a several page tables associated with it, corresponding to different regions, such as program text and data segments.

To understand how address translation works, imagine the following scenario: at some point, your program asks for data from location 1000. Figure 3-4 shows the steps required to complete the retrieval of this data. By choosing location 1000, you have identified which region the memory reference falls in, and this identifies which page table is involved. Location 1000 then helps the processor choose an entry within the table. For instance, if the page size is 512 bytes, 1000 falls within the second page (pages range from addresses 0–511, 512–1023, 1024–1535, etc.).

Therefore, the second table entry should hold the address of the page housing the value at location 1000.

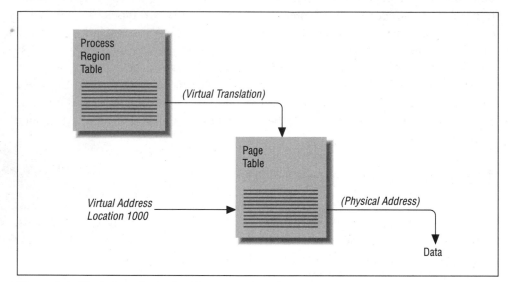

Figure 3-4: Virtual-to-physical address mapping

The operating system stores the page-table addresses virtually, so it's going to take a virtual-to-physical translation to locate the table in memory. One more virtual-to-physical translation, and we finally have the true address of location 1000. The memory reference can complete, and the processor can return to executing your program.

Translation Lookaside Buffer

As you can see, address translation through a page table is pretty complicated. It required two table lookups (maybe three) to locate our data. If every memory reference was that complicated, virtual memory computers would be horrible performers. Fortunately, locality of reference causes virtual address translations to group together; a program may repeat the same virtual page mapping millions of times a second. And where we have repeated use of the same data, we can apply a cache.

All modern virtual memory machines have a special cache called a *translation lookaside buffer* (TLB) for virtual-to-physical-memory-address translation. The two inputs to the TLB are an integer that identifies the program making the memory request and the virtual page requested. From the output pops a pointer to the physical page number. Virtual address in; physical address out. TLB lookups occur in parallel with instruction execution, so if the address data is in the TLB, memory references proceed quickly.

Like other kinds of caches, the TLB is limited in size. It doesn't contain enough entries to handle all the possible virtual-to-physical-address translations for all the programs that might run on your computer. Larger pools of address translations are kept out in memory, in the page tables. If your program asks for a virtual-to-physical-address translation, and the entry doesn't exist in the TLB, you suffer a *TLB miss*. The information needed may have to be generated (a new page may need to be created), or it may have to be retrieved from the page table.

The TLB is good for the same reason that other types of caches are good: it reduces the cost of memory references. But like other caches, there are pathological cases where the TLB can fail to deliver value. The easiest case to construct is one where every memory reference your program makes causes a TLB miss:

```
REAL X(10000000)
COMMON X
DO I=0,9999
  DO J=1,10000000,10000
    SUM = SUM + X(J+I)
  END DO
END DO
```

Assume that the TLB page size for your computer is less than 40 KB. Every time through the inner loop in the above example, the program asks for data that is 4 bytes*10,000 = 40,000 bytes away from the last reference. That is, each reference falls on a different memory page. This causes 1000 TLB misses in the inner loop, taken 1001 times, for a total of at least one million TLB misses. To add insult to injury, each reference is guaranteed to cause a data cache miss as well. Admittedly, no one would start with a loop like the one above. But presuming that the loop was any good to you at all, the restructured version in the code below would cruise through memory like a warm knife through butter:

```
REAL X(10000000)
COMMON X
DO I=1,10000000
  SUM = SUM + X(I)
END DO
```

The revised loop has unit stride, and TLB misses occur only every so often. Usually it is not necessary to explicitly tune programs to make good use of the TLB. Once a program is tuned to be "cache-friendly," it nearly always is tuned to be TLB friendly.

Because there is a performance benefit to keeping the TLB very small, the TLB entry often contains a length field. A single TLB entry can be over a megabyte in length and can be used to translate addresses stored in multiple virtual memory pages.

Page Faults

A page table entry also contains other information about the page it represents, including flags to tell whether the translation is valid, whether the associated page can be modified, and some information describing how new pages should be initialized. References to pages that aren't marked valid are called *page faults*.

Taking a worst-case scenario, say that your program asks for a variable from a particular memory location. The processor goes to look for it in the cache and finds it isn't there (cache miss), which means it must be loaded from memory. Next it goes to the TLB to find the physical location of the data in memory and finds there is no TLB entry (a TLB miss). Then it tries consulting the page table (and refilling the TLB), but finds that either there is no entry for your particular page or that the memory page has been shipped to disk (both are page faults). Each step of the memory hierarchy has shrugged off your request. A new page will have to be created in memory and possibly, depending on the circumstances, refilled from disk.

Although they take a lot of time, page faults aren't errors. Even under optimal conditions every program suffers some number of page faults. Writing a variable for the first time or calling a subroutine that has never been called can cause a page fault. This may be surprising if you have never thought about it before. The illusion is that your entire program is present in memory from the start, but some portions may never be loaded. There is no reason to make space for a page whose data is never referenced or whose instructions are never executed. Only those pages that are required to run the job get created or pulled in from the disk.*

The pool of physical memory pages is limited because physical memory is limited, so on a machine where many programs are lobbying for space, there will be a higher number of page faults. This is because physical memory pages are continually being recycled for other purposes. However, when you have the machine to yourself, and memory is less in demand, allocated pages tend to stick around for a while. In short, you can expect fewer page faults on a quiet machine. One trick to remember if you ever end up working for a computer vendor: always run short benchmarks twice. On some systems, the number of page faults will go down. This is because the second run finds pages left in memory by the first, and you won't have to pay for page faults again.†

---

* The term for this is *demand paging*.

† Text pages are identified by the disk device and block number from which they came.

Paging space (swap space) on the disk is the last and slowest piece of the memory hierarchy for most machines. In the worst-case scenario we saw how a memory reference could be pushed down to slower and slower performance media before finally being satisfied. If you step back, you can view the disk paging space as having the same relationship to main memory as main memory has to cache. The same kinds of optimizations apply too, and locality of reference is important. You can run programs that are larger than the main memory system of your machine, but sometimes at greatly decreased performance. When we look at memory optimizations in Chapter 8, we will concentrate on keeping the activity in the fastest parts of the memory system and avoiding the slow parts.

Improving Memory Performance

Given the importance, in the area of high performance computing, of the performance of a computer's memory subsystem, many techniques have been used to improve the performance of the memory systems of computers. The two attributes of memory system performance are generally *bandwidth* and *latency*. Some memory system design changes improve one at the expense of the other, and other improvements positively impact both bandwidth and latency. Bandwidth generally focuses on the best possible steady-state transfer rate of a memory system. Usually this is measured while running a long unit-stride loop reading or reading and writing memory.* Latency is a measure of the worst-case performance of a memory system as it moves a small amount of data such as a 32- or 64-bit word between the processor and memory. Both are important because they are an important part of most high performance applications.

Because memory systems are divided into components, there are different bandwidth and latency figures between different components as shown in Figure 3-5. The bandwidth rate between a cache and the CPU will be higher than the bandwidth between main memory and the cache, for instance. There may be several caches and paths to memory as well. Usually, the peak memory bandwidth quoted by vendors is the speed between the data cache and the processor.

In the rest of this section, we look at techniques to improve latency, bandwidth, or both.

Large Caches

As we mentioned at the start of this chapter, the disparity between CPU speeds and memory is growing. If you look closely, you can see vendors innovating in several ways. Some workstations are being offered with 4- MB data caches! This is

---

* See the STREAM section in Chapter 15 for measures of memory bandwidth.

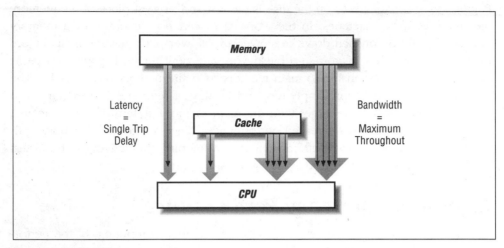

Figure 3-5: Simple memory system

larger than the main memory systems of machines just a few years ago. With a large enough cache, a small (or even moderately large) data set can fit completely inside and get incredibly good performance. Watch out for this when you are testing new hardware. When your program grows too large for the cache, the performance may drop off considerably, perhaps by a factor of 10 or more, depending on the memory access patterns. Interestingly, an increase in cache size on the part of vendors can render a benchmark obsolete.

Up to 1992, the Linpack 100×100 benchmark was probably the single most-respected benchmark to determine the average performance across a wide range of applications. In 1992, IBM introduced the IBM RS-6000 which had a cache large enough to contain the entire 100×100 matrix for the duration of the benchmark. For the first time, a workstation had performance on this benchmark on the same order of supercomputers. In a sense, with the entire data structure in a SRAM cache, the RS-6000 was operating like a Cray vector supercomputer. The problem was that the Cray could maintain and improve the performance for a 120×120 matrix, whereas the RS-6000 suffered a significant performance loss at this increased matrix size. Soon, all the other workstation vendors introduced similarly large caches, and the 100×100 Linpack benchmark ceased to be useful as an indicator of average application performance.

Wider Memory Systems

Consider what happens when a cache line is refilled from memory: consecutive memory locations from main memory are read to fill consecutive locations within the cache line. The number of bytes transferred depends on how big the line is— anywhere from 16 bytes to 256 bytes or more. We want the refill to proceed quickly because an instruction is stalled in the pipeline, or perhaps the processor is waiting for more instructions. In Figure 3-6, if we have two DRAM chips that provide us with 4 bits of data every 100 ns (remember cycle time), a cache fill of a 16-byte line takes 1600 ns.

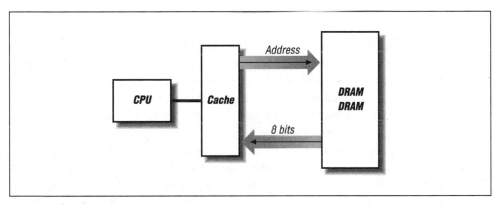

Figure 3-6: Narrow memory system

One way to make the cache-line fill operation faster is to "widen" the memory system as shown in Figure 3-7. Instead of having two rows of DRAMs, we create multiple rows of DRAMs. Now on every 100-ns cycle, we get 32 contiguous bits, and our cache-line fills are four times faster.

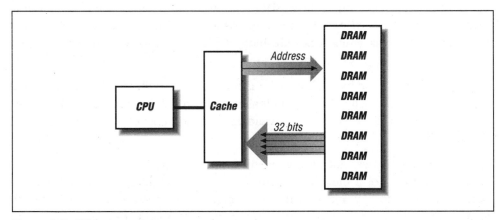

Figure 3-7: Wide memory system

We can improve the performance of a memory system by increasing the width of the memory system up to the length of the cache line, at which time we can fill the entire line in a single memory cycle. On the SGI Power Challenge series of systems, the memory width is 256 bits. The downside of a wider memory system is that DRAMs must be added in multiples. In many modern workstations and personal computers, memory is expanded in the form of single inline memory modules (SIMMs). SIMMs currently are either 30-, 72-, or 168-pin modules, each of which is made up of several DRAM chips ready to be installed into a memory subsystem.

Bypassing Cache

It's interesting that we have spent nearly an entire chapter on how great a cache is for high performance computers, and now we are going to bypass the cache to improve performance. As mentioned earlier, some types of processing result in non-unit strides (or bouncing around) through memory. These types of memory reference patterns bring out the worst-case behavior in cache-based architectures. It is these reference patterns that see improved performance by bypassing the cache. Inability to support these types of computations remains an area where traditional supercomputers can significantly outperform high-speed RISC processors. For this reason, RISC processors that are serious about number crunching may have special instructions that bypass data cache memory; the data are transferred directly between the processor and the main memory system.* In Figure 3-8 we have four banks of SIMMs that can do cache fills at 128 bits per 100 ns memory cycle. Remember that the data is available after 50 ns but we can't get more data until the DRAMs refresh 50–60 ns later. However, if we are doing 32-bit non-unit-stride loads and have the capability to bypass cache, each load will be satisfied from one of the four SIMMs in 50 ns. While that SIMM refreshed, another load can occur from any of the other three SIMMs in 50 ns. In a random mix of non-unit loads there is a 75% chance that the next load will fall on a "fresh" DRAM. If the load falls on a bank while it is refreshing, it simply has to wait until the refresh completes.

A further advantage of bypassing cache is that the data doesn't need to be moved through the SRAM cache. This operation can add from 10–50 ns to the load time for a single word. This also avoids invalidating the contents of an entire cache line in the cache.

Adding cache bypass, increasing memory-system widths, and adding banks increases the cost of a memory system. Computer-system vendors make an economic choice as to how many of these techniques they need to apply to get sufficient performance for their particular processor and system. Hence, as processor speed increases, vendors must add more of these memory system features to their commodity systems to maintain a balance between processor and memory-system speed.

---

* By the way, most machines have uncached memory spaces for process synchronization and I/O device registers. However, memory references to these locations bypass the cache because of the address chosen, not necessarily because of the instruction chosen.

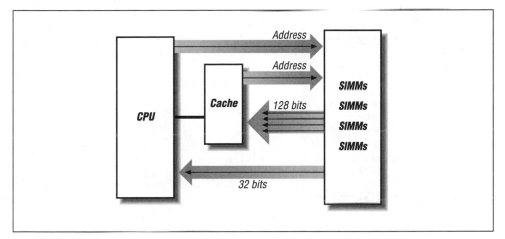

Figure 3-8: Bypassing cache

Interleaved and Pipelined Memory Systems

Vector supercomputers, such as the CRAY Y/MP and the Convex C3, are machines that depend on multibanked memory systems for performance. The C3, in particular, has a memory system with up to 256-way interleaving. Each interleave (or bank) is 64 bits wide. This is an expensive memory system to build, but it has some very nice performance characteristics. Having a large number of banks helps to reduce the chances of repeated access to the same memory bank. If you do hit the same bank twice in a row, however, the penalty is a delay of nearly 300 ns—a long time for a machine with a clock speed of 16 ns. So when things go well, they go very well.

However, having a large number of banks alone is not sufficient to feed a 16-ns processor using 50 ns DRAM. In addition to interleaving, the memory subsystem also needs to be pipelined. That is, the CPU must begin the second, third, and fourth load before the CPU has received the results of the first load as shown in Figure 3-9. Then each time it receives the results from bank "n," it must start the load from bank "n+4" to keep the pipeline fed. This way, after a brief startup delay, loads complete every 16 ns and so the memory system appears to operate at the clock rate of the CPU. This pipelined memory approach is facilitated by the 128-element vector registers in the C3 processor.

Using gather/scatter hardware, non-unit-stride operations can also be pipelined. The only difference for non-unit-stride operations is that the banks are not accessed in sequential order. With a random pattern of memory references, it's possible to reaccess a memory bank before it has completely refreshed from a previous access. This is called a *bank stall*.

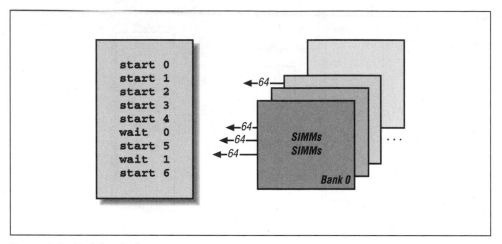

Figure 3-9: Multibanked memory system

Different access patterns are subject to bank stalls of varying severity. For instance, accesses to every fourth word in an eight-bank memory system would also be subject to bank stalls, though the recovery would occur sooner. References to every second word might not experience bank stalls at all; each bank may have recovered by the time its next reference comes around; it depends on the relative speeds of the processor and memory system. Irregular access patterns are sure to encounter some bank stalls.

In addition to the bank stall hazard, single-word references made directly to a multibanked memory system carry a greater latency than those of (successfully) cached memory accesses. This is because references are going out to memory that is slower than cache, and there may be additional address translation steps as well. However, banked memory references are pipelined. As long as references are started well enough in advance, several pipelined, multibanked references can be in flight at one time, giving you good throughput.

The CDC-205 system performed vector operations in a memory-to-memory fashion using a set of explicit memory pipelines. This system had superior performance for very long unit-stride vector computations. A single instruction could perform 65,000 computations using three memory pipes.

Software Managed Caches

Here's an interesting thought: if a vector processor can plan far enough in advance to start a memory pipe, why can't a RISC processor start a cache-fill before it really needs the data in those same situations? In a way, this is priming the cache to hide the latency of the cache-fill. If this could be done far enough in advance, it would appear that all memory references would operate at the speed of the cache.

This concept is called *prefetching* and it is supported using a special prefetch instruction available on many RISC processors. A prefetch instruction operates just like a standard load instruction, except that the processor doesn't wait for the cache to fill before the instruction completes. The idea is to prefetch far enough ahead of the computation to have the data ready in cache by the time the actual computation occurs. The following is an example of how this might be used:

```
DO I=1,1000000,8
  PREFETCH(ARR(I+8))
  DO J=0,7
    SUM=SUM+ARR(I+J)
  END DO
END DO
```

This is not the actual FORTRAN. Prefetching is usually done in the assembly code generated by the compiler when it detects that you are stepping through the array using a fixed stride. The compiler typically estimate how far ahead you should be prefetching. In the above example, if the cache-fills were particularly slow, the value 8 in I+8 could be changed to 16 or 32 while the other values changed accordingly.

In a processor that could only issue one instruction per cycle, there might be no payback to a prefetch instruction; it would take up valuable time in the instruction stream in exchange for an uncertain benefit. On a superscalar processor, however, a cache hint could be mixed in with the rest of the instruction stream and issued alongside other, real instructions. If it saved your program from suffering extra cache misses, it would be worth having.

Post-RISC Effects on Memory References

Memory operations typically access the memory during the execute phase of the pipeline on a RISC processor. On the post-RISC processor, things are no different than on a RISC processor except that many loads can be half finished at any given moment. On some current processors, up to 28 memory operations may be active with 10 waiting for off-chip memory to arrive. This is an excellent way to compensate for slow memory latency compared to the CPU speed. Consider the following loop:

```
        LOADI    R6,10000     Set the Iterations
        LOADI    R5,0         Set the index variable
LOOP:   LOAD     R1,R2(R5)    Load a value from memory
        INCR     R1           Add one to R1
        STORE    R1,R3(R5)    Store the incremented value back to memory
        INCR     R5           Add one to R5
        COMPARE  R5,R6        Check for loop termination
        BLT      LOOP         Branch if R5 < R6 back to LOOP
```

In this example, assume that it take 50 cycles to access memory. When the fetch/ decode puts the first load into the instruction reorder buffer (IRB), the load starts on the next cycle and then is suspended in the execute phase. However, the rest of the instructions are in the IRB. The `INCR R1` must wait for the load and the `STORE` must also wait. However, by using a rename register, the `INCR R5`, `COM-PARE`, and `BLT` can all be computed, and the fetch/decode goes up to the top of the loop and sends another load into the IRB for the next memory location that will have to wait. This looping continues until about 10 iterations of the loop are in the IRB. Then the first load actually shows up from memory and the `INCR R1` and `STORE` from the first iteration begins executing. Of course the store takes a while, but about that time the second load finishes, so there is more work to do and so on . . .

Like many aspects of computing, the post-RISC architecture, with its out-of-order and speculative execution, optimizes memory references. The post-RISC processor dynamically unrolls loops at execution time to compensate for memory subsystem delay. Assuming a pipelined multibanked memory system that can have multiple memory operations started before any complete (the HP PA-8000 can have 10 off-chip memory operations in flight at one time), the processor continues to dispatch memory operations until those operations begin to complete.

Unlike a vector processor or a prefetch instruction, the post-RISC processor does not need to anticipate the precise pattern of memory references so it can carefully control the memory subsystem. As a result, the post-RISC processor can achieve peak performance in a far-wider range of code sequences than either vector processors or in-order RISC processors with prefetch capability.

This implicit tolerance to memory latency makes the post-RISC processors ideal for use in the scalable shared-memory processors of the future, where the memory hierarchy will become even more complex than current processors with three levels of cache and a main memory.

Unfortunately, the one code segment that doesn't benefit significantly from the post-RISC architecture is the linked-list traversal. This is because the next address is never known until the previous load is completed so all loads are fundamentally serialized.

Dynamic RAM Technology Trends

Much of the techniques in this section have focused on how to deal with the imperfections of the dynamic RAM chip (although when your clock rate hits 300–600 MHz or 3–2 ns, even SRAM starts to look pretty slow). It's clear that the demand for more and more RAM will continue to increase, and gigabits and more DRAM will fit on a single chip. Because of this, significant work is underway to make new super DRAMs faster and more tuned to the extremely fast processors of the present and the future. Some of the technologies are relatively straightforward, and others require a major redesign of the way that processors and memories are manufactured.

Some DRAM improvements include:

- Fast page mode DRAM
- Extended data out RAM (EDO RAM)
- Synchronous DRAM (SDRAM)
- RAMBUS
- Cached DRAM (CDRAM)

Fast page mode DRAM saves time by allowing a mode in which the entire address doesn't have to be re-clocked into the chip for each memory operation. Instead, there is an assumption that the memory will be accessed sequentially (as in a cache-line fill), and only the low-order bits of the address are clocked in for successive reads or writes.

EDO RAM is a modification to output buffering on page mode RAM that allows it to operate roughly twice as quickly for operations other than refresh.

Synchronous DRAM is synchronized using an external clock that allows the cache and the DRAM to coordinate their operations. Also, SDRAM can pipeline the retrieval of multiple memory bits to improve overall throughput.

RAMBUS is a proprietary technology capable of 500 MB/sec data transfer. RAMBUS uses significant logic within the chip and operates at higher power levels than typical DRAM.

Cached DRAM combines a SRAM cache on the same chip as the DRAM. This tightly couples the SRAM and DRAM and provides performance similar to SRAM devices with all the limitations of any cache architecture. One advantage of the CDRAM approach is that the amount of cache is increased as the amount of DRAM is increased. Also when dealing with memory systems with a large number of interleaves, each interleave has its own SRAM to reduce latency, assuming the data requested was in the SRAM.

An even more advanced approach is to integrate the processor, SRAM, and DRAM onto a single chip clocked at say 5 GHz, containing 128 MB of data. Understandably, there is a wide range of technical problems to solve before this type of component is widely available for $200—but it's not out of the question. The manufacturing processes for DRAM and processors are already beginning to converge in some ways (RAMBUS). The biggest performance problem when we have this type of system will be, "What to do if you need 160 MB?"

Closing Notes

They say that the computer of the future will be a good memory system that just happens to have a CPU attached. As high performance microprocessor systems take over as *the* high performance computing engines, the problem of a cache-based memory system that uses DRAM for main memory must be solved. There are many architecture and technology efforts underway to transform workstation and personal computer memories to be as capable as supercomputer memories.

As CPU speed increases faster than memory speed, you will need the techniques in this book. Also, as you move into multiple processors, memory problems don't get better; usually they get worse. With many hungry processors always ready for more data, a memory subsystem can become extremely strained.

With just a little skill, we can often restructure memory accesses so that they play to your memory system's strengths instead of its weaknesses.

Exercises

1. The following code segment traverses a pointer chain:

   ```
   while ((p = (char *) *p) != NULL);
   ```

   How will such a code interact with the cache if all the references fall within a small portion of memory? How will the code interact with the cache if references are stretched across many megabytes?

2. How would the code in Exercise 1 behave on a multibanked memory system that has no cache?

3. A long time ago, people regularly wrote self-modifying code—programs that wrote into instruction memory and changed their own behavior. What would be the implications of self-modifying code on a machine with a Harvard memory architecture?

4. Assume a memory architecture with an L1 cache speed of 10 ns, L2 speed of 30 ns, and memory speed of 200 ns. Compare the average memory system performance with (1) L1 80%, L2 10%, and memory 10%; and (2) L1 85% and memory 15%.

5. On a computer system, run loops that process arrays of varying length from 16 to 16 million:

   ```
   ARRAY(I) = ARRAY(I) + 3
   ```

   How does the number of additions per second change as the array length changes? Experiment with REAL*4, REAL*8, INTEGER*4, and INTEGER*8.

Which has more significant impact on performance. larger array elements or integer versus floating-point? Try this on a range of different computers.

6. Create a two-dimensional array of 1024×1024. Loop through the array with rows as the inner loop and then again with columns as the inner loop. Perform a simple operation on each element. Do the loops perform differently? Why? Experiment with different dimensions for the array and see the performance impact.

7. Write a program that repeatedly executes timed loops of different sizes to determine the cache size for your system.

4

Floating-Point Numbers

Often when we want to make a point that nothing is sacred, we say, "one plus one does not equal two." This is designed to shock us and attack our fundamental assumptions about the nature of the universe. Well, in this chapter on floating-point numbers, we will learn that "0.1 + 0.1 does not always equal 0.2" when we use floating-point numbers for computations.

In this chapter we explore the limitations of floating-point numbers and how you as a programmer can write code to minimize the effect of these limitations. This chapter is just a brief introduction to a significant field of mathematics called *numerical analysis*.

Reality

The real world is full of real numbers. Quantities such as distances, velocities, masses, angles, and other quantities are all real numbers.* A wonderful property of real numbers is that they have unlimited accuracy. For example, when considering the ratio of the circumference of a circle to its diameter, we arrive at a value of 3.141592 .... The decimal value for *pi* does not terminate. Because real numbers have unlimited accuracy, even though we can't write it down, *pi* is still a real

---

* In high performance computing we often simulate the real world, so it is somewhat ironic that we use simulated real numbers (floating-point) in those simulations of the real world.

number. Some real numbers are *rational numbers* because they can be represented as the ratio of two integers, such as 1/3. Not all real numbers are rational numbers. Not surprisingly, those real numbers that aren't rational numbers are called irrational. You probably would not want to start an argument with an irrational number unless you have a lot of free time on your hands.

Unfortunately, on a piece of paper, or in a computer, we don't have enough space to keep writing the digits of *pi*. So what do we do? We decide that we only need so much accuracy and round real numbers to a certain number of digits. For example, if we decide on four digits of accuracy, our approximation of *pi* is 3.142. Some state legislature attempted to pass a law that *pi* was to be three. While this is often cited as evidence for the IQ of governmental entities, perhaps the legislature was just suggesting that we only need one digit of accuracy for *pi*. Perhaps they foresaw the need to save precious memory space on computers when representing real numbers.

Representation

Given that we cannot perfectly represent real numbers on digital computers, we must come up with a compromise that allows us to approximate real numbers.* There are a number of different ways that have been used to represent real numbers. The challenge in selecting a representation is the trade-off between space and accuracy and the tradeoff between speed and accuracy. In the field of high performance computing we generally expect our processors to produce a floating-point result every 600-MHz clock cycle. It is pretty clear that in most applications we aren't willing to drop this by a factor of 100 just for a little more accuracy. Before we discuss the format used by most high performance computers, we discuss some alternative (albeit slower) techniques for representing real numbers.

Binary Coded Decimal

In the earliest computers, one technique was to use *binary coded decimal* (BCD). In BCD, each base-10 digit was stored in four bits. Numbers could be arbitrarily long with as much precision as there was memory:

---

* Interestingly, analog computers have an easier time representing real numbers. Imagine a "water-adding" analog computer which consists of two glasses of water and an empty glass. The amount of water in the two glasses are perfectly represented real numbers. By pouring the two glasses into a third, we are adding the two real numbers perfectly (unless we spill some), and we wind up with a real number amount of water in the third glass. The problem with analog computers is knowing just how much water is in the glasses when we are all done. It is also problematic to perform 600 million additions per second using this technique without getting pretty wet. Try to resist the temptation to start an argument over whether quantum mechanics would cause the real numbers to be rational numbers. And don't point out the fact that even digital computers are really analog computers at their core. I am trying to keep the focus on floating-point values, and you keep drifting away!

```
123.45
0001 0010 0011 0100 0101
```

This format allows the programmer to choose the precision required for each variable. Unfortunately, it is difficult to build extremely high-speed hardware to perform arithmetic operations on these numbers. Because each number may be far longer than 32 or 64 bits, they did not fit nicely in a register. Much of the floating-point operations for BCD were done using loops in microcode. Even with the flexibility of accuracy on BCD representation, there was still a need to round real numbers to fit into a limited amount of space.

Another limitation of the BCD approach is that we store a value from 0–9 in a four-bit field. This field is capable of storing values from 0–15 so some of the space is wasted.

Rational Numbers

One intriguing method of storing real numbers is to store them as rational numbers. To briefly review mathematics, rational numbers are the subset of real numbers that can be expressed as a ratio of integer numbers. For example, 22/7 and 1/2 are rational numbers. Some rational numbers, such as 1/2 and 1/10, have perfect representation as base-10 decimals, and others, such as 1/3 and 22/7, can only be expressed as infinite-length base-10 decimals. When using rational numbers, each real number is stored as two integer numbers representing the numerator and denominator. The basic fractional arithmetic operations are used for addition, subtraction, multiplication, and division, as shown in Figure 4-1.

$$\frac{1}{3} \times \frac{30}{7} = \frac{30}{21} = \frac{10}{7}$$

$$\frac{1}{6} + \frac{1}{5} = \frac{5}{30} + \frac{6}{30} = \frac{11}{30}$$

$$\frac{14173}{21224} \times \frac{77234}{2121} = \frac{1094637482}{45016104} = \frac{547318741}{22508052}$$

Figure 4-1: Rational number mathematics

The limitation that occurs when using rational numbers to represent real numbers is that the size of the numerators and denominators tends to grow. For each addition, a common denominator must be found. To keep the numbers from becoming extremely large, during each operation, it is important to find the *greatest common divisor* (GCD) to reduce fractions to their most compact representation. When the values grow and there are no common divisors, either the large integer values must be stored using dynamic memory or some form of approximation must be used, thus losing the primary advantage of rational numbers.

For mathematical packages such as Maple or Mathematica that need to produce exact results on smaller data sets, the use of rational numbers to represent real numbers is at times a useful technique. The performance and storage cost is less significant than the need to produce exact results in some instances.

Fixed Point

If the desired number of decimal places is known in advance, it's possible to use fixed-point representation. Using this technique, each real number is stored as a scaled integer. This solves the problem that base-10 fractions such as 0.1 or 0.01 cannot be perfectly represented as a base-2 fraction. If you multiply 110.77 by 100 and store it as a scaled integer 11077, you can perfectly represent the base-10 fractional part (0.77). This approach can be used for values such as money, where the number of digits past the decimal point is small and known.

However, just because all numbers can be accurately represented it doesn't mean there are not errors with this format. When multiplying a fixed-point number by a fraction, you get digits that can't be represented in a fixed-point format, so some form of rounding must be used. For example, if you have $125.87 in the bank at 4% interest, your interest amount would be $5.0348. However, because your bank balance only has two digits of accuracy, they only give you $5.03, resulting in a balance of $130.90. Of course you probably have heard many stories of programmers getting rich depositing many of the remaining 0.0048 amounts into their own account. My guess is that banks have probably figured that one out by now, and the bank keeps the money for itself. But it does make one wonder if they round or truncate in this type of calculation.*

Mantissa/Exponent

The floating-point format that is most prevalent in high performance computing is a variation on scientific notation. In scientific notation the real number is represented using a mantissa, base, and exponent: 6.02×10^{23}.

---

* Perhaps banks round this instead of truncating, knowing that they will always make it up in teller machine fees.

The mantissa typically has some fixed number of places of accuracy. The mantissa can be represented in base 2, base 16, or BCD. There is generally a limited range of exponents, and the exponent can be expressed as a power of 2, 10, or 16.

The primary advantage of this representation is that it provides a wide overall range of values while using a fixed-length storage representation. The primary limitation of this format is that the difference between two successive values is not uniform. For example, assume that you can represent three base-10 digits, and your exponent can range from −10 to 10. For numbers close to zero, the "distance" between successive numbers is very small. For the number 1.72×10^{-10}, the next larger number is 1.73×10^{-10}. The distance between these two "close" small numbers is 0.000000000001. For the number 6.33×10^{10}, the next larger number is 6.34×10^{10}. The distance between these "close" large numbers is 100 million.

In Figure 4-2, we use two base-2 digits with an exponent ranging from −1 to 1.

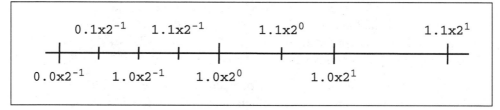

Figure 4-2: Distance between successive floating-point numbers

There are multiple equivalent representations of a number when using scientific notation:

```
6.00 X 10⁵
0.60 X 10⁶
0.06 X 10⁷
```

By convention, we shift the mantissa (adjust the exponent) until there is exactly one nonzero digit to the left of the decimal point. When a number is expressed this way, it is said to be "normalized." In the above list, only 6.00×10^5 is normalized. Figure 4-3 shows how some of the floating-point numbers from Figure 4-2 are not normalized.

While the mantissa/exponent has been the dominant floating-point approach for high performance computing, there were a wide variety of specific formats in use by computer vendors. Historically, each computer vendor had their own particular format for floating-point numbers. Because of this, a program executed on several different brands of computer would generally produce different answers. This

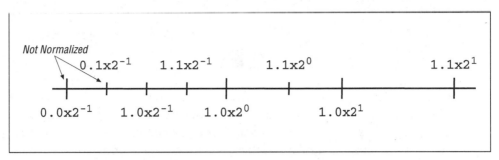

Figure 4-3: Normalized floating-point numbers

invariably led to heated discussions about which system provided the right answer and which system(s) were generating meaningless results.*

When storing floating-point numbers in digital computers, typically the mantissa is normalized, and then the mantissa and exponent are converted to base-2 and packed into a 32- or 64-bit word. If more bits were allocated to the exponent, the overall range of the format would be increased, and the number of digits of accuracy would be decreased. Also the base of the exponent could be base-2 or base-16. Using 16 as the base for the exponent increases the overall range of exponents, but because normalization must occur on four-bit boundaries, the available digits of accuracy are reduced on the average. Later we will see how the IEEE 754 standard for floating-point format represents numbers.

Effects of Floating-Point Representation

One problem with the mantissa/base/exponent representation is that not all base-10 numbers can be expressed perfectly as a base-2 number. For example, 1/2 and 0.25 can be represented perfectly as base-2 values, while 1/3 and 0.1 produce infinitely repeating base-2 decimals. These values must be rounded to be stored in the floating-point format. With sufficient digits of precision, this generally is not a problem for computations. However, it does lead to some anomalies where algebraic rules do not appear to apply. Consider the following example:

```
REAL*4 X,Y
X = 0.1
Y = 0
DO I=1,10
  Y = Y + X
ENDDO
IF ( Y .EQ. 1.0 ) THEN
```

---

* Interestingly, there was an easy answer to the question for many programmers. Generally they trusted the results from the computer they used to debug the code and dismissed the results from other computers as garbage.

```
    PRINT *,'Algebra is truth'
  ELSE
    PRINT *,'Not here'
  ENDIF
  PRINT *,1.0-Y
  END
```

At first glance, this appears simple enough. Mathematics tells us ten times 0.1 should be one. Unfortunately, because 0.1 cannot be represented exactly as a base-2 decimal, it must be rounded. It ends up being rounded down to the last bit. When ten of these slightly smaller numbers are added together, it does not quite add up to 1.0. When X and Y are REAL*4, the difference is about 10^{-7}, and when they are REAL*8, the difference is about 10^{-16}.

One possible method for comparing computed values to constants is to subtract the values and test to see how close the two values become. For example, one can rewrite the test in the above code to be:

```
  IF ( ABS(1.0-Y) .LT. 1E-6 ) THEN
    PRINT *,'Close enough for government work'
  ELSE
    PRINT *,'Not even close'
  ENDIF
```

The type of the variables in question and the expected error in the computation that produces Y determines the appropriate value used to declare that two values are close enough to be declared equal.

Another area where inexact representation becomes a problem is the fact that algebraic inverses do not hold with all floating-point numbers. For example, using REAL*4, the value (1.0/X) * X does not evaluate to 1.0 for 135 values of X from one to 1000. This can be a problem when computing the inverse of a matrix using LU-decomposition. LU-decomposition repeatedly does division, multiplication, addition, and subtraction. If you do the straightforward LU-decomposition on a matrix with integer coefficients that has an integer solution, there is a pretty good chance you won't get the exact solution when you run your algorithm. Discussing techniques for improving the accuracy of matrix inverse computation is best left to a numerical analysis text.

More Algebra That Doesn't Work

While the examples in the proceeding section focused on the limitations of multiplication and division, addition and subtraction are not, by any means, perfect. Because of the limitation of the number of digits of precision, certain additions or subtractions have no effect. Consider the following example using REAL*4 with 7 digits of precision:

```
X = 1.25E8
Y = X + 7.5E-3
IF ( X.EQ.Y ) THEN
   PRINT *,'Am I nuts or what?'
ENDIF
```

While both of these numbers are precisely representable in floating-point, adding them is problematic. Prior to adding these numbers together, their decimal points must be aligned as in Figure 4-4.

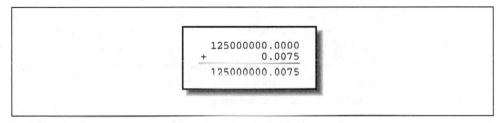

Figure 4-4: Loss of accuracy while aligning decimal points

Unfortunately, while we have computed the exact result, it cannot fit back into a **REAL*4** variable (7 digits of accuracy) without truncating the 0.0075. So after the addition, the value in **Y** is exactly 1.25E8. Even sadder, the addition could be performed *millions* of times, and the value for **Y** would still be 1.25E8.

Because of the limitation on precision, not all algebraic laws apply all the time. For instance, the answer you obtain from X+Y will be the same as Y+X, as per the commutative law for addition. Whichever operand you pick first, the operation yields the same result; they are mathematically equivalent. It also means that you can choose either of the following two forms and get the same answer:

```
(X + Y) + Z
(Y + X) + Z
```

However, this is not equivalent:

```
(Y + Z) + X
```

The third version isn't equivalent to the first two because the order of the calculations has changed. Again, the rearrangement is equivalent algebraically, but not computationally. By changing the order of the calculations, we have taken advantage of the associativity of the operations; we have made an *associative transformation* of the original code.

To understand why the order of the calculations matters, imagine that your computer can perform arithmetic significant to only five decimal places.

Also assume that the values of X, Y, and Z are .00005, .00005, and 1.0000, respectively. This means that:

```
(X + Y) + Z =   .00005 +   .00005 + 1.0000
            =   .0001            + 1.0000    = 1.0001
```

but:

```
(Y + Z) + X =   .00005 + 1.0000   +   .00005
            = 1.0000            +   .00005   = 1.0000
```

The two versions give slightly different answers. When adding Y+Z+X, the sum of the smaller numbers was insignificant when added to the larger number. But when computing X+Y+Z, we add the two small numbers first, and their combined sum is large enough to influence the final answer. For this reason, compilers that rearrange operations for the sake of performance generally only do so after the user has requested optimizations beyond the defaults.

For these reasons, the FORTRAN language is very strict about the exact order of evaluation of expressions. To be compliant, the compiler must ensure that the operations occur exactly as you express them.*

For Kernighan and Ritchie C, the operator precedence rules are different. Although the precedences between operators are honored (i.e., * comes before +, and evaluation generally occurs left to right for operators of equal precedence), the compiler is allowed to treat a few commutative operations (+, *, &, ^ and |) as if they were fully associative, *even* if they are parenthesized. For instance, you might tell the C compiler:

```
a = x + (y + z);
```

However, the C compiler is free to ignore you, and combine X, Y, and Z in any order it pleases.

Now armed with this knowledge, view the following harmless-looking code segment:

```
REAL*4 SUM,A(1000000)
SUM = 0.0
DO I=1,1000000
  SUM = SUM + A(I)
ENDDO
```

Begins to look like a nightmare waiting to happen. The accuracy of this sum depends of the relative magnitudes and order of the values in the array A. If we sort the array from smallest to largest and then perform the additions, we have a more accurate value. There are other algorithms for computing the sum of an array

---

* Often even if you didn't mean it.

that reduce the error without requiring a full sort of the data. Consult a good text-book on numerical analysis for the details on these algorithms.

If the range of magnitudes of the values in the array is relatively small, the straight-forward computation of the sum is probably sufficient.

Improving Accuracy Using Guard Digits

In this section we explore a technique to improve the precision of floating-point computations without using additional storage space for the floating-point numbers.

Consider the following example of a base-10 system with five digits of accuracy performing the following subtraction:

```
10.001 - 9.9993 = 0.0017
```

All of these values can be perfectly represented using our floating-point format. However, if we only have five digits of precision available while aligning the deci-mal points during the computation, the results end up with significant error as shown in Figure 4-5.

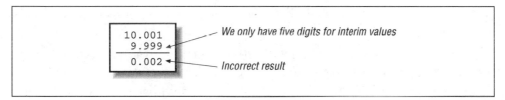

Figure 4-5: Need for guard digits

To perform this computation and round it correctly, we do not need to increase the number of significant digits for *stored* values. We do, however, need additional digits of precision while performing the computation.

The solution is to add extra *guard digits* which are maintained during the interim steps of the computation. In our case, if we maintained six digits of accuracy while aligning operands, and rounded before normalizing and assigning the final value, we would get the proper result. The guard digits only need to be present as part of the floating-point execution unit in the CPU. It is not necessary to add guard digits to the registers or to the values stored in memory.

It is not necessary to have an extremely large number of guard digits. At some point, the difference in the magnitude between the operands becomes so great that lost digits do not affect the addition or rounding results.

History of IEEE Floating-Point Format

Prior to the RISC microprocessor revolution, each vendor had their own floating-point formats based on their designers' views of the relative importance of range versus accuracy and speed versus accuracy. It was not uncommon for one vendor to carefully analyze the limitations of another vendor's floating-point format and use this information to convince users that theirs was the only "accurate" floating-point implementation. In reality none of the formats was perfect. The formats were simply imperfect in different ways.

During the 1980s the Institute for Electrical and Electronics Engineers (IEEE) produced a standard for the floating-point format. The title of the standard is "IEEE 754-1985 Standard for Binary Floating-Point Arithmetic." This standard provided the precise definition of a floating-point format and described the operations on floating-point values.

Because IEEE 754 was developed after a variety of floating-point formats had been in use for quite some time, the IEEE 754 working group had the benefit of examining the existing floating-point designs and taking the strong points, and avoiding the mistakes in existing designs. The IEEE 754 specification had its beginnings in the design of the Intel i8087 floating-point coprocessor. The i8087 floating-point format improved on the DEC VAX floating-point format by adding a number of significant features.

The near universal adoption of IEEE 754 floating-point format has occurred over a 10-year time period. The high performance computing vendors of the mid 1980s (Cray IBM, DEC, and Control Data) had their own proprietary floating-point formats that they had to continue supporting because of their installed user base. They really had no choice but to continue to support their existing formats. In the mid to late 1980s the primary systems that supported the IEEE format were RISC workstations and some coprocessors for microprocessors. Because the designers of these systems had no need to protect a proprietary floating-point format, they readily adopted the IEEE format. As RISC processors moved from general-purpose integer computing to high performance floating-point computing, the CPU designers found ways to make IEEE floating-point operations operate very quickly. In 10 years, the IEEE 754 has gone from a standard for floating-point coprocessors to the dominant floating-point standard for all computers. Because of this standard, we, the users, are the beneficiaries of a portable floating-point environment.

IEEE Floating-Point Standard

The IEEE 754 standard specified a number of different details of floating-point operations, including:

- Storage formats

- Precise specifications of the results of operations

- Special values

- Specified runtime behavior on illegal operations

Specifying the floating-point format to this level of detail insures that when a computer system is compliant with the standard, users can expect repeatable execution from one hardware platform to another when operations are executed in the same order.

IEEE Storage Format

The two most common IEEE floating-point formats in use are 32- and 64-bit numbers. Table 4-1 gives the general parameters of these data types.

Table 4-1: Parameters of IEEE 32- and 64-Bit Formats

IEEE75	FORTRAN	C	Bits	Exponent Bits	Mantissa Bits
Single	REAL*4	float	32	8	24
Double	REAL*8	double	64	11	53
Double-Extended	REAL*10	long double	>=80	>=15	>=64

In FORTRAN, the 32-bit format is usually called REAL, and the 64-bit format is usually called DOUBLE. However, some FORTRAN compilers double the sizes for these data types. For that reason, it is safest to declare your FORTRAN variables as REAL*4 or REAL*8. The double-extended format is not as well supported in compilers and hardware as the single- and double-precision formats. The bit arrangement for the single and double formats are shown in Figure 4-6.

Based on the storage layouts in Table 4-1, we can derive the ranges and accuracy of these formats, as shown in Table 4-2.

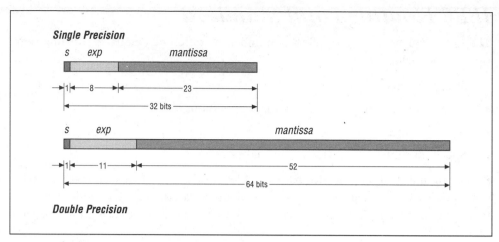

Figure 4-6: IEEE 754 floating-point formats

Table 4-2: Range and Accuracy of IEEE 32- and 64-Bit Formats

IEEE754	Minimum Normalized Number	Largest Finite Number	Base-10 Accuracy
Single	1.2E-38	3.4 E+38	6-9 digits
Double	2.2E-308	1.8 E+308	15-17 digits
Extended Double	3.4E-4932	1.2 E+4932	18-21 digits

The minimum normalized number is the smallest number which can be represented at full precision. IEEE format also supportes *subnormal* numbers, which are smaller than the minimum normalized number at a loss of precision. Using subnormal numbers, one can represent numbers as small as 2.0E-45 in the 32-bit format, but for numbers that small, the accuracy is reduced to 1–2 digits of base-10 accuracy.

In IEEE, if a computation yields a value larger than the largest finite number (called *overflow*), the special value infinity is returned.

Converting from Base-10 to IEEE Internal Format

We now examine how a 32-bit floating-point number is stored. The high-order bit is the sign of the number. Numbers are stored in a sign-magnitude format (i.e., not 2's - complement). The exponent is stored in the 8-bit field biased by adding 127 to the exponent. This results in an exponent ranging from -126 through +127.

The mantissa is converted into base-2 and normalized so that there is one nonzero digit to the left of the binary place, adjusting the exponent as necessary. The digits to the right of the binary point are then stored in the low-order 23 bits of the word. Because all numbers are normalized, there is no need to store the leading 1.

This gives a free extra bit of precision. Because this bit is dropped, it's no longer proper to refer to the stored value as the mantissa. In IEEE parlance, this mantissa minus its leading digit is called the *significand.*

Figure 4-7 shows an example conversion from base-10 to IEEE 32-bit format.

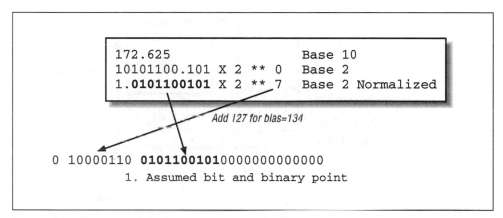

```
172.625                    Base 10
10101100.101 X 2 ** 0      Base 2
1.0101100101 X 2 ** 7      Base 2 Normalized
```

Add 127 for bias=134

```
0 10000110 01011001010000000000000
         1. Assumed bit and binary point
```

Figure 4-7: Converting from base-10 to IEEE 32-bit format

The 64-bit format is similar, except the exponent is 11 bits long, biased by adding 1023 to the exponent, and the significand is 54 bits long.

IEEE Operations

The IEEE standard specifies how computations are to be performed on floating-point values on the following operations:

- Addition

- Subtraction

- Multiplication

- Division

- Square root

- Remainder (modulo)

- Conversion to/from integer

- Conversion to/from printed base-10

These operations are specified in a machine-independent manner, giving flexibility to the CPU designers to implement the operations as efficiently as possible while maintaining compliance with the standard. During operations, the IEEE standard requires the maintenance of two guard digits and a sticky bit for intermediate values. The guard digits above and the sticky bit are used to indicate if any of the bits beyond the second guard digit is nonzero.

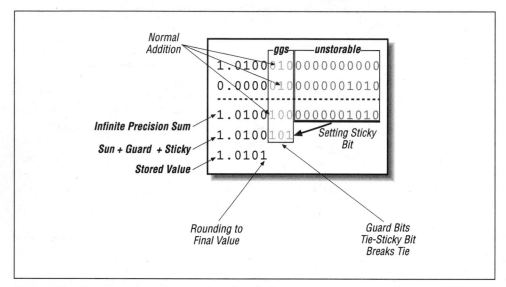

Figure 4-8: Computation using guard and sticky bits

In Figure 4-8, we have five bits of normal precision, two guard digits, and a sticky bit. Guard bits simply operate as normal bits—as if the significand were 25 bits. Guard bits participate in rounding as the extended operands are added. The sticky bit is set to 1 if any of the bits beyond the guard bits is nonzero in either operand.* Once the extended sum is computed, it is rounded so that the value stored in memory is the closest possible value to the extended sum including the guard digits. Table 4-3 shows all eight possible values of the two guard digits and the sticky bit and the resulting stored value with an explanation as to why.

Table 4-3: Extended Sums and Their Stored Values

Extended Sum	Stored Value	Why
1.0100 000	1.0100	Truncated based on guard digits
1.0100 001	1.0100	Truncated based on guard digits
1.0100 010	1.0100	Rounded down based on guard digits
1.0100 011	1.0100	Rounded down based on guard digits
1.0100 100	1.0100	Rounded down based on sticky bit

---

* If you are somewhat hardware-inclined and you think about it for a moment, you will soon come up with a way to properly maintain the sticky bit without ever computing the full "infinite precision sum." You just have to keep track as things get shifted around.

Table 4-3: Extended Sums and Their Stored Values (continued)

Extended Sum	Stored Value	Why
1.0100 101	1.0101	Rounded up based on sticky bit
1.0100 110	1.0101	Rounded up based on guard digits
1.0100 111	1.0101	Rounded up based on guard digits

The first priority is to check the guard digits. Never forget that the sticky bit is just a hint, not a real digit. So if we can make a decision without looking at the sticky bit, that is good. The only desision we are making is to round the last storable bit up or down. When that stored value is retrieved for the next computation, its guard digits are set to zeros. It is sometimes helpful to think of the stored value as having the guard digits, but set to zero.

So of our eight different extended sums, we must choose between two stored values. In the first two cases, the guard digits in the extended sum and stored value match exactly, so we just store it. For nonzero guard digits, we have to figure which is closer. When the guard digits are 01 the extended sum is one guard digit unit away from the truncated value. For 11 we are closest to the rounded-up value. However, when the guard digits are 10 we have the largest error and are right between the truncated and rounded-up values. It is at this point where we consult the value of the sticky bit to get a better indication of which stored value would be closer to our extended sum.

Two guard digits and the sticky bit in the IEEE format insures that operations yield the same rounding as if the intermediate result were computed using unlimited precision and then rounded to fit within the limits of precision of the final computed value.

At this point, you might be asking, "Why do I care about this minutiae?" At some level, unless you are a hardware designer, you don't care. But when you examine details like this, you can be assured of one thing: when they developed the IEEE floating-point standard, they looked at the details *very* carefully. The goal was to produce the most accurate possible floating-point standard within the constraints of a fixed-length 32- or 64-bit format. Because they did such a good job, it's one less thing you have to worry about. Besides, this stuff makes great exam questions.

Special Values

In addition to specifying the results of operations on numeric data, the IEEE standard also specifies the precise behavior on undefined operations such as dividing by zero. These results are indicated using several special values. These values are bit patterns that are stored in variables that are checked before operations are performed. The IEEE operations are all defined on these special values in addition to the normal numeric values. Table 4-4 summarizes the special values for a 32-bit IEEE floating-point number.

Table 4-4: Special Values for an IEEE 32-Bit Number

Special Value	Exponent	Significand
+ or - 0	00000000	0
Denormalized number	00000000	nonzero
NaN (Not a Number)	11111111	nonzero
+ or - Infinity	11111111	0

The value of the exponent and significand determines which type of special value this particular floating-point number represents. Zero is designed such that integer zero and floating-point zero are the same bit pattern.

Denormalized numbers can occur at some point as a number continues to get smaller, and the exponent has reached the minimum value. We could declare that minimum to be the smallest representable value. However, with denormalized values, we can continue by setting the exponent bits to zero and shifting the significand bits to the right, first adding the leading "1" that was dropped, then continuing to add leading zeros to indicate even smaller values. At some point the last nonzero digit is shifted off to the right, and the value becomes zero. This approach is called *gradual underflow* where the value keeps approaching zero and then eventually becomes zero. Not all implementations support denormalized numbers in hardware; they might trap to a software routine to handle these numbers at a significant performance cost.

At the top end of the biased exponent value, an exponent of all 1s can represent the *Not a Number* (NaN) value or infinity. Infinity occurs in computations roughly according to the principles of mathematics. If you continue to increase the magnitude of a number beyond the range of the floating-point format, once the range has been exceeded, the value becomes infinity. Once a value is infinity, further additions won't increase it, and subtractions won't decrease it. You can also produce the value infinity by dividing a nonzero value by zero. If you divide a nonzero value by infinity, you get zero as a result.

The NaN value indicates a number that is not mathematically defined. You can generate a NaN by dividing zero by zero, dividing infinity by infinity, or taking the square root of -1. The difference between infinity and NaN is that the NaN value has a nonzero significand. The NaN value is very sticky. Any operation that has a NaN as one of its inputs always produces a NaN result.

Exceptions and Traps

In addition to defining the results of computations that aren't mathematically defined, the IEEE standard provides programmers with the ability to detect when these special values are being produced. This way, programmers can write their code without adding extensive IF tests throughout the code checking for the magnitude of values. Instead they can register a trap handler for an event such as underflow and handle the event when it occurs. The exceptions defined by the IEEE standard include:

- Overflow to infinity
- Underflow to zero
- Division by zero
- Invalid operation
- Inexact operation

According to the standard, these traps are under the control of the user. In most cases, the compiler runtime library manages these traps under the direction from the user through compiler flags or runtime library calls. Traps generally have significant overhead compared to a single floating-point instruction, and if a program is continually executing trap code, it can significantly impact performance.

In some cases it's appropriate to ignore traps on certain operations. A commonly ignored trap is the underflow trap. In many iterative programs, it's quite natural for a value to keep reducing to the point where it "disappears." Depending on the application, this may or may not be an error situation so this exception can be safely ignored.

If you run a program and then it terminates, you see a message such as:

```
Overflow handler called 10,000,000 times
```

It probably means that you need to figure out why your code is exceeding the range of the floating-point format. It probably also means that your code is executiong more slowly because it is spending too much time in its error handlers.

Compiler Issues

The IEEE 754 floating-point standard does a good job describing how floating-point operations are to be performed. However, we generally don't write assembly language programs. When we write in a higher-level language such as FORTRAN, it's sometimes difficult to get the compiler to generate the assembly language you need for your application. The problems fall into two categories:

- The compiler is too conservative in trying to generate IEEE-compliant code and produces code that doesn't operate at the peak speed of the processor. On some processors, to fully support gradual underflow, extra instructions must be generated for certain instructions. If your code will never underflow, these instructions are unnecessary overhead.

- The optimizer takes liberties rewriting your code to improve its performance, eliminating some necessary steps. For example, if you have the following code:

```
Z = X + 500
Y = Z - 200
```

The optimizer may replace it with Y = X + 300. However, in the case of a value for X that is close to overflow, the two sequences may not produce the same result.

Sometimes a user prefers "fast" code that loosely conforms to the IEEE standard, and at other times the user will be writing a numerical library routine and need total control over each floating-point operation. Compilers have a challenge supporting the needs of both of these types of users. Because of the nature of the high performance computing market and benchmarks, often the "fast and loose" approach prevails in many compilers.

Closing Notes

While this is a relatively long chapter with a lot of technical detail, it does not even begin to scratch the surface of the IEEE floating-point format or the entire field of numerical analysis. We as programmers must be careful about the accuracy of our programs, lest the results become meaningless. Here are a few basic rules to get you started:

- Look for compiler options that relax or enforce strict IEEE compliance and choose the appropriate option for your program. You may even want to change these options for different portions of your program.

- Use REAL*8 for computations unless you are sure REAL*4 has sufficient precision. Given that REAL*4 has roughly 7 digits of precision, if the bottom digits become meaningless due to rounding and computations, you are in some danger of seeing the effect of the errors in your results. REAL*8 with 13 digits makes this much less likely to happen.

- Be aware of the relative magnitude of numbers when you are performing additions.

- When summing up numbers, if there is a wide range, sum from smallest to largest.

- Perform multiplications before divisions whenever possible.

- When performing a comparison with a computed value, check to see if the values are "close" rather than identical.

- Make sure that you are not performing any unnecessary type conversions during the critical portions of your code.

An excellent reference on floating-point issues and the IEEE format is "What Every Computer Scientist Should Know About Floating-Point Arithmetic," written by David Goldberg, in *ACM Computing Surveys* magazine (March 1991). This article gives examples of the most common problems with floating-point and outlines the solutions. It also covers the IEEE floating-point format very thoroughly. I also recommend you consult Dr. William Kahan's home page *(http://http.cs.berkeley.edu/~wkahan/)* for some excellent materials on the IEEE format and challenges using floating-point arithmetic. Dr. Kahan was one of the original designers of the Intel i8087 and the IEEE 754 floating-point format.

Exercises

1. Run the following code to count the number of inverses that are not perfectly accurate:

```
REAL*4 X,Y,Z
INTEGER I
I = 0
DO X=1.0,1000.0,1.0
  Y = 1.0 / X
  Z = Y * X
  IF ( Z .NE. 1.0 ) THEN
    I = I + 1
  ENDIF
ENDDO
PRINT *,'Found ',I
END
```

Change the type of the variables to **REAL*8** and repeat. Make sure to keep the optimization at a sufficiently low level (-O0) to keep the compiler from eliminating the computations.

2. Write a program to determine the number of digits of precision for **REAL*4** and **REAL*8**.

3. Write a program to demonstrate how summing an array forward to backward and backward to forward can yield a different result.

4. Assuming your compiler supports varying levels of IEEE compliance, take a significant computational code and test its overall performance under the various IEEE compliance options. Do the results of the program change?

II

Programming and Tuning Software

5

What a Compiler Does

The goal of an *optimizing compiler* is the efficient translation of a higher-level language into the fastest possible machine language that accurately represents the high-level language source. What makes a representation good is: it gives the correct answers, and it executes quickly.

Naturally, it makes no difference how fast a program runs if it doesn't produce the right answers.* But given an expression of a program that executes correctly, an optimizing compiler looks for ways to streamline it. As a first cut, this usually means simplifying the code, throwing out extraneous instructions, and sharing intermediate results between statements. More advanced optimizations seek to restructure the program and may actually make the code grow in size, though the number of instructions executed will (hopefully) shrink.

When it comes to finally generating machine language, the compiler has to know about the registers and rules for issuing instructions. For performance, it needs to understand the costs of those instructions and the latencies of machine resources, such as the pipelines. This is especially true for processors that can execute more than one instruction at a time. It takes a balanced instruction mix—the right proportion of floating-point, fixed point, memory and branch operations, etc.—to keep the machine busy.

Initially compilers were tools that allowed us to write in something more readable than assembly language. Today they border on artificial intelligence as they take our high-level source code and translate it into highly optimized machine language across a wide variety of single- and multiple- processor architectures. In the area of high performance computing, the compiler at times has a greater impact on the performance of our program than either the processor or memory architecture.

---

* However, you can sometimes trade accuracy for speed.

Throughout the history of high performance computing, if we are not satisfied with the performance of our program written in a high-level language, we will gladly rewrite all or part of the program in assembly language. Thankfully, today's compilers usually make that step unnecessary.

In this chapter we cover the basic operation of optimizing compilers. In a later chapter we will cover the techniques used to analyze and compile programs for advanced architectures such as parallel or vector processing systems. We start our look at compilers examining how the relationship between programmers and their compilers has changed over time.

History of Compilers

If you have been in high performance computing since its beginning in the 1950s, you have programmed in several languages during that time. During the 1950s and early 1960s, you programmed in assembly language. The constraint on memory and slow clock rates made every instruction precious. With small memories, overall program size was typically small, so assembly language was sufficient. Toward the end of the 1960s, programmers began writing more of their code in a high-level language such as FORTRAN. Writing in a high-level language made your work much more portable, reliable, and maintainable. Given the increasing speed and capacity of computers, the cost of using a high-level language was something most programmers were willing to accept. In the 1970s if a program spent a particularly large amount of time in a particular routine, or the routine was part of the operating system or it was a commonly used library, most likely it was written in assembly language.

During the late 1970s and early 1980s, *optimizing compilers* continued to improve to the point that all but the most critical portions of general-purpose programs were written in high-level languages. On the average, the compilers generate better code than most assembly language programmers. This was often because a compiler could make better use of hardware resources such as registers. In a processor with 16 registers, a programmer might adopt a convention regarding the use of registers to help keep track of what value is in what register. A compiler can use each register as much as it likes because it can precisely track when a register is available for another use.

However, during that time, high performance computer architecture was also evolving. Cray Research was developing vector processors at the very top end of the computing spectrum. Compilers were not quite ready to determine when these new vector instructions could be used. Programmers were forced to write assembly language or create highly hand-tuned FORTRAN that called the appropriate vector routines in their code. In a sense, vector processors turned back the clock when it came to trusting the compiler for a while. Programmers never lapsed completely into assembly language, but some of their FORTRAN started looking rather un-FORTRAN like. As the vector computers matured, their compilers became increasingly able to detect when vectorization could be performed. At some point, the compilers again became better than programmers on these architectures. These new compilers reduced the need for extensive directives or language extensions.*

The RISC revolution led to an increasing dependence on the compiler. Programming early RISC processors such as the Intel i860 was painful compared to CISC processors. Subtle differences in the way a program was coded in machine language could have a significant impact on the overall performance of the program. For example, a programmer might have to count the instruction cycles between a load instruction and the use of the results of the load in a computational instruction. As superscalar processors were developed, certain pairs of instructions could be issued simultaneously, and others had to be issued serially. Because there were a large number of different RISC processors produced, programmers did not have time to learn the nuances of wringing the last bit of performance out of each processor. It was much easier to lock the processor designer and the compiler writer together (hopefully they work for the same company) and have them hash out the best way to generate the machine code. Then everyone would use the compiler and get code that made reasonably good use of the hardware.

The compiler became an important tool in the processor design cycle. Processor designers had much greater flexibility in the types of changes they could make. For example, it would be a good design in the next revision of a processor to execute existing codes 10% slower than a new revision, but by recompiling the code, it would perform 65% faster. Of course it was important to actually provide that compiler when the new processor was shipped and have the compiler give that level of performance across a wide range of codes rather than just one particular benchmark suite.

Which Language to Optimize?

It has been said, "I don't know what language they will be using to program high performance computers 10 years from now, but we do know it will be called FORTRAN." At the risk of inciting outright warfare, we need to discuss the strengths and weaknesses of languages that are used for high performance computing. Most

---

* The Livermore Loops was a benchmark that specifically tested the capability of a compiler to effectively optimize a set of loops. In addition to being a performance benchmark, it was also a compiler benchmark.

computer scientists (not computational scientists) train on a steady diet of C, C++,* or some other language focused on data structures or objects. When students encounter high performance computing for the first time, there is an immediate desire to keep programming in their favorite language. However, to get the peak performance across a wide range of architectures, FORTRAN is the only practical language.

When students ask why this is, usually the first answer is, "Because it has always been that way." In one way this is correct. Physicists, mechanical engineers, chemists, structural engineers, and meteorologists do most programming on high performance computers. FORTRAN is the language of those fields. (When was the last time a computer science student wrote a properly working program that computed for a week?) So naturally the high performance computer vendors put more effort into making FORTRAN work well on their architecture.

This is not the only reason that FORTRAN is a better language, however. There are some fundamental elements that make C, C++, or any data structures-oriented language unsuitable for high performance programming. In a word, that problem is *pointers*. Pointers (or addresses) are the way good computer scientists construct linked lists, binary trees, binomial queues, and all those nifty data structures. The problem with pointers is that the effect of a pointer operation is known only at execution time when the value of the pointer is loaded from memory. Once an optimizing compiler sees a pointer, all bets are off. It cannot make any assumptions about the effect of a pointer operation at compile time. It must generate conservative (less optimized) code that simply does exactly the same operation in machine code that the high-level language described.

While the lack of pointers in FORTRAN is a boon to optimization, it seriously limits the programmer's ability to create data structures. In some applications, especially highly scalable network-based applications, the use of good data structures can significantly improve the overall performance of the application. To solve this, in the FORTRAN 90 specification, pointers have been added to FORTRAN. In some ways, this was an attempt by the FORTRAN community to keep programmers from beginning to use C in their applications for the data structure areas of their applications. If programmers begin to use pointers throughout their codes, their FORTRAN programs will suffer from the same problems that inhibit optimization in C programs. In a sense FORTRAN has given up its primary advantage over C by trying to be more like C. The debate over pointers is one reason that the adoption rate of FORTRAN 90 somewhat slowed. Many programmers prefer to do their data structure, communications, and other bookkeeping work in C, while doing the computations in FORTRAN 77.

---

* Just for the record, both the authors of this book are quite accomplished in C, C++, and FORTRAN, so they have no preconceived notions.

FORTRAN 90 also has strengths and weaknesses when compared to FORTRAN 77 on high performance computing platforms. FORTRAN 90 has a strong advantage over FORTRAN 77 in the area of improved semantics that enable more opportunities for advanced optimizations. This advantage is especially true on distributed memory systems on which data decomposition is a significant factor. (See Chapter 13, *Language Support for Performance.*) However, until FORTRAN 90 becomes popular, vendors won't be motivated to squeeze the last bit of performance out of FORTRAN 90.

So while FORTRAN 77 continues to be the mainstream language for high performance computing for the near future, other languages, like C and FORTRAN 90, have their limited and potentially increasing roles to play. In some ways the strongest potential challenger to FORTRAN in the long run may come in the form of a numerical tool set such as Matlab. However, packages such as Matlab have their own set of optimization challenges that must be overcome before they topple FORTRAN 77's domination.

Optimizing Compiler Tour

We will start by taking a walk through an optimizing compiler to see one at work. We think it's interesting, and if you can empathize with the compiler, you will be a better programmer; you will know what the compiler wants from you, and what it can do on its own.

Compilation Process

The compilation process is typically broken down into a number of identifiable steps, as shown in Figure 5-1. While not all compilers are implemented in exactly this way, it helps to understand the different functions a compiler must perform:

1. A precompiler or preprocessor phase is where some simple textual manipulation of the source code is performed. The preprocessing step can be processing of include files and making simple string substitutions throughout the code.

2. The lexical analysis phase is where the incoming source statements are decomposed into tokens such as variables, constants, comments, or language elements.

3. The parsing phase is where the input is checked for syntax, and the compiler translates the incoming program into an intermediate language that is ready for optimization.

4. One or more optimization passes are performed on the intermediate language.

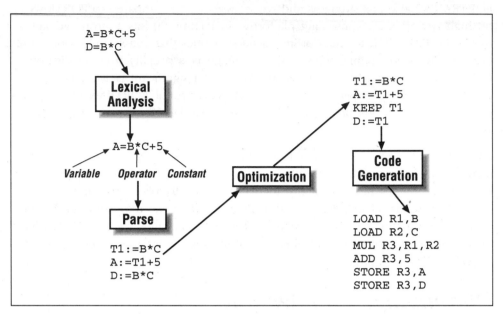

Figure 5-1: Basic compiler processes

5. An object code generator translates the intermediate language into assembly code, taking into consideration the particular architectural details of the processor in question.

As compilers become more and more sophisticated in order to wring the last bit of performance from the processor, some of these steps (especially the optimization and code-generation steps) become more and more blurred. In this chapter, we focus on the traditional optimizing compiler, and in later chapters we will look more closely at how modern compilers do more sophisticated optimizations.

Intermediate Language Representation

Because we are most interested in the optimization of our program, we start our discussion at the output of the parse phase of the compiler. The parse phase output is in the form of an an *intermediate language* (IL) that is somewhere between a high-level language and assembly language. The intermediate language expresses the same calculations that were in the original program, in a form the compiler can manipulate more easily. Furthermore, instructions that aren't present in the source, such as address expressions for array references, become visible along with the rest of the program, making them subject to optimizations too.

How would an intermediate language look? In terms of complexity, it's similar to assembly code but not so simple that the definitions* and uses of variables are lost. We'll need definition and use information to analyze the flow of data through the program. Typically, calculations are expressed as a stream of *quadruples*—statements with exactly one operator, (up to) two operands, and a result.† Presuming that anything in the original source program can be recast in terms of quadruples, we have a usable intermediate language. To give you an idea of how this works, We're going to rewrite the statement below as a series of four quadruples:

```
A = -B + C * D / E
```

Taken all at once, this statement has four operators and four operands: /, *, +, and – (negate), and B, C, D, and E. This is clearly too much to fit into one quadruple. We need a form with exactly one operator and, at most, two operands per statement. The recast version that follows manages to do this, employing temporary variables to hold the intermediate results:

```
T1 = D / E
T2 = C * T1
T3 = -B
A  = T3 + T2
```

A workable intermediate language would, of course, need some other features, like pointers. We're going to suggest that we create our own intermediate language to investigate how optimizations work. To begin, we need to establish a few rules:

- Instructions consist of one opcode, two operands, and a result. Depending on the instruction, the operands may be empty.

- Assignments are of the form X := Y op Z, meaning X gets the result of op applied to Y and Z.

- All memory references are explicit load from or store to "temporaries" tn.

- Logical values used in branches are calculated separately from the actual branch.

- Jumps go to absolute addresses.

If we were building a compiler, we'd need to be a little more specific. For our purposes, this will do. Consider the following bit of C code:

```
while (j < n) {
    k = k + j * 2;
    m = j * 2;
```

---

* By "definitions," we mean the assignment of values: not declarations.

† More generally, code can be cast as *n*-tuples. It depends on the level of the intermediate language.

```
        j++;
    }
```

This loop translates into the intermediate language representation shown here:

```
A::    t1    := j
       t2    := n
       t3    := t1 < t2
       jmp (B) t3
       jmp (C) TRUE

B::    t4    := k
       t5    := j
       t6    := t5 * 2
       t7    := t4 + t6
       k     := t7
       t8    := j
       t9    := t8 * 2
       m     := t9
       t10   := j
       t11   := t10 + 1
       j     := t11
       jmp (A) TRUE
C::
```

Each C source line is represented by several IL statements. On many RISC processors, our IL code is so close to machine language that we could turn it directly into object code.* Often the lowest optimization level does a literal translation from the intermediate language to machine code. When this is done, the code generally is very large and performs very poorly. Looking at it, you can see places to save a few instructions. For instance, j gets loaded into temporaries in four places; surely we can reduce that. We have to do some analysis and make some optimizations.

Basic Blocks

After generating our intermediate language, we want to cut it into *basic blocks*. These are code sequences that start with an instruction that either follows a branch or is itself a target for a branch. Put another way, each basic block has one entrance (at the top) and one exit (at the bottom). Figure 5-2 represents our IL code as a group of three basic blocks. Basic blocks make code easier to analyze. By restricting flow of control within a basic block from top to bottom and eliminating all the branches, we can be sure that if the first statement gets executed, the second one does too, and so on. Of course, the branches haven't disappeared, but we have forced them outside the blocks in the form of the connecting arrows— the *flow graph*.

---

* See Appendix B, *Looking at Assembly Language*, for some examples of machine code translated directly from intermediate language.

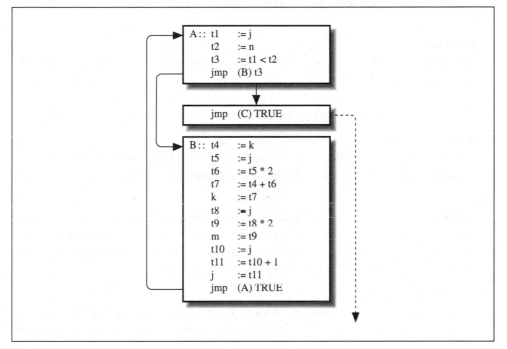

Figure 5-2: Intermediate language divided into basic blocks

We are now free to extract information from the blocks themselves. For instance, we can say with certainty which variables a given block uses and which variables it defines (sets the value of). We might not be able to do that if the block contained a branch. We can also gather the same kind of information about the calculations it performs. After we have analyzed the blocks so that we know what goes in and what comes out, we can modify them to improve performance and just worry about the interaction between blocks.

Optimization Levels

There are a wide variety of optimization techniques, and they are not all applicable in all situations. So the user is typically given some choices as to whether or not particular optimizations are performed. Often this is expressed in the form of an *optimization level* that is specified on the compiler as a command-line option such as –O3.

The different levels of optimization controlled by a compiler flag may include the following:

No optimization

Generates machine code directly from the intermediate language, which can be very large and slow code. The primary uses of no optimization are for debuggers and establishing the correct program output. Because every operation is done precisely as the user specified, it must be right.

Basic optimizations

Similar to those described in this chapter. They generally work to minimize the intermediate language and generate fast compact code.

Interprocedural analysis

Looks beyond the boundaries of a single routine for optimization opportunities. This optimization level might include extending a basic optimization such as copy propagation across multiple routines. Another result of this technique is procedure inlining where it will improve performance.

Runtime profile analysis

It is possible to use runtime profiles to help the compiler generate improved code based on its knowledge of the patterns of runtime execution gathered from profile information.

Floating-point optimizations

The IEEE floating-point standard (IEEE 754) specifies precisely how floating-point operations are performed and the precise side effects of these operations. The compiler may identify certain algebraic transformations that increase the speed of the program (such as replacing a division with a reciprocal and a multiplication) but might change the output results from the unoptimized code.

Data flow analysis

Identifies potential parallelism between instructions, blocks, or even successive loop iterations.

Advanced optimization

May include automatic vectorization, parallelization, or data decomposition on advanced architecture computers.

These optimizations might be controlled by several different compiler options. It often takes some time to figure out the best combination of compiler flags for a particular code or set of codes. In some cases, programmers compile different routines using different optimization settings for best overall performance.

Classical Optimizations

Once the intermediate language is broken into basic blocks, there are a number of optimizations that can be performed on the code in these blocks. Some optimizations are very simple and affect a few tuples within a basic block. Other optimizations move code from one basic block to another without altering the program results. For example, it is often valuable to move a computation from the body of a loop to the code immediately preceding the loop.

In this section, we are going to list classical optimizations by name and tell you what they are for. We're not suggesting that *you* make the changes; most compilers since the mid-1980s automatically perform these optimizations at all but their lowest optimization level. As we said at the start of the chapter, if you understand what the compiler can (and can't) do, you will become a better programmer because you will be able to play to the compiler's strengths.

Copy Propagation

To start, let's look at a technique for untangling calculations. Take a look at the following segment of code: notice the two computations involving X.

```
X = Y
Z = 1.0 + X
```

As written, the second statement requires the results of the first before it can proceed—you need X to calculate Z. Unnecessary dependencies could translate into a delay at runtime.* With a little bit of rearrangement we can make the second statement independent of the first, by *propagating* a copy of Y. The new calculation for Z uses the value of Y directly:

```
X = Y
Z = 1.0 + Y
```

Notice that we left the first statement, X=Y, intact. You may ask, "Why keep it?" The problem is that we can't tell whether the value of X is needed elsewhere. That is something for another analysis to decide. If it turns out that no other statement needs the new value of X, the assignment is eliminated later by dead code removal.

---

* This code is an example of a *flow dependence*. I describe dependencies in detail in Chapter 9, *Understanding Parallelism*.

Constant Folding

A clever compiler can find constants throughout your program. Some of these are "obvious" constants like those defined in parameter statements. Others are less obvious, such as local variables that are never redefined. When you combine them in a calculation, you get a *constant expression*. The little program below has two constants, I and K:

```
PROGRAM MAIN
INTEGER I,K
PARAMETER (I = 100)
K = 200
J = I + K
END
```

Because I and K are constant individually, the combination I+K is constant, which means that J is a constant too. The compiler reduces constant expressions like I+K into constants with a technique called *constant folding*.

How does constant folding work? You can see that it is possible to examine every path along which a given variable could be defined en route to a particular basic block. If you discover that all paths lead back to the same value, that is a constant; you can replace all references to that variable with that constant. This replacement has a ripple-through effect. If the compiler finds itself looking at an expression that is made up solely of constants, it can evaluate the expression at compile time and replace it with a constant. After several iterations, the compiler will have located most of the expressions that are candidates for constant folding.

A programmer can sometimes improve performance by making the compiler aware of the constant values in your application. For example, in the following code segment:

```
X = X * Y
```

the compiler may generate quite different runtime code if it knew that Y was 0, 1, 2, or 175.32. If it does not know the value for Y, it must generate the most conservative (not necessarily the fastest) code sequence. A programmer can communicate these values through the use of the **PARAMETER** statement in FORTRAN. By the use of a parameter statment, the compiler knows the values for these constants at runtime. Another example we have seen is:

```
DO I = 1,10000
  DO J=1,IDIM
   .....
  ENDDO
ENDDO
```

After looking at the code, it's clear that IDIM was either 1, 2, or 3, depending on the data set in use. Clearly if the compiler knew that IDIM was 1, it could generate much simpler and faster code.

Dead Code Removal

Programs often contain sections of *dead code* that have no effect on the answers and can be removed. Occasionally, dead code is written into the program by the author, but a more common source is the compiler itself; many optimizations produce dead code that needs to be swept up afterwards.

Dead code comes in two types:

- Instructions that are unreachable

- Instructions that produce results that are never used

You can easily write some unreachable code into a program by directing the flow of control around it—permanently. If the compiler can tell it's unreachable, it will eliminate it. For example, it's impossible to reach the statement I = 4 in this program:

```
PROGRAM MAIN
I = 2
WRITE (*,*) I
STOP
I = 4
WRITE (*,*) I
END
```

The compiler throws out everything after the STOP statement and probably gives you a warning. Unreachable code produced by the compiler during optimization will be quietly whisked away.

Computations with local variables can produce results that are never used. By analyzing a variable's definitions and uses, the compiler can see whether any other part of the routine references it. Of course the compiler can't tell the ultimate fate of variables that are passed between routines, external or common, so those computations are always kept (as long as they are reachable).* In the following program, computations involving k contribute nothing to the final answer and are good candidates for dead code elimination:

```
main ()
{
  int i,k;
```

---

* If a compiler does sufficient interprocedural analysis, it can even optimize variables across routine boundaries. Interprocedural analysis can be the bane of benchmark codes trying to time a computation without using the results of the computation.

```
    i = k = 1;
    i += 1;
    k += 2;
    printf ("%d\n",i);
}
```

Dead code elimination has often produced some amazing benchmark results from poorly written benchmarks. See the exercises at the end of the chapter for an example of this type of code.

Strength Reduction

Operations or expressions have time costs associated with them. Sometimes it's possible to replace a more expensive calculation with a cheaper one. We call this *strength reduction*. The following code fragment contains two expensive operations:

```
    REAL X,Y
    Y = X**2
    J = K*2
```

For the exponentiation operation on the first line, the compiler generally makes an embedded mathematical subroutine library call. In the library routine, X is converted to a logarithm, multiplied, then converted back. Overall, raising X to a power is expensive—taking perhaps hundreds of machine cycles. The key is to notice that X is being raised to a small integer power. A much cheaper alternative would be to express it as X*X, and pay only the cost of multiplication. The second statement shows integer multiplication of a variable K by 2. Adding K+K yields the same answer, but takes less time.

There are many opportunities for compiler-generated strength reductions; these are just a couple of them. We will see an important special case when we look at induction variable simplification. Another example of a strength reduction is replacing multiplications by integer powers of two by logical shifts.

Variable Renaming

In Chapter 2, *High Performance Microprocessors*, we talked about register renaming. Some processors can make runtime decisions to replace all references to register 1 with register 2, for instance, to eliminate bottlenecks. Register renaming keeps instructions that are recycling the same registers for different purposes from having to wait until previous instructions have finished with them.

The same situation can occur in programs—the same variable (i.e., memory location) can be recycled for two unrelated purposes. For example, see the variable x in the following fragment:

```
x  = y * z;
q  = r + x + x;
x  = a + b;
```

When the compiler recognizes that a variable is being recycled, and that its current and former uses are independent, it can substitute a new variable to keep the calculations separate:

```
x0 = y * z;
q  = r + x0 + x0;
x  = a + b;
```

Variable renaming is an important technique because it clarifies that calculations are independent of each other, which increases the number of things that can be done in parallel.

Common Subexpression Elimination

Subexpressions are pieces of expressions. For instance, A+B is a subexpression of C*(A+B). If A+B appears in several places, like it does below, we call it a *common subexpression*:

```
D = C * (A + B)
E = (A + B)/2.
```

Rather than calculate A + B twice, the compiler can generate a temporary variable and use it wherever A + B is required:

```
temp = A + B
D = C * temp
E = temp/2.
```

Different compilers go to different lengths to find common subexpressions. Most pairs, such as A+B, are recognized. Some can recognize reuse of intrinsics, such as SIN(X). Don't expect the compiler to go too far though. Subexpressions like A+B+C are not computationally equivalent to reassociated forms like B+C+A, even though they are algebraically the same. In order to provide predictable results on computations, FORTRAN must either perform operations in the order specified by the user or reorder them in a way to guarantee exactly the same result. Sometimes the user doesn't care which way A+B+C associates, but the compiler cannot assume the user does not care.

Address calculations provide a particularly rich opportunity for common subexpression elimination. You don't see the calculations in the source code; they're generated by the compiler. For instance, a reference to an array element `A(I,J)` may translate into an intermediate language expression such as:

```
address(A) + (I-1)*sizeof_datatype(A)
+ (J-1)*sizeof_datatype(A) * column_dimension(A)
```

If `A(I,J)` is used more than once, we have multiple copies of the same address computation. Common subexpression elimination will (hopefully) discover the redundant computations and group them together.

Loop-Invariant Code Motion

Loops are where many high performance computing programs spend a majority of their time. The compiler looks for every opportunity to move calculations out of a loop body and into the surrounding code. Expressions that don't change after the loop is entered (*loop-invariant expressions*) are prime targets. The following loop has two loop-invariant expressions:

```
DO I=1,N
  A(I) = B(I) + C * D
  E = G(K)
ENDDO
```

Below, we have modified the expressions to show how they can be moved to the outside:

```
temp = C * D
DO I=1,N
  A(I) = B(I) + temp
ENDDO
E = G(K)
```

It is possible to move code before or after the loop body. As with common subexpression elimination, address arithmetic is a particularly important target for loop-invariant code motion. Slowly changing portions of index calculations can be pushed into the suburbs, to be executed only when needed.

Induction Variable Simplification

Loops can contain what are called *induction variables*. Their value changes as a linear function of the loop iteration count. For example, `K` is an induction variable in the following loop. Its value is tied to the loop index:

```
DO I=1,N
  K = I*4 + M
    ...
ENDDO
```

Induction variable simplification replaces calculations for variables like K with simpler ones. Given a starting point and the expression's first derivative, you can arrive at K's value for the *n*th iteration by stepping through the *n-1* intervening iterations:

```
K = M
DO I=1,N
  K = K + 4
   ...
ENDDO
```

The two forms of the loop aren't equivalent; the second won't give you the value of K given any value of I. Because you can't jump into the middle of the loop on the *n*th iteration, K always takes on the same values it would have if we had kept the original expression.

Induction variable simplification probably wouldn't be a very important optimization, except that array address calculations look very much like the calculation for K in the example above. For instance, the address calculation for A(I) within a loop iterating on the variable I looks like this:

```
address = base_address(A) + (I-1) * sizeof_datatype(A)
```

Performing all that math is unnecessary. The compiler can create a new induction variable for references to A and simplify the address calculations:

```
outside the loop...
address = base_address(A) - (1 * sizeof_datatype(A))
inside the loop...
address = address + sizeof_datatype(A)
```

Induction variable simplification is especially useful on processors that can automatically increment a register each time it is used as a pointer for a memory reference. While stepping through a loop, the memory reference and the address arithmetic can both be squeezed into a single instruction—a great savings.

Object Code Generation

Precompilation, lexical analysis, parsing, and many optimization techniques are somewhat portable, but code generation is very specific to the target processor. In some ways this phase is where compilers earn their keep on single-processor RISC systems.

Anything that isn't handled in hardware has to be addressed in software. That means if the processor can't resolve resource conflicts, such as overuse of a register or pipeline, then the compiler is going to have to take care of it. Allowing the compiler to take care of it isn't necessarily a bad thing—it's a design decision. A complicated compiler and simple, fast hardware might be cost effective for certain applications. Two processors at opposite ends of this spectrum are the MIPS R2000 and the HP PA-8000. The first depends heavily on the compiler to schedule instructions and fairly distribute resources. The second manages both things at runtime, though both depend on the compiler to provide a balanced instruction mix.

In all computers, register selection is a challenge because, in spite of their numbers, registers are precious. You want to be sure that the most active variables become register resident at the expense of others. On machines without register renaming (see Chapter 2), you have to be sure that the compiler doesn't try to recycle registers too quickly, otherwise the processor has to delay computations as it waits for one to be freed.

Some instructions in the repertoire also save your compiler from having to issue others. Examples are auto-increment for registers being used as array indices or conditional assignments in lieu of branches. These both save the processor from extra calculations and make the instruction stream more compact.

Lastly, there are opportunities for increased parallelism. Programmers generally think serially, specifying steps in logical succession. Unfortunately, serial source code makes serial object code. A compiler that hopes to efficiently use the parallelism of the processor will have to be able to move instructions around and find operations that can be issued side by side. This is one of the biggest challenges for compiler writers today. As superscalar and *very long instruction word* (VLIW) designs become capable of executing more instructions per clock cycle, the compiler will have to dig deeper for operations that can execute at the same time.

Closing Notes

This chapter has been a basic introduction into how an optimizing compiler operates. However, this is not the last we will talk about compilers. In order to perform the automatic vectorization, parallelization, and data decomposition, compilers must further analyze the source code. As we encounter these topics, we will discuss the compiler impacts and how programmers can best interact with compilers.

For single-processor modern RISC architectures, compilers usually generate better code than most assembly language programmers. Instead of compensating for a simplistic compiler by adding hand optimizations, we as programmers must keep our programs simple so as not to confuse the compiler. By understanding the patterns that compilers are quite capable of optimizing, we can focus on writing straightforward programs that are portable and understandable.

Exercises

1. Does your compiler recognize dead code in the program below? How can you be sure? Does the compiler give you a warning?

   ```
   main()
   {
       int k=1;
       if (k == 0)
           printf ("This statement is never executed.\n");
   }
   ```

2. Compile the following code and execute it under various optimization levels. Try to guess the different types of optimizations that are being performed to improve the performance as the optimization is increased.

   ```
   REAL*8 A(1000000)
   DO I=1,1000000
      A(I) = 3.1415927
   ENDDO
   DO I=1,1000000
      A(I) = A(I) * SIN(A(I)) + COS(A(I))
   ENDDO
   PRINT *,"All Done"
   ```

3. Take the following code segment and compile it at various optimization levels. Look at the generated assembly language code (-S option on some compilers) and find the effects of each optimization level on the machine language. Time the program to see the performance at the different optimization levels. If you have access to multiple architectures, look at the code generated using the same optimization levels on different architectures.

   ```
   REAL*8 A(1000000)
   COMMON/BLK/A
    .... Call Time
   DO I=1,1000000
      A(I) = A(I) + 1.234
   ENDDO
    .... Call Time
   END
   ```

   Why is it necessary to put the array into a common block?

6

Timing
and Profiling

Perhaps getting your code to produce the right answers is enough. After all, if you only plan to use the program once in a while, or if it only takes a few minutes to run, execution time isn't going to matter that much. But it might not always be that way. Typically, people start taking interest in the runtime of their programs for two reasons:

- The workload has increased.

- They are considering a new machine.

It's clear why you might care about the performance of your program if the workload increases. Trying to cram 25 hours of computing time into a 24-hour day is an administrative nightmare. But why should people who are considering a new machine care about the runtime? After all, the new machine is presumably faster than the old one, so everything should take less time. The reason is that when people are evaluating new machines, they need a basis of comparison—a benchmark. People often use familiar programs as benchmarks. It makes sense: you want a benchmark to be representative of the kind of work you do, and nothing is more representative of the work you do than the work you do!

Benchmarking sounds easy enough, provided you have timing tools. And you already know the meaning of time.* You just want to be sure that what those tools are reporting is the same as what you think you're getting; especially if you have never used the tools before. To illustrate, imagine if someone took your watch and replaced it with another that expressed time in some funny units or three overlapping sets of hands. It would be very confusing; you might have a problem reading

---

* Time is money.

it at all. You would also be justifiably nervous about conducting your affairs by a watch you don't understand.

UNIX timing tools are like the six-handed watch, reporting three different kinds of time measurements. They aren't giving conflicting information—they just present more information than you can jam into a single number. Again, the trick is learning to read the watch. That's what the first part of this chapter is about. We'll investigate the different types of measurements that determine how a program is doing. In Chapter 16, *Running Your Own Benchmarks*, we apply what we've learned when we talk about how to conduct a formal benchmark.

If you plan to tune a program, you need more than timing information. Where is time being spent—in a single loop, subroutine call overhead, or with memory problems? For tuners, the latter sections of this chapter discuss how to profile code at the procedural and statement levels. We also discuss what profiles mean and how they predict the approach you have to take when, and if, you decide to tweak the code for performance, and what your chances for success will be.

Timing

We assume that your program runs correctly. It would be rather ridiculous to time a program that's not running right, though this doesn't mean it doesn't happen. Depending on what you are doing, you may be interested in knowing how much time is spent overall, or you may be looking at just a portion of the program. We show you how to time the whole program first, and then talk about timing individual loops or subroutines.

Timing a Whole Program

Under UNIX, you can time program execution by placing the *time* command before everything else you normally type on the command line. When the program finishes, a timing summary is produced. For instance, if your program is called *foo*, you can time its execution by typing **time foo**. If you are using the C shell or Korn shell, *time* is one of the shell's built-in commands. With a Bourne shell, *time* is a separate command executable in */bin*. In any case, the following information appears at the end of the run:

- User time
- System time
- Elapsed time

These timing figures are easier to understand with a little background. As your program runs, it switches back and forth between two fundamentally different modes: *user mode* and *kernel mode*. The normal operating state is user mode. It is in user mode that the instructions the compiler generated on your behalf get executed, in addition to any subroutine library calls linked with your program.* It might be enough to run in user mode forever, except that programs generally need other services, such as I/O, and these require the intervention of the operating system—the kernel. A kernel service request made by your program, or perhaps an event from outside your program, causes a switch from user mode into kernel mode.

Time spent executing in the two modes is accounted for separately. The *user time* figure describes time spent in user mode. Similarly, *system time* is a measure of the time spent in kernel mode. As far as user time goes, each program on the machine is accounted for separately. That is, you won't be charged for activity in somebody else's application. System time accounting works the same way, for the most part; however, you can, in some instances, be charged for some system services performed on other people's behalf, in addition to your own. Incorrect charging occurs because your program may be executing at the moment some outside activity causes an interrupt. This seems unfair, but take consolation in the fact that it works both ways: other users may be charged for your system activity too, for the same reason.

Taken together, user time and system time are called *CPU time*. Generally, the user time is far greater than the system time. You would expect this because most applications only occasionally ask for system services. In fact, a disproportionately large system time probably indicates some trouble. For instance, programs that are repeatedly generating exception conditions, such as page faults, misaligned memory references, or floating-point exceptions, use an inordinate amount of system time. Time spent doing things like seeking on a disk, rewinding a tape, or waiting for characters at the terminal doesn't show up in CPU time. That's because these activities don't require the CPU; the CPU is free to go off and execute other programs.

The third piece of information (corresponding to the third set of hands on the watch), *elapsed time*, is a measure of the actual (wall clock) time that has passed since the program was started. For programs that spend most of their time computing, the elapsed time should be close to the CPU time. Reasons why elapsed time might be greater are:

- You are timesharing the machine with other active programs.†

---

* Cache miss time is buried in here too.

† The *uptime* command gives you a rough indication of the other activity on your machine. The last three fields tell the average number of processes ready to run during the last 1, 5, and 15 minutes, respectively.

- Your application performs a lot of I/O.

- Your application requires more memory bandwidth than is available on the machine.

- Your program was paging or swapped.

People often record the CPU time and use it as an estimate for elapsed time. Using CPU time is okay on a single CPU machine, provided you have seen the program run when the machine was quiet and noticed the two numbers were very close together. But for multiprocessors, the total CPU time can be far different from the elapsed time. Whenever there is a doubt, wait until you have the machine to yourself and time your program then, using elapsed time. It is very important to produce timing results that can be verified using another run when the results are being used to make important purchasing decisions.

If you are running on a Berkeley UNIX derivative, the C shell's built-in *time* command can report a number of other useful statistics. The default form of the output is shown in Figure 6-1. Check with your *csh* manual page for more possibilities.

In addition to figures for CPU and elapsed time, *csh* time command produces information about CPU utilization, page faults, swaps, blocked I/O operations (usually disk activity), and some measures of how much physical memory our program occupied when it ran. We describe each of them in turn.

Percent utilization

Percent utilization corresponds to the ratio of elapsed time to CPU time. As we mentioned above, there can be a number of reasons why the CPU utilization wouldn't be 100% or mighty close. You can often get a hint from the other fields as to whether it is a problem with your program or whether you were sharing the machine when you ran it.

Average real memory utilization

The two *average memory utilization* measurements shown in Figure 6-1 characterize the program's resource requirements as it ran.

The first measurement, *shared-memory space*, accounts for the average amount of *real* memory taken by your program's text segment—the portion that holds the machine instructions. It is called "shared" because several concurrently running copies of a program can share the same text segment (to save memory). Years ago, it was possible for the text segment to consume a significant portion of the memory system, but these days, with memory sizes starting around 32 MB, you have to compile a pretty huge source program and use every bit of it to create a shared-memory usage figure big enough to cause concern. The shared-memory

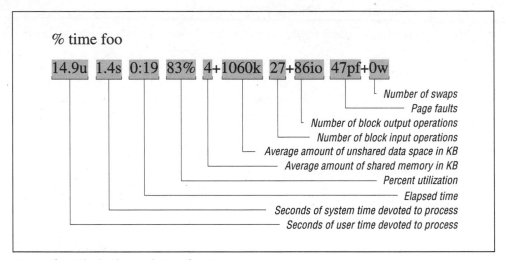

Figure 6-1: The built-in csh time function

space requirement is usually quite low relative to the amount of memory available on your machine.

The second average memory utilization measurement, *unshared-memory space*, describes the average *real* storage dedicated to your program's data structures as it ran. This storage includes saved local variables and COMMON for FORTRAN, and static and external variables for C. We stress the word "real" here and above because these numbers talk about physical memory usage, taken over time. It may be that you have allocated arrays with 1 trillion elements (virtual space), but if your program only crawls into a corner of that space, your runtime memory requirements will be pretty low.

What the unshared-memory space measurement doesn't tell you, unfortunately, is your program's demand for memory at its greediest. An application that requires 100 MB 1/10th of the time and 1 KB the rest of the time appears to need only 10 MB on average—not a revealing picture of the program's memory requirements.

Blocked I/O operations

The two figures for *blocked I/O* operations primarily describe disk usage, though tape devices and some other peripherals may also be used with blocked I/O. Character I/O operations, such as terminal input and output, do not appear here. A large number of blocked I/O operations could explain a lower-than-expected CPU utilization.

Page faults and swaps

An unusually high number of *page faults* or any *swaps* probably indicates a system choked for memory, which would also explain a longer-than-expected elapsed time. It may be that other programs are competing for the same space. And don't forget that even under optimal conditions, every program suffers some number of page faults, as explained in Chapter 3, *Memory*. Techniques for minimizing page faults are described in Chapter 8, *Loop Optimizations*.

Timing a Portion of the Program

For some benchmarking or tuning efforts, measurements taken on the "outside" of the program tell you everything you need to know. But if you are trying to isolate performance figures for individual loops or portions of the code, you may want to include timing routines on the inside too. The basic technique is simple enough:

1. Record the time before you start doing X.
2. Do X.
3. Record the time at completion of X.
4. Subtract the start time from the completion time.

If, for instance, X's primary job is to calculate particle positions, divide by the total time to obtain a number for particle positions/second. You have to be careful though; too many calls to the timing routines, and the observer becomes part of the experiment. The timing routines take time too, and their very presence can increase instruction cache miss or paging. Furthermore, you want X to take a significant amount of time so that the measurements are meaningful. Paying attention to the time between timer calls is really important because the clock used by the timing functions has a limited resolution. An event that occurs within a fraction of a second is hard to measure with any accuracy.

Getting Time Information

In this section, we discuss methods for getting various timer values during the execution of your program.

For FORTRAN programs, a library timing function found on many machines is called *etime*, which takes a two-element REAL*4 array as an argument and fills the slots with the user CPU time and system CPU time, respectively. The value returned by the function is the sum of the two. Here's how *etime* is often used:

```
real*4 tarray(2), etime
real*4 start, finish

start  = etime(tarray)
```

```
finish = etime(tarray)

write (*,*) 'CPU time: ', finish - start
```

Not every vendor supplies an *etime* function; in fact, one doesn't provide a timing routine for FORTRAN at all. Try it first. If it shows up as an undefined symbol when the program is linked, you can use the following C routine. It provides the same functionality as *etime*:

```
#include <sys/times.h>
#define TICKS   100.

float etime (parts)
struct {
        float user;
        float system;
} *parts;
{
        struct tms local;
        times (&local);
        parts->user   = (float) local.tms_utime/TICKS;
        parts->system = (float) local.tms_stime/TICKS;
        return (parts->user + parts->system);
}
```

There are a couple of things you might have to tweak to make it work. First of all, linking C routines with FORTRAN routines on your computer may require you to add an underscore (_) after the function name. This changes the entry to `float etime_ (parts)`. Furthermore, you might have to adjust the `TICKS` parameter. We assumed that the system clock had a resolution of 1/100 of a second (true for the Hewlett-Packard machines that this version of *etime* was written for). 1/60 is very common. On an RS-6000 the number would be 1000. You may find the value in a file named */usr/include/sys/param.h* on your machine, or you can determine it empirically.

A C routine for retrieving the wall time using calling *gettimeofday* is shown below. It is suitable for use with either C or FORTRAN programs as it uses call-by-value parameter passing:

```
#include <stdio.h>
#include <stdlib.h>
#include <sys/time.h>

void hpcwall(double *retval)
{
  static long zsec = 0;
  static long zusec = 0;
  double esec;
  struct timeval tp;
  struct timezone tzp;
```

```
    gettimeofday(&tp, &tzp);

    if ( zsec == 0 ) zsec = tp.tv_sec;
    if ( zusec == 0 ) zusec = tp.tv_usec;

    *retval = (tp.tv_sec - zsec) + (tp.tv_usec - zusec ) * 0.000001 ;
}

void hpcwall_(double *retval) { hpcwall(retval); } /* Other convention */
```

Given that you will often need both CPU and wall time, and you will be continually computing the difference between successive calls to these routines, you may want to write a routine to return the elapsed wall and CPU time upon each call as follows:

```
        SUBROUTINE HPCTIM(WTIME,CTIME)
        IMPLICIT NONE
*
        REAL WTIME,CTIME
        COMMON/HPCTIMC/CBEGIN,WBEGIN
        REAL*8 CBEGIN,CEND,WBEGIN,WEND
        REAL ETIME,CSCRATCH(2)
*
        CALL HPCWALL(WEND)
        CEND=ETIME(CSCRATCH)
*
        WTIME = WEND - WBEGIN
        CTIME = CEND - CBEGIN
*
        WBEGIN = WEND
        CBEGIN = CEND
        END
```

Using Timing Information

You can get a lot information from the timing facilities on a UNIX machine. Not only can you tell how long it takes to perform a given job, but you can also get hints about whether the machine is operating efficiently, or whether there is some other problem that needs to be factored in, such as inadequate memory.

Once the program is running with all anomalies explained away, you can record the time as a baseline. If you are tuning, the baseline will be a reference with which you can tell how much (or little) tuning has improved things. If you are benchmarking, you can use the baseline to judge how much overall incremental performance a new machine will give you. But remember to watch the other figures—paging, CPU utilization, etc. These may differ from machine to machine for reasons unrelated to raw CPU performance. You want to be sure you are getting the full picture. In Chapter 15, *Using Published Benchmarks*, and Chapter 16 we talk about benchmarking in more detail.

Subroutine Profiling

Sometimes you want more detail than the overall timing of the application. But you don't have time to modify the code to insert several hundred *etime* calls into your code. Profiles are also very useful when you have been handed a strange 20,000-line application program and told to figure out how it works and then improve its performance.

Most compilers provide a facility to automatically insert timing calls into your code at the entry and exit of each routine at compile time. While your program runs, the entry and exit times are recorded and then dumped into a file. A separate utility summarizes the execution patterns and produces a report that shows the percentage of the time spent in each of your routines and the library routines.

The profile gives you a sense of the shape of the execution profile. That is, you can see that 10% of the time is spent in subroutine **A**, 5% in subroutine **B**, etc. Naturally, if you add all of the routines together they should account for 100% of the overall time spent. From these percentages you can construct a picture—a *profile*—of how execution is distributed when the program runs. Though not representative of any particular profiling tool, the histograms in Figure 6-2 and Figure 6-3 depict these percentages, sorted from left to right, with each vertical column representing a different routine. They help illustrate different profile shapes.

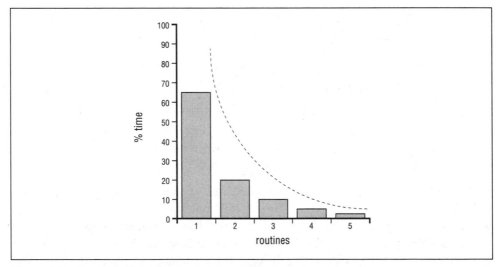

Figure 6-2: Sharp profile—dominated by routine 1

A *sharp profile* says that most of the time is spent in one or two procedures, and if you want to improve the program's performance you should focus your efforts on tuning those procedures. A minor optimization in a heavily executed line of code can sometimes have a great effect on the overall runtime, given the right opportunity. A *flat profile,** on the other hand, tells you that the runtime is spread across many routines, and effort spent optimizing any one or two will have little benefit in speeding up the program. Of course, there are also programs whose execution profile falls somewhere in the middle.

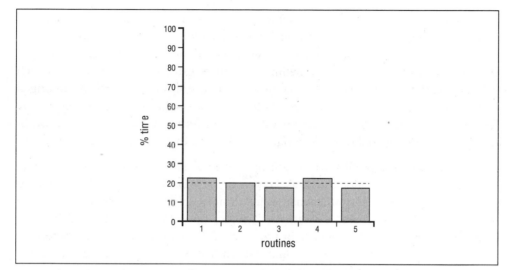

Figure 6-3: Flat profile—no routine predominates

We cannot predict with absolute certainty what you are likely to find when you profile your programs, but there are some general trends. For instance, engineering and scientific codes built around matrix solutions often exhibit very sharp profiles. The runtime is dominated by the work performed in a handful of routines. To tune the code, you need to focus your efforts on those routines to make them more efficient. It may involve restructuring loops to expose parallelism, providing hints to the compiler, or rearranging memory references. In any case, the challenge is tangible; you can see the problems you have to fix.

There are limits to how much tuning one or two routines will improve your runtime, of course. An often quoted rule of thumb is *Amdahl's Law*, derived from remarks made in 1967 by one of the designers of the IBM 360 series, and founder of Amdahl Computer, Gene Amdahl. Strictly speaking, his remarks were about the performance potential of parallel computers, but people have adapted Amdahl's Law to describe other things too. For our purposes, it goes like this: Say you have a program with two parts, one that can be optimized so that it goes infinitely fast

---

* The term "flat profile" is a little overloaded. We are using it to describe a profile that shows an even distribution of time throughout the program. You will also see the label flat profile used to draw distinction from a call graph profile, as described below.

and another that can't be optimized at all. Even if the optimizable portion makes up 50% of the initial runtime, at best you will be able to cut the total runtime in half. That is, your runtime will eventually be dominated by the portion that can't be optimized. This puts an upper limit on your expectations when tuning.

Even given the finite return on effort suggested by Amdahl's Law, tuning a program with a sharp profile can be rewarding. Programs with flat profiles are much more difficult to tune. These are often system codes, nonnumeric applications, and varieties of numerical codes without matrix solutions. It takes a global tuning approach to reduce, to any justifiable degree, the runtime of a program with a flat profile. For instance, you can sometimes optimize instruction cache usage, which is complicated because of the program's equal distribution of activity among a large number of routines. It can also help to reduce subroutine call overhead by folding callees into callers. Occasionally, you can find a memory reference problem that is endemic to the whole program—and one that can be fixed all at once.

When you look at a profile, you might find an unusually large percentage of time spent in the library routines such as `log`, `exp`, or `sin`. Often these functions are done in software routines rather than inline. You may be able to rewrite your code to eliminate some of these operations. Another important pattern to look for is when a routine takes far longer than you expect. Unexpected execution time may indicate you are accessing memory in a pattern that is bad for performance or that some aspect of the code cannot be optimized properly.

In any case, to get a profile, you need a profiler. One or two *subroutine profilers* come standard with the software development environments on all UNIX machines. We discuss two of them: *prof* and *gprof*. In addition, we mention a few line-by-line profilers. Subroutine profilers can give you a general overall view of where time is being spent. You probably should start with *prof*, if you have it (most machines do). Otherwise, use *gprof*. After that, you can move to a line-by-line profiler if you need to know which statements take the most time.

prof

prof is the most common of the UNIX profiling tools. In a sense, it is an extension of the compiler, linker, and object libraries, plus a few extra utilities, so it is hard to look at any one thing and say "this profiles your code." *prof* works by periodically sampling the program counter as your application runs. To enable profiling, you must recompile and relink using the -**p** flag. For example, if your program has two modules, *stuff.c* and *junk.c*, you need to compile and link according to the following code:

```
% cc stuff.c -p -O -c
% cc junk.c -p -O -c
% cc stuff.o junk.o -p -o stuff
```

This creates a *stuff* binary that is ready for profiling. You don't need to do anything special to run it. Just treat it normally by entering `stuff`. Because runtime statistics are being gathered, it takes a little longer than usual to execute.* At completion, there is a new file called *mon.out* in the directory where you ran it. This file contains the history of *stuff* in binary form, so you can't look at it directly. Use the *prof* utility to read *mon.out* and create a profile of *stuff.* By default, the information is written to your screen on standard output, though you can easily redirect it to a file:

```
% prof stuff > stuff.prof
```

To explore how the *prof* command works, we have created the following ridiculous little application, *loops.c.* It contains a main routine and three subroutines for which you can predict the time distribution just by looking at the code.

```
main () {
    int 1;
    for (1=0;1<1000;1++) {
        if (1 == 2*(1/2)) foo ();
        bar();
        baz();
    }
}
foo (){
    int j;
    for (j=0;j<200;j++)
}
bar () {
    int i;
    for (i=0;i<200;i++);
}
baz () {
    int k;
    for (k=0;k<300;k++);
}
```

Again, you need to compile and link *loops* with the **-p** flag, run the program, and then run the *prof* utility to extract a profile, as follows:

```
% cc loops.c -p -o loops
% ./loops
% prof loops > loops.prof
```

The following example shows what a *loops.prof* should look like. There are six columns.

---

* Remember: code with profiling enabled takes longer to run. You should recompile and relink the whole thing *without* the -p flag when you have finished profiling.

```
%Time Seconds Cumsecs  #Calls  msec/call  Name
 56.8    0.50    0.50    1000      0.500   _baz
 27.3    0.24    0.74    1000      0.240   _bar
 15.9    0.14    0.88     500      0.28    _foo
  0.0    0.00    0.88       1      0.      _creat
  0.0    0.00    0.88       2      0.      _profil
  0.0    0.00    0.88       1      0.      _main
  0.0    0.00    0.88       3      0.      _getenv
  0.0    0.00    0.88       1      0.      _strcpy
  0.0    0.00    0.88       1      0.      _write
```

The columns can be described as follows:

`%Time`

Percentage of CPU time consumed by this routine

`Seconds`

CPU time consumed by this routine

`Cumsecs`

A running total of time consumed by this and all preceding routines in the list

`Calls`

The number of times this particular routine was called

`msec/call`

Seconds divided by number of calls giving the average length of time taken by each invocation of the routine

`Name`

The name of this routine

The top three routines listed are from *loops.c* itself. You can see an entry for the "main" routine more than halfway down the list. Depending on the vendor, the names of the routines may contain leading or trailing underscores, and there will always be some routines listed you don't recognize. These are contributions from the C library and possibly the FORTRAN libraries, if you are using FORTRAN. Profiling also introduces some overhead into the run, and often shows up as one or two subroutines in the *prof* output. In this case, the entry for `_profil` represents code inserted by the linker for collecting runtime profiling data.

If it was our intention to tune *loops*, we would consider a profile like the one in the figure above to be a fairly good sign. The lead routine takes 50% of the runtime, so at least there is a chance we could do something with it that would have a significant impact on the overall runtime. (Of course with a program as trivial as *loops*, there is plenty we can do, since *loops* does nothing.)

gprof

Just as it's important to know how time is distributed when your program runs, it's also valuable to be able to tell who called who in the list of routines. Imagine, for instance, if something labeled **_exp** showed up high in the list in the *prof* output. You might say: "Hmmm, I don't remember calling anything named **exp( )**. I wonder where that came from." A call tree helps you find it.

Subroutines and functions can be thought of as members of a family tree. The top of the tree, or root, is actually a routine that precedes the main routine you coded for the application. It calls your main routine, which in turn calls others, and so on, all the way down to the leaf nodes of the tree. This tree is properly known as a *call graph.** The relationship between routines and nodes in the graph is one of parents and children. Nodes separated by more than one hop are referred to as ancestors and descendants.

Figure 6-4 graphically depicts the kind of call graph you might see in a small application. **main** is the parent or ancestor of most of the rest of the routines. **G** has two parents, **E** and **C**. Another routine, **A**, doesn't appear to have any ancestors or descendants at all. This problem can happen when routines are not compiled with profiling enabled, or when they aren't invoked with a subroutine call— such as would be the case if **A** were an exception handler.

The UNIX profiler that can extract this kind of information is called *gprof.* It replicates the abilities of *prof,* plus it gives a call graph profile so you can see who calls whom, and how often. The call graph profile is handy if you are trying to figure out how a piece of code works or where an unknown routine came from, or if you are looking for candidates for subroutine inlining.

To use call graph profiling you need go through the same steps as with *prof,* except that a **-pg** flag is substituted for the **-p** flag.† Additionally, when it comes time to produce the actual profile, you use the *gprof* utility instead of *prof.* One other difference is that the name of the statistics file is *gmon.out* instead of *mon.out*:

```
% cc -pg stuff.c -c
% cc stuff.o -pg -o stuff
% stuff
% gprof stuff > stuff.gprof
```

---

* It doesn't have to be a tree. Any subroutine can have more than one parent. Furthermore, recursive subroutine calls introduce cycles into the graph, in which a child calls one of its parents.

† On HP machines, the flag is –G.

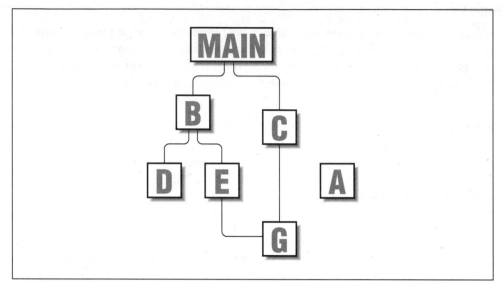

Figure 6-4: Simple call graph

The output from *gprof* is divided into three sections:

- Call graph profile

- Timing profile

- Index

The first section textually maps out the call graph. The second section lists routines, the percentage of time devoted to each, the number of calls, etc. (similar to *prof*). The third section is a cross reference so that you can locate routines by number, rather than by name. This section is especially useful for large applications because routines are sorted based on the amount of time they use, and it can be difficult to locate a particular routine by scanning for its name. Let's invent another trivial application to illustrate how *gprof* works. Figure 6-5 shows a short piece of FORTRAN code, along with a diagram of how the routines are connected together. Subroutines A and B are both called by MAIN, and, in turn, each calls C. The following example shows a section of the output from *gprof*'s call graph profile:*

---

* In the interest of conserving space, we clipped out the section most relevant to our discussion and included it in this example. There was a lot more to it, including calls of setup and system routines, the likes of which you will see when you run *gprof*.

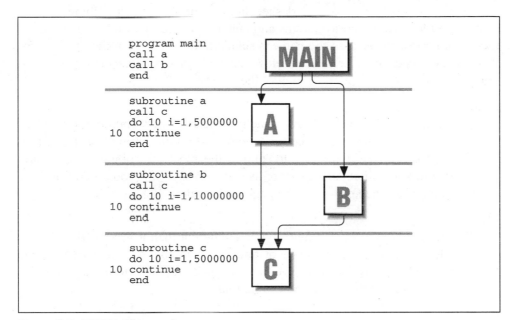

Figure 6-5: FORTRAN example

index	%time	self	descendants	called/total called+self called/total	parents name index children
....			....		....
		0.00	8.08	1/1	_main [2]
[3]	99.9	0.00	8.08	1	_MAIN_ [3]
		3.23	1.62	1/1	_b_ [4]
		1.62	1.62	1/1	_a_ [5]
		3.23	1.62	1/1	_MAIN_ [3]
[4]	59.9	3.23	1.62	1	_b_ [4]
		1.62	0.00	1/2	_c_ [6]
		1.62	1.62	1/1	_MAIN_ [3]
[5]	40.0	1.62	1.62	1	_a_ [5]
		1.62	0.00	1/2	_c_ [6]
		1.62	0.00	1/2	_a_ [5]
		1.62	0.00	1/2	_b_ [4]
[6]	39.9	3.23	0.00	2	_c_ [6]

Sandwiched between each set of dashed lines is information describing a given routine and its relationship to parents and children. It is easy to tell which routine the block represents because the name is shifted farther to the left than the others. Parents are listed above, children below. As with *prof,* underscores are tacked onto the labels.* A description of each of the columns follows:

index

> You will notice that each routine name is associated with a number in brackets ([n]). This is a cross-reference for locating the routine elsewhere in the profile. If, for example, you were looking at the block describing _MAIN_ and wanted to know more about one of its children, say _a_, you could find it by scanning down the left side of the page for its index, [5].

%time

> The meaning of the %time field is a little different than it was for *prof.* In this case it describes the percentage of time spent in this routine *plus* the time spent in all of its children. It gives you a quick way to determine where the busiest sections of the call graph can be found.

self

> Listed in seconds, the self column has different meanings for parents, the routine in question, and its children. Starting with the middle entry—the routine itself—the self figure shows how much overall time was dedicated to the routine. In the case _b_, for instance, this amounts to 3.23 seconds.

> Each self column entry shows the amount of time that can be attributed to calls from the parents. If you look at routine _c_, for example, you will see that it consumed a total time of 3.23 seconds. But note that it had two parents: 1.62 seconds of the time was attributable to calls from _a_, and 1.62 seconds to _b_.

> For the children, the self figure shows how much time was spent executing each child due to calls from this routine. The children may have consumed more time overall, but the only time accounted for is time-attributable to calls from this routine. For example, _c_ accumulated 3.23 seconds overall, but if you look at the block describing _b_, you see _c_ listed as a child with only 1.62 seconds. That's the total time spent executing _c_ on behalf of _b_.

---

* You may have noticed that there are two main routines: _MAIN_ and _main. In a FORTRAN program, _MAIN_ is the actual FORTRAN main routine. It's called as a subroutine by _main, provided from a system library at link time. When you're profiling C code, you won't see _MAIN_.

descendants

As with the self column, figures in the descendants column have different meanings for the routine, its parents, and children. For the routine itself, it shows the number of seconds spent in all of its descendants.

For the routine's parents, the descendants figure describes how much time spent in the routine can be traced back to calls by each parent. Looking at routine _c_ again, you can see that of its total time, 3.23 seconds, 1.62 seconds were attributable to each of its two parents, _a_ and _b_.

For the children, the descendants column shows how much of the child's time can be attributed to calls from this routine. The child may have accumulated more time overall, but the only time displayed is time associated with calls from this routine.

calls

The calls column shows the number of times each routine was invoked, as well as the distribution of those calls associated with both parents and children. Starting with the routine itself, the figure in the calls column shows the total number of entries into the routine. In situations where the routine called itself, you will also see a +n immediately appended, showing that additional n calls were made recursively.

Parent and child figures are expressed as ratios. For the parents, the ratio m/n says "of the n times the routine was called, m of those calls came from this parent." For the child, it says "of the n times this child was called, m of those calls came from this routine."

gprof's Flat Profile

As we mentioned previously, *gprof* also produces a timing profile (also called a "flat" profile, just to confuse things) similar to the one produced by *prof*. A few of the fields are different from *prof*, and there is some extra information, so it will help if we explain it briefly. The following example shows the first few lines from a *gprof* flat profile for *stuff*. You will recognize the top three routines from the original program. The others are library functions included at link-time.

% time	cumulative seconds	self seconds	calls	self ms/call	total ms/call	name
39.9	3.23	3.23	2	1615.07	1615.07	_c_ [6]
39.9	6.46	3.23	1	3230.14	4845.20	_b_ [4]
20.0	8.08	1.62	1	1620.07	3235.14	_a_ [5]
0.1	8.09	0.01	3	3.33	3.33	_ioctl [9]
0.0	8.09	0.00	64	0.00	0.00	.rem [12]
0.0	8.09	0.00	64	0.00	0.00	_f_clos [177]
0.0	8.09	0.00	20	0.00	0.00	_sigblock [178]
...	....	....	.	.	.	......

Here's what each column means:

`%time`

> Again, we see a field that describes the runtime for each routine as a percentage of the overall time taken by the program. As you might expect, all the entries in this column should total 100% (nearly).

`cumulative seconds`

> For any given routine, the column called "cumulative seconds" tallies a running sum of the time taken by all the preceding routines plus its own time. As you scan towards the bottom, the numbers asymptotically approach the total runtime for the program.

`self seconds`

> Each routine's individual contribution to the runtime.

`calls`

> The number of times this particular routine was called.

`self ms/call`

> Seconds spent inside the routine, divided by the number of calls. This gives the average length of time taken by each invocation of the routine. The figure is presented in milliseconds.

`total ms/call`

> Seconds spent inside the routine plus its descendants, divided by the number of calls.

`name`

> The name of the routine. Notice that the cross-reference number appears here too.

Accumulating the Results of Several gprof Runs

It is possible to accumulate statistics from multiple runs so that you can get a picture of how a program is doing with a variety of data sets. For instance, say that you wanted to profile an application—call it *bar*—with three different sets of input data. You could perform the runs separately, saving the *gmon.out* files as you go, and then combine the results into a single profile at the end:

```
% f77 -pg bar.f -o bar
% bar < data1.input
% mv gmon.out gmon.1
% bar < data2.input
% mv gmon.out gmon.2
% bar < data3.input
% gprof bar -s gmon.1 gmon.2 gmon.out > gprof.summary.out
```

In the example profile, each run along the way creates a new *gmon.out* file that we renamed to make room for the next one. At the end, *gprof* combines the information from each of the data files to produce a summary profile of *bar* in the file *gprof.summary.out*. Additionally (you don't see it here), *gprof* creates a file named *gmon.sum* that contains the merged data from the original three data files. *gmon.sum* has the same format as *gmon.out*, so you can use it as input for other merged profiles down the road.

In form, the output from a merged profile looks exactly the same as for an individual run. There are a couple of interesting things you will note, however. For one thing, the `main` routine appears to have been invoked more than once—one time for each run, in fact. Furthermore, depending on the application, multiple runs tend to either smooth the contour of the profile or exaggerate its features. You can imagine how this might happen. If a single routine is consistently called while others come and go as the input data changes, it takes on increasing importance in your tuning efforts.

A Few Words About Accuracy

For processors running at 600 MHz and more, the time between 60 Hz and 100 Hz samples is a veritable eternity. Furthermore, you can experience quantization errors when the sampling frequency is fixed, as is true of steady 1/100th or 1/60th of a second samples. To take an exaggerated example, assume that the timeline in Figure 6-6 shows alternating calls to two subroutines, BAR and FOO. The tick marks represent the sample points for profiling.

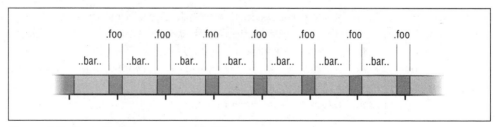

Figure 6-6: Quantization errors in profiling

BAR and FOO take turns running. In fact, BAR takes more time than FOO. But because the sampling interval closely matches the frequency at which the two subroutines alternate, we get a quantizing error: most of the samples happen to be taken while FOO is running. Therefore, the profile tells us that FOO took more CPU time than BAR.

We have described the tried and true UNIX subroutine profilers that have been available for years. In many cases, vendors have much better tools available for the asking or for a fee. If you are doing some serious tuning, ask your vendor representative to look into other tools for you.

Basic Block Profilers

There are several good reasons to desire a finer level of detail than you can see with a subroutine profiler. For humans trying to understand how a subroutine or function is used, a profiler that tells which lines of source code were actually executed, and how often, is invaluable; a few clues about where to focus your tuning efforts can save you time. Also, such a profiler saves you from discovering that a particularly clever optimization makes no difference because you put it in a section of code that never gets executed.

As part of an overall strategy, a subroutine profile can direct you to a handful of routines that account for most of the runtime, but it takes a *basic block profiler** to get you to the associated source code lines.

Basic block profilers can also provide compilers with information they need to perform their own optimizations. Most compilers work in the dark. They can restructure and unroll loops, but they cannot tell when it will pay off. Worse yet, misplaced optimizations often have an adverse effect of slowing down the code! This can be the result of added instruction cache burden, wasted tests introduced by the compiler, or incorrect assumptions about which way a branch would go at runtime. If the compiler can automatically interpret the results of a basic block profile, or if you can supply the compiler with hints, it often means a reduced runtime with little effort on your part.

There are several basic block profilers in the world. The closest thing to a standard, *tcov*, is shipped with Sun workstations; it's standard because the installed base is so big. On MIPS-based workstations, such as those from Silicon Graphics and DEC, the profiler (packaged as an extension to *prof*) is called *pixie*. We explain briefly how to run each profiler using a reasonable set of switches. You can consult your manual pages for other options.

tcov

tcov, available on Sun workstations and other SPARC machines that run SunOS, gives execution statistics that describe the number of times each source statement was executed. It is very easy to use. Assume for illustration that we have a source program called *foo.c*. The following steps create a basic block profile:

---

* A basic block is a section of code with only one entrance and one exit. If you know how many times the block was entered, you know how many times each of the statements in the block was executed, which gives you a line-by-line profile. The concept of a basic block is explained in detail in Chapter 5, *What a Compiler Does*.

```
% cc -a foo.c -o foo
% foo
% tcov foo.c
```

The **-a** option tells the compiler to include the necessary support for *tcov*.* Several files are created in the process. One called *foo.d* accumulates a history of the execution frequencies within the program *foo*. That is, old data is updated with new data each time *foo* is run, so you can get an overall picture of what happens inside *foo*, given a variety of data sets. Just remember to clean out the old data if you want to start over. The profile itself goes into a file called *foo.tcov*.

Let's look at an illustration. Below is a short C program that performs a bubble sort of 10 integers:

```
int n[] = {23,12,43,2,98,78,2,51,77,8};
main ()
  {
    int i, j, ktemp;
    for (i=10; i>0; i--) {
      for (j=0; j<i; j++) {
        if (n[j] < n[j+1]) {
          ktemp = n[j+1], n[j+1] = n[j], n[j] = ktemp;
        }
      }
    }
  }
```

tcov produces a basic block profile that contains execution counts for each source line, plus some summary statistics (not shown):

```
           int n[] = {23,12,43,2,98,78,2,51,77,8};
           main ()
   1 ->    {
             int i, j, ktemp;
  10 ->       for (i=10; i>0; i--) {
  10,    55 ->      for (j=0; j<i; j++) {
  55 ->         if (n[j] < n[j+1]) {
  23 ->           ktemp = n[j+1], n[j+1] = n[j], n[j] = ktemp;
                 }
               }
             }
   1 ->    }
```

The numbers to the left tell you the number of times each block was entered. For instance, you can see that the routine was entered just once, and that the highest count occurs at the test `n[j] < n[j+1]`. *tcov* shows more than one count on a line in places where the compiler has created more than one block.

---

* On Sun Solaris systems, the **-xa** option is used.

pixie

pixie is a little different from *tcov*. Rather than reporting the number of times each source line was executed, *pixie* reports the number of machine clock cycles devoted to executing each line. In theory, you could use this to calculate the amount of time spent per statement, although anomalies like cache misses are not represented.

pixie works by "pixifying" an executable file that has been compiled and linked in the normal way. Below we run *pixie* on *foo* to create a new executable called *foo.pixie*:

```
% cc foo.c -o foo
% pixie foo
% foo.pixie
% prof -pixie foo
```

Also created was a file named *foo.Addrs*, which contains addresses for the basic blocks within *foo*. When the new program, *foo.pixie*, is run, it creates a file called *foo.Counts*, containing execution counts for the basic blocks whose addresses are stored in *foo.Addrs*. *pixie* data accumulates from run to run. The statistics are retrieved using *prof* and a special **-pixie** flag.

pixie's default output comes in three sections and shows:

- Cycles per routine

- Procedure invocation counts

- Cycles per basic line

Below, we have listed the output of the third section for the bubble sort:

```
procedure (file)            line bytes      cycles     %   cum %

main (foo.c)                   7    44         605  12.11   12.11
_cleanup (flsbuf.c)           59    20         500  10.01   22.13
fclose (flsbuf.c)             81    20         500  10.01   32.14
fclose (flsbuf.c)             94    20         500  10.01   42.15
_cleanup (flsbuf.c)           54    20         500  10.01   52.16
fclose (flsbuf.c)             76    16         400   8.01   60.17
main (foo.c)                  10    24         298   5.97   66.14
main (foo.c)                   8    36         207   4.14   70.28
....                          ..    ..          ..   ...    ...
```

Here you can see three entries for the **main** routine from *foo.c*, plus a number of system library routines. The entries show the associated line number and the number of machine cycles dedicated to executing that line as the program ran. For instance, line 7 of *foo.c* took 605 cycles (12% of the runtime).

Virtual Memory

In addition to the negative performance impact due to cache misses, the virtual memory system can also slow your program down if it is too large to fit in the memory of the system or is competing with other large jobs for scarce memory resources.

Under most UNIX implementations, the operating system automatically pages pieces of a program that are too large for the available memory out to the *swap area*. The program won't be tossed out completely; that only happens when memory gets extremely tight, or when your program has been inactive for a while. Rather, individual pages are placed in the swap area for later retrieval. First of all, you need to be aware that this is happening if you don't already know about it. Second, if it is happening, the memory access patterns are critical. When references are too widely scattered, your runtime will be completely dominated by disk I/O.

If you plan in advance, you can make a virtual memory system work for you when your program is too large for the physical memory on the machine. The techniques are exactly the same as those for tuning a software-managed out-of-core solution, or loop nests. The process of "blocking" memory references so that data consumed in neighborhoods uses a bigger portion of each virtual memory page before rotating it out to disk to make room for another.*

Gauging the Size of Your Program and the Machine's Memory

How can you tell if you are running out-of-core? There are ways to check for paging on the machine, but perhaps the most straightforward check is to compare the size of your program against the amount of available memory. You do this with the *size* command:

```
% size myprogram
```

On a System V UNIX machine, the output looks something like this:

```
53872 + 53460 + 10010772 = 10118104
```

On a Berkeley UNIX derivative you see something like this:

```
text      data      bss         hex       decimal
53872     53460     10010772    9a63d8    10118104
```

---

* We examine the techniques for blocking in Chapter 8.

The first three fields describe the amount of memory required for three different portions of your program. The first, text, accounts for the machine instructions that make up your program. The second, data, includes initialized values in your program such as the contents of data statements, common blocks, externals, character strings, etc. The third component, `bss`, *(block started by symbol),* is usually the largest. It describes an uninitialized data area in your program. This area would be made of common blocks that are not set by a block data. The last field is a total for all three sections added together, in bytes.*

Next, you need to know how much memory you have in your system. Unfortunately, there isn't a standard UNIX command for this. On the RS/6000, */etc/lscfg* tells you. On an SGI machine, */etc/hinv* does it. Many System V UNIX implementations have an */etc/memsize* command. On any Berkeley derivative, you can type:

```
% ps aux
```

This command gives you a listing of all the processes running on the machine. Find the process with the largest value in the `%MEM`. Divide the value in the `RSS` field by the percentage of memory used to get a rough figure for how much memory your machine has:

```
memory = RSS/(%MEM/100)
```

For instance, if the largest process shows 5% memory usage and a resident set size (RSS) of 840 KB, your machine has 840000/(5/100) = 16 MB of memory.† If the answer from the size command shows a total that is anywhere near the amount of memory you have, you stand a good chance of paging when you run—especially if you are doing other things on the machine at the same time.

Checking for Page Faults

Your system's performance monitoring tools tell you if programs are paging. Some paging is OK; page faults and "page-ins" occur naturally as programs run. Also, be careful if you are competing for system resources along with other users. The picture you get won't be the same as when you have the computer to yourself.

To check for paging activity on a Berkeley UNIX derivative, use the *vmstat* command. Commonly people invoke it with a time increment so that it reports paging at regular intervals:

---

* Warning: The *size* command won't give you the full picture if your program allocates memory dynamically, or keeps data on the stack. This area is especially important for C programs and FORTRAN programs that create large arrays that are not in COMMON.

† You could also reboot the machine!It will tell you how much memory is available when it comes up.

```
% vmstat 5
```

This command produces output every five seconds:

procs			memory		page						disk				faults			cpu		
r	b	w	avm	fre	re	at	pi	po	fr	de	sr	s0	d1	d2	d3	in	sy	cs	us	sy	id
0	0	0	824	21568	0	0	0	0	0	0	0	0	0	0	0	20	37	13	0	1	98
0	0	0	840	21508	0	0	0	0	0	0	0	1	0	0	0	251	186	156	0	10	90
0	0	0	846	21460	0	0	0	0	0	0	0	2	0	0	0	248	149	152	1	9	89
0	0	0	918	21444	0	0	0	0	0	0	0	4	0	0	0	258	143	152	2	10	89

Lots of valuable information is produced. For our purposes, the important fields are `avm` or *active virtual memory*, the `fre` or *free real memory*, and the `pi` and `po` numbers showing paging activity. When the `fre` figure drops to near zero, and the `po` field shows a lot of activity, it's an indication that the memory system is overworked.

On a SysV machine, paging activity can be seen with the *sar* command:

```
% sar -r 5 5
```

This command shows you the amount of free memory and swap space presently available. If the free memory figure is low, you can assume that your program is paging:

```
Sat Apr 18 20:42:19
[r] freemem freeswap
       4032    82144
```

As we mentioned earlier, if you must run a job larger than the size of the memory on your machine, the same sort of advice that applied to conserving cache activity applies to paging activity.* Try to minimize the stride in your code, and where you can't, blocking memory references helps a whole lot.

A note on memory performance monitoring tools: you should check with your workstation vendor to see what they have available beyond *vmstat* or *sar*. There may be much more sophisticated (and often graphical) tools that can help you understand how your program is using memory.

Closing Notes

We have seen some of the tools for timing and profiling. Even though it seems like we covered a lot, there are other kinds of profiles we would like to be able to cover—cache miss measurements, runtime dependency analysis, flop measurements, and so on. These profiles are good when you are looking for particular

---

* By the way, are you getting the message "Out of memory?" If you are running *csh*, try typing `unlimit` to see if the message goes away. Otherwise, it may mean that you don't have enough swap space available to run the job.

anomalies, such as cache miss or floating-point pipeline utilization. Profilers for these quantities exist for some machines, but they aren't widely distributed.

One thing to keep in mind: when you profile code you sometimes get a very limited view of the way a program is used. This is especially true if it can perform many types of analyses for many different sets of input data. Working with just one or two profiles can give you a distorted picture of how the code operates overall. Imagine the following scenario: someone invites you to take your very first ride in an automobile. You get in the passenger's seat with a sketch pad and a pen, and record everything that happens. Your observations include some of the following:

- The radio is always on.

- The windshield wipers are never used.

- The car moves only in a forward direction.

The danger is that, given this limited view of the way a car is operated, you might want to disconnect the radio's on/off knob, remove the windshield wipers, and eliminate the reverse gear. This would come as a real surprise to the next person who tries to back the car out on a rainy day! The point is that unless you are careful to gather data for *all kinds* of uses, you may not really have a picture of how the program operates. A single profile is fine for tuning a benchmark, but you may miss some important details on a multipurpose application. Worse yet, if you optimize it for one case and cripple it for another, you may do far more harm than good.

Profiling, as we saw in this chapter, is pretty mechanical. Tuning requires insight. It's only fair to warn you that it isn't always rewarding. Sometimes you pour your soul into a clever modification that actually *increases* the runtime. Argh! What went wrong? You'll need to depend on your profiling tools to answer that.

Exercises

1. Profile the following program using *gprof*. Is there any way to tell how much of the time spent in routine c was due to recursive calls?

```
main()
{
    int i, n=10;
    for (i=0; i<1000; i++) {
        c(n);
        a(n);
    }
}
c(n)
```

```
int n;
{
    if (n > 0) {
        a(n-1);
        c(n-1);
    }
}
a(n)
int n;
{
    c(n);
}
```

2. Profile an engineering code (floating-point intensive) with full optimization on and off. How does the profile change? Can you explain the change?

3. Write a program to determine the overhead of the *getrusage* and the *ctime* calls. Other than consuming processor time, how can making a system call to check the time too often alter the application performance?

7

Eliminating Clutter

We have looked at code from the compiler's point of view and at how to profile code to find the trouble spots. This is good information, but if you are dissatisfied with a code's performance, you might still be wondering what to do about it. One possibility is that your code is too obtuse for the compiler to optimize properly. Excess code, too much modularization, or even previous optimization-related "improvements" can clutter up your code and confuse the compilers. Clutter is anything that contributes to the runtime without contributing to the answer. It comes in two forms:

Things that contribute to overhead
Subroutine calls, indirect memory references, tests within loops, wordy tests, type conversions, variables preserved unnecessarily

Things that restrict compiler flexibility
Subroutine calls, indirect memory references, tests within loops, ambiguous pointers

It's not a mistake that some of the same items appear in both lists. Subroutine calls or if-statements within loops can both bite and scratch you by taking too much time and by creating *fences*—places in the program where instructions that appear before can't be safely intermixed with instructions that appear after, at least not without a great deal of care. The goal of this chapter is to show you how to eliminate clutter, so you can restructure what's left over for the fastest execution. We save a few specific topics that might fit here, especially those regarding memory references, for later chapters where they are treated as subjects by themselves.

Before we start, we'll remind you: as you look for ways to improve what you have, keep your eyes and mind open to the possibility that there might be a fundamentally better way to do something—a more efficient sorting technique, random number generator, or solver. A different algorithm may buy you far more speed than tuning. Algorithms are beyond the scope of this book, but what we are discussing here should help you recognize "good" code, or help you to code a new algorithm to get the best performance.

Subroutine Calls

A typical corporation is full of frightening examples of overhead. Say your department has prepared a stack of paperwork to be completed by another department. What do you have to do to transfer that work? First, you have to be sure that your portion is completed; you can't ask them to take over if the materials they need aren't ready. Next, you need to package the materials—data, forms, charge numbers, and the like. And finally comes the official transfer. Upon receiving what you sent, the other department has to unpack it, do their job, repackage it, and send it back.

A lot of time gets wasted moving work between departments. Of course, if the overhead is minimal compared to the amount of useful work being done, it won't be that big a deal. But it might be more efficient for small jobs to stay within one department. The same is true of subroutine and function calls. If you only enter and exit modules once in a relative while, the overhead of saving registers and preparing argument lists won't be significant. However, if you are repeatedly calling a few small subroutines, the overhead can buoy them to the top of the profile. It might be better if the work stayed where it was, in the calling routine.

Additionally, subroutine calls inhibit compiler flexibility. Given the right opportunity, you'd like your compiler to have the freedom to intermix instructions that aren't dependent upon each other. These are found on either side of a subroutine call, in the caller and callee. But the opportunity is lost when the compiler can't peer into subroutines and functions. Instructions that might overlap very nicely have to stay on their respective sides of the artificial fence.

It helps if we illustrate the challenge that subroutine boundaries present with an exaggerated example. The following loop runs very well on a wide range of processors:

```
DO I=1,N
   A(I) = A(I) + B(I) * C
ENDDO
```

The code below performs the same calculations, but look at what we have done:

```
DO I=1,N
   CALL MADD (A(I), B(I), C)
ENDDO
SUBROUTINE MADD (A,B,C)
```

```
A = A + B * C
RETURN
END
```

Each iteration calls a subroutine to do a small amount of work that was formerly within the loop. This is a particularly painful example because it involves floating-point calculations. The resulting loss of parallelism, coupled with the procedure call overhead, might produce code that runs 100 times slower. Remember, these operations are pipelined, and it takes a certain amount of "wind-up" time before the throughput reaches one operation per clock cycle. If there are few floating-point operations to perform between subroutine calls, the time spent winding up and winding down pipelines figures prominently.

Subroutine and function calls complicate the compiler's ability to efficiently manage COMMON and `external` variables, delaying until the last possible moment actually storing them in memory. The compiler uses registers to hold the "live" values of many variables. When you make a call, the compiler cannot tell whether the subroutine will be changing variables that are declared as `external` or COMMON. Therefore, it's forced to store any modified `external` or COMMON variables back into memory so that the callee can find them. Likewise, after the call has returned, the same variables have to be reloaded into registers because the compiler can no longer trust the old, register-resident copies. The penalty for saving and restoring variables can be substantial, especially if you are using lots of them. It can also be unwarranted if variables that ought to be local are specified as `external` or COMMON, as in the following code:

```
COMMON /USELESS/ K
DO K=1,1000
  IF (K .EQ. 1) CALL AUX
ENDDO
```

In this example, K has been declared as a COMMON variable. It is used only as a do-loop counter, so there really is no reason for it to be anything but local. However, because it is in a COMMON block, the call to AUX forces the compiler to store and reload K each iteration. This is because the side effects of the call are unknown.

So far, it looks as if we are preparing a case for huge main programs without any subroutines or functions! Not at all. Modularity is important for keeping source code compact and understandable. And frankly, the need for maintainability and modularity is always more important than the need for *small* performance improvements. However, there are a few approaches for streamlining subroutine calls that don't require you to scrap modular coding techniques: macros and procedure inlining.

Remember, if the function or subroutine does a reasonable amount of work, procedure call overhead isn't going to matter very much. However, if one small routine appears as a leaf node in one of the busiest sections of the call graph, you
might want to think about inserting it in appropriate places in the program.

Macros

Macros are little procedures that are substituted inline at compile time. Unlike subroutines or functions, which are included once during the link, macros are replicated every place they are used. When the compiler makes its first pass through
your program, it looks for patterns that match previous macro definitions and
expands them inline. In fact, in later stages, the compiler sees an expanded macro
as source code.

Macros are part of both C and FORTRAN (although the FORTRAN notion of a
macro, the *statement function*, is reviled by the FORTRAN community, and won't
survive much longer).* For C programs, macros are created with a `#define` construct, as demonstrated here:

```
#define average(x,y) ((x+y)/2)
main ()
{
    float q = 100, p = 50;
    float a;
    a = average(p,q);
    printf ("%f\n",a);
}
```

The first compilation step for a C program is a pass through the C preprocessor,
cpp. This happens automatically when you invoke the compiler. *cpp* expands
`#define` statements inline, replacing the pattern matched by the macro definition.
In the program above, the statement:

```
a = average(p,q);
```

gets replaced with:

```
a = ((p+q)/2);
```

You have to be careful how you define the macro because it literally replaces the
pattern located by *cpp*. For instance, if the macro definition said:

```
#define multiply(a,b) (a*b)
```

---

* The statement function has been eliminated in FORTRAN 90.

and you invoked it as:

```
c = multiply(x+t,y+v);
```

the resulting expansion would be `x+t*y+v`—probably not what you intended.

If you are a C programmer you may be using macros without being conscious of it. Many C header files (*.h*) contain macro definitions. In fact, some "standard" C library functions are really defined as macros in the header files. For instance, the function *getchar* can be linked in when you build your program. If you have a statement:

```
#include <stdio.h>
```

in your file, *getchar* is replaced with a macro definition at compile time, replacing the C library function.

You can make *cpp* macros work for FORTRAN programs too.* For example, a FORTRAN version of the C program above might look like this:

```
#define AVERAG(X,Y) ((X+Y)/2)
C
      PROGRAM MAIN
      REAL A,P,Q
      DATA P,Q /50.,100./
      A = AVERAG(P,Q)
      WRITE (*,*) A
      END
```

Without a little preparation, the **#define** statement is rejected by the FORTRAN compiler. The program first has to be preprocessed through *cpp* to replace the use of **AVERAG** with its macro definition. It makes compilation a two-step procedure, but that shouldn't be too much of a burden, especially if you are building your programs under the control of the *make* utility. We would also suggest you store FORTRAN programs containing *cpp* directives under *filename.F* to distinguish them from unadorned FORTRAN. Just be sure you make your changes only to the *.F* files and not to the output from *cpp*. This is how you would preprocess FOR-TRAN *.F* files by hand:

```
% /lib/cpp -P < average.F > average.f
% f77 average.f -c
```

The FORTRAN compiler never sees the original code. Instead, the macro definition is substituted inline as if you had typed it yourself:

```
C
      PROGRAM MAIN
      REAL A,P,Q
```

---

* Some programmers use the standard UNIX *m4* preprocessor for FORTRAN.

```
DATA P,Q /50.,100./
A - ((P+Q)/2)
WRITE (*,*) A
END
```

By the way, some FORTRAN compilers recognize the *.F* extension already, making the two-step process unnecessary. If the compiler sees the *.F* extension it invokes *cpp* automatically, compiles the output, and throws away the intermediate *f* file. Try compiling a *.F* on your computer to see if it works.

Also, be aware that macro expansions may make source lines extend past column 72, which will probably make your FORTRAN compiler complain (or worse: it might pass unnoticed). Some compilers support input lines longer than 72 characters. On the Sun compilers the **-e** option allows extended input lines up to 132 characters long.

Procedure Inlining

Macro definitions tend to be pretty short, usually just a single statement. Sometimes you have slightly longer (but not too long) bits of code that might also benefit from being copied inline, rather than called as a subroutine or function. Again, the reason for doing this is to eliminate procedure call overhead and expose parallelism. If your compiler is capable of *inlining* subroutine and function definitions into the modules that call them, then you have a very natural, very portable way to write modular code without suffering the cost of subroutine calls.

Depending on the vendor, you can ask the compiler for procedure inlining by:

- Specifying which routines should be inlined on the compiler's command line
- Putting inlining directives into the source program
- Letting the compiler inline automatically

The directives and compile line options are not standard, so you have to check your compiler documentation. Unfortunately, you may learn that there is no such feature ("yet," always yet), or that it's an expensive extra. The third form of inlining in the list, automatic, is available from just a few vendors. Automatic inlining depends on a sophisticated compiler that can view the definitions of several modules at once.

There are some words of caution with regard to procedure inlining. You can easily do too much of it. If everything and anything is ingested into the body of its parents, the resulting executable may be so large that it repeatedly spills out of the instruction cache and becomes a net performance loss. Our advice is that you use the caller/callee information profilers give you and make some intelligent decisions about inlining, rather than trying to inline every subroutine available. Again, small routines that are called often are generally the best candidates for inlining.

Branches

People sometimes take a week to make a decision, so we can't fault a computer if it takes a few tens of nanoseconds. However, if an if-statement appears in some heavily traveled section of the code, you might get tired of the delay. There are two basic approaches to reducing the impact of branches:

- Streamline them.

- Move them out to the computational suburbs. Particularly, get them out of loops.

In this section we show you some easy ways to reorganize conditionals so they execute more quickly.

Branches Within Loops

Numerical codes usually spend most of their time in loops, so you don't want anything inside a loop that doesn't have to be there, especially an if-statement. Not only do if-statements gum up the works with extra instructions, they can force a strict order on the iterations of a loop. Of course, you can't always avoid conditionals. Sometimes, though, people place them in loops to process events that could have been handled outside, or even ignored.

To take you back a few years, the following code shows a loop with a test for a value close to zero:

```
PARAMETER (SMALL = 1.E-20)
DO I=1,N
  IF (ABS(A(I)) .GE. SMALL) THEN
    B(I) = B(I) + A(I) * C
  ENDIF
ENDDO
```

The idea was that if the multiplier, `A(I)`, were reasonably small, there would be no reason to perform the math in the center of the loop. Because floating-point operations weren't pipelined on many machines, a comparison and a branch was cheaper; the test would save time. On an older CISC or early RISC processor, a comparison and branch is probably still a savings. But on other architectures, it costs a lot less to just perform the math and skip the test. Eliminating the branch eliminates a control dependency and allows the compiler to pipeline more arithmetic operations. Of course, the answer could change slightly if the test is eliminated. It then becomes a question of whether the difference is significant. Here's another example where a branch isn't necessary. The loop finds the absolute value of each element in an array:

```
DO I=1,N
  IF (A(I) .LT. 0.) A(I) = -A(I)
ENDDO
```

But why perform the test at all? On most machines, it's quicker to perform the `abs()` operation on every element of the array.

We do have to give you a warning, though: if you are coding in C, the absolute value, `fabs()`, is a subroutine call. In this particular case, you are better off leaving the conditional in the loop.*

When you can't always throw out the conditional, there are things you can do to minimize negative performance. First, we have to learn to recognize which conditionals within loops can be restructured and which cannot. Conditionals in loops fall into several categories:

- Loop invariant conditionals

- Loop index dependent conditionals

- Independent loop conditionals

- Dependent loop conditionals

- Reductions

- Conditionals that transfer control

Let's look at these types in turn.

Loop Invariant Conditionals

The following loop contains an *invariant* test:

```
DO I=1,K
  IF (N .EQ. 0) THEN
    A(I) = A(I) + B(I) * C
  ELSE
    A(I) = 0.
  ENDIF
ENDDO
```

"Invariant" means that the outcome is always the same. Regardless of what happens to the variables A, B, C, and I, the value of N won't change, so neither will the outcome of the test.

---

* The machine representation of a floating-point number starts with a *sign bit*. If the bit is 0, the number is positive. If it is 1, the number is negative. The fastest absolute value function is one that merely "ands" out the sign bit. See macros in */usr/include/macros.h* and */usr/include/math.h*.

You can recast the loop by making the test outside and replicating the loop body twice—once for when the test is true, and once for when it is false, as in the following example:

```
IF (N .EQ. 0) THEN
  DO I=1,K
    A(I) = A(I) + B(I) * C
  ENDDO
ELSE
  DO I=1,K
    A(I) = 0
  ENDDO
ENDIF
```

The effect on the runtime is dramatic. Not only have we eliminated K-1 copies of the test, we have also assured that the computations in the middle of the loop are not control-dependent on the if-statement, and are therefore much easier for the compiler to pipeline.

We remember helping someone optimize a program with loops containing similar conditionals. They were checking to see whether debug output should be printed each iteration inside an otherwise highly optimizable loop. We can't fault the person for not realizing how much this slowed the program down. Performance wasn't important at the time. The programmer was just trying to get the code to produce good answers. But later on, when performance mattered, by cleaning up invariant conditionals, we were able to speed up the program by a factor of 100.

Loop Index Dependent Conditionals

For *loop index dependent* conditionals, the test is true for certain ranges of the loop index variables. It isn't always true or always false, like the conditional we just looked at, but it does change with a predictable pattern, and one that we can use to our advantage. The following loop has two index variables, I and J.

```
DO I=1,N
  DO J=1,N
    IF (J .LT. I)
      A(J,I) = A(J,I) + B(J,I) * C
    ELSE
      A(J,I) = 0.0
    ENDIF
  ENDDO
ENDDO
```

Notice how the if-statement partitions the iterations into distinct sets: those for which it is true and those for which it is false. You can take advantage of the predictability of the test to restructure the loop into several loops—each custom-made for a different partition:

```
DO I=1,N
  DO J=1,I-1
      A(J,I) = A(J,I) + B(J,I) * C
  ENDDO
  DO J=I,N
      A(J,I) = 0.0
  ENDDO
ENDDO
```

The new version will almost always be faster. A possible exception is when N is a small value, like 3, in which case we have created more clutter. But then, the loop probably has such a small impact on the total runtime that it won't matter which way it's coded.

Independent Loop Conditionals

It would be nice if you could optimize every loop by partitioning it. But more often than not, the conditional doesn't directly depend on the value of the index variables. Although an index variable may be involved in addressing an array, it doesn't create a recognizable pattern in advance—at least not one you can see when you are writing the program. Here's such a loop:

```
DO I=1,N
  DO J=1,N
    IF (B(J,I) .GT. 1.0) A(J,I) = A(J,I) + B(J,I) * C
  ENDDO
ENDDO
```

There is not much you can do about this type of conditional. But because every iteration is independent, the loop can be unrolled or can be performed in parallel.

Dependent Loop Conditionals

When the conditional is based on a value that changes with each iteration of the loop, the compiler has no choice but to execute the code exactly as written. For instance, the following loop has an if-statement with built-in scalar recursion:

```
DO I=1,N
  IF (X .LT. A(I)) X = X + B(I)*2.
ENDDO
```

You can't know which way the branch will go for the next iteration until you are done with the current iteration. To recognize the dependency, try to unroll the loop slightly by hand. If you can't start the second test until the first has finished, you have a *dependent loop* conditional. You may want to look at these types of loops to see if you can eliminate the iteration-to-iteration value.

Reductions

Keep an eye out for loops in which the if-statement is performing a *max* or *min* function on a array. This is a *reduction*, so called because it reduces a array to a scalar result (the previous example was a reduction too, by the way). Again, we are getting a little bit ahead of ourselves, but since we are talking about if-statements in loops, I want to introduce a trick for restructuring reductions `max` and `min` to expose more parallelism. The following loop searches for the maximum value, z, in the array a by going through the elements one at a time:

```
for (i=0; i<n; i++)
    z = a[i] > z ? a[i] : z;
```

As written, it's recursive like the loop from the previous section. You need the result of a given iteration before you can proceed to the next. However, since we are looking for the greatest element in the whole array, and since that will be the same element (essentially) no matter how we go about looking for it, we can restructure the loop to check several elements at a time (we assume n is evenly divisible by 2 and do not include the preconditioning loop):

```
z0 = 0.;
z1 = 0.;
for (i=0; i< n-1; i+=2) {
   z0 = z0 < a[i]   ? a[i]   : z0;
   z1 = z1 < a[i+1] ? a[i+1] : z1;
}
z = z0 < z1 ? z1 : z0;
```

Do you see how the new loop calculates two new maximum values each iteration? These maximums are then compared with one another, and the winner becomes the new official *max*. It's analogous to a play-off arrangement in a Ping-Pong tournament. Whereas the old loop was more like two players competing at a time while the rest sat around, the new loop runs several matches side by side. In general this particular optimization is not a good one to code by hand. On parallel processors, the compiler performs the reduction in its own way. If you hand-code similar to this example, you may inadvertently limit the compiler's flexibility on a parallel system.

Conditionals That Transfer Control

Let's step back a second. Have you noticed a similarity among all the loops so far? We have looked only at a particular type of conditional, *conditional assignments*—based on the outcome of the test, a variable gets reassigned. Of course, not every conditional ends up in an assignment. You can have statements that transfer flow of control, such as subroutine calls or `goto` statements. In the following example, the programmer is carefully checking before dividing by zero.

However, this test has an extremely negative impact on the performance because it forces the iterations to be done precisely in order:

```
DO I=1,N
  DO J=1,N
    IF (B(J,I) .EQ. 0 ) THEN
      PRINT *,I,J
      STOP
    ENDIF
    A(J,I) = A(J,I) / B(J,I)
  ENDDO
ENDDO
```

Avoiding these tests is one of the reasons that the designers of the IEEE floating-point standard added the trap feature for operations such as dividing by zero. These traps allow the programmer in a performance-critical section of the code to achieve maximum performance yet still detect when an error occurs.

Other Clutter

Clutter comes in many forms. Consider the previous sections as having dealt with large pieces of junk you might find in the front hall closet: an ironing board, hockey sticks, and pool cues. Now we are down to the little things: a widowed checker, a tennis ball, and a hat nobody owns. We want to mention a few of them here. We apologize in advance for changing subjects a lot, but that's the nature of cleaning out a closet!

Data Type Conversions

Statements that contain runtime type conversions suffer a little performance penalty each time the statement is executed. If the statement is located in a portion of the program where there is a lot of activity, the total penalty can be significant.

People have their reasons for writing applications with mixed typing. Often it is a matter of saving memory space, memory bandwidth, or time. In the past, for instance, double-precision calculations took twice as long as their single-precision counterparts, so if some of the calculations could be arranged to take place in single precision, there could be a performance win.* But any time saved by performing part of the calculations in single precision and part in double precision has to

---

* Nowadays, single-precision calculations can take *longer* than double-precision calculations from register to register.

be measured against the additional overhead caused by the runtime type conversions. In the following code, the addition of A(I) to B(I) is *mixed type*:

```
INTEGER NUMEL, I
PARAMETER (NUMEL = 1000)
REAL*8 A(NUMEL)
REAL*4 B(NUMEL)
DO I=1,NUMEL
  A(I) = A(I) + B(I)
ENDDO
```

In each iteration, B(I) has to be promoted to double precision before the addition can occur. You don't see the promotion in the source code, but it's there, and it takes time.

C programmers beware: in Kernighan and Ritchie (K&R) C, all floating-point calculations in C programs take place in double precision—even if all the variables involved are declared as *float*. It is possible for you to write a whole K+R application in one precision, yet suffer the penalty of many type conversions.

Another data type–related mistake is to use character operations in IF tests. On many systems, character operations have poorer performance than integer operations since they may be done via procedure calls. Also, the optimizers may not look at code using character variables as a good candidate for optimization. For example, the following code:

```
DO I=1,10000
  IF ( CHVAR(I) .EQ. 'Y' ) THEN
    A(I) = A(I) + B(I)*C
  ENDIF
ENDDO
```

might be better written using an integer variable to indicate whether or not a computation should be performed:

```
DO I=1,10000
  IF ( IFLAG(I) .EQ. 1 ) THEN
    A(I) = A(I) + B(I)*C
  ENDIF
ENDDO
```

Another way to write the code, assuming the IFLAG variable was 0 or 1, would be as follows:

```
DO I=1,10000
  A(I) = A(I) + B(I)*C*IFLAG(I)
ENDDO
```

The last approach might actually perform slower on some computer systems than the approach using the IF and the integer variable.

Doing Your Own Common Subexpression Elimination

So far we have given your compiler the benefit of the doubt. *Common subexpression elimination*—the ability of the compiler to recognize repeated patterns in the code and replace all but one with a temporary variable—probably works on your machine for simple expressions. In the following lines of code, most compilers would recognize `a+b` as a common subexpression:

```
c = a + b + d
e = q + a + b
```

becomes:

```
temp = a + b
c = temp + d
e = q + temp
```

Substituting for `a+b` eliminates some of the arithmetic. If the expression is reused many times, the savings can be significant. However, a compiler's ability to recognize common subexpressions is limited, especially when there are multiple components, or their order is permuted. A compiler might not recognize that `a+b+c` and `c+b+a` are equivalent.* For important parts of the program, you might consider doing common subexpression elimination of complicated expressions by hand. This guarantees that it gets done. It compromises beauty somewhat, but there are some situations where it is worth it.

Here's another example in which the function *sin* is called twice with the same argument:

```
x = r*sin(a)*cos(b);
y = r*sin(a)*sin(b);
z = r*cos(a);
```

becomes:

```
temp = r*sin(a);
x = temp*cos(b);
y = temp*sin(b);
z = r*cos(a);
```

We have replaced one of the calls with a temporary variable. We agree, the savings for eliminating one transcendental function call out of five won't win you a Nobel prize, but it does call attention to an important point: compilers typically do not perform common subexpression elimination over subroutine or function calls.

---

* And because of overflow and round-off errors in floating-point, in some situations they might not be equivalent.

The compiler can't be sure that the subroutine call doesn't change the state of the argument or some other variables that it can't see.

The only time a compiler might eliminate common subexpressions containing function calls is when they are intrinsics, as in FORTRAN. This can be done because the compiler can assume some things about their side effects. You, on the other hand, can see into subroutines, which means you are better qualified than the compiler to group together common subexpressions involving subroutines or functions.

Doing Your Own Code Motion

All of these optimizations have their biggest payback within loops because that's where all of a program's activity is concentrated. One of the best ways to cut down on runtime is to move unnecessary or repeated (invariant) instructions out of the main flow of the code and into the suburbs. For loops, it's called *hoisting* instructions when they are pulled out from the top and *sinking* when they are pushed down below. Here's an example:

```
DO I=1,N
  A(I) = A(I) / SQRT(X*X + Y*Y)
ENDDO
```

becomes:

```
TEMP = 1 / SQRT(X*X + Y*Y)
DO I=1,N
  A(I) = A(I) * TEMP
ENDDO
```

We hoisted an expensive, invariant operation out of the loop and assigned the result to a temporary variable. Notice, too, that we made an algebraic simplification when we exchanged a division for multiplication by an inverse. The multiplication will execute much more quickly. Your compiler might be smart enough to make these transformations itself, assuming you have instructed the compiler that these are legal transformations; but without crawling through the assembly language, you can't be positive. Of course, if you rearrange code by hand and the runtime for the loop suddenly goes down, you will know that the compiler has been sandbagging all along.

Sometimes you want to sink an operation below the loop. Usually, it's some calculation performed each iteration but whose result is only needed for the last. To illustrate, here's a sort of loop that is different from the ones we have been looking at. It searches for the final character in a character string:

```
while (*p != ' ')
   c = *p++;
```

becomes:

```
while (*p++ != ' ');
c = *(p-1);
```

The new version of the loop moves the assignment of c beyond the last iteration. Admittedly, this transformation would be a reach for a compiler and the savings wouldn't even be that great. But it illustrates the notion of sinking an operation very well.

Again, hoisting or sinking instructions to get them out of loops is something your compiler should be capable of doing. But often you can slightly restructure the calculations yourself when you move them to get an even greater benefit.

Handling Array Elements in Loops

Here's another area where you would like to trust the compiler to do the right thing. When making repeated use of an array element within a loop, you want to be charged just once for loading it from memory. Take the following loop as an example. It reuses X(I) twice:

```
DO I=1,N
   XOLD(I) = X(I)
   X(I)    = X(I) + XINC(I)
ENDDO
```

In reality, the steps that go into retrieving X(I) are just additional common subexpressions: an address calculation (possibly) and a memory load operation. You can see that the operation is repeated by rewriting the loop slightly:

```
DO I=1,N
   TEMP    = X(I)
   XOLD(I) = TEMP
   X(I)    = TEMP + XINC(I)
ENDDO
```

FORTRAN compilers *should* recognize that the same X(I) is being used twice and that it only needs to be loaded once, but compilers aren't always so smart. You sometimes have to create a temporary scalar variable to hold the value of an array element over the body of a loop. This is particularly true when there are subroutine calls or functions in the loop, or when some of the variables are **external** or **COMMON**. Make sure to match the types between the temporary variables and the other variables. You don't want to incur type conversion overhead just because you are "helping" the compiler. For C compilers, the same kind of indexed expressions are an even greater challenge. Consider this code:

```
doinc(int xold[],int x[],int xinc[],int n)
{
  for (i=0; i<n; i++) {
    xold[i] = x[i];
    x[i]    = x[i] + xinc[i];
  }
}
```

Unless the compiler can see the definitions of `x`, `xinc`, and `xold`, it has to assume that they are pointers leading back to the same storage, and repeat the loads and stores. In this case, introducing temporary variables to hold the values `x`, `xinc`, and `xold` is an optimization the compiler wasn't free to make.

Interestingly, while putting scalar temporaries in the loop is useful for RISC and superscalar machines, it doesn't help code that runs on parallel hardware. A parallel compiler looks for opportunities to eliminate the scalars or, at the very least, to replace them with temporary vectors. If you run your code on a parallel machine from time to time, you might want to be careful about introducing scalar temporary variables into a loop. A dubious performance gain in one instance could be a real performance loss in another.

Closing Notes

In this chapter, we introduced tuning techniques for eliminating program clutter—anything that contributes to the runtime without contributing to the answer. We saw many examples of tuning techniques—enough that you may be asking yourself, "What's left?" Well, as we will see in the upcoming chapters, there are a couple of ways we can help the compiler:

- Find more parallelism

- Use memory as effectively as possible

Sometimes this means we make changes that are not beautiful. However, they are often quick.

Exercises

1. How would you simplify the following loop conditional?

```
DO I=1,N
  A(I) = A(I) * B
  IF (I .EQ. N/2) A(I) = 0.
ENDDO
```

2. The following loop is taken from this chapter. Time it on your computer, both with and without the test. Run it with three sets of data: one with all A(I)s less than SMALL, one with all A(I)s greater than SMALL, and one with an even split. When is it better to leave the test in the loop, if ever?

```
PARAMETER (SMALL = 1.E-20)
DO I=1,N
  IF (ABS(A(I)) .GE. SMALL) THEN
    B(I) = B(I) + A(I) * C
  ENDIF
ENDDO
```

3. Write a simple program that calls a simple subroutine in its inner loop. Time the program execution. Then tell the compiler to inline the routine and test the performance again. Finally, modify the code to perform the operations in the body of the loop and time the code. Which option ran faster? You may have to look at the generated machine code to figure out why.

8

Loop Optimizations

In nearly all high performance applications, loops are where the majority of the execution time is spent. In the last chapter we examined ways in which application developers introduced clutter into loops, possibly slowing those loops down. In this chapter we focus on techniques used to improve the performance of these "clutter-free" loops. Sometimes the compiler is clever enough to generate the faster versions of the loops, and other times we have to do some rewriting of the loops ourselves to help the compiler.

It's important to remember that one compiler's performance enhancing modifications are another compiler's clutter. When you make modifications in the name of performance you must make sure you're helping by testing the performance with and without the modifications. Also, when you move to another architecture you need to make sure that any modifications aren't hindering performance. For this reason, you should choose your performance-related modifications wisely. You should also keep the original (simple) version of the code for testing on new architectures. Also if the benefit of the modification is small, you should probably keep the code in its most simple and clear form.

We look at a number of different loop optimization techniques, including:

- Loop unrolling

- Nested loop optimization

- Loop interchange

- Memory reference optimization

- Blocking

- Out-of-core solutions

Someday, it may be possible for a compiler to perform all these loop optimizations automatically. Typically loop unrolling is performed as part of the normal compiler optimizations. Other optimizations may have to be triggered using explicit compile-time options. As you contemplate making manual changes, look carefully at which of these optimizations can be done by the compiler. Also run some tests to determine if the compiler optimizations are as good as hand optimizations.

Operation Counting

Before you begin to rewrite a loop body or reorganize the order of the loops, you must have some idea of what the body of the loop does for each iteration. *Operation counting* is the process of surveying a loop to understand the operation mix. You need to count the number of loads, stores, floating-point, integer, and library calls per iteration of the loop. From the count, you can see how well the operation mix of a given loop matches the capabilities of the processor. Of course, operation counting doesn't guarantee that the compiler will generate an efficient representation of a loop.* But it generally provides enough insight to the loop to direct tuning efforts.

Bear in mind that an instruction mix that is balanced for one machine may be imbalanced for another. Processors on the market today can generally issue some combination of one to four operations per clock cycle. Address arithmetic is often embedded in the instructions that reference memory. Because the compiler can replace complicated loop address calculations with simple expressions (provided the pattern of addresses is predictable), you can often ignore address arithmetic when counting operations.†

---

* Take a look at the assembly language output to be sure, which may be going a bit overboard. To get an assembly language listing on most machines, compile with the –S flag. On an RS/6000, use the –qlist flag.

† The compiler reduces the complexity of loop index expressions with a technique called *induction variable simplification*. See Chapter 5, *What a Compiler Does*.

Let's look at a few loops and see what we can learn about the instruction mix:

```
DO I=1,N
  A(I,J,K) = A(I,J,K) + B(J,I,K)
ENDDO
```

This loop contains one floating-point addition and three memory references (two loads and a store). There are some complicated array index expressions, but these will probably be simplified by the compiler and executed in the same cycle as the memory and floating-point operations. For each iteration of the loop, we must increment the index variable and test to determine if the loop has completed.

A 3:1 ratio of memory references to floating-point operations suggests that we can hope for no more than 1/3 peak floating-point performance from the loop unless we have more than one path to memory. That's bad news, but good information. The ratio tells us that we ought to consider memory reference optimizations first.

The loop below contains one floating-point addition and two memory operations—a load and a store. Operand B(J) is loop-invariant, so its value only needs to be loaded once, upon entry to the loop:

```
DO I=1,N
  A(I) = A(I) + B(J)
ENDDO
```

Again, our floating-point throughput is limited, though not as severely as in the previous loop. The ratio of memory references to floating-point operations is 2:1.

The next example shows a loop with better prospects. It performs element-wise multiplication of two vectors of complex numbers and assigns the results back to the first. There are six memory operations (four loads and two stores) and six floating-point operations (two additions and four multiplications):

```
for (i=0; i<n; i++) {
    xr[i] = xr[i] * yr[i] - xi[i] * yi[i];
    xi[i] = xr[i] * yi[i] + xi[i] * yr[i];
}
```

It appears that this loop is roughly balanced for a processor that can perform the same number of memory operations and floating-point operations per cycle. However, it might not be. Many processors perform a floating-point multiply and add in a single instruction. If the compiler is good enough to recognize that the multiply-add is appropriate, this loop may also be limited by memory references; each iteration would be compiled into two multiplications and two multiply-adds.

Again, operation counting is a simple way to estimate how well the requirements of a loop will map onto the capabilities of the machine. For many loops, you often find the performance of the loops dominated by memory references, as we have seen in the last three examples. This suggests that memory reference tuning is very important.

Basic Loop Unrolling

The most basic form of loop optimization is loop unrolling. It is so basic that most of today's compilers do it automatically if it looks like there's a benefit. There has been a great deal of clutter introduced into old dusty-deck FORTRAN programs in the name of loop unrolling that now serves only to confuse and mislead today's compilers.

We're not suggesting that you unroll any loops by hand. The purpose of this section is twofold. First, once you are familiar with loop unrolling, you might recognize code that was unrolled by a programmer (not you) some time ago and simplify the code. Second, you need to understand the concepts of loop unrolling so that when you look at generated machine code, you recognize unrolled loops.

The primary benefit in loop unrolling is to perform more computations per iteration. At the end of each iteration, the index value must be incremented, tested, and the control is branched back to the top of the loop if the loop has more iterations to process. By unrolling the loop, there are less "loop-ends" per loop execution. Unrolling also reduces the overall number of branches significantly and gives the processor more instructions between branches (i.e., it increases the size of the basic blocks).

For illustration, consider the following loop. It has a single statement wrapped in a do-loop:

```
DO I=1,N
   A(I) = A(I) + B(I) * C
ENDDO
```

You can unroll the loop, as we have below, giving you the same operations in fewer iterations with less loop overhead. You can imagine how this would help on any computer. Because the computations in one iteration do not depend on the computations in other iterations, calculations from different iterations can be executed together. On a superscalar processor, portions of these four statements may actually execute in parallel:

```
DO I=1,N,4
   A(I)   = A(I)   + B(I)   * C
   A(I+1) = A(I+1) + B(I+1) * C
   A(I+2) = A(I+2) + B(I+2) * C
   A(I+3) = A(I+3) + B(I+3) * C
ENDDO
```

However, this loop is not *exactly* the same as the previous loop. The loop is unrolled four times, but what if N is not divisible by 4? If not, there will be one, two, or three spare iterations that don't get executed. To handle these extra iterations, we add another little loop to soak them up. The extra loop is called a *preconditioning loop*:

```
II = IMOD (N,4)
DO I=1,II
  A(I) = A(I) + B(I) * C
ENDDO

DO I=1+II,N,4
  A(I)   = A(I)   + B(I)   * C
  A(I+1) = A(I+1) + B(I+1) * C
  A(I+2) = A(I+2) + B(I+2) * C
  A(I+3) = A(I+3) + B(I+3) * C
ENDDO
```

The number of iterations needed in the preconditioning loop is the total iteration count modulo for this unrolling amount. If, at runtime, N turns out to be divisible by 4, there are no spare iterations, and the preconditioning loop isn't executed.

Speculative execution in the post-RISC architecture can reduce or eliminate the need for unrolling a loop that will operate on values that must be retrieved from main memory. Because the load operations take such a long time relative to the computations, the loop is naturally unrolled. While the processor is waiting for the first load to finish, it may speculatively execute three to four iterations of the loop ahead of the first load, effectively unrolling the loop in the Instruction Reorder Buffer.

Qualifying Candidates for Loop Unrolling

Assuming a large value for N, the previous loop was an ideal candidate for loop unrolling. The iterations could be executed in any order, and the loop innards were small. But as you might suspect, this isn't always the case; some kinds of loops can't be unrolled so easily. Additionally, the way a loop is used when the program runs can disqualify it for loop unrolling, even if it looks promising.

In this section we are going to discuss a few categories of loops that are generally not prime candidates for unrolling, and give you some ideas of what you can do about them. We talked about several of these in the previous chapter as well, but they are also relevant here.

Loops with Low Trip Counts

To be effective, loop unrolling requires a fairly large number of iterations in the original loop. To understand why, picture what happens if the total iteration count is low, perhaps less than 10, or even less than 4. With a trip count this low, the preconditioning loop is doing a proportionately large amount of the work. It's not supposed to be that way. The preconditioning loop is supposed to catch the few leftover iterations missed by the unrolled, main loop. However, when the trip count is low, you make one or two passes through the unrolled loop, plus one or two passes through the preconditioning loop. In other words, you have more clutter; the loop shouldn't have been unrolled in the first place.

Probably the only time it makes sense to unroll a loop with a low trip count is when the number of iterations is constant and known at compile time. For instance, suppose you had the following loop:

```
PARAMETER (NITER = 3)
DO I=1,NITER
  A(I) = B(I) * C
ENDDO
```

Because **NITER** is hardwired to 3, you can safely unroll to a depth of 3 without worrying about a preconditioning loop. In fact, you can throw out the loop structure altogether and leave just the unrolled loop innards:

```
PARAMETER (NITER = 3)
A(1) = B(1) * C
A(2) = B(2) * C
A(3) = A(3) * C
```

Of course, if a loop's trip count is low, it probably won't contribute significantly to the overall runtime, unless you find such a loop at the center of a larger loop. Then you either want to unroll it completely or leave it alone.

Fat Loops

Loop unrolling helps performance because it fattens up a loop with more calculations per iteration. By the same token, if a particular loop is already fat, unrolling isn't going to help. The loop overhead is already spread over a fair number of instructions. In fact, unrolling a fat loop may even slow your program down because it increases the size of the text segment, placing an added burden on the memory system (we'll explain this in greater detail shortly). A good rule of thumb is to look elsewhere for performance when the loop innards exceed three or four statements.

Loops Containing Procedure Calls

As with fat loops, loops containing subroutine or function calls generally aren't good candidates for unrolling. There are several reasons. First, they often contain a fair number of instructions already. And if the subroutine being called is fat, it makes the loop that calls it fat as well. The size of the loop may not be apparent when you look at the loop; the function call can conceal many more instructions.

Second, when the calling routine and the subroutine are compiled separately, it's impossible for the compiler to intermix instructions. A loop that is unrolled into a series of function calls behaves much like the original loop, before unrolling.

Last, function call overhead is expensive. Registers have to be saved; argument lists have to be prepared. The time spent calling and returning from a subroutine can be much greater than that of the loop overhead. Unrolling to amortize the cost of the loop structure over several calls doesn't buy you enough to be worth the effort.

The general rule when dealing with procedures is to first try to eliminate them in the "remove clutter" phase, and when this has been done, check to see if unrolling gives an additional performance improvement.

Loops with Branches in Them

In the previous chapter we showed you how to eliminate certain types of branches, but of course, we couldn't get rid of them all. In cases of iteration-independent branches, there might be some benefit to loop unrolling. The IF test becomes part of the operations that must be counted to determine the value of loop unrolling. Below is a doubly nested loop. The inner loop tests the value of B(J,I):

```
DO I=1,N
  DO J=1,N
    IF (B(J,I) .GT. 1.0) A(J,I) = A(J,I) + B(J,I) * C
  ENDDO
ENDDO
```

Each iteration is independent of every other, so unrolling it won't be a problem. We'll just leave the outer loop undisturbed:

```
    II = IMOD (N,4)
    DO I=1,N
      DO  J=1,II
        IF (B(J,I) .GT. 1.0)
+         A(J,I) = A(J,I) + B(J,I) * C
      ENDDO
      DO J=II+1,N,4
        IF (B(J,I)    .GT. 1.0)
```

```
+        A(J,I)   = A(J,I)   + B(J,I)   * C
         IF (B(J+1,I) .GT. 1.0)
+        A(J+1,I) = A(J+1,I) + B(J+1,I) * C
         IF (B(J+2,I) .GT. 1.0)
+        A(J+2,I) = A(J+2,I) + B(J+2,I) * C
         IF (B(J+3,I) .GT. 1.0)
+        A(J+3,I) = A(J+3,I) + B(J+3,I) * C
      ENDDO
   ENDDO
```

This approach works particularly well if the processor you are using supports conditional execution. As described earlier, conditional execution can replace a branch and an operation with a single conditionally executed assignment. On a superscalar processor with conditional execution, this unrolled loop executes quite nicely.

Nested Loops

When you embed loops within other loops, you create a *loop nest*. The loop or loops in the center are called the *inner* loops. The surrounding loops are called *outer* loops. Depending on the construction of the loop nest, we may have some flexibility in the ordering of the loops. At times, we can swap the outer and inner loops with great benefit. In the next sections we look at some common loop nestings and the optimizations that can be performed on these loop nests.

Often when we are working with nests of loops, we are working with multidimensional arrays. Computing in multidimensional arrays can lead to non-unit-stride memory access. Many of the optimizations we perform on loop nests are meant to improve the memory access patterns.

First, we examine the computation-related optimizations followed by the memory optimizations.

Outer Loop Unrolling

If you are faced with a loop nest, one simple approach is to unroll the inner loop. Unrolling the innermost loop in a nest isn't any different from what we saw above. You just pretend the rest of the loop nest doesn't exist and approach it in the normal way. However, there are times when you want to apply loop unrolling not just to the inner loop, but to outer loops as well—or perhaps only to the outer loops. Here's a typical loop nest:

```
for (i=0; i<n; i++)
    for (j=0; j<n; j++)
        for (k=0; k<n; k++)
            a[i][j][k] = a[i][j][k] + b[i][j][k] * c;
```

To unroll an outer loop, you pick one of the outer loop index variables and replicate the innermost loop body so that several iterations are performed at the same time, just like we saw in the previous section. The difference is in the index variable for which you unroll. In the code below, we have unrolled the middle (j) loop twice:

```
for (i=0; i<n; i++)
    for (j=0; j<n; j+=2)
        for (k=0; k<n; k++) {
            a[i][j][k]   = a[i][j][k]   + b[i][k][j]   * c;
            a[i][j+1][k] = a[i][j+1][k] + b[i][k][j+1] * c;
        }
```

We left the k loop untouched; however, we could unroll that one, too. That would give us outer *and* inner loop unrolling at the same time:

```
for (i=0; i<n; i++)
    for (j=0; j<n; j+=2)
        for (k=0; k<n; k+=2) {
            a[i][j][k]     = a[i][j][k]     + b[i][k][j]     * c;
            a[i][j+1][k]   = a[i][j+1][k]   + b[i][k][j+1]   * c;
            a[i][j][k+1]   = a[i][j][k+1]   + b[i][k+1][j]   * c;
            a[i][j+1][k+1] = a[i][j+1][k+1] + b[i][k+1][j+1] * c;
        }
```

We could even unroll the i loop too, leaving eight copies of the loop innards. (Notice that we completely ignored preconditioning; in a real application, of course, we couldn't.)

Outer Loop Unrolling to Expose Computations

Say that you have a doubly nested loop and that the inner loop trip count is low—perhaps 4 or 5 on average. Inner loop unrolling doesn't make sense in this case because there won't be enough iterations to justify the cost of the preconditioning loop. However, you may be able to unroll an outer loop. Consider this loop, assuming that M is small and N is large:

```
DO I=1,N
  DO J=1,M
    A(J,I) = B(J,I) + C(J,I) * D
  ENDDO
ENDDO
```

Unrolling the I loop gives you lots of floating-point operations that can be overlapped:

```
II = IMOD (N,4)
DO I=1,II
  DO J=1,M
    A(J,I)   = B(J,I)   + C(J,I) * D
```

```
      ENDDO
    ENDDO

    DO I=II,N,4
      DO J=1,M
        A(J,I)   = B(J,I)   + C(J,I)   * D
        A(J,I+1) = B(J,I+1) + C(J,I+1) * D
        A(J,I+2) = B(J,I+2) + C(J,I+2) * D
        A(J,I+3) = B(J,I+3) + C(J,I+3) * D
      ENDDO
    ENDDO
```

In this particular case, there is bad news to go with the good news: unrolling the outer loop causes strided memory references on A, B, and C. However, it probably won't be too much of a problem because the inner loop trip count is small, so it naturally groups references to conserve cache entries.

Outer loop unrolling can also be helpful when you have a nest with recursion in the inner loop, but not in the outer loops. In this next example, there is a first-order linear recursion in the inner loop:

```
    DO J=1,M
      DO I=2,N
        A(I,J) = A(I,J) + A(I-1,J) * B
      ENDDO
    ENDDO
```

Because of the recursion, we can't unroll the inner loop, but we can work on several copies of the outer loop at the same time. When unrolled, it looks like this:

```
    JJ = IMOD (M,4)
    DO J=1,JJ
      DO I=2,N
        A(I,J) = A(I,J) + A(I-1,J) * B
      ENDDO
    ENDDO

    DO J=1+JJ,M,4
      DO I=2,N
        A(I,J)   = A(I,J)   + A(I-1,J)   * B
        A(I,J+1) = A(I,J+1) + A(I-1,J+1) * B
        A(I,J+2) = A(I,J+2) + A(I-1,J+2) * B
        A(I,J+3) = A(I,J+3) + A(I-1,J+3) * B
      ENDDO
    ENDDO
```

You can see the recursion still exists in the I loop, but we have succeeded in finding lots of work to do anyway.

Sometimes the reason for unrolling the outer loop is to get a hold of much larger chunks of things that can be done in parallel. If the outer loop iterations are independent, and the inner loop trip count is high, then each outer loop iteration represents a significant, parallel chunk of work. On a single CPU that doesn't matter much, but on a tightly coupled multiprocessor, it can translate into a tremendous increase in speeds.

Loop Interchange

Loop interchange is a technique for rearranging a loop nest so that the right stuff is at the center. What the right stuff is depends upon what you are trying to accomplish. In many situations, loop interchange also lets you swap high trip count loops for low trip count loops, so that activity gets pulled into the center of the loop nest.*

Loop Interchange to Move Computations to the Center

When someone writes a program that represents some kind of real-world model, they often structure the code in terms of the model. This makes perfect sense. The computer is an analysis tool; you aren't writing the code on the computer's behalf. However, a model expressed naturally often works on one point in space at a time, which tends to give you insignificant inner loops—at least in terms of the trip count. For performance, you might want to interchange inner and outer loops to pull the activity into the center, where you can then do some unrolling. Let's illustrate with an example. Here's a loop where KDIM time-dependent quantities for points in a two-dimensional mesh are being updated:

```
PARAMETER (IDIM = 1000, JDIM = 1000, KDIM = 3)
  ...
DO I=1,IDIM
  DO J=1,JDIM
    DO K=1,KDIM
      D(K,J,I) = D(K,J,I) + V(K,J,I) * DT
    ENDDO
  ENDDO
ENDDO
```

In practice, KDIM is probably equal to 2 or 3, where J or I, representing the number of points, may be in the thousands. The way it is written, the inner loop has a very low trip count, making it a poor candidate for unrolling.

By interchanging the loops, you update one quantity at a time, across all of the points. For tuning purposes, this moves larger trip counts into the inner loop and allows you to do some strategic unrolling:

---

* It's also good for improving memory access patterns, as we will see in the next section.

```
DO K=1,KDIM
  DO J=1,JDIM
    DO I=1,IDIM
      D(K,J,I) = D(K,J,I) + V(K,J,I) * DT
    ENDDO
  ENDDO
ENDDO
```

This example is straightforward; it's easy to see that there are no inter-iteration dependencies. But how can you tell, in general, when two loops can be interchanged? Interchanging loops might violate some dependency, or worse, only violate it occasionally, meaning you might not catch it when optimizing. Can we interchange the loops below?

```
DO I=1,N-1
  DO J=2,N
    A(I,J) = A(I+1,J-1) * B(I,J)
    C(I,J) = B(J,I)
  ENDDO
ENDDO
```

While it is possible to examine the loops by hand and determine the dependencies, it is much better if the compiler can make the determination. Very few single-processor compilers automatically perform loop interchange. However, the compilers for high-end vector and parallel computers generally interchange loops if there is some benefit and if interchanging the loops won't alter the program results.*

Memory Access Patterns

The best pattern is the most straightforward: increasing and unit sequential. For an array with a single dimension, stepping through one element at a time will accomplish this. For multiply-dimensioned arrays, access is fastest if you iterate on the array subscript offering the smallest *stride* or step size. In FORTRAN programs, this is the leftmost subscript; in C, it is the rightmost. The FORTRAN loop below has unit stride, and therefore will run quickly:

```
DO J=1,N
  DO I=1,N
    A(I,J) = B(I,J) + C(I,J) * D
  ENDDO
ENDDO
```

In contrast, the next loop is slower because its stride is N (which, we assume, is greater than 1). As N increases from one to the length of the cache line (adjusting

---

* When the compiler performs automatic parallel optimization, it prefers to run the outermost loop in parallel to minimize overhead and unroll the innermost loop to make best use of a superscalar or vector processor. For this reason, the compiler needs to have some flexibility in ordering the loops in a loop nest.

for the length of each element), the performance worsens. Once N is longer than the length of the cache line (again adjusted for element size), the performance won't decrease:

```
DO J=1,N
  DO I=1,N
    A(J,I) = B(J,I) + C(J,I) * D
  ENDDO
ENDDO
```

Here's a unit-stride loop like the previous one, but written in C:

```
for (i=0; i<n; i++)
    for (j=0; j<n; j++)
        a[i][j] = a[i][j] + c[i][j] * d;
```

Unit stride gives you the best performance because it conserves cache entries. Recall how a data cache works.* Your program makes a memory reference; if the data is in the cache, it gets returned immediately. If not, your program suffers a cache miss while a new cache line is fetched from main memory, replacing an old one. The line holds the values taken from a handful of neighboring memory locations, including the one that caused the cache miss. If you loaded a cache line, took one piece of data from it, and threw the rest away, you would be wasting a lot of time and memory bandwidth. However, if you brought a line into the cache and consumed everything in it, you would benefit from a large number of memory references for a small number of cache misses. This is exactly what you get when your program makes unit-stride memory references.

The worst-case patterns are those that jump through memory, especially a large amount of memory, and particularly those that do so without apparent rhyme or reason (viewed from the outside). On jobs that operate on very large data structures, you pay a penalty not only for cache misses, but for TLB misses too.† It would be nice to be able to rein these jobs in so that they make better use of memory. Of course, you can't eliminate memory references; programs have to get to their data one way or another. The question is, then: how can we restructure memory access patterns for the best performance?

In the next few sections, we are going to look at some tricks for restructuring loops with strided, albeit predictable, access patterns. The tricks will be familiar; they are mostly loop optimizations from the last chapter, used here for different reasons. The underlying goal is to minimize cache and TLB misses as much as possible. You will see that we can do quite a lot, although some of this is going to be ugly.

---

* See Chapter 3, *Memory*.

† The Translation Lookaside Buffer (TLB) is a cache of translations from virtual memory addresses to physical memory addresses. For more information, refer back to Chapter 3.

Loop Interchange to Ease Memory Access Patterns

Loop interchange is a good technique for lessening the impact of strided memory references. Let's revisit our FORTRAN loop with non-unit stride. The good news is that we can easily interchange the loops; each iteration is independent of every other:

```
DO J=1,N
  DO I=1,N
    A(J,I) = B(J,I) + C(J,I) * D
  ENDDO
ENDDO
```

After interchange, A, B, and C are referenced with the leftmost subscript varying most quickly. This modification can make an important difference in performance. We traded three N-strided memory references for unit strides:

```
DO I=1,N
  DO J=1,N
    A(J,I) = B(J,I) + C(J,I) * D
  ENDDO
ENDDO
```

Matrix Multiplication

Matrix multiplication is a common operation we can use to explore the options that are available in optimizing a loop nest. A programmer who has just finished reading a linear algebra textbook would probably write matrix multiply as it appears in the example below:

```
DO I=1,N
  DO J=1,N
    SUM = 0
    DO K=1,N
      SUM = SUM + A(I,K) * B(K,J)
    ENDDO
    C(I,J) = SUM
  ENDDO
ENDDO
```

The problem with this loop is that the A(I,K) will be non-unit stride. Each iteration in the inner loop consists of two loads (one non-unit stride), a multiplication, and an addition.

Given the nature of the matrix multiplication, it might appear that you can't eliminate the non-unit stride. However, with a simple rewrite of the loops all the memory accesses can be made unit stride:

```
DO J=1,N
 DO I=1,N
   C(I,J) = 0.0
 ENDDO
ENDDO

DO K=1,N
  DO J=1,N
    SCALE = B(K,J)
    DO I=1,N
      C(I,J) = C(I,J) + A(I,K) * SCALE
    ENDDO
  ENDDO
ENDDO
```

Now, the inner loop accesses memory using unit stride. Each iteration performs
two loads, one store, a multiplication, and an addition. When comparing this to
the previous loop, the non-unit stride loads have been eliminated, but there is an
additional store operation. Assuming that we are operating on a cache-based system, and the matrix is larger than the cache, this extra store won't add much to the
execution time. The store is to the location in C(I,J) that was used in the load.
In most cases, the store is to a line that is already in the in the cache. The B(K,J)
becomes a constant scaling factor within the inner loop.

When Interchange Won't Work

In the matrix multiplication code, we encountered a non-unit stride and were able
to eliminate it with a quick interchange of the loops. Unfortunately, life is rarely
this simple. Often you find some mix of variables with unit and non-unit strides, in
which case interchanging the loops moves the damage around, but doesn't make
it go away.

The loop to perform a matrix transpose represents a simple example of this
dilemma:

```
DO I=1,N                        DO 20 J=1,M
  DO J=1,M                        DO 10 I=1,N
    A(J,I) = B(I,J)                   A(J,I) = B(I,J)
  ENDDO                           ENDDO
ENDDO                           ENDDO
```

Whichever way you interchange them, you will break the memory access pattern
for either A or B. Even more interesting, you have to make a choice between

strided loads vs. strided stores: which will it be?* We really need a general method for improving the memory access patterns for *both* A and B, not one or the other. We'll show you such a method in the next section.

Blocking to Ease Memory Access Patterns

Blocking is another kind of memory reference optimization. As with loop interchange, the challenge is to retrieve as much data as possible with as few cache misses as possible. We'd like to rearrange the loop nest so that it works on data in little neighborhoods, rather than striding through memory like a man on stilts. Given the following vector sum, how can we rearrange the loop?

```
DO I=1,N
  DO J=1,N
    A(J,I) = A(J,I) + B(I,J)
  ENDDO
ENDDO
```

This loop involves two vectors. One is referenced with unit stride, the other with a stride of N. We can interchange the loops, but one way or another we still have N-strided array references on either A or B, either of which is undesirable. The trick is to *block* references so that you grab a few elements of A, and then a few of B, and then a few of A, and so on—in neighborhoods. We make this happen by combining inner and outer loop unrolling:

```
DO I=1,N,2
  DO J=1,N,2
    A(J,I)     = A(J,I)     + B(I,J)
    A(J+1,I)   = A(J+1,I)   + B(I,J+1)
    A(J,I+1)   = A(J,I+1)   + B(I+1,J)
    A(J+1,I+1) = A(J+1,I+1) + B(I+1,J+1)
  ENDDO
ENDDO
```

Use your imagination so we can show why this helps. Usually, when we think of a two-dimensional array, we think of a rectangle or a square (see Figure 8-1). Remember, to make programming easier, the compiler provides the illusion that two-dimensional arrays A and B are rectangular plots of memory as in Figure 8-1. Actually, memory is sequential storage. In FORTRAN, a two-dimensional array is constructed in memory by logically lining memory "strips" up against each other, like the pickets of a cedar fence. (It's the other way around in C: rows are stacked

---

* I can't tell you which is the better way to cast it; it depends on the brand of computer. Some perform better with the loops left as they are, sometimes by more than a factor of two. Others perform better with them interchanged. The difference is in the way the processor handles updates of main memory from cache.

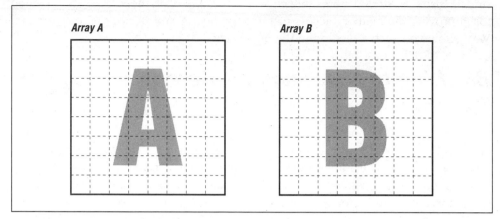

Figure 8-1: Arrays A and B

on top of one another.) Array storage starts at the upper left, proceeds down to the bottom, and then starts over at the top of the next column. Stepping through the array with unit stride traces out the shape of a backwards "N," repeated over and over, moving to the right.

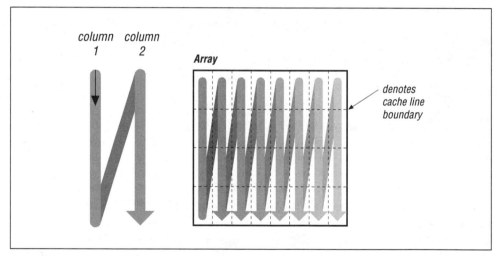

Figure 8-2: How array elements are stored

Imagine that the thin horizontal lines of Figure 8-2 cut memory storage into pieces the size of individual cache entries. Picture how the loop will traverse them. Because of their index expressions, references to A go from top to bottom (in the backwards "N" shape), consuming every bit of each cache line, but references to B dash off to the right, using one piece of each cache entry and discarding the rest (see Figure 8-3, top). This low usage of cache entries will result in a high number of cache misses.

If we could somehow rearrange the loop so that it consumed the arrays in small rectangles, rather than strips, we could conserve some of the cache entries that are being discarded. This is exactly what we accomplished by unrolling both the inner and outer loops, as in the following example. Array A is referenced in several strips side by side, from top to bottom, while B is referenced in several strips side by side, from left to right (see Figure 8-3, bottom). This improves cache performance and lowers runtime.

For really big problems, more than cache entries are at stake. On virtual memory machines, memory references have to be translated through a TLB. If you are dealing with large arrays, TLB misses, in addition to cache misses, are going to add to your runtime.

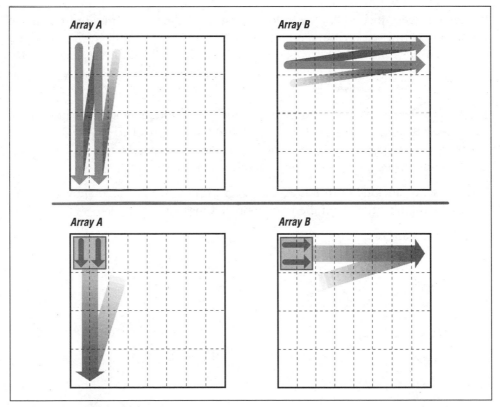

Figure 8-3: 2×2 squares

Here's something that may surprise you. In the code below, we rewrite this loop yet again, this time blocking references at two different levels: in 2×2 squares to save cache entries, and by cutting the original loop in two parts to save TLB entries:

```
DO I=1,N,2
  DO J=1,N/2,2
    A(J,I) = A(J,I) + B(I,J)
    A(J+1,I) = A(J+1,I) + B(I+1,J)
    A(J,I+1) = A(J,I+1) + B(I+1,J)
    A(J+1,I+1) = A(J+1,I+1) + B(I+1,J+1)
  ENDDO
ENDDO
DO I=1,N,2
  DO J=N/2+1,N,2
    A(J,I) = A(J,I) + B(I,J)
    A(J+1,I) = A(J+1,I) + B(I+1,J)
    A(J,I+1) = A(J,I+1) + B(I+1,J)
    A(J+1,I+1) = A(J+1,I+1) + B(I+1,J+1)
  ENDDO
ENDDO
```

You might guess that adding more loops would be the wrong thing to do. But if you work with a reasonably large value of N, say 512, you will see a significant increase in performance. This is because the two arrays A and B are each 256 KB × 8 bytes = 2 MB when N is equal to 512—larger than can be handled by the TLBs and caches of most processors.

The two boxes in Figure 8-4 illustrate how the first few references to A and B look superimposed upon one another in the blocked and unblocked cases. Unblocked references to B zing off through memory, eating through cache and TLB entries. Blocked references are more sparing with the memory system.

You can take blocking even further for larger problems. This code shows another method that limits the size of the inner loop and visits it repeatedly:

```
II = MOD (N,16)
JJ = MOD (N,4)

DO I=1,N
  DO J=1,JJ
    A(J,I) = A(J,I) + B(J,I)
  ENDDO
ENDDO

DO I=1,II
  DO J=JJ+1,N
      A(J,I) = A(J,I) + B(J,I)
      A(J,I) = A(J,I) + 1.0D0
  ENDDO
ENDDO

DO I=II+1,N,16
  DO J=JJ+1,N,4
```

```
      DO K=I,I+15
        A(J,K)   = A(J,K)   + B(K,J)
        A(J+1,K) = A(J+1,K) + B(K,J+1)
        A(J+2,K) = A(J+2,K) + B(K,J+2)
        A(J+3,K) = A(J+3,K) + B(K,J+3)
      ENDDO
    ENDDO
  ENDDO
```

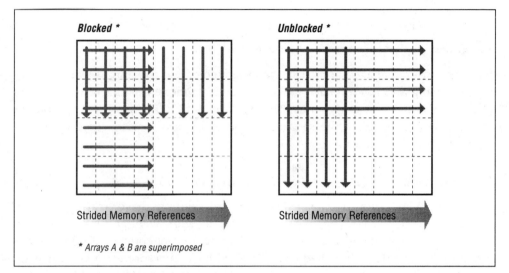

Figure 8-4: Picture of unblocked versus blocked references

Where the inner I loop used to execute N iterations at a time, the new K loop executes only 16 iterations. This divides and conquers a large memory address space by cutting it into little pieces.

While these blocking techniques begin to have diminishing returns on single-processor systems, on large multiprocessor systems with nonuniform memory access (NUMA), there can be significant benefit in carefully arranging memory accesses to maximize reuse of both cache lines and main memory pages.

Again, the combined unrolling and blocking techniques we just showed you are for loops with *mixed stride* expressions. They work very well for loop nests like the one we have been looking at. However, if all array references are strided the same way, you will want to try loop unrolling or loop interchange first.

Programs That Require More Memory Than You Have

People occasionally have programs whose memory size requirements are so great that the data can't fit in memory all at once. At any time, some of the data has to reside outside of main memory on secondary (usually disk) storage. These out-of-core solutions fall into two categories:

- Software-managed, out-of-core solutions

- Virtual memory–managed, out-of-core solutions

With a software-managed approach, the programmer has recognized that the problem is too big and has modified the source code to move sections of the data out to disk for retrieval at a later time. The other method depends on the computer's memory system handling the secondary storage requirements on its own, sometimes at a great cost in runtime.

Software-Managed, Out-of-Core Solutions

Most codes with software-managed, out-of-core solutions have adjustments; you can tell the program how much memory it has to work with, and it takes care of the rest. It is important to make sure the adjustment is set correctly. Code that was tuned for a machine with limited memory could have been ported to another without taking into account the storage available. Perhaps the whole problem will fit easily.

If we are writing an out-of-core solution, the trick is to group memory references together so that they are localized. This usually occurs naturally as a side effect of partitioning, say, a matrix factorization into groups of columns. Blocking references the way we did in the previous section also corrals memory references together so you can treat them as memory "pages." Knowing when to ship them off to disk entails being closely involved with what the program is doing.

Closing Notes

Loops are the heart of nearly all high performance programs. The first goal with loops is to express them as simply and clearly as possible (i.e., eliminates the clutter). Then, use the profiling and timing tools to figure out which routines and loops are taking the time. Once you find the loops that are using the most time, try to determine if the performance of the loops can be improved.

First try simple modifications to the loops that don't reduce the clarity of the code. You can also experiment with compiler options that control loop optimizations.

Once you've exhausted the options of keeping the code looking clean, and if you still need more performance, resort to hand-modifying to the code. Typically the loops that need a little hand-coaxing are loops that are making bad use of the memory architecture on a cache-based system. Hopefully the loops you end up changing are only a few of the overall loops in the program.

However, before going too far optimizing on a single processor machine, take a look at how the program executes on a parallel system. Sometimes the modifications that improve performance on a single-processor system confuses the parallel-processor compiler. The compilers on parallel and vector systems generally have more powerful optimization capabilities, as they must identify areas of your code that will execute well on their specialized hardware. These compilers have been interchanging and unrolling loops automatically for some time now.

Exercises

1. Why is an unrolling amount of three or four iterations generally sufficient for simple vector loops on a RISC processor? What relationship does the unrolling amount have to floating-point pipeline depths?

2. On a processor that can execute one floating-point multiply, one floating-point addition/subtraction, and one memory reference per cycle, what's the best performance you could expect from the following loop?

```
DO I = 1,10000
  A(I) = B(I) * C(I) - D(I) * E(I)
ENDDO
```

3. Try unrolling, interchanging, or blocking the loop in subroutine **BAZFAZ** to increase the performance. What method or combination of methods works best? Look at the assembly language created by the compiler to see what its approach is at the highest level of optimization. (Note: Compile the main routine and **BAZFAZ** separately; adjust **NTIMES** so that the untuned run takes about one minute; and use the compiler's default optimization level.)

```
        PROGRAM MAIN
        IMPLICIT NONE
        INTEGER M,N,I,J
        PARAMETER (N = 512, M = 640, NTIMES = 500)
        DOUBLE PRECISION Q(N,M), R(M,N)
    C
        DO I=1,M
          DO J=1,N
            Q(J,I) = 1.0D0
            R(I,J) = 1.0D0
          ENDDO
        ENDDO
```

```
C
      DO I=1,NTIMES
        CALL BAZFAZ (Q,R,N,M)
      ENDDO
      END

      SUBROUTINE BAZFAZ (Q,R,N,M)
      IMPLICIT NONE
      INTEGER M,N,I,J
      DOUBLE PRECISION Q(N,M), R(N,M)
C
      DO I=1,N
        DO J=1,M
          R(I,J) = Q(I,J) * R(J,I)
        ENDDO
      ENDDO
C
      END
```

4. Code the matrix multiplication algorithm in the "straightforward" manner and compile it with various optimization levels. See if the compiler performs any type of loop interchange.

   Try the same experiment with the following code:

   ```
   DO I=1,N
     DO J=1,N
       A(I,J) = A(I,J) + 1.3
     ENDDO
   ENDDO
   ```

   Do you see a difference in the compiler's ability to optimize these two loops? If you see a difference, explain it.

5. Code the matrix multiplication algorithm both the ways shown in this chapter. Execute the program for a range of values for N. Graph the execution time divided by N^3 for values of N ranging from 50×50 to 500×500. Explain the performance you see.

III

Shared-Memory Parallel Processors

9

Understanding Parallelism

In a sense, we have been talking about parallelism from the beginning of the book. Instead of calling it "parallelism," we have been using words like "pipelined," "superscalar," and "compiler flexibility." As we move into programming on multiprocessors, we must increase our understanding of parallelism in order to understand how to effectively program these systems. In short, as we gain more parallel resources, we need to find more parallelism in our code.

When we talk of parallelism, we need to understand the concept of *granularity*. The granularity of parallelism indicates the size of the computations that are being performed at the same time between synchronizations. Some examples of parallelism in order of increasing grain size are:

- When performing a 32-bit integer addition, using a carry lookahead adder, you can partially add bits 0 and 1 at the same time as bits 2 and 3.

- On a pipelined processor, while decoding one instruction, you can fetch the next instruction.

- On a two-way superscalar processor, you can execute any combination of an integer and a floating-point instruction in a single cycle.

- On a multiprocessor, you can divide the iterations of a loop among the four processors of the system.

- You can split a large array across four workstations attached to a network. Each workstation can operate on its local information and then exchange boundary values at the end of each time step.

In this chapter, we start at *instruction-level parallelism* (pipelined and superscalar) and move toward *thread-level parallelism*, which is what we need for multiprocessor systems. It is important to note that the different levels of parallelism are generally not in conflict. Increasing thread parallelism at a coarser grain size often exposes more fine-grained parallelism.

The following is a loop that has plenty of parallelism:

```
DO I=1,16000
  A(I) = B(I) * 3.14159
ENDDO
```

We have expressed the loop in a way that would imply that A(1) must be computed first, followed by A(2), and so on. However, once the loop was completed, it would not have mattered if A(16000), were computed first followed by A(15999), and so on. The loop could have computed the even values of I and then computed the odd values of I. It would not even make a difference if all 16,000 of the iterations were computed simultaneously using a 16,000-way superscalar processor.* If the compiler has flexibility in the order in which it can execute the instructions that make up your program, it can execute those instructions simultaneously when parallel hardware is available.

One technique that computer scientists use to formally analyze the potential parallelism in an algorithm is to characterize how quickly it would execute with an "infinite-way" superscalar processor.

Not all loops contain as much parallelism as this simple loop. We need to identify the things that limit the parallelism in our codes and remove them whenever possible. In previous chapters we have already looked at removing clutter and rewriting loops to simplify the body of the loop.

This chapter also supplements Chapter 5, *What a Compiler Does*, in many ways. We looked at the mechanics of compiling code, all of which apply here, but we didn't answer all of the "whys." Basic block analysis techniques form the basis for the work the compiler does when looking for more parallelism. Looking at two pieces of data, instructions, or data and instructions, a modern compiler asks the question, "Do these things depend on each other?" The three possible answers are yes, no, and we don't know. The third answer is effectively the same as a yes, because a compiler has to be conservative whenever it is unsure whether it is safe to tweak the ordering of instructions.

Helping the compiler recognize parallelism is one of the basic approaches specialists take in tuning code. A slight rewording of a loop or some supplementary information supplied to the compiler can change a "we don't know" answer into an opportunity for parallelism. To be certain, there are other facets to tuning as

---

* Interestingly, this is not as far-fetched as it might seem. On a *single instruction multiple data* (SIMD) computer such as the Connection CM-2 with 16,384 processors, it would take three instruction cycles to process this entire loop. See Chapter 12, *Large-Scale Parallel Computing*, for more details on this type of architecture.

well, such as optimizing memory access patterns so that they best suit the hardware, or recasting an algorithm. And there is no single best approach to every problem; any tuning effort has to be a combination of techniques.

Dependencies

Imagine a symphony orchestra where each musician plays without regard to the conductor or the other musicians. At the first tap of the conductor's baton, each musician goes through all of his or her sheet music. Some finish far ahead of others, leave the stage, and go home. The cacophony wouldn't resemble music (come to think of it, it would resemble experimental jazz) because it would be totally uncoordinated. Of course this isn't how music is played. A computer program, like a musical piece, is woven on a fabric that unfolds in time (though perhaps woven more loosely). Certain things must happen before or along with others, and there is a rate to the whole process.

With computer programs, whenever event A must occur before event B can, we say that B is *dependent* on A. We call the relationship between them a *dependency*. Sometimes dependencies exist because of calculations or memory operations; we call these *data dependencies*. Other times, we are waiting for a branch or do-loop exit to take place; this is called a *control dependency*. Each is present in every program to varying degrees. The goal is to eliminate as many dependencies as possible. Rearranging a program so that two chunks of the computation are less dependent exposes *parallelism*, or opportunities to do several things at once.

Control Dependencies

Just as variable assignments can depend on other assignments, a variable's value can also depend on the *flow of control* within the program. For instance, an assignment within an if-statement can occur only if the conditional evaluates to *true*. The same can be said of an assignment within a loop. If the loop is never entered, no statements inside the loop are executed.

When calculations occur as a consequence of the flow of control, we say there is a *control dependency*, as in the code below and shown graphically in Figure 9-1. The assignment located inside the block-if may or may not be executed, depending on the outcome of the test X .NE. 0. In other words, the value of Y depends on the flow of control in the code around it. Again, this may sound to you like a concern for compiler designers, not programmers, and that's mostly true. But there are times when you might want to move control-dependent instructions around to get expensive calculations out of the way (provided your compiler isn't smart enough to do it for you). For example, say that Figure 9-2 represents a little section of your program. Flow of control enters at the top and goes through two

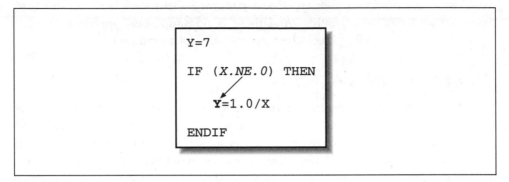

Figure 9-1: Control dependency

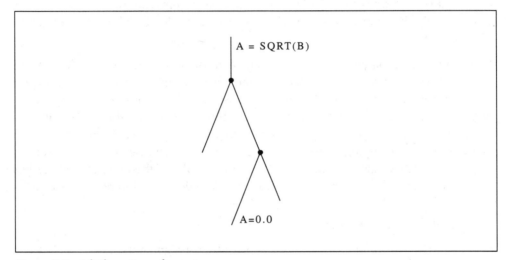

Figure 9-2: A little section of your program

branch decisions. Furthermore, say that there is a square root operation at the entry point, and that the flow of control almost always goes from the top, down to the leg containing the statement A=0.0. This means that the results of the calculation A=SQRT(B) are almost always discarded because A gets a new value of 0.0 each time through. A square root operation is always "expensive" because it takes a lot of time to execute. The trouble is that you can't just get rid of it; occasionally it's needed. However, you could move it out of the way and continue to observe the control dependencies by making two copies of the square root operation along the less traveled branches, as shown in Figure 9-3. This way the SQRT would execute only along those paths where it was actually needed.

This kind of instruction scheduling will be appearing in compilers (and even hardware) more and more as time goes on. A variation on this technique is to calculate results that might be needed at times when there is a gap in the instruction stream

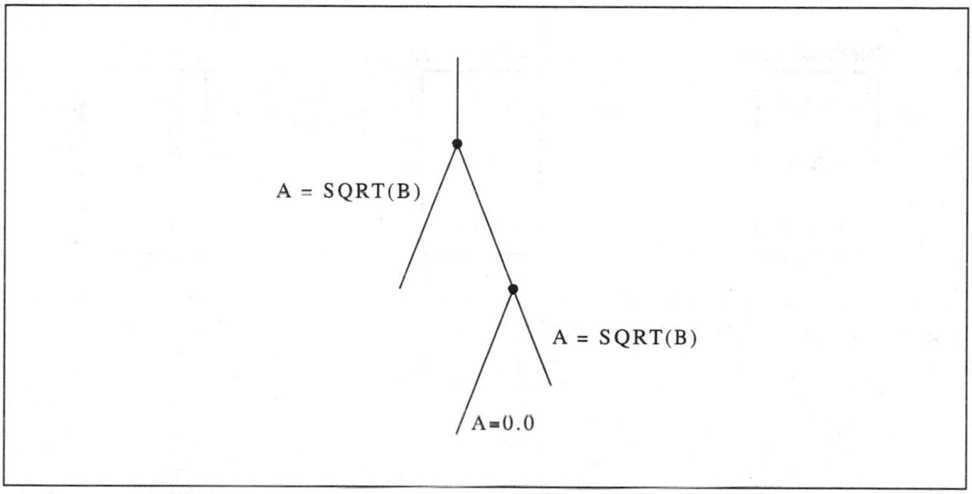

A = SQRT(B)

A = SQRT(B)

A=0.0

Figure 9-3: Expensive operation moved so that it's rarely executed

(because of dependencies), thus using some spare cycles that might otherwise be wasted.

Data Dependencies

A calculation that is in some way bound to a previous calculation is said to be *data dependent* upon that calculation. In the code below, the value of B is data dependent on the value of A. That's because you can't calculate B until the value of A is available:

```
A = X + Y + COS(Z)
B = A * C
```

This dependency is easy to recognize, but others are not so simple. At other times, you must be careful not to rewrite a variable with a new value before every other computation has finished using the old value. We can group all data dependencies into three categories: (1) flow dependencies, (2) antidependencies, and (3) output dependencies. Figure 9-4 contains some simple examples to demonstrate each type of dependency. In each example, we use an arrow that starts at the source of the dependency and ends at the statement that must be delayed by the dependency. The key problem in each of these dependencies is that the second statement can't execute until the first has completed. Obviously in the particular output dependency example, the first computation is dead code and can be eliminated unless there is some intervening code that needs the values. There are other techniques to eliminate either output or antidependencies. The following example contains a flow dependency followed by an output dependency.

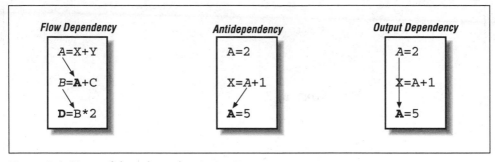

Figure 9-4: Types of data dependencies

```
X = A / B
Y = X + 2.0
X = D - E
```

While we can't eliminate the flow dependency, the output dependency can be eliminated by using a scratch variable:

```
Xtemp = A / B
Y = Xtemp + 2.0
X = D - E
```

As the number of statements and the interactions between those statements increase, we need a better way to identify and process these dependencies. Figure 9-5 shows four statements with four dependencies.

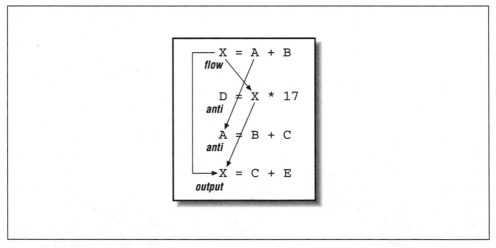

Figure 9-5: Multiple dependencies

None of the second through fourth instructions can be started before the first instruction completes.

Forming a DAG

One method for analyzing a sequence of instructions is to organize it into a *directed acyclic graph* (DAG).* Like the instructions it represents, a DAG describes all of the calculations and relationships between variables. The data flow within a DAG proceeds in one direction; most often a DAG is constructed from top to bottom. Identifiers and constants are placed at the "leaf" nodes—the ones on the top. Operations, possibly with variable names attached, make up the internal nodes. Variables appear in their final states at the bottom. The DAG's edges order the relationships between the variables and operations within it. All data flow proceeds from top to bottom.

To construct a DAG, the compiler takes each intermediate language tuple and maps it onto one or more nodes. For instance, those tuples that represent binary operations, such as addition (X=A+B), form a portion of the DAG with two inputs (A and B) bound together by an operation (+). The result of the operation may feed into yet other operations within the basic block (and the DAG) as shown in Figure 9-6.

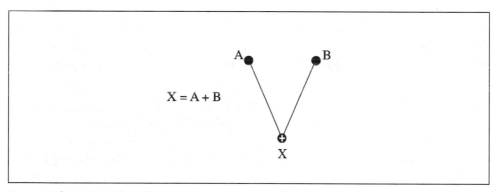

Figure 9-6: A trivial data flow graph

For a basic block of code, we build our DAG in the order of the instructions. The DAG for the previous four instructions is shown in Figure 9-7. This particular example has many dependencies, so there is not much opportunity for parallelism. Figure 9-8 shows a more straightforward example shows how constructing a DAG can identify parallelism.

From this DAG, we can determine that instructions 1 and 2 can be executed in parallel. Because we see the computations that operate on the values A and B

---

* A *graph* is a collection of nodes connected by edges. By *directed*, we mean that the edges can only be traversed in specified directions. The word *acyclic* means that there are no cycles in the graph; that is, you can't loop anywhere within it.

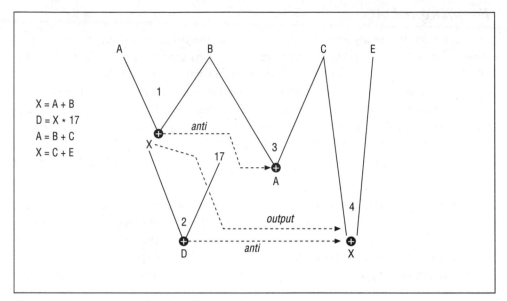

Figure 9-7: A more complex data flow graph

while processing instruction 4, we can eliminate a common subexpression during the construction of the DAG. If we can determine that Z is the only variable that is used outside this small block of code, we can assume the Y computation is dead code.

By constructing the DAG, we take a sequence of instructions and determine which must be executed in a particular order and which can be executed in parallel. This type of data flow analysis is very important in the codegeneration phase on super-scalar processors. We have introduced the concept of dependencies and how to use data flow to find opportunities for parallelism in code sequences within a basic block. We can also use data flow analysis to identify dependencies, opportunities for parallelism, and dead code between basic blocks.

Uses and Definitions

As the DAG is constructed, the compiler can make lists of variable *uses* and *definitions*, as well as other information, and apply these to global optimizations across many basic blocks taken together. Looking at the DAG in Figure 9-8, we can see that the variables defined are Z, Y, X, C, and D, and the variables used are A and B. Considering many basic blocks at once, we can say how far a particular variable definition reaches—where its value can be seen. From this we can recognize situations where calculations are being discarded, where two uses of a given variable are completely independent, or where we can overwrite register-resident values without saving them back to memory. We call this investigation *data flow analysis*.

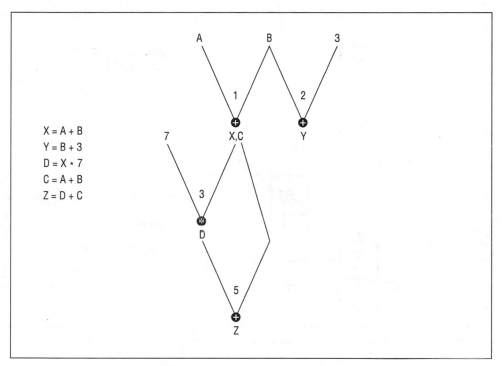

Figure 9-8: Extracting parallelism from a DAG

To illustrate, suppose that we have the flow graph in Figure 9-9. Beside each basic block we've listed the variables it uses and the variables it defines. What can data flow analysis tell us?

Notice that a value for A is defined in block X but only used in block Y. That means that A is dead upon exit from block Y or immediately upon taking the right-hand branch leaving X; none of the other basic blocks uses the value of A. That tells us that any associated resources, such as a register, can be freed for other uses.

Looking at Figure 9-9 we can see that D is defined in basic block X, but never used. This means that the calculations defining D can be discarded.

Something interesting is happening with the variable G. Blocks X and W both use it, but if you look closely you'll see that the two uses are distinct from one another, meaning that they can be treated as two independent variables.

A compiler featuring advanced instruction scheduling techniques might notice that W is the only block that uses the value for E, and so move the calculations defining E out of block Y and into W, where they are needed.

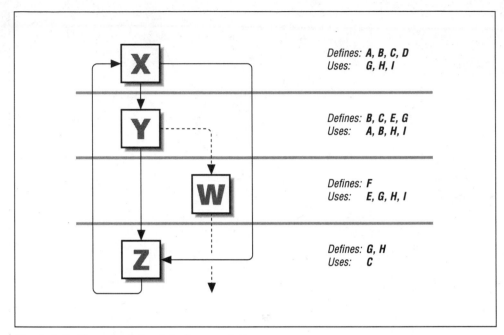

Figure 9-9: Flow graph for data flow analysis

In addition to gathering data about variables, the compiler can also keep information about subexpressions. Examining both together, it can recognize cases where redundant calculations are being made (across basic blocks), and substitute previously computed values in their place. If, for instance, the expression `H*I` appears in blocks **X**, **Y**, and **W**, it could be calculated just once in block **X** and propagated to the others that use it.

Loops

Loops are the center of activity for many applications, so there is often a high payback for simplifying or moving calculations outside, into the computational suburbs. Early compilers for parallel architectures used pattern matching to identify the bounds of their loops. This limitation meant that a hand-constructed loop using if-statements and goto-statements would not be correctly identified as a loop. Because modern compilers use data flow graphs, it's practical to identify loops as a particular subset of nodes in the flow graph. To a data flow graph, a hand constructed loop looks the same as a compiler-generated loop. Optimizations can therefore be applied to either type of loop.

Once we have identified the loops, we can apply the same kinds of data-flow analysis we applied above. Among the things we are looking for are calculations that are unchanging within the loop and variables that change in a predictable (linear) fashion from iteration to iteration.

How does the compiler identify a loop in the flow graph? Fundamentally, two conditions have to be met:

- A given node has to dominate all other nodes within the suspected loop. This means that all paths to any node in the loop have to pass through one particular node, the dominator. The dominator node forms the header at the top of the loop.

- There has to be a cycle in the graph. Given a dominator, if we can find a path back to it from one of the nodes it dominates, we have a loop. This path back is known as the *back edge* of the loop.

The flow graph in Figure 9-10 contains one loop and one red herring. You can see that node B dominates every node below it in the subset of the flow graph. That satisfies Condition 1 and makes it a candidate for a loop header. There is a path from E to B, and B dominates E, so that makes it a back edge, satisfying Condition 2. Therefore, the nodes B, C, D, and E form a loop. The loop goes through an array of linked list start pointers and traverses the lists to determine the total number of nodes in all lists. Letters to the extreme right correspond to the basic block numbers in the flow graph.

At first glance, it appears that the nodes C and D form a loop too. The problem is that C doesn't dominate D (and vice versa), because entry to either can be made from B, so condition 1 isn't satisfied. Generally, the flow graphs that come from code segments written with even the weakest appreciation for a structured design offer better loop candidates.

After identifying a loop, the compiler can concentrate on that portion of the flow graph, looking for instructions to remove or push to the outside. Certain types of subexpressions, such as those found in array index expressions, can be simplified if they change in a predictable fashion from one iteration to the next.

In the continuing quest for parallelism, loops are generally our best sources for large amounts of parallelism. However, loops also provide new opportunities for those parallelism-killing dependencies.

Loop-Carried Dependencies

The notion of data dependence is particularly important when we look at loops, the hub of activity inside numerical applications. A well-designed loop can produce millions of operations that can all be performed in parallel. However, a single misplaced dependency in the loop can force it all to be run in serial. So the stakes are higher when looking for dependencies in loops.

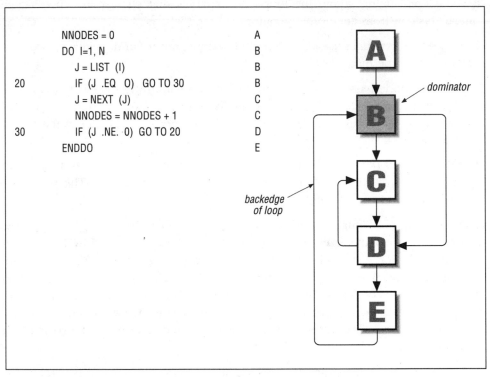

```
            NNODES = 0                     A
            DO I=1, N                      B
               J = LIST (I)                B
   20          IF (J .EQ  0)  GO TO 30     B
               J = NEXT (J)                C
               NNODES = NNODES + 1         C
   30          IF (J .NE. 0) GO TO 20      D
            ENDDO                          E
```

Figure 9-10: Flow graph with a loop in it

Some constructs are completely independent, right out of the box. The question we want to ask is "Can two different iterations execute at the same time, or is there a data dependency between them?" Consider the following loop:

```
DO I=1,N
   A(I) = A(I) + B(I)
ENDDO
```

For any two values of I and K, can we calculate the value of A(I) and A(K) at the same time? Below, we have manually unrolled several iterations of the previous loop, so they can be executed together:

```
A(I)   = A(I)   + B(I)
A(I+1) = A(I+1) + B(I+1)
A(I+2) = A(I+2) + B(I+2)
```

You can see that none of the results are used as an operand for another calculation. For instance, the calculation for A(I+1) can occur at the same time as the calculation for A(I) because the calculations are independent; you don't need the results of the first to determine the second. In fact, mixing up the order of the calculations won't change the results in the least. Relaxing the serial order imposed on these calculations makes it possible to execute this loop very quickly on parallel hardware.

Flow Dependencies

For comparison, look at the next code fragment:

```
DO I=2,N
  A(I) = A(I-1) + B(I)
ENDDO
```

This loop has the regularity of the previous example, but one of the subscripts is changed. Again, it's useful to manually unroll the loop and look at several iterations together:

```
A(I)   = A(I-1) + B(I)
A(I+1) = A(I)   + B(I+1)
A(I+2) = A(I+1) + B(I+2)
```

In this case, there is a dependency problem. The value of A(I+1) depends on the value of A(I), the value of A(I+2) depends on A(I+1), and so on; every iteration depends on the result of a previous one. Dependencies that extend back to a previous calculation and perhaps a previous iteration (like this one), are loop carried *flow dependencies* or *backward dependencies*. You often see such dependencies in applications that perform Gaussian elimination on certain types of matrices, or numerical solutions to systems of differential equations. However, it is impossible to run such a loop in parallel (as written); the processor must wait for intermediate results before it can proceed.

In some cases, flow dependencies are impossible to fix; calculations are so dependent upon one another that we have no choice but to wait for previous ones to complete. Other times, dependencies are a function of the way the calculations are expressed. For instance, the loop above can be changed to reduce the dependency. By replicating some of the arithmetic, we can make it so that the second and third iterations depend on the first, but not on one another. The operation count goes up—we have an extra addition that we didn't have before—but we have reduced the dependency between iterations:

```
DO I=2,N,2
  A(I)   = A(I-1) + B(I)
  A(I+1) = A(I-1) + B(I) + B(I+1)
ENDDO
```

The speed increase on a workstation won't be great (most machines run the recast loop more slowly). However, some parallel computers can trade off additional calculations for reduced dependency and chalk up a net win.

Antidependencies

It's a different story when there is a loop-carried antidependency, as in the code below:

```
DO I=1,N
   A(I)   = B(I)   * E
   B(I)   = A(I+2) * C
ENDDO
```

In this loop, there is an antidependency between the variable `A(I)` and the variable `A(I+2)`. That is, you must be sure that the instruction that uses `A(I+2)` does so before the previous one redefines it. Clearly, this is not a problem if the loop is executed serially, but remember, we are looking for opportunities to overlap instructions. Again, it helps to pull the loop apart and look at several iterations together. We have recast the loop by making many copies of the first statement, followed by copies of the second:

```
A(I)   = B(I)   * E
A(I+1) = B(I+1) * E
A(I+2) = B(I+2) * E
...
B(I)   = A(I+2) * C   ← assignment makes use of the new
B(I+1) = A(I+3) * C       value of A(I+2) incorrect.
B(I+2) = A(I+4) * C
```

The reference to `A(I+2)` needs to access an "old" value, rather than one of the new ones being calculated. If you perform all of the first statement followed by all of the second statement, the answers will be wrong. If you perform all of the second statement followed by all of the first statement, the answers will also be wrong. In a sense, to run the iterations in parallel, you must either save the `A` values to use for the second statement or store all of the `B` value in a temporary area until the loop completes.

We can also directly unroll the loop and find *some* parallelism:

```
1   A(I)   = B(I)   * E
2   B(I)   = A(I+2) * C   →
3   A(I+1) = B(I+1) * E   |  Output dependency
4   B(I+1) = A(I+3) * C   |
5   A(I+2) = B(I+2) * E   ←
6   B(I+2) = A(I+4) * C
```

Statements 1–4 could all be executed simultaneously. Once those statements completed execution, statements 5–8 could execute in parallel. Using this approach, there are sufficient intervening statements between the dependent statements that we can see some parallel performance improvement from a superscalar RISC processor.

Output Dependencies

The third class of data dependencies, *output dependencies*, is of particular interest to users of parallel computers, particularly multiprocessors. Output dependencies involve getting the right values to the right variables when all calculations have been completed. Otherwise, an output dependency is violated. The loop below assigns new values to two elements of the vector **A** with each iteration:

```
DO I=1,N
  A(I)   = C(I) * 2.
  A(I+2) = D(I) + E
ENDDO
```

As always, we won't have any problems if we execute the code sequentially. But if several iterations are performed together, and statements are reordered, then incorrect values can be assigned to the last elements of **A**. For example, in the naive vectorized equivalent below, `A(I+2)` takes the wrong value because the assignments occur out of order:

```
A(I)   = C(I)   * 2.
A(I+1) = C(I+1) * 2.
A(I+2) = C(I+2) * 2.
A(I+2) = D(I)   + E     ← Output dependency violated
A(I+3) = D(I+1) + E
A(I+4) = D(I+2) + E
```

Whether or not you have to worry about output dependencies depends on whether you are actually parallelizing the code. Your compiler will be conscious of the danger, and will be able to generate legal code—and possibly even fast code, if it's clever enough. But output dependencies occasionally become a problem for programmers.

Dependencies Within an Iteration

We have looked at dependencies that cross iteration boundaries but we haven't looked at dependencies within the same iteration. Consider the following code fragment:

```
DO I = 1,N
  D = B(I) * 17
  A(I) = D + 14
ENDDO
```

When we look at the loop, the variable D has a flow dependency. The second statement cannot start until the first statement has completed. At first glance this might appear to limit parallelism significantly. When we look closer and manually unroll several iterations of the loop, the situation gets worse:

```
D = B(I) * 17
A(I) = D + 14
D = B(I+1) * 17
A(I+1) = D + 14
D = B(I+2) * 17
A(I+2) = D + 14
```

Now, the variable D has flow, output, and antidependencies. It looks like this loop has no hope of running in parallel. However, there is a simple solution to this problem at the cost of some extra memory space, using a technique called *promoting a scalar to a vector*. We define D as an array with N elements and rewrite the code as follows:

```
DO I = 1,N
  D(I) = B(I) * 17
  A(I) = D(I) + 14
ENDDO
```

Now the iterations are all independent and can be run in parallel. Within each iteration, the first statement must run before the second statement.

Reductions

The sum of an array of numbers is one example of a *reduction*—so called because it reduces a vector to a scalar. The following loop to determine the total of the values in an array certainly looks as though it might be able to be run in parallel:

```
SUM = 0.0
DO I=1,N
  SUM = SUM + A(I)
ENDDO
```

However, if we perform our unrolling trick, it doesn't look very parallel:

```
SUM = SUM + A(I)
SUM = SUM + A(I+1)
SUM = SUM + A(I+2)
```

This loop also has all three types of dependencies and looks impossible to parallelize. If we are willing to accept the potential effect of rounding, we can add some parallelism to this loop as follows (again we did not add the preconditioning loop):

```
SUM0 = 0.0
SUM1 = 0.0
SUM2 = 0.0
SUM3 = 0.0
```

```
DO I=1,N,4
   SUM0 = SUM0 + A(I)
   SUM1 = SUM1 + A(I+1)
   SUM2 = SUM2 + A(I+2)
   SUM3 = SUM3 + A(I+3)
ENDDO
SUM = SUM0 + SUM1 + SUM2 + SUM3
```

Again, this is not precisely the same computation, but all four partial sums can be computed independently. The partial sums are combined at the end of the loop.

Loops that look for the maximum or minimum elements in an array, or multiply all the elements of an array, are also reductions. Likewise, some of these can be reorganized into partial results, as with the sum, to expose more computations. Note that the maximum and minimum are associative operators, so the results of the reorganized loop are identical to the sequential loop.

Ambiguous References

Every dependency we have looked at so far has been clear cut; you could see exactly what you were dealing with by looking at the source code. But other times, describing a dependency isn't so easy. Recall this loop from the "Antidependencies" section earlier in this chapter:

```
DO I=1,N
   A(I)   = B(I) * E
   B(I)   = A(I+2) * C
ENDDO
```

Because each variable reference is solely a function of the index, I, it's clear what kind of dependency we are dealing with. Furthermore, we can describe how far apart (in iterations) a variable reference is from its definition. This is called the *dependency distance*. A negative value represents a flow dependency; a positive value means there is an antidependency. A value of zero says that no dependency exists between the reference and the definition. In this loop, the dependency distance for A is +2 iterations.

However, array subscripts may be functions of other variables besides the loop index. It may be difficult to tell the distance between the use and definition of a particular element. It may even be impossible to tell whether the dependency is a flow dependency or an antidependency, or whether a dependency exists at all. Consequently, it may be impossible to determine if it's safe to overlap execution of different statements, as in the following loop:

```
DO I=1,N
   A(I)   = B(I) * E
   B(I)   = A(I+K) * C      ← K unknown
ENDDO
```

If the loop made use of `A(I+K)`, where the value of `K` was unknown, we wouldn't be able to tell (at least by looking at the code) anything about the kind of dependency we might be facing. If `K` is zero, we have a dependency within the iteration and no loop-carried dependencies. If `K` is positive we have an antidependency with distance `K`. Depending on the value for `K`, we might have enough parallelism for a superscalar processor. If `K` is negative, we have a loop-carried flow dependency, and we may have to execute the loop serially.

Ambiguous references, like `A(I+K)` above, have an effect on the parallelism we can detect in a loop. From the compiler perspective, it may be that this loop does contain two independent calculations that the author whimsically decided to throw into a single loop. But when they appear together, the compiler has to treat them conservatively, as if they were interrelated. This has a big effect on performance. If the compiler has to assume that consecutive memory references may ultimately access the same location, the instructions involved cannot be overlapped. One other option is for the compiler to generate two versions of the loop and check the value for `K` at runtime to determine which version of the loop to execute.

A similar situation occurs when we use integer index arrays in a loop. The loop below contains only a single statement, but you can't be sure that any iteration is independent without knowing the contents of the `K` and `J` arrays:

```
DO I=1,N
   A(K(I)) = A(K(I)) + B(J(I)) * C
ENDDO
```

For instance, what if all of the values for `K(I)` were the same? This causes the same element of the array `A` to be rereferenced with each iteration! That may seem ridiculous to you, but the compiler can't tell.

With code like this, it's common for every value of `K(I)` to be unique. This is called a *permutation*. If you can tell a compiler that it is dealing with a permutation, the penalty is lessened in some cases. Even so, there is insult being added to injury. Indirect references require more memory activity than direct references, and this slows you down.

Pointer Ambiguity in Numerical C Applications

FORTRAN compilers depend on programmers to observe aliasing rules. That is, programmers are not supposed to modify locations through pointers that may be aliases of one another. They can become aliases in several ways, such as when two dummy arguments receive pointers to the same storage locations:

```
CALL BOB (A,A)
   ...
END
```

```
SUBROUTINE BOB (X,Y)   ← X,Y become aliases
```

C compilers don't enjoy the same restrictions on aliasing. In fact, there are cases where aliasing could be desirable. Additionally, C is blessed with pointer types, increasing the opportunities for aliasing to occur. This means that a C compiler has to approach operations through pointers more conservatively than a FORTRAN compiler would. Let's look at some examples to see why.

The following loop nest looks like a FORTRAN loop cast in C. The arrays are declared or allocated all at once at the top of the routine, and the starting address and leading dimensions are visible to the compiler. This is important because it means that the storage relationship between the array elements is well known. Hence, you could expect good performance:

```
#define N ...
double a[N][N], c[N][N], d;
for (i=0; i<N; i++)
    for (j=0; j<N; j++)
        a[i][j] = a[i][j] + c[j][i] * d;
```

Now imagine what happens if you allocate the rows dynamically. This makes the address calculations more complicated. The loop nest hasn't changed; however, there is no guaranteed stride that can get you from one row to the next. This is because the storage relationship between the rows is unknown:

```
#define N ...
double *a[N], *c[N], d;
for (i=0; i<N; i++) {
    a[i] = (double *) malloc (N*sizeof(double));
    c[i] = (double *) malloc (N*sizeof(double));
}
for (i=0; i<N; i++)
    for (j=0; j<N; j++)
        a[i][j] = a[i][j] + c[j][i] * d;
```

In fact, your compiler knows even less than you might expect about the storage relationship. For instance, how can it be sure that references to a and c aren't aliases? It may be obvious to you that they're not. You might point out that *malloc* never overlaps storage. But the compiler isn't free to assume that. Who knows? You may be substituting your own version of *malloc*!

Let's look at a different example, where storage is allocated all at once, though the declarations are not visible to all routines that are using it. The following subroutine **bob** performs the same computation as our previous example. However, because the compiler can't see the declarations for a and c (they're in the main routine), it doesn't have enough information to be able to overlap memory references from successive iterations; the references could be aliases:

```
#define N ...
main()
{
    double a[N][N], c[N][N], d;
    ...
    bob (a,c,d,N);
}
bob (double *a,double *c,double d,int n)
{
    int i,j;
    double *ap, *cp;
    for (i=0;i<n;i++) {
        ap = a + (i*n);
        cp = c + i;
        for (j=0; j<n; j++)
            *(ap+j) = *(ap+j) + *(cp+(j*n)) * d;
    }
}
```

To get the best performance, make available to the compiler as many details about the size and shape of your data structures as possible. Pointers, whether in the form of formal arguments to a subroutine or explicitly declared, can hide important facts about how you are using memory. The more information the compiler has, the more it can overlap memory references. This information can come from compiler directives or from making declarations visible in the routines where performance is most critical.

Closing Notes

You already knew there was a limit to the amount of parallelism in any given program. Now you know why. Clearly, if a program had no dependencies, you could execute the whole thing at once, given suitable hardware. But programs aren't infinitely parallel; they are often hardly parallel at all. This is because they contain dependencies of the types we saw above.

When we are writing and/or tuning our loops, we have a number of (sometimes conflicting) goals to keep in mind:

- Balance memory operations and computations.

- Minimize unnecessary operations.

- Access memory using unit stride if at all possible.

- Allow all of the loop iterations to be computed in parallel.

In the coming chapters, we will begin to learn more about executing our programs on parallel multiprocessors. At some point we will escape the bonds of compiler automatic optimization and begin to explicitly code the parallel portions of our code.

To learn more about compilers and dataflow, read *The Art of Compiler Design: Theory and Practice* by Thomas Pittman and James Peters (Prentice Hall).

Exercises

1. Identify the dependencies (if there are any) in the following loops. Can you think of ways to organize each loop for more parallelism?

    (a)
    ```
    DO I=1,N-2
      A(I+2) = A(I) + 1.
    ENDDO
    ```

    (b)
    ```
    DO I=1,N-1,2
      A(I+1) = A(I) + 1.
    ENDDO
    ```

    (c)
    ```
    DO I=2,N
      A(I) = A(I-1) * 2.
      B = A(I-1)
    ENDDO
    ```

    (d)
    ```
    DO I=1,N
      IF(N .GT. M)
        A(I) = 1.
    ENDDO
    ```

    (e)
    ```
    DO I=1,N
      A(I,J) = A(I,K) + B
    ENDDO
    ```

    (f)
    ```
    DO I=1,N-1
      A(I+1,J) = A(I,K) + B
    ENDDO
    ```

    (g)
    ```
    for (i=0; i<n; i++)
      a[i] = b[i];
    ```

2. Imagine that you are a parallelizing compiler, trying to generate code for the loop below. Why are references to **A** a challenge? Why would it help to know that **K** is equal to zero? Explain how you could partially vectorize the statements involving **A** if you knew that **K** had an absolute value of at least 8.

    ```
    DO I=1,N
      E(I,M) = E(I-1,M+1) - 1.0
      B(I)   = A(I+K) * C
      A(I)   = D(I) * 2.0
    ENDDO
    ```

3. The following three statements contain a flow dependency, an antidependency and an output dependency. Can you identify each? Given that you are allowed to reorder the statements, can you find a permutation that produces

the same values for the variables C and B? Show how you can reduce the dependencies by combining or rearranging calculations and using temporary variables.

```
B = A + C
B = C + D
C = B + D
```

In this chapter:
- *Symmetric Multiprocessing Hardware*
- *Multiprocessor Software Concepts*
- *Techniques for Multithreaded Programs*
- *A Real Example*
- *Closing Notes*

10

Shared-Memory Multiprocessors

In the mid-1980s, shared-memory multiprocessors were pretty expensive and pretty rare. Now, as hardware costs are dropping, they are becoming commonplace. Many home computer systems in the under-$3000 range have a socket for a second CPU. Home computer operating systems are providing the capability to use more than one processor to improve system performance. Rather than specialized resources locked away in a central computing facility, these shared-memory processors are often viewed as a logical extension of the desktop. These systems run the same operating system (UNIX or NT) as the desktop and many of the same applications from a workstation will execute on these multiprocessor servers.

Typically a workstation will have from 1 to 4 processors and a server system will have 4 to 64 processors. Shared-memory multiprocessors have a significant advantage over other multiprocessors because all the processors share the same view of the memory, as shown in Figure 10-1.

These processors are also described as *uniform memory access* (also known as UMA) systems. This designation indicates that memory is equally accessible to all processors with the same performance.

The popularity of these systems is not due simply to the demand for high performance computing. These systems are excellent at providing high throughput for a multiprocessing load, and function effectively as high-performance database servers, network servers, and Internet servers. Within limits, their throughput is increased linearly as more processors are added.

In this book we are not so interested in the performance of database or Internet servers. That is too passé; buy more processors, get better throughput. We are interested in pure, raw, unadulterated compute speed for *our* high performance

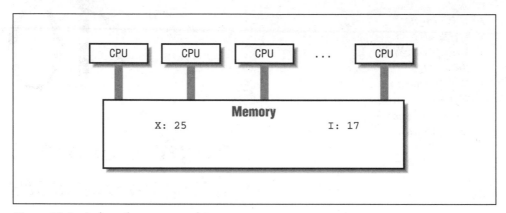

Figure 10-1: A shared-memory multiprocessor

application. Instead of running hundreds of small jobs, we want to utilize all $750,000 worth of hardware for our single job.

The challenge is to find techniques that make a program that takes an hour to complete using one processor, complete in less than a minute using 64 processors. This is not trivial. Throughout this book so far, we have been on an endless quest for parallelism. In this and the remaining chapters, we will begin to see the payoff for all of your hard work and dedication!

The cost of a shared-memory multiprocessor can range from $4000 to $30 million. Some example systems include multiple-processor Intel systems from a wide range of vendors, SGI Power Challenge Series, HP/Convex C-Series, DEC AlphaServers, Cray vector/parallel processors, and Sun Enterprise systems. The SGI Origin 2000, HP/Convex Exemplar, Data General AV-20000, and Sequent NUMAQ-2000 all are uniform-memory, symmetric multiprocessing systems that can be linked to form even larger shared nonuniform memory-access systems. Among these systems, as the price increases, the number of CPUs increases, the performance of individual CPUs increases, and the memory performance increases.

In this chapter we will study the hardware and software environment in these systems and learn how to execute our programs on these systems.

Symmetric Multiprocessing Hardware

In Figure 10-1, we viewed an ideal shared-memory multiprocessor. In this section, we look in more detail at how such a system is actually constructed. The primary advantage of these systems is the ability for any CPU to access all of the memory and peripherals. Furthermore, the systems need a facility for deciding among themselves who has access to what, and when, which means there will have to be hardware support for arbitration. The two most common architectural underpinnings for symmetric multiprocessing are *buses* and *crossbars*. The bus is the simplest of the two approaches. Figure 10-2 shows processors connected using a bus. A bus can be thought of as a set of parallel wires connecting the components of the computer (CPU, memory, and peripheral controllers), a set of protocols for communication, and some hardware to help carry it out. A bus is less expensive to build, but because all traffic must cross the bus, as the load increases, the bus eventually becomes a performance bottleneck.

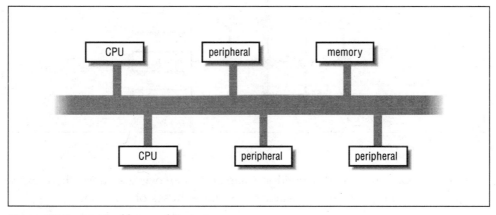

Figure 10-2: A typical bus architecture

A crossbar is a hardware approach to eliminate the bottleneck caused by a single bus. A crossbar is like several buses running side by side with attachments to each of the modules on the machine—CPU, memory, and peripherals. Any module can get to any other by a path through the crossbar, and multiple paths may be active simultaneously. In the 4×5 crossbar of Figure 10-3, for instance, there can be four active data transfers in progress at one time. In the diagram it looks like a patchwork of wires, but there is actually quite a bit of hardware that goes into constructing a crossbar. Not only does the crossbar connect parties that wish to communicate, but it must also actively arbitrate between two or more CPUs that want access to the same memory or peripheral. In the event that one module is too popular, it's the crossbar that decides who gets access and who doesn't. Crossbars have the best performance because there is no single shared bus. However, they are more expensive to build, and their cost increases as the number of ports is increased. Because of their cost, crossbars typically are only found at the high end of the price and performance spectrum.

Whether the system uses a bus or crossbar, there is only so much memory bandwidth to go around; four or eight processors drawing from one memory system can quickly saturate all available bandwidth. All of the techniques that improve

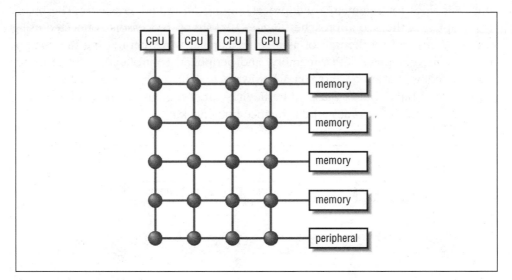

Figure 10-3: A crossbar

memory performance (as described in Chapter 3, *Memory*) also apply here in the design of the memory subsystems attached to these buses or crossbars.

The Effect of Cache

The most common multiprocessing system is made up of commodity processors connected to memory and peripherals through a bus. Interestingly, the fact that these processors make use of cache somewhat mitigates the bandwidth bottleneck on a bus-based architecture. By connecting the processor to the cache and viewing the main memory through the cache, we significantly reduce the memory traffic across the bus. In this architecture, most of the memory accesses across the bus take the form of cache line loads and flushes. To understand why, consider what happens when the cache hit rate is very high. In Figure 10-4, a high cache hit rate eliminates some of the traffic that would have otherwise gone out across the bus or crossbar to main memory. Again, it is the notion of "locality of reference" that makes the system work. If you assume that a fair number of the memory references will hit in the cache, the equivalent attainable main memory bandwidth is more than the bus is actually capable of. This assumption explains why multiprocessors are designed with less bus bandwidth than the sum of what the CPUs can consume at once.

Imagine a scenario where two CPUs are accessing different areas of memory using unit stride. Both CPUs access the first element in a cache line at the same time. The bus arbitrarily allows one CPU access to the memory. The first CPU fills a cache line and begins to process the data. The instant the first CPU has completed

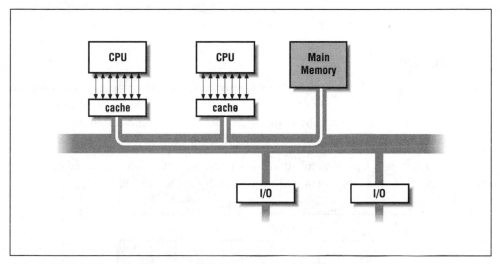

Figure 10-4: High cache hit rate reduces main memory traffic

its cache line fill, the cache line fill for the second CPU begins. Once the second cache line fill has completed, the second CPU begins to process the data in its cache line. If the time to process the data in a cache line is longer than the time to fill a cache line, the cache line fill for processor two completes before the next cache line request arrives from processor one. Once the initial conflict is resolved, both processors appear to have conflict-free access to memory for the remainder of their unit-stride loops.

In actuality, on some of the fastest bus-based systems, the memory bus is sufficiently fast that up to 20 processors can access memory using unit stride with very little conflict. If the processors are accessing memory using non-unit stride, bus and memory bank conflict becomes apparent, with fewer processors.

This bus architecture combined with local caches is very popular for general-purpose multiprocessing loads. The memory reference patterns for database or Internet servers generally consist of a combination of time periods with a small working set, and time periods that access large data structures using unit stride. Scientific codes tend to perform more non-unit-stride access than general-purpose codes. For this reason, the most expensive parallel-processing systems targeted at scientific codes tend to use crossbars connected to multibanked memory systems.

The main memory system is better shielded when a larger cache is used. For this reason, multiprocessors sometimes incorporate a two-tier cache system, where each processor uses its own small on-chip local cache, backed up by a larger second board-level cache with as much as 4 MB of memory. Only when neither can satisfy a memory request, or when data has to be written back to main memory, does a request go out over the bus or crossbar.

Coherency

Now, what happens when one CPU of a multiprocessor running a single program in parallel changes the value of a variable, and another CPU tries to read it? Where does the value come from? These questions are interesting because there can be multiple copies of each variable, and some of them can hold old or stale values.

For illustration, say that you are running a program with a shared variable **A**. Processor 1 changes the value of **A** and Processor 2 goes to read it.

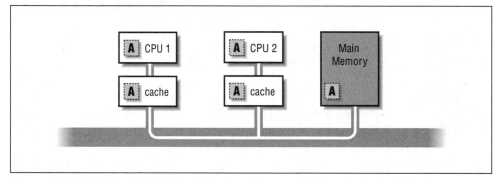

Figure 10-5: Multiple copies of variable A

In Figure 10-5, if Processor 1 is keeping **A** as a register-resident variable, then Processor 2 doesn't stand a chance of getting the correct value when it goes to look for it. There is no way that 2 can know the contents of 1's registers; so assume, at the very least, that Processor 1 writes the new value back out. Now the question is, where does the new value get stored? Does it remain in Processor 1's cache? Is it written to main memory? Does it get updated in Processor 2's cache?

Really, we are asking what kind of *cache coherency protocol* the vendor uses to assure that all processors see a uniform view of the values in "memory." It generally isn't something that the programmer has to worry about, except that in some cases, it can affect performance. The approaches used in these systems are similar to those used in single-processor systems with some extensions. The most straightforward cache coherency approach is called a *write-through policy*: variables written into cache are simultaneously written into main memory. As the update takes place, other caches in the system see the main memory reference being performed. This can be done because all of the caches continuously monitor (also known as *snooping*) the traffic on the bus, checking to see if each address is in their cache. If a cache "notices" that it contains a copy of the data from the locations being written, it may either *invalidate* its copy of the variable or obtain new values (depending on the policy) One thing to note is that a write-through cache demands a fair amount of main memory bandwidth since each write goes out over the main memory bus. Furthermore, successive writes to the same location or bank are subject to the main memory cycle time and can slow the machine down.

A more sophisticated cache coherency protocol is called *copyback* or *writeback*. The idea is that you write values back out to main memory only when the cache housing them needs the space for something else. Updates of cached data are coordinated between the caches, by the caches, without help from the processor. Copyback caching also uses hardware that can monitor (snoop) and respond to the memory transactions of the other caches in the system. The benefit of this method over the write-through method is that memory traffic is reduced considerably. Let's walk through it to see how it works.

Cache Line States

For this approach to work, each cache must maintain a state for each line in its cache. The possible states used in the example include:

Modified
> This cache line needs to be written back to memory.

Exclusive
> There are no other caches that have this cache line.

Shared
> There are read-only copies of this line in two or more caches.

Empty/Invalid
> This cache line doesn't contain any useful data.

This particular coherency protocol is often called *MESI*. Other cache coherency protocols are more complicated, but these states give you an idea how multiprocessor writeback cache coherency works.

We start where a particular cache line is in memory and in none of the writeback caches on the systems. The first cache to ask for data from a particular part of memory completes a normal memory access; the main memory system returns data from the requested location in response to a cache miss. The associated cache line is marked *exclusive*, meaning that this is the only cache in the system containing a copy of the data; it is the owner of the data. If another cache goes to main memory looking for the same thing, the request is intercepted by the first cache, and the data is returned from the first cache—not main memory. Once an interception has occurred and the data is returned, the data is marked *shared* in both of the caches.

When a particular line is marked shared, the caches have to treat it differently than they would if they were the exclusive owners of the data—especially if any of them wants to modify it. In particular, a write to a shared cache entry is preceded by a broadcast message to all the other caches in the system. It tells them to invalidate their copies of the data. The one remaining cache line gets marked as *modified* to signal that it has been changed, and that it must be returned to main memory when the space is needed for something else. By these mechanisms, you can maintain cache coherence across the multiprocessor without adding tremendously to the memory traffic.

By the way, even if a variable is not shared, it's possible for copies of it to show up in several caches. On a symmetric multiprocessor, your program can bounce around from CPU to CPU. If you run for a little while on this CPU, and then a little while on that, your program will have operated out of separate caches. That means that there can be several copies of seemingly unshared variables scattered around the machine. Operating systems often try to minimize how often a process is moved between physical CPUs during context switches. This is one reason not to overload the available processors in a system.

Data Placement

There is one more pitfall regarding shared memory we have so far failed to mention. It involves data movement. Although it would be convenient to think of the multiprocessor memory as one big pool, we have seen that it is actually a carefully crafted system of caches, coherency protocols, and main memory. The problems come when your application causes lots of data to be traded between the caches. Each reference that falls out of a given processor's cache (especially those that require an update in another processor's cache) has to go out on the bus.

Often, it's slower to get memory from another processor's cache than from the main memory because of the protocol and processing overhead involved. Not only do we need to have programs with high locality of reference and unit stride, we also need to minimize the data that must be moved from one CPU to another.

Multiprocessor Software Concepts

Now that we have examined the way shared-memory multiprocessor hardware operates, we need to examine how software operates on these types of computers. We still have to wait until the next chapters to begin making our FORTRAN programs run in parallel. For now, we use C programs to examine the fundamentals of multiprocessing and multithreading. There are several techniques used to implement multithreading, so the topics we will cover include:

- Operating system–supported multiprocessing
- User space multithreading
- Operating system-supported multithreading

The last of these is what we primarily will use to reduce the walltime of our applications.

Operating System–Supported Multiprocessing

Most modern general-purpose operating systems support some form of multiprocessing. Multiprocessing doesn't require more than one physical CPU; it is simply the operating system's ability to run more than one *process* on the system. The operating system context-switches between each process at fixed time intervals, or on interrupts or input-output activity. For example, in UNIX, if you use the *ps* command, you can see the processes on the system:

```
% ps -a
    PID TTY        TIME CMD
  28410 pts/34    0:00 tcsh
  28213 pts/38    0:00 xterm
  10488 pts/51    0:01 telnet
  28411 pts/34    0:00 xbiff
  11123 pts/25    0:00 pine
   3805 pts/21    0:00 elm
   6773 pts/44    5:48 ansys
    ...
% ps -a | grep ansys
   6773 pts/44    6:00 ansys
```

For each process we see the process identifier (PID), the terminal that is executing the command, the amount of CPU time the command has used, and the name of the command. The PID is unique across the entire system. Most UNIX commands are executed in a separate process. In the above example, most of the processes are waiting for some type of event, so they are taking very few resources except for memory. Process 6773* seems to be executing and using resources. Running *ps* again confirms that the CPU time is increasing for the *ansys* process:

```
% vmstat 5
 procs     memory            page            disk          faults      cpu
 r b w   swap  free re mf pi po fr de sr f0 s0 -- --  in   sy   cs us sy id
 3 0 0 353624 45432  0  0  1  0  0  0  0  0  0  0 461 5626 354 91  9  0
 3 0 0 353248 43960  0 22  0  0  0  0  0  0 14  0 518 6227 385 89 11  0
```

---

* ANSYS is a commonly used structural-analysis package.

Running the *vmstat 5* command tells us many things about the activity on the system. First, there are three runnable processes. If we had one CPU, only one would actually be running at a given instant. To allow all three jobs to progress, the operating system time-shares between the processes. Assuming equal priority, each process executes about 1/3 of the time. However, this system is a two-processor system, so each process executes about 2/3 of the time. Looking across the *vmstat* output, we can see paging activity (*pi, po*), context switches (*cs*), overall user time (*us*), system time (*sy*), and idle time (*id*).

Each process can execute a completely different program. While most processes are completely independent, they can cooperate and share information using interprocess communication (pipes, sockets) or various operating system-supported shared-memory areas. We generally don't use multiprocessing on these shared-memory systems as a technique to increase single-application performance. We will explore techniques that use multiprocessing coupled with communication to improve performance on scalable parallel processing systems in Chapter 12, *Large-Scale Parallel Computing*.

Multiprocessing software

In this section, we explore how programs access multiprocessing features.* In this example, the program creates a new process using the *fork()* function. The new process (child) prints some messages and then changes its identity using *exec()* by loading a new program. The original process (parent) prints some messages and then waits for the child process to complete:

```
int globvar;    /* A global variable */

main () {

  int pid,status,retval;
  int stackvar;    /* A stack variable */

  globvar = 1;
  stackvar = 1;
  printf("Main - calling fork globvar=%d stackvar=%d\n",globvar,stackvar);
  pid = fork();
  printf("Main - fork returned pid=%d\n",pid);
  if ( pid == 0 ) {
    printf("Child - globvar=%d stackvar=%d\n",globvar,stackvar);
    sleep(1);
    printf("Child - woke up globvar=%d stackvar=%d\n",globvar,stackvar);
    globvar = 100;
    stackvar = 100;
```

---

* These examples are written in C using the POSIX 1003.1 application programming interface. This example runs on most UNIX systems and on other POSIX-compliant systems including OpenNT, Open-VMS, and many others.

```
        printf("Child - modified globvar=%d stackvar=%d\n",globvar,stackvar);
        retval = execl("/bin/date", (char *) 0 );
        printf("Child - WHY ARE WE HERE retval=%d\n",retval);
    } else {
        printf("Parent - globvar=%d stackvar=%d\n",globvar,stackvar);
        globvar = 5;
        stackvar = 5;
        printf("Parent - sleeping globvar=%d stackvar=%d\n",globvar,stackvar);
        sleep(2);
        printf("Parent - woke up globvar=%d stackvar=%d\n",globvar,stackvar);
        printf("Parent - waiting for pid=%d\n",pid);
        retval = wait(&status);
        status = status >> 8;   /* Return code in bits 15-8 */
        printf("Parent - status=%d retval=%d\n",status,retval);
    }
}
```

The key to understanding this code is to understand how the *fork()* function operates. The simple summary is that the *fork()* function is called once in a process and returns twice, once in the original process and once in a newly created process. The newly created process is an identical copy of the original process. All the variables (local and global) have been duplicated. Both processes have access to all of the open files of the original process. Figure 10-6 shows how the fork operation creates a new process.

The only difference between the processes is that the return value from the *fork()* function call is 0 in the new (child) process and the process identifier (shown by the *ps* command) in the original (parent) process. This is the program output:

```
recs % cc -o fork fork.c
recs % fork
Main - calling fork globvar=1 stackvar=1
Main - fork returned pid=19336
Main - fork returned pid=0
Parent - globvar=1 stackvar=1
Parent - sleeping globvar=5 stackvar=5
Child - globvar=1 stackvar=1
Child - woke up globvar=1 stackvar=1
Child - modified globvar=100 stackvar=100
Thu Nov  6 22:40:33
Parent - woke up globvar=5 stackvar=5
Parent - waiting for pid=19336
Parent - status=0 retval=19336
recs %
```

Tracing this through, first the program sets the global and stack variable to one and then calls *fork()*. During the *fork()* call, the operating system suspends the process, makes an exact duplicate of the process, and then restarts both processes. You can see two messages from the statement immediately after the fork. The first line is coming from the original process, and the second line is coming from the new process. If you were to execute a *ps* command at this moment in time, you

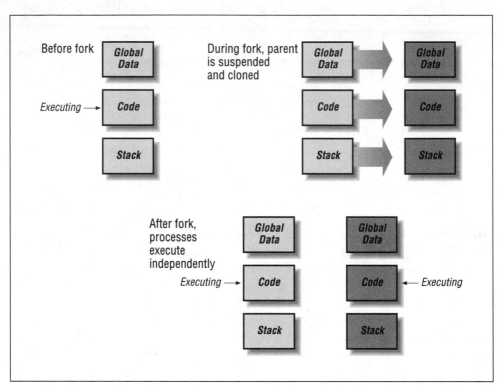

Figure 10-6: How a fork operates

would see two processes running called "fork." One would have a process identifier of 19336.

As both processes start, they execute an IF-THEN-ELSE and begin to perform different actions in the parent and child. Notice that *globvar* and *stackvar* are set to 5 in the parent, and then the parent sleeps for two seconds. At this point, the child begins executing. The values for *globvar* and *stackvar* are unchanged in the child process. This is because these two processes are operating in completely independent memory spaces. The child process sleeps for one second and sets its copies of the variables to 100. Next, the child process calls the *execl()* function to overwrite its memory space with the UNIX date program. Note that the *execl()* never returns; the date program takes over all of the resources of the child process. If you were to do a *ps* at this moment in time, you still see two processes on the system but process 19336 would be called "date." The *date* command executes, and you can see its output.*

---

* It's not uncommon for a human parent process to "fork" and create a human child process that initially seems to have the same identity as the parent. It's also not uncommon for the child process to change its overall identity to be something very different from the parent at some later point. Usually

The parent wakes up after a brief two-second sleep and notices that its copies of global and local variables have not been changed by the action of the child process. The parent then calls the *wait()* function to determine if any of its children exited. The *wait()* function returns which child has exited and the status code returned by that child process (in this case, process 19336).

User Space Multithreading

A *thread* is different from a process. When you add threads, they are added to the existing process rather than starting in a new process. Processes start with a single thread of execution and can add or remove threads throughout the duration of the program. Unlike processes, which operate in different memory spaces, all threads in a process share the same memory space. Figure 10-7 shows how the creation of a thread differs from the creation of a process. Not all of the memory space in a process is shared between all threads. In addition to the global area that is shared across all threads, each thread has a *thread private* area for its own local variables. It's important for programmers to know when they are working with shared variables and when they are working with local variables.

When attempting to speed up high performance computing applications, threads have the advantage over processes in that multiple threads can cooperate and work on a shared data structure to hasten the computation. By dividing the work into smaller portions and assigning each smaller portion to a separate thread, the total work can be completed more quickly.

Multiple threads are also used in high performance database and Internet servers to improve the overall *throughput* of the server. With a single thread, the program can either be waiting for the next network request or reading the disk to satisfy the previous request. With multiple threads, one thread can be waiting for the next network transaction while several other threads are waiting for disk I/O to complete.

The following is an example of a simple multithreaded application.* It begins with a single master thread that creates three additional threads. Each thread prints some messages, accesses some global and local variables, and then terminates:

```
#define _REENTRANT      /* basic lines for threads */
#include <stdio.h>
#include <pthread.h>
```

---

human children wait 13 years or so before this change occurs, but in UNIX, this happens in a few microseconds. So, in some ways, in UNIX, there are many parent processes that are "disappointed" because their children did not turn out like them!

* This example uses the IEEE POSIX standard interface for a thread library. If your system supports POSIX threads, this example should work. If not, there should be similar routines on your system for each of the thread functions.

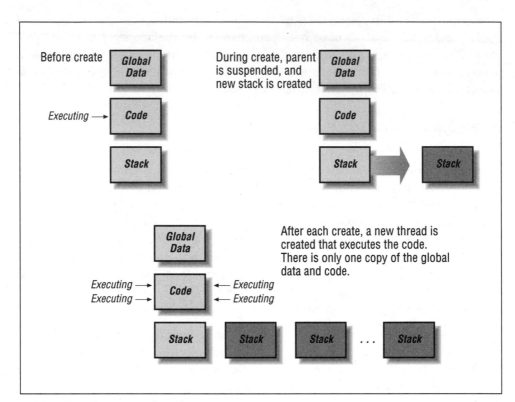

Figure 10-7: Creating a thread

```
#define THREAD_COUNT 3
void *TestFunc(void *);
int globvar;                      /* A global variable */
int index[THREAD_COUNT];          /* Local zero-based thread index */
pthread_t thread_id[THREAD_COUNT];  /* POSIX Thread IDs */

main() {
  ipt i,retval;
  pthread_t tid;

  globvar = 0;
  printf("Main - globvar=%d\n",globvar);
  for(i=0;i<THREAD_COUNT;i++) {
    index[i] = i;
    retval = pthread_create(&tid,NULL,TestFunc,(void *) index[i]);
    printf("Main - creating i=%d tid=%d retval=%d\n",i,tid,retval);
    thread_id[i] = tid;
  }
  printf("Main thread - threads started globvar=%d\n",globvar);
  for(i=0;i<THREAD_COUNT;i++) {
    printf("Main - waiting for join %d\n",thread_id[i]);
    retval = pthread_join( thread_id[i], NULL ) ;
    printf("Main - back from join %d retval=%d\n",i,retval);
```

```
    }
    printf("Main thread - threads completed globvar=%d\n",globvar);
}

void *TestFunc(void *parm) {
    int me,self;

    me = (int) parm;   /* My own assigned thread ordinal */
    self = pthread_self();   /* The POSIX Thread library thread number */
    printf("TestFunc me=%d - self=%d globvar=%d\n",me,self,globvar);
    globvar = me + 15;
    printf("TestFunc me=%d - sleeping globvar=%d\n",me,globvar);
    sleep(2);
    printf("TestFunc me=%d - done param=%d globvar=%d\n",me,self,globvar);
}
```

The global shared areas in this case are those variables declared in the static area outside the *main()* code. The local variables are any variables declared within a routine. When threads are added, each thread gets its own function call stack. In C, the *automatic* variables that are declared at the beginning of each routine are allocated on the stack. As each thread enters a function, these variables are separately allocated on that particular thread's stack. So these are the *thread-local* variables.

Unlike the *fork()* function, the *pthread_create()* function creates a new thread, and then control is returned to the calling thread. One of the parameters of the *pthread_create()* is the name of a function.

New threads begin execution in the function *TestFunc()* and the thread finishes when it returns from this function. When this program is executed, it produces the following output:

```
recs % cc -o create1 -lpthread -lposix4 create1.c
recs % create1
Main - globvar=0
Main - creating i=0 tid=4 retval=0
Main - creating i=1 tid=5 retval=0
Main - creating i=2 tid=6 retval=0
Main thread - threads started globvar=0
Main - waiting for join 4
TestFunc me=0 - self=4 globvar=0
TestFunc me=0 - sleeping globvar=15
TestFunc me=1 - self=5 globvar=15
TestFunc me=1 - sleeping globvar=16
TestFunc me=2 - self=6 globvar=16
TestFunc me=2 - sleeping globvar=17
TestFunc me=2 - done param=6 globvar=17
TestFunc me=1 - done param=5 globvar=17
TestFunc me=0 - done param=4 globvar=17
Main - back from join 0 retval=0
Main - waiting for join 5
Main - back from join 1 retval=0
```

```
Main - waiting for join 6
Main - back from join 2 retval=0
Main thread - threads completed globvar=17
recs %
```

You can see the threads getting created in the loop. The master thread completes the *pthread_create()* loop, executes the second loop, and calls the *pthread_join()* function. This function suspends the master thread until the specified thread completes. The master thread is waiting for Thread 4 to complete. Once the master thread suspends, one of the new threads is started. Thread 4 starts executing. Initially the variable *globvar* is set to 0 from the main program. The *self, me,* and *param* variables are thread-local variables, so each thread has its own copy. Thread 4 sets *globvar* to 15 and goes to sleep. Then Thread 5 begins to execute and sees *globvar* set to 15 from Thread 4; Thread 5 sets *globvar* to 16, and goes to sleep. This activates Thread 6, which sees the current value for *globvar* and sets it to 17. Then Threads 6, 5, and 4 wake up from their sleep, all notice the latest value of 17 in *globvar,* and return from the *TestFunc()* routine, ending the threads.

All this time, the master thread is in the middle of a *pthread_join()* waiting for Thread 4 to complete. As Thread 4 completes, the *pthread_join()* returns. The master thread then calls *pthread_join()* repeatedly to ensure that all three threads have been completed. Finally, the master thread prints out the value for *globvar* that contains the latest value of 17.

To summarize, when an application is executing with more than one thread, there are shared global areas and thread private areas. Different threads execute at different times, and they can easily work together in shared areas.

Limitations of user space multithreading

Multithreaded applications were around long before multiprocessors existed. It is quite practical to have multiple threads with a single CPU. As a matter of fact, the previous example would run on a system with any number of processors, including one. If you look closely at the code, it performs a sleep operation at each critical point in the code. One reason to add the sleep calls is to slow the program down enough that you can actually see what is going on. However, these sleep calls also have another effect. When one thread enters the sleep routine, it causes the thread library to search for other "runnable" threads. If a runnable thread is found, it begins executing immediately while the calling thread is "sleeping." This is called a *user-space thread context switch.* The process actually has one operating system thread shared among several logical user threads. When library routines (such as *sleep*) are called, the thread library* jumps in and reschedules threads.

We can explore this effect by substituting the following *SpinFunc()* function, replacing *TestFunc()* function in the *pthread_create()* call in the previous example:

```
void *SpinFunc(void *parm)      {
  int me;
  me =  (int) parm;
  printf("SpinFunc me=%d - sleeping %d seconds ...\n", me, me+1);
  sleep(me+1);
  printf("SpinFunc me=%d - wake globvar=%d...\n", me, globvar);
  globvar ++;
  printf("SpinFunc me=%d - spinning globvar=%d...\n", me, globvar);
  while(globvar < THREAD_COUNT ) ;
  printf("SpinFunc me=%d - done globvar=%d...\n", me, globvar);
  sleep(THREAD_COUNT+1);
}
```

If you look at the function, each thread entering this function prints a message and goes to sleep for 1, 2, and 3 seconds. Then the function increments *globvar* (initially set to 0 in main) and begins a while-loop, continuously checking the value of *globvar*. As time passes, the second and third threads should finish their *sleep()*, increment the value for *globvar*, and begin the while-loop. When the last thread reaches the loop, the value for *globvar* is 3 and all the threads exit the loop. However, this isn't what happens:

```
recs % create2 &
[1] 23921
recs %
Main - globvar=0
Main - creating i=0 tid=4 retval=0
Main - creating i=1 tid=5 retval=0
Main - creating i=2 tid=6 retval=0
Main thread - threads started globvar=0
Main - waiting for join 4
SpinFunc me=0 - sleeping 1 seconds ...
SpinFunc me=1 - sleeping 2 seconds ...
SpinFunc me=2 - sleeping 3 seconds ...
SpinFunc me=0 - wake globvar=0...
SpinFunc me=0 - spinning globvar=1...

recs % ps
   PID TTY       TIME CMD
 23921 pts/35   0:09 create2
recs % ps
   PID TTY       TIME CMD
```

---

* The *pthreads* library supports both user-space threads and operating-system threads, as we shall soon see. Another popular early threads package was called *cthreads*.

```
   23921 pts/35    1:16 create2
recs % kill -9 23921
[1]    Killed                  create2
recs %
```

We run the program in the background* and everything seems to run fine. All the threads go to sleep for 1, 2, and 3 seconds. The first thread wakes up and starts the loop waiting for *globvar* to be incremented by the other threads. Unfortunately, with user space threads, there is no automatic time sharing. Because we are in a CPU loop that never makes a system call, the second and third threads never get scheduled so they can complete their *sleep()* call. To fix this problem, we need to make the following change to the code:

```
while(globvar < THREAD_COUNT ) sleep(1) ;
```

With this sleep† call, Threads 2 and 3 get a chance to be "scheduled." They then finish their sleep calls, increment the *globvar* variable, and the program terminates properly.

You might ask the question, "Then what is the point of user space threads?" Well, when there is a high performance database server or Internet server, the multiple logical threads can overlap network I/O with database I/O and other background computations. This technique is not so useful when the threads all want to perform simultaneous CPU-intensive computations. To do this, you need threads that are created, managed, and scheduled by the operating system rather than a user library.

Operating System-Supported Multithreading

When the operating system supports multiple threads per process, you can begin to use these threads to do simultaneous computational activity. There is still no requirement that these applications be executed on a multiprocessor system. When an application that uses four operating system threads is executed on a single processor machine, the threads execute in a time-shared fashion. If there is no other load on the system, each thread gets 1/4 of the processor. While there are good reasons to have more threads than processors for noncompute applications, it's not a good idea to have more active threads than processors for compute-intensive applications because of thread-switching overhead. (For more detail on the effect of too many threads, see Appendix D, *How FORTRAN Manages Threads at Runtime.*)

---

* Because we know it will hang and ignore interrupts.

† Some thread libraries support a call to a *routine sched_yield()* that checks for runnable threads. If it finds a runnable thread, it runs the thread. If no thread is runnable, it returns immediately to the calling thread. This routine allows a thread that has the CPU to ensure that other threads make progress during CPU-intensive periods of its code.

If you are using the POSIX threads library, it is a simple modification to request that your threads be created as operating-system rather rather than user threads, as the following code shows:

```
#define _REENTRANT     /* basic 3-lines for threads */
#include <stdio.h>
#include <pthread.h>

#define THREAD_COUNT 2
void *SpinFunc(void *);
int globvar;                        /* A global variable */
int index[THREAD_COUNT];            /* Local zero-based thread index */
pthread_t thread_id[THREAD_COUNT];    /* POSIX Thread IDs */
pthread_attr_t attr;                /* Thread attributes NULL=use default */

main() {
  int i,retval;
  pthread_t tid;

  globvar = 0;
  pthread_attr_init(&attr);        /* Initialize attr with defaults */
  pthread_attr_setscope(&attr, PTHREAD_SCOPE_SYSTEM);
  printf("Main - globvar=%d\n",globvar);
  for(i=0;i<THREAD_COUNT;i++) {
    index[i] = i;
    retval = pthread_create(&tid,&attr,SpinFunc,(void *) index[i]);
    printf("Main - creating i=%d tid=%d retval=%d\n",i,tid,retval);
    thread_id[i] = tid;
  }
  printf("Main thread - threads started globvar=%d\n",globvar);
  for(i=0;i<THREAD_COUNT;i++) {
    printf("Main - waiting for join %d\n",thread_id[i]);
    retval = pthread_join( thread_id[i], NULL ) ;
    printf("Main - back from join %d retval=%d\n",i,retval);
  }
  printf("Main thread - threads completed globvar=%d\n",globvar);
}
```

The code executed by the master thread is modified slightly. We create an "attribute" data structure and set the PTHREAD_SCOPE_SYSTEM attribute to indicate that we would like our new threads to be created and scheduled by the operating system. We use the attribute information on the call to *pthread_create()*. None of the other code has been changed. The following is the execution output of this new program:

```
recs % create3
Main - globvar=0
Main - creating i=0 tid=4 retval=0
SpinFunc me=0 - sleeping 1 seconds ...
Main - creating i=1 tid=5 retval=0
Main thread - threads started globvar=0
Main - waiting for join 4
```

```
SpinFunc me=1 - sleeping 2 seconds ...
SpinFunc me=0 - wake globvar=0...
SpinFunc me=0 - spinning globvar=1...
SpinFunc me=1 - wake globvar=1...
SpinFunc me=1 - spinning globvar=2...
SpinFunc me=1 - done globvar=2...
SpinFunc me=0 - done globvar=2...
Main - back from join 0 retval=0
Main - waiting for join 5
Main - back from join 1 retval=0
Main thread - threads completed globvar=2
recs %
```

Now the program executes properly. When the first thread starts spinning, the operating system is context switching between all three threads. As the threads come out of their *sleep()*, they increment their shared variable, and when the final thread increments the shared variable, the other two threads instantly notice the new value (because of the cache coherency protocol) and finish the loop. If there are fewer than three CPUs, a thread may have to wait for a time-sharing context switch to occur before it notices the updated global variable.

With operating-system threads and multiple processors, a program can realistically break up a large computation between several independent threads and compute the solution more quickly. Of course this presupposes that the computation could be done in parallel in the first place.

Techniques for Multithreaded Programs

Given that we have multithreaded capabilities and multiprocessors, we must still convince the threads to work together to accomplish some overall goal. Often we need some ways to coordinate and cooperate between the threads. There are several important techniques that are used while the program is running with multiple threads, including:

- Fork-join (or create-join) programming
- Synchronization using a critical section with a lock, semaphore, or mutex
- Barriers

Each of these techniques has an overhead associated with it. Because these overheads are necessary to go parallel, we must make sure that we have sufficient work to make the benefit of parallel operation worth the cost.

Fork-Join Programming

This approach is the simplest method of coordinating your threads. As in the earlier examples in this chapter, a master thread sets up some global data structures that describe the tasks each thread is to perform and then use the *pthread_create()* function to activate the proper number of threads. Each thread checks the global data structure using its thread-id as an index to find its task. The thread then performs the task and completes. The master thread waits at a *pthread_join()* point, and when a thread has completed, it updates the global data structure and creates a new thread. These steps are repeated for each major iteration (such as a time-step) for the duration of the program:

```
for(ts=0;ts<10000;ts++) {   /* Time Step Loop */
    /* Setup tasks */
    for (ith=0;ith<NUM_THREADS;ith++) pthread_create(..,work_routine,..)
    for (ith=0;ith<NUM_THREADS;ith++) pthread_join(...)
}
work_routine() {
    /* Perform Task */
    return;
}
```

The shortcoming of this approach is the overhead cost associated with creating and destroying an operating system thread for a potentially very short task.

The other approach is to have the threads created at the beginning of the program and to have them communicate amongst themselves throughout the duration of the application. To do this, they use such techniques as critical sections or barriers.

Synchronization

Synchronization is needed when there is a particular operation to a shared variable that can only be performed by one processor at a time. For example, in previous *SpinFunc()* examples, consider the line:

```
globvar++;
```

In assembly language, this takes at least three instructions:

```
LOAD    R1,globvar
ADD     R1,1
STORE   R1,globvar
```

What if *globvar* contained 0, Thread 1 was running, and, at the precise moment it completed the LOAD into Register R1 and before it had completed the ADD or STORE instructions, the operating system interrupted the thread and switched to Thread 2? Thread 2 catches up and executes all three instructions using its registers: loading 0, adding 1 and storing the 1 back into *globvar*. Now Thread 2 goes to sleep and Thread 1 is restarted at the ADD instruction. Register R1 for Thread 1 contains the previously loaded value of 0; Thread 1 adds 1 and then stores 1 into *globvar*. What is wrong with this picture? We meant to use this code to count the number of threads that have passed this point. Two threads passed the point, but because of a bad case of bad timing, our variable indicates only that one thread passed. This is because the increment of a variable in memory is not *atomic*. That is, halfway through the increment, something else can happen.

Another way we can have a problem is on a multiprocessor when two processors execute these instructions simultaneously. They both do the LOAD, getting 0. Then they both add 1 and store 1 back to memory.* Which processor actually got the honor of storing *their* 1 back to memory is simply a race.

We must have some way of guaranteeing that only one thread can be in these three instructions at the same time. If one thread has started these instructions, all other threads must wait to enter until the first thread has exited. These areas are called *critical sections*. On single-CPU systems, there was a simple solution to critical sections: you could turn off interrupts for a few instructions and then turn them back on. This way you could guarantee that you would get all the way through before a timer or other interrupt occurred:

```
INTOFF                  // Turn off Interrupts
LOAD    R1,globvar
ADD     R1,1
STORE   R1,globvar
INTON                   // Turn on Interrupts
```

However, this technique does not work for longer critical sections or when there is more than one CPU. In these cases, you need a lock, a semaphore, or a mutex. Most thread libraries provide this type of routine. To use a mutex, we have to make some modifications to our example code:

```
    ...
pthread_mutex_t my_mutex;        /* MUTEX data structure */
    ...

main() {
    ...
    pthread_attr_init(&attr);     /* Initialize attr with defaults */
    pthread_mutex_init (&my_mutex, NULL);
    .... pthread_create( ... )
        ...
}
void *SpinFunc(void *parm)       {
    ...
    pthread_mutex_lock (&my_mutex);
    globvar ++;
```

---

* Boy, this is getting pretty picky. How often will either of these events really happen? Well, if it crashes your airline reservation system every 100,000 transactions or so, that would be way too often.

```
        pthread_mutex_unlock (&my_mutex);
        while(globvar < THREAD_COUNT ) ;
        printf("SpinFunc me=%d - done globvar=%d...\n", me, globvar);
        ...
    }
```

The mutex data structure must be declared in the shared area of the program. Before the threads are created, *pthread_mutex_init* must be called to initialize the mutex. Before *globvar* is incremented, we must lock the mutex and after we finish updating *globvar* (three instructions later), we unlock the mutex. With the code as shown above, there will never be more than one processor executing the *globvar++* line of code, and the code will never hang because an increment was missed. Semaphores and locks are used in a similar way.

Interestingly, when using user space threads, an attempt to lock an already locked mutex, semaphore, or lock can cause a thread context switch. This allows the thread that "owns" the lock a better chance to make progress toward the point where they will unlock the critical section. Also, the act of unlocking a mutex can cause the thread waiting for the mutex to be dispatched by the thread library.

Barriers

Barriers are different than critical sections. Sometimes in a multithreaded application, you need to have all threads arrive at a point before allowing any threads to execute beyond that point. An example of this is a *time-based simulation*. Each task processes its portion of the simulation but must wait until all of the threads have completed the current time step before any thread can begin the next time step. Typically threads are created, and then each thread executes a loop with one or more barriers in the loop. The rough pseudocode for this type of approach is as follows:

```
main() {
  for (ith=0;ith<NUM_THREADS;ith++) pthread_create(..,work_routine,..)
  for (ith=0;ith<NUM_THREADS;ith++) pthread_join(...) /* Wait a long time */
  exit()
}

work_routine() {

  for(ts=0;ts<10000;ts++) {  /* Time Step Loop */
        /* Compute total forces on particles */
    wait_barrier();
        /* Update particle positions based on the forces */
    wait_barrier();
  }
  return;
}
```

In a sense, our *SpinFunc()* function implements a barrier. It sets a variable initially to 0. Then as threads arrive, the variable is incremented in a critical section. Immediately after the critical section, the thread spins until the precise moment that all the threads are in the spin loop, at which time all threads exit the spin loop and continue on.

For a critical section, only one processor can be executing in the critical section at the same time. For a barrier, all processors must arrive at the barrier before any of the processors can leave.

A Real Example

In all of the above examples, we have focused on the mechanics of shared memory, thread creation, and thread termination. We have used the *sleep()* routine to slow things down sufficiently to see interactions between processes. But we want to go very fast, not just learn threading for threading's sake.

The example code below uses the multithreading techniques described in this chapter to speed up a sum of a large array. The *hpcwall* routine is from Chapter 6, *Timing and Profiling*.

This code allocates a four-million-element double-precision array and fills it with random numbers between 0 and 1. Then using one, two, three, and four threads, it sums up the elements in the array:

```
#define _REENTRANT     /* basic 3-lines for threads */
#include <stdio.h>
#include <stdlib.h>
#include <pthread.h>

#define MAX_THREAD 4
void *SumFunc(void *);
int ThreadCount;                    /* Threads on this try */
double GlobSum;                     /* A global variable */
int index[MAX_THREAD];              /* Local zero-based thread index */
pthread_t thread_id[MAX_THREAD];    /* POSIX Thread IDs */
pthread_attr_t attr;                /* Thread attributes NULL=use default */
pthread_mutex_t my_mutex;           /* MUTEX data structure */

#define MAX_SIZE 4000000
double array[MAX_SIZE];             /* What we are summing... */
void hpcwall(double *);

main() {
  int i,retval;
  pthread_t tid;
  double single,multi,begtime,endtime;

  /* Initialize things */
```

```
   for (i=0; i<MAX_SIZE; i++) array[i] = drand48();
   pthread_attr_init(&attr);        /* Initialize attr with defaults */
   pthread_mutex_init (&my_mutex, NULL);
   pthread_attr_setscope(&attr, PTHREAD_SCOPE_SYSTEM);

   /* Single threaded sum */
   GlobSum = 0;
   hpcwall(&begtime);
   for(i=0; i<MAX_SIZE;i++) GlobSum = GlobSum + array[i];
   hpcwall(&endtime);
   single = endtime - begtime;
   printf("Single sum=%lf time=%lf\n",GlobSum,single);

   /* Use different numbers of threads to accomplish the same thing */
   for(ThreadCount=2;ThreadCount<=MAX_THREAD; ThreadCount++) {
     printf("Threads=%d\n",ThreadCount);
     GlobSum = 0;
     hpcwall(&begtime);
     for(i=0;i<ThreadCount;i++) {
       index[i] = i;
       retval = pthread_create(&tid,&attr,SumFunc,(void *) index[i]);
       thread_id[i] = tid;
     }
     for(i=0;i<ThreadCount;i++) retval = pthread_join(thread_id[i],NULL);
     hpcwall(&endtime);
     multi = endtime - begtime;
     printf("Sum=%lf time=%lf\n",GlobSum,multi);
     printf("Efficiency = %lf\n",single/(multi*ThreadCount));
   } /* End of the ThreadCount loop */
}

void *SumFunc(void *parm)        {
  int i,me,chunk,start,end;
  double LocSum;

  /* Decide which iterations belong to me */
  me =  (int) parm;
  chunk = MAX_SIZE / ThreadCount;
  start = me * chunk;
  end = start + chunk;  /* C-Style - actual element + 1 */
  if ( me == (ThreadCount-1) ) end = MAX_SIZE;
  printf("SumFunc me=%d start=%d end=%d\n",me,start,end);

  /* Compute sum of our subset*/
  LocSum = 0;
  for(i=start;i<end;i++ ) LocSum = LocSum + array[i];

  /* Update the global sum and return to the waiting join */
  pthread_mutex_lock (&my_mutex);
  GlobSum = GlobSum + LocSum;
  pthread_mutex_unlock (&my_mutex);
}
```

First, the code performs the sum using a single thread using a for-loop. Then for each of the parallel sums, it creates the appropriate number of threads that call *SumFunc()*. Each thread starts in *SumFunc()* and initially chooses an area to operation in the shared array. The "strip" is chosen by dividing the overall array up evenly among the threads with the last thread getting a few extra if the division has a remainder.

Then, each thread independently performs the sum on its area. When a thread has finished its computation, it uses a mutex to update the global sum variable with its contribution to the global sum:

```
recs % addup
Single sum=7999998000000.000000 time=0.256624
Threads=2
SumFunc me=0 start=0 end=2000000
SumFunc me=1 start=2000000 end=4000000
Sum=7999998000000.000000 time=0.133530
Efficiency = 0.960923
Threads=3
SumFunc me=0 start=0 end=1333333
SumFunc me=1 start=1333333 end=2666666
SumFunc me=2 start=2666666 end=4000000
Sum=7999998000000.000000 time=0.091018
Efficiency = 0.939829
Threads=4
SumFunc me=0 start=0 end=1000000
SumFunc me=1 start=1000000 end=2000000
SumFunc me=2 start=2000000 end=3000000
SumFunc me=3 start=3000000 end=4000000
Sum=7999998000000.000000 time=0.107473
Efficiency = 0.596950
recs %
```

There are some interesting patterns. Before you interpret the patterns, you must know that this system is a three-processor Sun Enterprise 3000. Note that as we go from one to two threads, the time is reduced to one-half. That is a good result given how much it costs for that extra CPU. We characterize how well the additional resources have been used by computing an efficiency factor that should be 1.0. This is computed by multiplying the wall time by the number of threads. Then the time it takes on a single processor is divided by this number. If you are using the extra processors well, this evaluates to 1.0. If the extra processors are used pretty well, this would be about 0.9. If you had two threads, and the computation did not speed up at all, you would get 0.5.

At two and three threads, wall time is dropping, and the efficiency is well over 0.9. However, at four threads, the wall time increases, and our efficiency drops very dramatically. This is because we now have more threads than processors. Even though we have four threads that could execute, they must be time-sliced between three processors.* This is even worse that it might seem. As threads are switched, they move from processor to processor and their caches must also move from processor to processor, further slowing performance. This cache-thrashing effect is not too apparent in this example because the data structure is so large, most memory references are not to values previously in cache.

It's important to note that because of the nature of floating-point (see Chapter 4, *Floating-Point Numbers*), the parallel sum may not be the same as the serial sum. To perform a summation in parallel, you must be willing to tolerate these slight variations in your results.

Closing Notes

As they drop in price, multiprocessor systems are becoming far more common. These systems have many attractive features, including good price/performance, compatibility with workstations, large memories, high throughput, large shared memories, fast I/O, and many others. While these systems are strong in multiprogrammed server roles, they are also an affordable high performance computing resource for many organizations. Their cache-coherent shared-memory model allows multithreaded applications to be easily developed.

We have also examined some of the software paradigms that must be used to develop multithreaded applications. While you hopefully will never have to write C code with explicit threads like the examples in this chapter, it is nice to understand the fundamental operations at work on these multiprocessor systems. Using the FORTRAN language with an automatic parallelizing compiler, we have the advantage that these and many more details are left to the FORTRAN compiler and runtime library. At some point, especially on the most advanced architectures, you may have to explicitly program a multithreaded program using the types of techniques shown in this chapter.

One trend that has been predicted for some time is that we will begin to see multiple cache-coherent CPUs on a single chip once the ability to increase the clock rate on a single chip slows down. Imagine that your new $2000 workstation has four 1-GHz processors on a single chip. Sounds like a good time to learn how to write multithreaded programs!

---

* It is important to match the number of runnable threads to the available resources. In compute code, when there are more threads than available processors, the threads compete among themselves, causing unnecessary overhead and reducing the efficiency of your computation. See Appendix D for more details.

Exercises

1. Experiment with the fork code in this chapter. Run the program multiple times and see how the order of the messages changes. Explain the results.

2. Experiment with the create1 and create3 codes in this chapter. Remove all of the *sleep()* calls. Execute the programs several times on single and multiprocessor systems. Can you explain why the output changes from run to run in some situations and doesn't change in others?

3. Experiment with the parallel sum code in this chapter. In the *SumFunc()* routine, change the for-loop to:

   ```
   for(i=start;i<end;i++ ) GlobSum = GlobSum + array[i];
   ```

   Remove the three lines at the end that get the mutex and update the Glob-Sum. Execute the code. Explain the difference in values that you see for GlobSum. Are the patterns different on a single processor and a multiprocessor? Explain the performance impact on a single processor and a multiprocessor.

4. Explain how the following code segment could cause deadlock—two or more processes waiting for a resource that can't be relinquished:

   ```
        . . .
   call lock    (lword1)
   call lock    (lword2)
        . . .
   call unlock (lword1)
   call unlock (lword2)
        .

        .

        .
   call lock    (lword2)
   call lock    (lword1)
        . . .
   call unlock (lword2)
   call unlock (lword1)
        . . .
   ```

5. If you were to code the functionality of a spin-lock in C, it might look like this:

   ```
   while (!lockword);
   lockword = !lockword;
   ```

   As you know from the first sections of the book, the same statements would be compiled into explicit loads and stores, a comparison, and a branch. There's a danger that two processes could each load lockword, find it unset, and continue on as if they owned the lock (we have a race condition). This suggests that spin-locks are implemented differently—that they're not merely the two lines of C above. How do you suppose they are implemented?

11

Programming Shared-Memory Multiprocessors

In Chapter 10, *Shared-Memory Multiprocessors*, we examined the hardware used to implement shared-memory parallel processors and the software environment for a programmer who is using threads explicitly. In this chapter, we view these processors from a simpler vantage point. When programming these systems in FORTRAN, you have the advantage of the compiler's support of these systems. At the top end of ease of use, we can simply add a flag or two on the compilation of our well-written code, set an environment variable, and voilá, we are executing in parallel. If you want some more control, you can add directives to particular loops where you know better than the compiler how the loop should be executed.* First we examine how well-written loops can benefit from automatic parallelism. Then we will look at the types of directives you can add to your program to assist the compiler in generating parallel code. While this chapter refers to running your code in parallel, most of the techniques apply to the vector-processor supercomputers as well.

Automatic Parallelization

So far in the book, we've covered the tough things you need to know to do parallel processing. At this point, assuming that your loops are clean, they use unit stride, and the iterations can all be done in parallel, all you have to do is turn on a

---

* If you have skipped all the other chapters in the book and jumped to this one, don't be surprised if some of the terminology is unfamiliar. While all those chapters seemed to contain endless boring detail, they did contain some basic terminology. So those of us who read all those chapters have some common terminology needed for this chapter. If you don't go back and read all the chapters, don't complain about the big words we keep using in this chapter!

compiler flag and buy a good parallel processor. For example, look at the following code:

```
PARAMETER(NITER=300,N=1000000)
REAL*8 A(N),X(N),B(N),C
DO ITIME=1,NITER
  DO I=1,N
      A(I) = X(I) + B(I) * C
  ENDDO
  CALL WHATEVER(A,X,B,C)
ENDDO
```

Here we have an iterative code that satisfies all the criteria for a good parallel loop. On a good parallel processor with a modern compiler, you are two flags away from executing in parallel. On Sun Solaris systems, the **autopar** flag turns on the automatic parallelization, and the **loopinfo** flag causes the compiler to describe the particular optimization performed for each loop. To compile this code under Solaris, you simply add these flags to your f77 call:

```
E6000: f77 -O3 -autopar -loopinfo -o daxpy daxpy.f
daxpy.f:
"daxpy.f", line 6: not parallelized, call may be unsafe
"daxpy.f", line 8: PARALLELIZED
E6000: /bin/time daxpy

real        30.9
user        30.7
sys          0.1
E6000:
```

If you simply run the code, it's executed using one thread. However, the code is enabled for parallel processing for those loops that can be executed in parallel. To execute the code in parallel, you need to set the UNIX environment to the number of parallel threads you wish to use to execute the code. On Solaris, this is done using the **PARALLEL** variable:

```
E6000: setenv PARALLEL 1
E6000: /bin/time daxpy

real        30.9
user        30.7
sys          0.1
E6000: setenv PARALLEL 2
E6000: /bin/time daxpy

real        15.6
user        31.0
sys          0.2
E6000: setenv PARALLEL 4
E6000: /bin/time daxpy
```

```
real      8.2
user      32.0
sys        0.5
E6000: setenv PARALLEL 8
E6000: /bin/time daxpy

real      4.3
user      33.0
sys        0.8
```

Speedup is the term used to capture how much faster the job runs using N processors compared to the performance on one processor. It is computed by dividing the single processor time by the multiprocessor time for each number of processors. Figure 11-1 shows the wall time and speedup for this application.

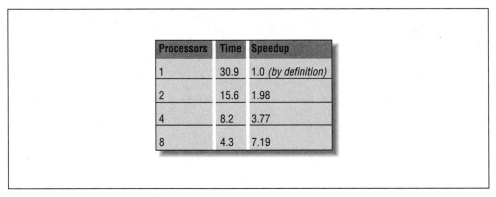

Processors	Time	Speedup
1	30.9	1.0 *(by definition)*
2	15.6	1.98
4	8.2	3.77
8	4.3	7.19

Figure 11-1: Improving performance by adding processors

Figure 11-2 shows this information graphically, plotting speedup versus the number of processors.

Note that for a while we get nearly perfect speedup, but we begin to see a measurable drop in speedup at four and eight processors. There are several causes for this. In all parallel applications, there is some portion of the code that can't run in parallel. During those nonparallel times, the other processors are waiting for work and aren't contributing to efficiency. This nonparallel code begins to affect the overall performance as more processors are added to the application.

So you say, "this is more like it!" and immediately try to run with 12 and 16 threads. Now, we see the graph in Figure 11-4 and the data from Figure 11-3.

What has happened here? Things were going so well, and then they slowed down. We are running this program on a 16-processor system, and there are eight other active threads, as indicated below:

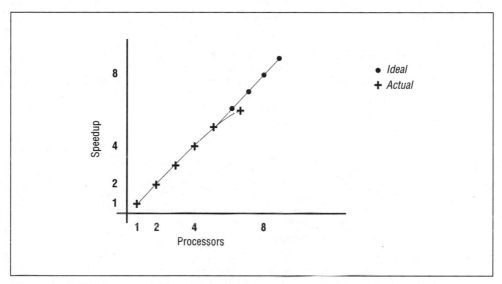

Figure 11-2: Ideal and actual performance improvement

Processors	Time	Speedup
1	30.9	1.0 *(by definition)*
2	15.6	1.98
4	8.2	3.77
8	4.3	7.19
12	14.2	2.18
16	57.0	0.57

Figure 11-3: Increasing the number of threads

```
E6000:uptime
  4:00pm  up 19 day(s), 37 min(s), 5 users, load average: 8.00, 8.05, 8.14
E6000:
```

Once we pass eight threads, there are no available processors for our threads. So the threads must be time-shared between the processors, significantly slowing the overall operation. By the end, we are executing 16 threads on eight processors,

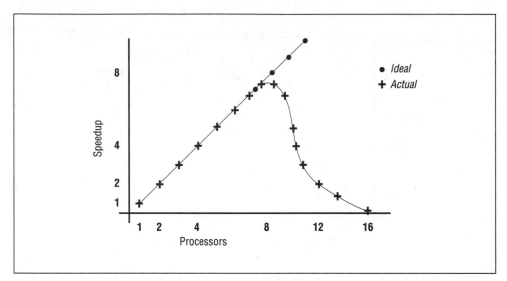

Figure 11-4: Diminishing returns

and our performance is slower than with one thread. So it is important that you don't create too many threads in these types of applications.*

Compiler Considerations

Improving performance by turning on automatic parallelization is an example of the "smarter compiler" we discussed in earlier chapters. The addition of a single compiler flag has triggered a great deal of analysis on the part of the compiler including:

- Which loops can execute in parallel, producing the exact same results as the sequential executions of the loops? This is done by checking for dependencies that span iterations. A loop with no inter-iteration dependencies is called a *DOALL* loop.

- Which loops are worth executing in parallel? Generally very short loops gain no benefit and may execute more slowly when executing in parallel. As with loop unrolling, parallelism always has a cost. It is best used when the benefit far outweighs the cost.

- In a loop nest, which loop is the best candidate to be parallelized? Generally the best performance occurs when we parallelize the outermost loop of a loop

---

* In Appendix D, *How FORTRAN Manages Threads at Runtime*, when we look at how the FORTRAN runtime library operates on these systems it will be much clearer why having more threads than available processors has such a negative impact on performance.

nest. This way the overhead associated with beginning a parallel loop is amortized over a longer parallel loop duration.

- Can and should the loop nest be interchanged? The compiler may detect that the loops in a nest can be done in any order. One order may work very well for parallel code while giving poor memory performance. Another order may give unit stride but perform poorly with multiple threads. The compiler must analyze the cost/benefit of each approach and make the best choice.

- How do we break up the iterations among the threads executing a parallel loop? Are the iterations short with uniform duration, or long with wide variation of execution time? We will see that there are a number of different ways to accomplish this. When the programmer has given no guidance, the compiler must make an educated guess.

Even though it seems complicated, the compiler can do a surprisingly good job on a wide variety of codes. It is not magic, however. For example, in the following code we have a loop-carried flow dependency:

```
PROGRAM DEP
PARAMETER(NITER=300,N=1000000)
REAL*4 A(N)

DO ITIME=1,NITER
  CALL WHATEVER(A)
  DO I=2,N
     A(I) = A(I-1) + A(I) * C
  ENDDO
ENDDO
END
```

When we compile the code, the compiler gives us the following message:

```
E6000: f77 -O3 -autopar -loopinfo -o dep dep.f
dep.f:
"dep.f", line 6: not parallelized, call may be unsafe
"dep.f", line 8: not parallelized, unsafe dependence (a)
E6000:
```

The compiler throws its hands up in despair, and lets you know that the loop at Line 8 had an unsafe dependence, and so it won't automatically parallelize the loop. When the code is executed below, adding a thread does not affect the execution performance:

```
E6000:setenv PARALLEL 1
E6000:/bin/time dep

real        18.1
user        18.1
sys          0.0
E6000:setenv PARALLEL 2
```

```
E6000:/bin/time dep

real        18.3
user        18.2
sys          0.0
E6000:
```

A typical application has many loops. Not all the loops are executed in parallel. It's a good idea to run a profile of your application, and in the routines that use most of the CPU time, check to find out which loops are not being parallelized. Within a loop nest, the compiler generally chooses only one loop to execute in parallel.

Other Compiler Flags

In addition to the flags shown above, you may have other compiler flags available to you that apply across the entire program:

- You may have a compiler flag to enable the automatic parallelization of *reduction* operations. Because the order of additions can affect the final value when computing a sum of floating-point numbers, the compiler needs permission to parallelize summation loops.

- Flags that relax the compliance with IEEE floating-point rules may also give the compiler more flexibility when trying to parallelize a loop. However, you must be sure that it's not causing accuracy problems in other areas of your code.

- Often a compiler has a flag called "unsafe optimization" or "assume no dependencies." While this flag may indeed enhance the performance of an application with loops that have dependencies, it almost certainly produces incorrect results.

There is some value in experimenting with a compiler to see the particular combination that will yield good performance across a variety of applications. Then that set of compiler options can be used as a starting point when you encounter a new application.

Assisting the Compiler

If it were all that simple, you wouldn't need this book. While compilers are extremely clever, there is still a lot of ways to improve the performance of your code without sacrificing its portability. Instead of converting the whole program to C and using a thread library, you can assist the compiler by adding compiler directives to our source code.

Compiler directives are typically inserted in the form of stylized FORTRAN comments. This is done so that a nonparallelizing compiler can ignore them and just look at the FORTRAN code, *sans* comments. This allows to you tune your code for parallel architectures without letting it run badly on a wide range of single-processor systems.

There are two categories of parallel-processing comments:

- Assertions

- Manual parallelization directives

Assertions tell the compiler certain things that you as the programmer know about the code that it might not guess by looking at the code. Through the assertions, you are attempting to assuage the compiler's doubts about whether or not the loop is eligible for parallelization. When you use directives, you are taking full responsibility for the correct execution of the program. You are telling the compiler what to parallelize and how to do it. You take full responsibility for the output of the program. If the program produces meaningless results, you have no one to blame but yourself.

Assertions

In a previous example, we compiled a program and received the following output:

```
E6000: f77 -O3 -autopar -loopinfo -o dep dep.f
dep.f:
"dep.f", line 6: not parallelized, call may be unsafe
"dep.f", line 8: not parallelized, unsafe dependence (a)
E6000:
```

An uneducated programmer who has not read this book (or has not looked at the code) might exclaim, "What unsafe dependence, I never put one of those in my code!" and quickly add a *no dependencies* assertion. This is the essence of an assertion. Instead of telling the compiler to simply parallelize the loop, the programmer is telling the compiler that its conclusion that there is a dependence is incorrect. Usually the net result is that the compiler does indeed parallelize the loop.

We will briefly review the types of assertions that are typically supported by these compilers. An assertion is generally added to the code using a stylized comment.

No dependencies

A *no dependencies* or *ignore dependencies* directive tells the compiler that references don't overlap. That is, it tells the compiler to generate code that may execute incorrectly if there *are* dependencies. You're saying, "I know what I'm doing;

it's OK to overlap references." A no dependencies directive might help the following loop:

```
DO I=1,N
  A(I) = A(I+K) * B(I)
ENDDO
```

If you know that k is greater than −1 or less than −n, you can get the compiler to parallelize the loop:

```
C$ASSERT NO_DEPENDENCIES
       DO I=1,N
         A(I) = A(I+K) * B(I)
       ENDDO
```

Of course, blindly telling the compiler that there are no dependencies is a prescription for disaster. If k equals −1, the example above becomes a recursive loop.

Relations

You will often see loops that contain some potential dependencies, making them bad candidates for a no dependencies directive. However, you may be able to supply some local facts about certain variables. This allows partial parallelization without compromising the results. In the code below, there are two potential dependencies because of subscripts involving k and j:

```
for (i=0; i<n; i++) {
    a[i] = a[i+k] * b[i];
    c[i] = c[i+j] * b[i];
}
```

Perhaps we know that there are no conflicts with references to a[i] and a[i+k]. But maybe we aren't so sure about c[i] and c[i+j]. Therefore, we can't say in general that there are no dependencies. However, we may be able to say something explicit about k (like "k is always greater than −1"), leaving j out of it. This information about the relationship of one expression to another is called a *relation assertion*. Applying a relation assertion allows the compiler to apply its optimization to the first statement in the loop, giving us partial parallelization.*

Again, if you supply inaccurate testimony that leads the compiler to make unsafe optimizations, your answer may be wrong.

---

* Notice that, if you were tuning by hand, you could split this loop into two: one parallelizable and one not.

Permutations

As we have seen elsewhere, when elements of an array are indirectly addressed, you have to worry about whether or not some of the subscripts may be repeated. In the code below, are the values of K(I) all unique? Or are there duplicates?

```
DO I=1,N
   A(K(I)) = A(K(I)) + B(I) * C
END DO
```

If you know there are no duplicates in K (i.e., that A(K(I)) is a permutation), you can inform the compiler so that iterations can execute in parallel. You supply the information using a *permutation assertion*.

No equivalences

Equivalenced arrays in FORTRAN programs provide another challenge for the compiler. If any elements of two equivalenced arrays appear in the same loop, most compilers assume that references could point to the same memory storage location and optimize very conservatively. This may be true even if it is abundantly apparent to you that there is no overlap whatsoever.

You inform the compiler that references to equivalenced arrays are safe with a *no equivalences* assertion. Of course, if you don't use equivalences, this assertion has no effect.

Trip count

Each loop can be characterized by an average number of iterations. Some loops are never executed or go around just a few times. Others may go around hundreds of times:

```
C$ASSERT TRIPCOUNT>100
      DO I=L,N
         A(I) = B(I) + C(I)
      END DO
```

Your compiler is going to look at every loop as a candidate for unrolling or parallelization. It's working in the dark, however, because it can't tell which loops are important and tries to optimize them all. This can lead to the surprising experience of seeing your runtime go up after optimization!

A *trip count assertion* provides a clue to the compiler that helps it decide how much to unroll a loop or when to parallelize a loop.* Loops that aren't important can be identified with low or zero trip counts. Important loops have high trip counts.

---

* The assertion is made either by hand or from a profiler.

Inline substitution

If your compiler supports procedure inlining, you can use directives and command-line switches to specify how many nested levels of procedures you would like to inline, thresholds for procedure size, etc. The vendor will have chosen reasonable defaults.

Assertions also let you choose subroutines that you think are good candidates for inlining. However, subject to its thresholds, the compiler may reject your choices. Inlining could expand the code so much that increased memory activity would claim back gains made by eliminating the procedure call. At higher optimization levels, the compiler is often capable of making its own choices for inlining candidates, provided it can find the source code for the routine under consideration.

Some compilers support a feature called *interprocedural analysis*. When this is done, the compiler looks across routine boundaries for its data flow analysis. It can perform significant optimizations across routine boundaries, including automatic inlining, constant propagation, and others.

No side effects

Without interprocedural analysis, when looking at a loop, if there is a subroutine call in the middle of the loop, the compiler has to treat the subroutine as if it will have the worst possible side effects. Also, it has to assume that there are dependencies that prevent the routine from executing simultaneously in two different threads.

Many routines (especially functions) don't have any side effects and can execute quite nicely in separate threads because each thread has its own private call stack and local variables. If the routine is meaty, there will be a great deal of benefit in executing it in parallel.

Your computer may allow you to add a directive that tells you if successive subroutine calls are independent:

```
C$ASSERT NO_SIDE_EFFECTS
      DO I=1,N
        CALL BIGSTUFF (A,B,C,I,J,K)
      END DO
```

Even if the compiler has all the source code, use of common variables or equivalences may mask call independence.

Manual Parallelism

At some point, you get tired of giving the compiler advice and hoping that it will reach the conclusion to parallelize your loop. At that point you move into the realm of manual parallelism. Luckily the programming model provided in FORTRAN insulates you from much of the details of exactly how multiple threads are managed at runtime. You generally control explicit parallelism by adding specially formatted comment lines to your source code. There are a wide variety of formats of these directives. In this section, we use the syntax that is part of the OpenMP (see *www.openmp.org*) standard. You generally find similar capabilities in each of the vendor compilers. The precise syntax varies slightly from vendor to vendor. (That alone is a good reason to have a standard.)

The basic programming model is that you are executing a section of code with either a single thread or multiple threads. The programmer adds a directive to summon additional threads at various points in the code. The most basic construct is called the *parallel region*.

Parallel regions

In a parallel region, the threads simply appear between two statements of straight-line code. A very trivial example might be the following using the OpenMP directive syntax:

```
        PROGRAM ONE
        EXTERNAL OMP_GET_THREAD_NUM, OMP_GET_MAX_THREADS
        INTEGER  OMP_GET_THREAD_NUM, OMP_GET_MAX_THREADS
        IGLOB = OMP_GET_MAX_THREADS()
        PRINT *,'Hello There'
C$OMP PARALLEL PRIVATE(IAM), SHARED(IGLOB)
        IAM = OMP_GET_THREAD_NUM()
        PRINT *, 'I am ', IAM, ' of ', IGLOB
C$OMP END PARALLEL
        PRINT *,'All Done'
        END
```

The C$OMP is the sentinel that indicates that this is a directive and not just another comment. The output of the program when run looks as follows:

```
% setenv OMP_NUM_THREADS 4
% a.out
Hello There
I am 0 of 4
I am 3 of 4
I am 1 of 4
I am 2 of 4
All Done
%
```

Execution begins with a single thread. As the program encounters the PARALLEL directive, the other threads are activated to join the computation. So in a sense, as execution passes the first directive, one thread becomes four. Four threads execute the two statements between the directives. As the threads are executing independently, the order in which the print statements are displayed is somewhat random. The threads wait at the END PARALLEL directive until all threads have arrived. Once all threads have completed the parallel region, a single thread continues executing the remainder of the program.

In Figure 11-5, the PRIVATE(IAM) indicates that the IAM variable is not shared across all the threads but instead, each thread has its own private version of the variable. The IGLOB variable is shared across all the threads. Any modification of IGLOB appears in all the other threads instantly, within the limitations of the cache coherency.

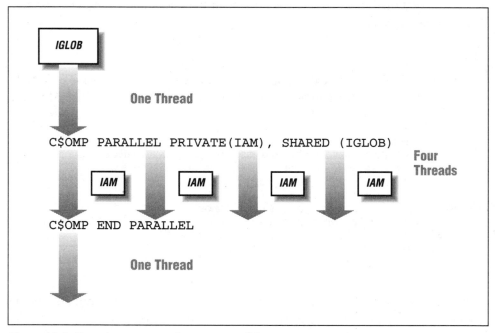

Figure 11-5: Data interactions during a parallel region

During the parallel region, the programmer typically divides the work among the threads. This pattern of going from single-threaded to multithreaded execution may be repeated many times throughout the execution of an application.

Because input and output are generally not thread-safe, to be completely correct, we should indicate that the print statement in the parallel section is only to be executed on one processor at any one time. We use a directive to indicate that this section of code is a critical section. A lock or other synchronization mechanism ensures that no more than one processor is executing the statements in the critical section at any one time:

```
C$OMP CRITICAL
        PRINT *, 'I am ', IAM, ' of ', IGLOB
C$OMP END CRITICAL
```

Parallel loops

Quite often the areas of the code that are most valuable to execute in parallel are loops. Consider the following loop:

```
DO I=1,1000000
  TMP1 = ( A(I) ** 2 ) + ( B(I) ** 2 )
  TMP2 = SQRT(TMP1)
  B(I) = TMP2
ENDDO
```

To manually parallelize this loop, we insert a directive at the beginning of the loop:

```
C$OMP PARALLEL DO
        DO I=1,1000000
          TMP1 = ( A(I) ** 2 ) + ( B(I) ** 2 )
          TMP2 = SQRT(TMP1)
          B(I) = TMP2
        ENDDO
C$OMP END PARALLEL DO
```

When this statement is encountered at runtime, the single thread again summons the other threads to join the computation. However, before the threads can start working on the loop, there are a few details that must be handled. The **PARALLEL DO** directive accepts the data classification and scoping clauses as in the parallel section directive earlier. We must indicate which variables are shared across all threads and which variables have a separate copy in each thread. It would be a disaster to have **TMP1** and **TMP2** shared across threads. As one thread takes the square root of **TMP1**, another thread would be resetting the contents of **TMP1**. **A(I)** and **B(I)** come from outside the loop, so they must be shared. We need to augment the directive as follows:

```
C$OMP PARALLEL DO SHARED(A,B) PRIVATE(I,TMP1,TMP2)
        DO I=1,1000000
          TMP1 = ( A(I) ** 2 ) + ( B(I) ** 2 )
          TMP2 = SQRT(TMP1)
          B(I) = TMP2
        ENDDO
C$OMP END PARALLEL DO
```

The iteration variable I also must be a thread-private variable. As the different threads increment their way through their particular subset of the arrays, they don't want to be modifying a global value for I.

There are a number of other options as to how data will be operated on across the threads. This summarizes some of the other data semantics available:

Firstprivate

> These are thread-private variables that take an initial value from the global variable of the same name immediately before the loop begins executing.

Lastprivate

> These are thread-private variables except that the thread that executes the last iteration of the loop copies its value back into the global variable of the same name.

Reduction

> This indicates that a variable participates in a reduction operation that can be safely done in parallel. This is done by forming a partial reduction using a local variable in each thread and then combining the partial results at the end of the loop.

Each vendor may have different terms to indicate these data semantics, but most support all of these common semantics. Figure 11-6 shows how the different types of data semantics operate.

Now that we have the data environment set up for the loop, the only remaining problem that must be solved is which threads will perform which iterations. It turns out that this is not a trivial task, and a wrong choice can have a significant negative impact on our overall performance.

Iteration scheduling

There are two basic techniques (along with a few variations) for dividing the iterations in a loop between threads. We can look at two extreme examples to get an idea of how this works:

```
C VECTOR ADD
      DO IPROB=1,10000
         A(IPROB) = B(IPROB) + C(IPROB)
      ENDDO

C PARTICLE TRACKING
      DO IPROB=1,10000
         RANVAL = RAND(IPROB)
         CALL ITERATE_ENERGY(RANVAL)
      ENDDO
```

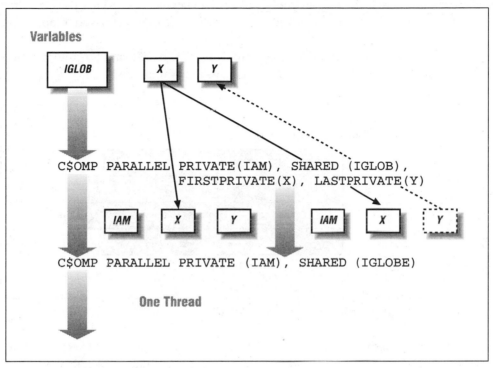

Figure 11-6: Variables during a parallel region

In both loops, all the computations are independent, so if there were 10,000 processors, each processor could execute a single iteration. In the vector-add example, each iteration would be relatively short, and the execution time would be relatively constant from iteration to iteration. In the particle tracking example, each iteration chooses a random number for an initial particle position and iterates to find the minimum energy. Each iteration takes a relatively long time to complete, and there will be a wide variation of completion times from iteration to iteration.

These two examples are effectively the ends of a continuous spectrum of the iteration scheduling challenges facing the FORTRAN parallel runtime environment:

Static
> At the beginning of a parallel loop, each thread takes a fixed continuous portion of iterations of the loop based on the number of threads executing the loop.

Dynamic
> With dynamic scheduling, each thread processes a chunk of data and when it has completed processing, a new chunk is processed. The chunk size can be varied by the programmer, but is fixed for the duration of the loop.

These two example loops can show how these iteration scheduling approaches might operate when executing with four threads. In the vector-add loop, static scheduling would distribute iterations 1–2500 to Thread 0, 2501–5000 to Thread 1, 5001–7500 to Thread 2, and 7501–10000 to Thread 3. In Figure 11-7, the mapping of iterations to threads is shown for the static scheduling option.

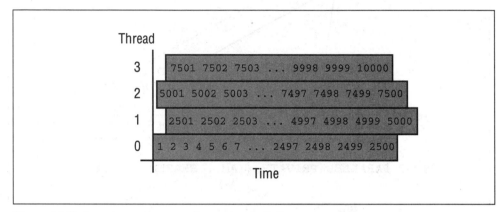

Figure 11-7: Iteration assignment for static scheduling

Since the loop body (a single statement) is short with a consistent execution time, static scheduling should result in roughly the same amount of overall work (and time if you assume a dedicated CPU for each thread) assigned to each thread per loop execution.

An advantage of static scheduling may occur if the entire loop is executed repeatedly. If the same iterations are assigned to the same threads that happen to be running on the same processors, the cache might actually contain the values for A, B, and C from the previous loop execution.* The runtime pseudo-code for static scheduling in the first loop might look as follows:

```
C VECTOR ADD - Static Scheduled
    ISTART = (THREAD_NUMBER * 2500 ) + 1
    IEND = ISTART + 2499
    DO ILOCAL = ISTART,IEND
      A(ILOCAL) = B(ILOCAL) + C(ILOCAL)
    ENDDO
```

It's not always a good strategy to use the static approach of giving a fixed number of iterations to each thread. If this is used in the second loop example, long and varying iteration times would result in poor load balancing. A better approach is to

---

* The operating system and runtime library actually go to some lengths to try to make this happen. This is another reason not to have more threads than available processors, which causes unnecessary context switching.

have each processor simply get the next value for IPROB each time at the top of the loop.

That approach is called *dynamic scheduling*, and it can adapt to widely varying iteration times. In Figure 11-8, the mapping of iterations to processors using dynamic scheduling is shown. As soon as a processor finishes one iteration, it processes the next available iteration in order.

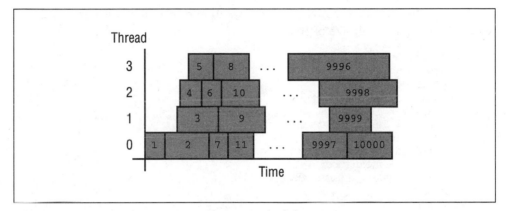

Figure 11-8: Iteration assignment in dynamic scheduling

If a loop is executed repeatedly, the assignment of iterations to threads may vary due to subtle timing issues that affect threads. The pseudo-code for the dynamic scheduled loop at runtime is as follows:

```
C PARTICLE TRACKING - Dynamic Scheduled
      IPROB = 0
      WHILE (IPROB <= 10000 )
        BEGIN_CRITICAL_SECTION
          IPROB = IPROB + 1
          ILOCAL = IPROB
        END_CRITICAL_SECTION
        RANVAL - RAND(ILOCAL)
        CALL ITERATE_ENERGY(RANVAL)
      ENDWHILE
```

ILOCAL is used so that each thread knows which iteration is currently processing. The IPROB value is altered by the next thread executing the critical section.

While the dynamic iteration scheduling approach works well for this particular loop, there is a significant negative performance impact if the programmer were to use the wrong approach for a loop. For example, if the dynamic approach were used for the vector-add loop, the time to process the critical section to determine which iteration to process may be larger than the time to actually process the iteration. Furthermore, any cache affinity of the data would be effectively lost because of the virtually random assignment of iterations to processors.

In between these two approaches are a wide variety of techniques that operate on a chunk of iterations. In some techniques the chunk size is fixed, and in others it varies during the execution of the loop. In this approach, a chunk of iterations are grabbed each time the critical section is executed. This reduces the scheduling overhead, but can have problems in producing a balanced execution time for each processor. The runtime is modified as follows to perform the particle tracking loop example using a chunk size of 100:

```
IPROB = 1
CHUNKSIZE = 100
WHILE (IPROB <= 10000 )
  BEGIN_CRITICAL_SECTION
    ISTART = IPROB
    IPROB = IPROB + CHUNKSIZE
  END_CRITICAL_SECTION
  DO ILOCAL = ISTART,ISTART+CHUNKSIZE-1
    RANVAL = RAND(ILOCAL)
    CALL ITERATE_ENERGY(RANVAL)
  ENDDO
ENDWHILE
```

The choice of chunk size is a compromise between overhead and termination imbalance. Typically the programmer must get involved through directives in order to control chunk size.

Part of the challenge of iteration distribution is to balance the cost (or existence) of the critical section against the amount of work done per invocation of the critical section. In the ideal world, the critical section would be free, and all scheduling would be done dynamically. Parallel/vector supercomputers with hardware assistance for load balancing can nearly achieve the ideal using dynamic approaches with relatively small chunk size.

Because the choice of loop iteration approach is so important, the compiler relies on directives from the programmer to specify which approach to use. The following example shows how we can request the proper iteration scheduling for our loops:

```
C VECTOR ADD
C$OMP PARALLEL DO PRIVATE(IPROB) SHARED(A,B,C) SCHEDULE(STATIC)
      DO IPROB=1,10000
          A(IPROB) = B(IPROB) + C(IPROB)
      ENDDO
C$OMP END PARALLEL DO
C PARTICLE TRACKING
C$OMP PARALLEL DO PRIVATE(IPROB,RANVAL) SCHEDULE(DYNAMIC)
      DO IPROB=1,10000
```

```
        RANVAL = RAND(IPROB)
        CALL ITERATE_ENERGY(RANVAL)
      ENDDO
C$OMP END PARALLEL DO
```

Closing Notes

Using data flow analysis and other techniques, modern compilers can peer through the clutter that we programmers innocently put into our code and see the patterns of the actual computations. In the field of high performance computing, having great parallel hardware and a lousy automatic parallelizing compiler generally results in no sales. Too many of the benchmark rules allow only a few compiler options to be set.

Physicists and chemists are interested in physics and chemistry, not computer science. If it takes 1 hour to execute a chemistry code without modifications and after six weeks of modifications the same code executes in 20 minutes, which is better? Well from a chemist's point of view, one took an hour, and the other took 1008 hours and 20 minutes, so the answer is obvious.* Although if the program were going to be executed thousands of times, the tuning might be a win for the programmer. The answer is even more obvious if it again takes six weeks to tune the program every time you make a modification to the program.

In some ways, assertions have become less popular than directives. This is due to two factors: (1) compilers are getting better at detecting parallelism even if they have to rewrite some code to do so, and (2) there are two kinds of programmers: those who know exactly how to parallelize their codes and those who turn on the "safe" auto-parallelize flags on their codes. Assertions fall in the middle ground, somewhere between where the programmer does not want to control all the details but kind of feels that the loop can be parallelized.

You can get online documentation of the OpenMP syntax used in these examples at *www.openmp.org*.

Exercises

1. Take a static, highly parallel program with a relative large inner loop. Compile the application for parallel execution. Execute the application increasing the threads. Examine the behavior when the number of threads exceed the avail-

---

* On the other hand, if the person is a computer scientist, improving the performance might result in anything from a poster session at a conference to a journal article! This makes for lots of intra-departmental masters degree projects.

able processors. See if different iteration scheduling approaches make a differ-ence.

2. Take the following loop and execute with several different iteration scheduling choices. For chunk-based scheduling, use a large chunk size, perhaps 100,000. See if any approach performs better than static scheduling:

```
DO I=1,4000000
  A(I) = B(I) * 2.34
ENDDO
```

3. Execute the following loop for a range of values for N from 1 to 16 million:

```
DO I=1,N
  A(I) = B(I) * 2.34
ENDDO
```

Run the loop in a single processor. Then force the loop to run in parallel. At what point do you get better performance on multiple processors? Do the number of threads affect your observations?

4. Use an explicit parallelization directive to execute the following loop in paral-lel with a chunk size of 1:

```
        J = 0
C$OMP PARALLEL DO PRIVATE(I) SHARED(J) SCHEDULE(DYNAMIC)
        DO I=1,1000000
          J = J + 1
        ENDDO
        PRINT *, J
C$OMP END PARALLEL DO
```

Execute the loop with a varying number of threads, including one. Also com-pile and execute the code in serial. Compare the output and execution times. What do the results tell you about cache coherency? About the cost of moving data from one cache to another, and about critical section costs?

IV

Scalable
Parallel Processing

12

Large-Scale Parallel Computing

The parallel-processing systems that use high performance RISC processors and a uniform shared-memory model are relatively easy to program. These are the most common high performance computers encountered by programmers. Because of the bus bandwidth or the cost of a large crossbar, these systems are generally limited to somewhere between 8–64 processors.

There are many applications whose performance can be improved by using more than one processor. Often the people interested in these applications can afford to spend significant resources on these systems. Often these problems are some type of simulation. Simulations of molecules, weather systems, economies, or fluid flow all have a parallel quality to them, like the systems they represent. Atoms don't take turns interacting, as in a computer program running on a serial computer. They all interact with one another, all at the same time.

In this chapter, we include the following topics:

- A discussion of our ability to take advantage of an ever-increasing number of processors

- A summary of interconnection technologies

- A taxonomy of parallel architectures

- A survey of existing scalable architectures

The field of scalable computing, though several decades old, is still struggling to reach maturity. Questions about how people should express their models haven't been settled. Nor is there any kind of agreement on what architectures are best. So in a sense, this chapter is less a statement of the way things are and more a tour of the battlefield. In this chapter, we focus on the theoretical and technical details of these systems. In the next chapter, we examine the programming environments that can be used on these systems.

Amdahl's Law

One question that you should ask at this point is, "How far can we go?" The answer to the question depends on the application. Gene Amdahl, architect of the IBM 360 computers, developed what is now called Amdahl's Law to characterize how well an application can make use of scalable parallel processors.

Whether running on a parallel computer or not, nearly every program has a mixture of parts that are serial and parts that are parallel. An engineering analysis is a good example. The setup portion may be very serial: data is read in, a matrix is populated. If there is little opportunity to overlap execution, the setup portion can't benefit from having multiple CPUs at its disposal. The solution phase, on the other hand, will often be highly parallel.

Amdahl's Law looks at how much of the program can be run in parallel and how much of the program must be run using only a single processor. For an example, let's say we have an application that executes in 100 minutes, and it could run in parallel for 95 of the 100 minutes. Once the ratio of parallel to serial time is established, it puts an upper bound on the possible speedup for this application using more processors. In this example, assume that we used so many processors that the parallel portion of the code executed in the blink of an eye. Because of the serial portion of the code, the overall runtime would be five minutes (plus a blink of an eye). So by purchasing an infinite number of processors, we have improved the performance of the application by a factor of 20. Figure 12-1 shows a graph of speedup versus number of processors. We see that there is a diminishing benefit to adding more processors, as the serial portion of the code becomes the dominant factor in execution time. When Amdahl's Law was first discussed, it seemed to show that large-scale parallel processors were pretty pointless. Surveys of existing code put the percentage of the code that could run in parallel for typical appli-

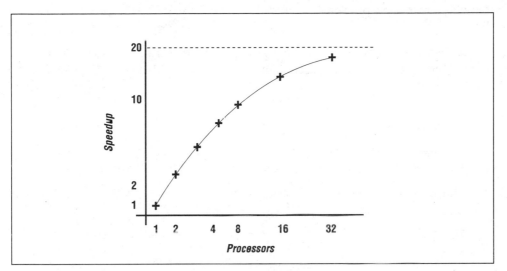

Figure 12-1: Amdahl's Law for a 95% parallel application

cations anywhere from 60%–95%. Beyond eight or so processors, there was not much point. (How could you argue with a law!)*

While Amdahl's Law is not *wrong*, there were two flawed assumptions made when it was used to conclude that massive parallelism is pointless:

- Because parallel processors were not available, programmers never bothered to try to make their code more parallel. As these systems became available, much effort went into rethinking how applications performed computations to maximize the computations that could be done in parallel.

- Often when you doubled the size of your problem, the serial portion took twice as much time, and the parallel portion took four or eight times longer. This disparity in the relative increase in time meant that the application spent more time (as a percentage) in the parallel portion of the application. As the memory and processor capability increased, scientists started solving larger problems. So by making a problem larger, a 95% parallel problem became a 99% parallel, and then a 99.9% parallel problem. These were not "violations" of Amdahl's Law. In fact, Amdahl's Law predicted that the last case could run up to 1000 times faster on a sufficiently large parallel processor.

Given the fact that potential speedup is so often affected by problem size, there are new "laws" that have been proposed that capture this effect. These laws are called Gustafson's Law and Ni's Law. Gustafson's Law addresses how the increasing sizes of a program affected its scalability. Ni's Law summarizes the interaction

---

* I think there is a song about this, "I fought Amdahl's Law and the law won." Or something like that.

between increasing problem size and the ability to execute the program in parallel.

There also have been advances such as data-flow analysis in compilers that make it possible to detect and extract parallelism from code that is difficult to find by examining the code manually.

More Bad News

Even though we have applications that could spend 99.9% or more of their time in parallel, there are still significant problems that can limit the overall speedup:

- The need to access globally shared information or transfer information from one processor to another

- Difficulty dividing the parallel computation evenly between so many processors

Often, running a program on multiple processors requires overhead that would not be necessary if there were only one processor. Programs usually have to be structured specifically for parallelism, so that there is enough to do to keep multiple processors busy without spending an inordinate amount of time coordinating or passing information between them. The job of splitting out the parallel parts for execution on multiple CPUs is called *problem decomposition.*

An application may be parallelized with a particular architecture in mind. For instance, it may be a massively parallel machine containing thousands of small processors, a traditional multiprocessor with four (or so) CPUs, or a network of workstations. In many cases, the effort spent parallelizing an application for one type of machine is transferable to another. The difference is often the granularity of the decomposed parts: the amount of work each processor does before it completes, communicates, or goes back to the well for more.

Another problem is communication. At some point, these processors must do something together or you might just as well use a room full of unconnected video games to do your computation. This generally requires some form of interprocessor communication. This communication is also an overhead that would not be necessary if the problem were run on a single processor. So, even during the parallel portions of the code, there are overhead factors that limit speedup. Generally, as the number of processors increases, the relative impact of the overhead also increases. This is another version of the law of diminishing returns with increasing processors.

Interconnect Technology

There is an interesting correspondence between high performance networking and high performance computing. In some sense, all the parallel processors we have been talking about so far are variations on the idea of "network of workstations." Most popular parallel processors are based on commodity RISC processors connected together to solve large problems collectively. Interestingly, there are many technologies that high performance parallel processors and high-end network equipment share. There are examples of a technology that was developed with an eye to network equipment that was eventually used to develop a parallel processor, and vice versa.

Fundamentally, processors must communicate with each other while working on a large common problem. Sometimes this communication is through shared memory and sometimes it is a message from one CPU to another. For multiple CPUs and memories to communicate, there must be some form of interconnect. In a sense it does not make much difference whether we connect CPUs to memory as in Figure 12-2, or connect nodes (each with a CPU and memory) to one another as in Figure 12-3.

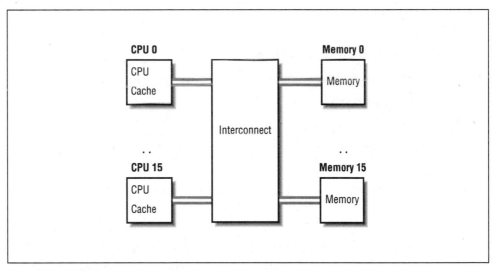

Figure 12-2: Connecting processors to memory

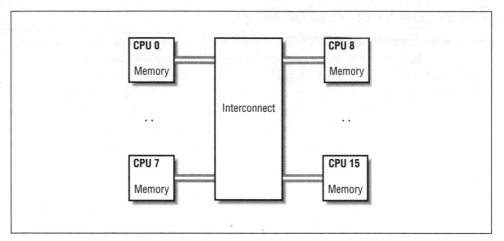

Figure 12-3: Connecting nodes to one another

One can view the interconnect as a network connecting all the entities that make up the parallel processing system. There are a number of different interconnection topologies, including the following:

- Bus architecture

- Crossbar

- Pipelined multistep communications

- Multistage interconnection network

- Mesh and toroid connections

- Hypercubes

- Irregular topologies

Each of these has advantages and disadvantages in terms of latency, bandwidth, scalability, and ease of manufacture. We discuss each in turn.

Bus architecture

We have already discussed the bus architecture. It's simple to build and allows easy expansion. The bus architecture is essentially a broadcast interconnect because every component that is connected to the bus can watch (or snoop) every operation that occurs on the bus. This makes it relatively straightforward to implement cache coherency across the bus. The primary limitation of the bus architecture is its ability to scale as more processors are added.

The bus architecture is similar to Ethernet in network technology. Ethernet is a broadcast technology; all systems connected to the network can "snoop" on all data that is being transferred across the network. Ethernet is inexpensive and works very well, but does not scale well to large amounts of traffic.

Crossbar

We have also discussed the crossbar interconnect. Like a network switch, the crossbar provides multiple independent paths from the processors to the memory. Generally, it is possible to push more data through a crossbar because of the multiple paths. However, some form of broadcast capability is needed to implement cache coherency. On a crossbar, the cache coherency requests can either be copied to all of the ports of the crossbar or there can be a separate bus for it.

Crossbars can scale better than bus-based systems in the area of data transfer rates. However, they are more expensive to build and they become quite costly as the number of processors is increased.

Neither the bus nor crossbar can scale sufficiently to support thousands of processors, so we must turn to more exotic interconnection networks to support these extremely large systems.

Pipelined multistep communications

As we move to a more scalable interconnect, we generally lose the ability to directly connect to all of the memory of the system. There may be several steps in the path from source to destination. As we will later see in the mesh architecture, there can be many (20–50) steps that messages must take on the trip from source to destination.

At each step, the message encounters a piece of hardware that is called a router. The purpose of a router is to take an incoming message and forward it out the appropriate link towards its destination. A router can be hardware or some combination of hardware and software, as shown in Figure 12-4. If we had to wait for a complete message at every step, this would significantly slow the communication capability. Also, we would need enough memory at each router to store several messages.

To minimize the latency of a message crossing an interconnection network, in most of the current interconnects the message transfer is pipelined at each stage. Let's look at an example of the source sending a request to the destination. As the message is sent to Router A, the first two bits of the message select the second output port of Router A. These bits are stripped off, and the rest of the message is sent out the second output port. As the message arrives at Router B, the next two bits of the message are stripped off, and select the third output port of the router. At Router C, the next two bits of the message select the fourth output port. In each router, two bits are stripped off and the rest of the bits of the message are

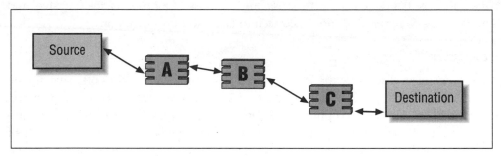

Figure 12-4: Pipelined multistage interconnection

delivered to the destination. In this example, the first six bits of the message would be "011011" to select the second (01), third (10), and fourth (11) router ports for the successive routers. Using this approach, there is very little latency added by the extra stage.* This approach dynamically establishes a "temporary connection" between the nodes. When the data transfer is finished, the resources used by the connection are available for other communications.

Multistage interconnection network

A multistage interconnection network (MIN) is an interconnect that can scale beyond a bus or a crossbar. A MIN is essentially a network of small crossbars. In Figure 12-5, eight four-way crossbars are linked to create a 32-way crossbar. This has an advantage in that it is less expensive to build than a 32-way crossbar with dedicated connections between all pairs of nodes. However, there may be some contention if Node 0 on the left wants to communicate with Node 4 on the right at the exact same time that Node 1 on the left wants to communicate with Node 7 on the right. On a crossbar, these communications could occur simultaneously. However, in a crossbar, if both Nodes 1 and 3 on the left wanted to communicate with Node 5 on the right, there would be contention.

A single 4×4 crossbar allows four nodes to communicate with one step. A MIN consisting of eight 4×4 crossbars connects 32 nodes at the cost of one additional step. However, if the communications are pipelined, the negative impact of the extra step can be minimized.

---

* Interestingly, high performance network switching equipment uses a similar approach. Because the destination addresses are in the beginning of network packets, once a switch has received the first part of a packet, it quickly determines its destination and begins sending the data to the destination even before the rest of the data has been received. The primary difference in a network switch is that it doesn't strip off the header bits when it passes the data on.

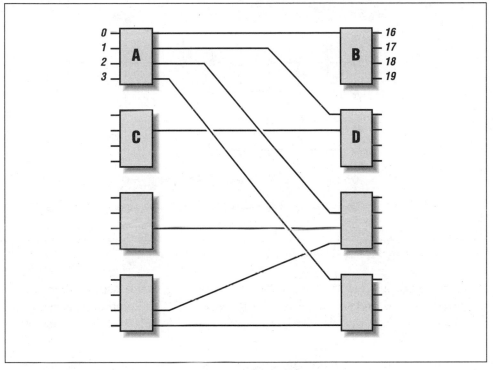

Figure 12-5: Multistage interconnection network

Mesh and toroid connections

A mesh is easy to visualize: it looks like a window screen extending in two or three dimensions. Each node has four or six directly connected Cartesian neighbors, depending on whether the machine is two-dimensional or three-dimensional. To move data from Node A to Node B, you map a Cartesian (X,Y) route through the mesh as shown in Figure 12-6. Similar to the MIN, the first bits of the message are used at each router to determine whether the message is routed north, south, east, or west. Then the bits are stripped off, and the rest of the message continues on.

You can visualize this process as a worm working its way through the mesh, turning left, turning right, and going straight. As the head of the "worm" moves through the mesh, all the data simultaneously trails right behind. Like the MIN, the message establishes the connection and uses the connection in a pipelined fashion. This technique of pipelining the data while the connection is being established was called *wormhole routing* by its inventor, William Dally of MIT.

Prior to wormhole routing, the mesh topology was not very popular because of the number of hops that were necessary on the average. If a two-dimensional

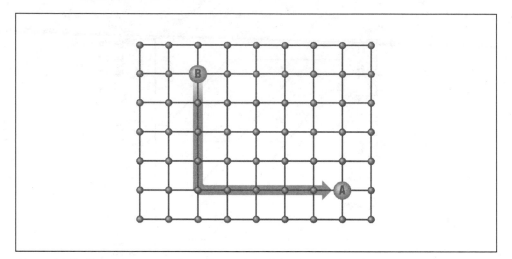

Figure 12-6: Mapping a route through a strictly Cartesian mesh

mesh were constructed to connect 256 processors, the worst-case number of hops required for two processors (upper-left to lower-right) to communicate would be 30. However, with wormhole routing, each hop only required 1–2 extra bits of time.

A variation on the mesh topology is the toroid topology. Figure 12-7 shows a two-dimensional toroid interconnect. A toroid adds a "wrap-around" link from the far left node to the far right node. This is done in each dimension. The advantage of this approach is that it reduces the worst-case number of hops by 50%. There are two ways this can happen. If the loops are bidirectional, the message can be sent in the direction that yields the shortest route. If loops are uni-directional, toroids still maintain an advantage when you consider the fact that most often we see two messages exchanged between a pair of processors. In our 256-processor computer, if we are sending from the upper left to lower right, it still takes 30 steps. However, the return message takes the looped links back and arrives in two steps. So the total hop count for our request and its reply is 32. But because we have moved two messages, the average hop count per message is 16.

Three-dimensional meshes and toroids have a shorter worst-case hop count than their two-dimensional versions. However, the two-dimensional interconnects are easier to build, and wormhole routing makes the number of hops less of a negative factor.

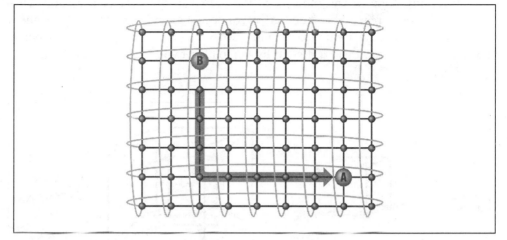

Figure 12-7: A two-dimensional toroid

Hypercubes

In the days before wormhole routing, the number of hops a message took from its source to its destination were significant. Each message had to pass completely across a hop to the next node before it could begin moving across the next hop. In this environment, the goal is to find an interconnect that minimizes the number of hops and is still reasonably easy to build. Figure 12-8 shows a number of different interconnection topologies that can connect four nodes.

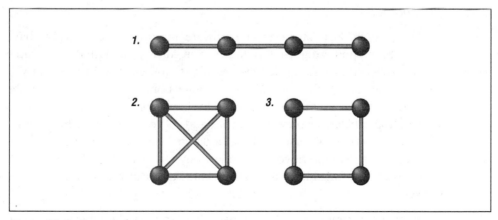

Figure 12-8: Four nodes

A good compromise is to arrange the processors into an *n*-dimensional cube. For instance, with four processors, you could build a 2-cube (the number of nodes, N, is 2^n). A 3-cube would be a volume composed of eight processors. The longest path from any node to any other is n hops—two in the case of a 2-cube. This turns out to be a reasonable number of connections, and it scales well. Higher-dimensional cubes are formed by joining two lower-dimensional cubes together. For instance, you can build a 4-cube by combining two 3-cubes as shown in Figure 12-9.

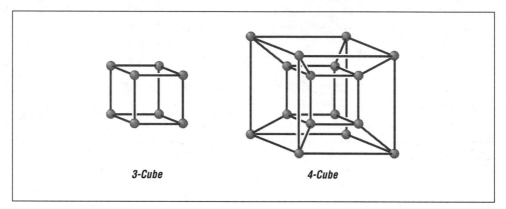

3-Cube   **4-Cube**

Figure 12-9: A 3-cube and a 4-cube

If you scale it to 1024 processors (this is a 10 cube), the longest path between any two nodes is ten hops, and the total number of connections is $2^{(n-1)*n}$ = 5120. To compare, if we build a two-dimensional mesh with 1024 nodes, the longest path between any two nodes is 64 hops.

Irregular topologies

As our ability to build fast interconnect hardware improves, we can also have enough power to support irregular topologies. Sun Microsystems had a research project called the S3MP that supported an irregular topology. The idea is that you have computer building blocks with an S3MP connection. You could connect the systems in a simple ring or star topology for light-duty applications. If you wanted more bandwidth and better latency, you could add more routers and more links. The S3MP system could make use of these additional links and get better bandwidth and latency. At some point you would just buy a bunch of CPU boxes, place them in a rack, add the maximum number of links, and call it a scalable parallel processing system.

While this architecture may seem a bit futuristic, it's probably the general direction in which systems will go. Users can purchase compute power and interconnect bandwidth as they go. Also, if the nodes of a scalable parallel processing system were the same hardware as a workstation, this would be a cost-effective and, thus, very appealing solution.

Summary of interconnection topologies

In parallel processing (and networking), we have lots of nodes that all want to communicate with each other. A wide range of techniques is used to connect these nodes. Each approach has its strengths and weaknesses. One of the fundamental choices a parallel processing company makes is which interconnect to use. Interestingly, this effect is so significant that sometimes a computer is named after its interconnect. For example, Cray's first scalable parallel processor was named the "T3D" for its three-dimensional toroid interconnect. The BBN-GP1000 was called the "Butterfly" because when its interconnect was drawn on paper, it looked somewhat like a butterfly.* And the nCUBE company is so named because it uses the n-cube interconnect. Before that a company called Hypercube marketed a computer called the Hypercube that used a hypercube interconnect.

In addition to categorizing parallel processors by their interconnect, we can categorize them by the way they execute instructions and access data. In the next section, we examine a taxonomy that categorizes the capabilities of these computers.

A Taxonomy of Parallel Architectures

We need some simple terminology that refers to a class of parallel processing systems. Michael Flynn developed the taxonomy as shown in Figure 12-10. This taxonomy is based on the number of simultaneous independent streams of instructions and data. When looking at a parallel architecture, you could either identify a single instruction (SI) stream or multiple instruction (MI) streams. For data you could find either a single data (SD) stream or multiple data (MD) streams coming from memory.

There are some grey areas in Flynn's taxonomy, but it has persisted as a way of broadly categorizing parallel processing architectures. The classic workstation is clearly a single instruction and single data (SISD) architecture. Array processors use a matrix of processors, all simultaneously performing the same instruction on their own local data (SIMD).† A network of workstations (NOW) communicating through message passing is clearly a MIMD processor.

There is a debate as to whether or not a uniform memory parallel processor such as those described in Chapter 10, *Shared-Memory Multiprocessors*, are MISD or MIMD computers.

---

* Kind of like one of those "ink-blot" tests.

† Here's an illustration: the largest SIMD machine in the world runs every weekday around noon, when the aerobics and exercise programs come on the air. The host calls out the instructions: "left, and down, and up, then right . . . ," while thousands follow along in lock step.

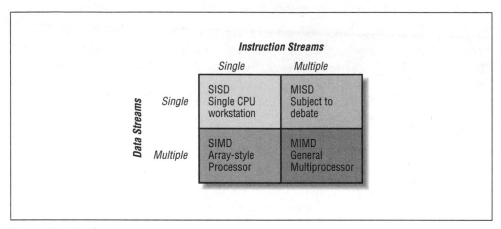

Figure 12-10: Flynn's taxonomy

One faction in the debate counts each connection between a CPU and its cache as an independent memory stream, and, therefore, it is clearly a MIMD architecture. The other faction sees that there is a single memory, and because of the cache coherency the data from the caches, in one sense, are coming to and from that single memory; hence, these systems exhibit the MISD architecture. If there were no coherency between the caches, it would probably be easier to agree that these systems are MIMD architectures. Figure 12-11 shows both sides of the argument.

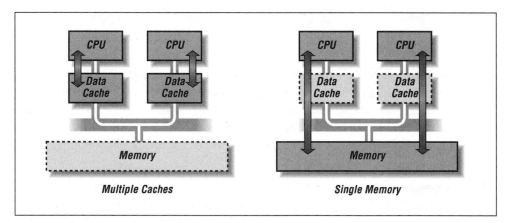

Figure 12-11: Single or multiple data streams?

There are four types of parallel architectures you are likely to encounter:

- MIMD (or MISD) with shared uniform memory

- MIMD with shared nonuniform memory
- MIMD with distributed memory
- SIMD with distributed memory

In the next sections, we look at some of the existing scalable parallel processing systems. In the next chapter, we begin to examine how they are programmed.

A Survey of Parallel Architectures

There is always a conflict between uniform-memory multiprocessors and scalable parallel processors.* Since scalable processors are harder to build, harder to program, and usually more expensive, they must provide significantly more power than the best uniform-memory multiprocessor. There are quite a few examples of scalable processor companies that went out of business because a new 16-processor, uniform-memory system was faster and cheaper than their old 64-processor scalable system.

Looking at this fact, one might conclude that the best idea is just to wait for a few years rather than learn to use scalable systems. There are two reasons that this is typically not done:

- Sometimes the problem is actually important and you need the answer now, not two years from now.
- The newest scalable systems are made up of multiple multiprocessor uniform memory systems. Once the techniques for scalable computing are mastered, we can throw very large numbers of processors at the problem for a real increase in speed.

Another potential trend that might occur is that the competition in the single processor market will fall off due to the extremely high cost of developing new processors. At some point, it may take three or four years to double single-processor performance rather than the 18 months it has taken for many years.† If the pace of innovation in single-processor systems slows, there will certainly be renewed interest in scalable computing systems.

---

* A rough working definition of how many processors it takes to qualify as "scalable" would be: A scalable parallel-processing system is one that supports significantly more processors than a bus- or crossbar-based system. There isn't a fixed number of processors that qualifies as scalable. A processor count considered "scalable" five years ago might not be considered scalable today because of improvements in bus and crossbar technology.

† I am *not* predicting this will happen. The end of this performance trend (Moore's Law) has been predicted incorrectly too many times over the course of history. But it *might* actually happen some day.

The Top 500 Report

An excellent resource that examines the relative success of particular high performance computer architectures is the "Top 500 Report." This report lists the 500 most powerful computer sites in the world. One URL for this report is *http://www.netlib.org/benchmark/top500.html*, and there are mirror sites in Europe and Japan. By looking at this report, one gets some indication of the relative success of a particular architecture in the high performance computing field. For example, this report contains the following information:

- In 1997, the fastest computer in the world was a distributed-memory MIMD system with 9152 Pentium CPUs installed at Sandia National Labs.

- In 1997, the second fastest computer in the world was a Cray T3E shared-memory MIMD system with 1248 DEC Alpha processors.

- In 1993, of the 500 fastest computers, none was a pure SMP multiprocessor, 344 were parallel/vector supercomputers, and 156 were scalable parallel processors.

- In 1997, of the fastest 500 computers, 66 were pure SMP multiprocessors, 71 were parallel/vector supercomputers, and 362 were scalable parallel processors.

It's fascinating to see the trends in the data. As of this writing, it is clear that scalable systems and scalable systems with multi-CPU nodes are becoming the dominant architecture at the top-level high performance computing sites, as shown in Figure 12-12. Now we will look at some parallel processing systems and their architecture.

Shared Uniform Memory MIMD

These systems were described in Chapter 10 and Chapter 11. They are popular because of their ease of use and good price/performance. Table 12-1 summarizes some of the features of the systems available as of this writing.

Table 12-1: Features of Shared Uniform Memory Systems

System	Processor	Max. CPUs	Memory Bandwidth
SGI Power Challenge	MIPS-R10000	36	1.2 GB/sec (bus)
DEC 8400	Alpha-21164	14	1.8 GB/sec (bus)
Sun E6000	UltraSparc-2	30	2.5 GB/sec (bus)
Sun E10000	UltraSparc-2	64	13 GB/sec (crossbar)
HP Exemplar	PA-8000	16	15 GB/sec (crossbar)
Cray T90	Cray Vector	32	800GB/sec (crossbar)

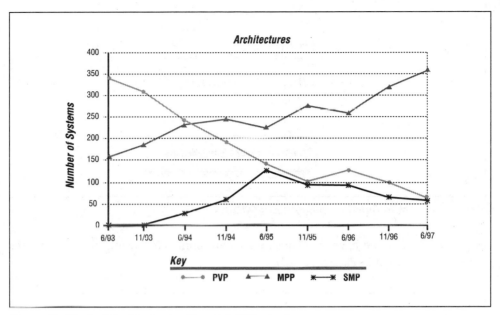

Figure 12-12: Architecture versus time: top 500 report

The pricing of these systems is a combination of the memory bandwidth and the aggregate performance of the processors.

Shared Non-Uniform Memory MIMD Systems

Given the success of the shared-memory programming model, it's not surprising that many vendors of scalable systems maintain the shared memory paradigm. However, to go beyond the crossbar, something must give. What is typically sacrificed is the uniform memory access found in the bus- and crossbar-based systems. The resulting system is called a *Non-Uniform Memory Access* (NUMA) system. In a NUMA system, the processors have direct access to all the memory located anywhere in the system. However, some memory may appear to be slower than other memory. A simple view of this is shown in Figure 12-13.

Different areas of memory (typically determined by the memory address) have different sharing and performance semantics. The global shared memory may or not be cache-coherent across processors.

On these types of systems, to achieve peak performance, one must use local memory whenever practical and only use global (or remote) memory sparingly. While this diagram shows the programming model, it's not the way most systems are implemented. Usually you have a set of nodes that each contain one or more

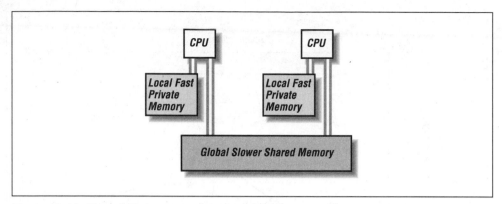

Figure 12-13: Non-uniform memory access (NUMA)

processors and some memory. These nodes are connected using one of the interconnects described in Figure 12-14.

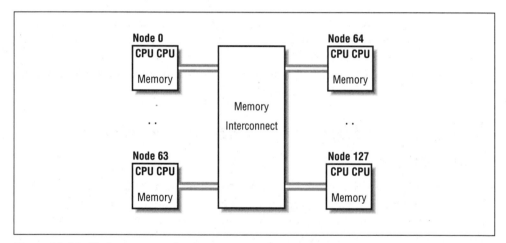

Figure 12-14: Nodes connected using a memory interconnect

In this example, we have two CPUs and memory on each node. References to the memory within the node are satisfied quickly without using the interconnect. References to the memories on the other nodes must be sent across the interconnect. These remote references take longer than the local references; this is the "nonuniform" part of the NUMA architecture.

Another interesting trend in these types of systems is how many processors are present in a node. Early scalable systems had one processor per node. Today they have up to 16 processors per node. Each node acts as a cache-coherent uniform memory multiprocessor with access to the slower remote memories.

Cache Coherence

As mentioned before, some scalable shared-memory systems implement a cache coherency protocol across the interconnect, and some do not. The advantage of cache coherence is that programmers, operating systems, and applications are used to working with cache-coherent systems so there are fewer surprises (other than the fact that some memory is slower). The term that the industry uses to refer to these systems is *cache-coherent nonuniform memory access* (ccNUMA).

The primary vendors of this type of system are the companies who are successful in the symmetric multiprocessing systems. Table 12-2 lists companies that have scalable cache-coherent systems.

Table 12-2: Scalable Cache-Coherent Systems

System	Processor	CPUs/Node	Max CPUs	Max Bandwidth
Data General AV-20000	Pentium	4	32	1GB/Sec
Sequent NUMAQ-2000	Pentium	4	32	1GB/Sec
SGI Origin-2000	MIPS-R10000	2	128	80GB/Sec
HP Exemplar X-Class	PA-8000	16	256	246GB/Sec

The Kendall Square company marketed a cache-coherent shared-memory system using a proprietary processor called the KSR-1, which could, theoretically, scale to 1088 nodes.

The belief that ccNUMA can provide scalable performance for business applications is one of the factors fueling the investment in this approach.

ccNUMA Implementation

Providing the illusion of a simple integrated memory system to a distributed-memory computer is a challenging problem. Uniform shared-memory multiprocessors have the crossbar or bus that makes cache coherency much simpler. Every cache must "see" every possible memory operation to determine that the operation is being done on a location that it currently has in its cache. On a bus, since all caches are connected to the same bus, they simply "snoop" (or continuously monitor) the bus and can see every memory transaction regardless of which processor issued the memory operation. A crossbar is somewhat more difficult. A crossbar must broadcast its cache coherency operations to all the ports of the crossbar to notify all of the caches. On a scalable system with 64 or more separate memories and 128 processor caches, broadcasting every cache operation to all these components is not practical.

An alternative to snooping or broadcast is directory-based caching. In this approach, processors can find out who else is sharing access to the same data and perform cache coherency operations only with those processors. One form of directory-based cache coherency is known as *scalable coherent interface* (SCI), defined in IEEE standards project (P1596). SCI-based systems track data ownership with a doubly linked list, stringing together each node holding a copy of a particular piece of data. A processor wishing to modify data has to coordinate with all other processors in the list. This means traversing the directory list and possibly adding or deleting itself. Once the data is in the caches, it's managed by the caches. When a processor makes a request for data that is already out in some other processor's cache, the memory subsystem replies with a pointer to the head of a list of processors, rather than the requested data. When this list is received, the processor that is trying to access the data communicates with all the processors that have the data in cache to obtain or get exclusive access to it. The HP Exemplar, Sequent NUMAQ-2000, and Data General AV-20000 systems use variants of the SCI caching mechanism. The HP Exemplar uses multiple SCI rings to enhance its overall bandwidth.

There are other schemes, too. The KSR-1 implemented a technique called *ALLCACHE*. With ALLCACHE, instead of having local caches and a global memory, all data in the system is stored in one of the nodes in the cache. If a processor needed data that wasn't in its cache, using a directory system, it retrieves the data from the other cache. This data stays in the current processor cache until it's needed by another processor. Instead of data moving from memory to cache and then back to memory, it simply migrates from one cache to another across the machine. The term used to describe this general approach to distributed cache-coherent memory is called COMA, or *cache-only memory architecture*.

Shared Memory Without Cache Coherency

It's possible to program a scalable shared-memory system that doesn't support cache coherency. If cache coherency isn't required, the memory architecture can be much simpler and the interconnection bandwidth can be spent moving data rather than exchanging cache messages.* However, these systems can be more difficult to program because the programmer must be more aware of when multiple processors may be accessing the same remote memory simultaneously. Also, it's more difficult to support the needs for business applications without cache coherency.

The current system that implements noncoherent shared memory is the Cray T3E system. The Cray T3E supports up to 2048 processors. Each node consists of two DEC Alpha 21164 processors and a local memory. The nodes are connected using a three-dimensional toroid interconnect. The overall bandwidth of the system is on

---

* It's not like the authors have any personal opinions about this.

the order of 122 GB/sec and the interconnect supports extremely low-latency loads and stores from remote memory.

Another interesting system that supported scalable shared memory without cache coherency was the BBN TC-2000. Originally, this system could expand to 256 Motorola MC88100 processors with one processor per node card. A later version with two Motorola 604 processors per card could expand to 512 processors. Remote memory was accessed through a multistage interconnection network (MIN).

Distributed-Memory MIMD Architecture

At some point, the programmer has so clearly decomposed the problem that all that is necessary is a whole lot of processors with some basic communication ability. The program is fully aware when it needs to communicate with other processors. For these types of applications, convienences like shared cache-coherent memory are not necessary.

These applications can execute on the distributed-memory MIMD computers. There are a number of programming environments that work very effectively on these computers. High Performance FORTRAN (HPF), Parallel Virtual Machine (PVM), and Message Passing Interface (MPI) are all examples of popular programming environments for these systems. These programming environments are discussed in Chapter 13, *Language Support for Performance*.

Interestingly, the techniques used in programming these computers can also improve performance on the other architectures as well. Even though communication between threads is simpler on the shared-memory parallel architectures, it can have a significant performance impact if it's done too often. By decomposing an application on a distributed-memory MIMD system, the developer identifies (and tries to minimize) the communication that must be performed as part of the application. Programs ported to HPF, PVM, or MPI often run very well on shared-memory architectures.

Networks of Workstations

The most basic instance of a distributed-memory MIMD machine is a network of workstations (NOW).* This approach is popular because is doesn't cost a lot to

---

* An interesting application that pushed the concept of NOW to the limits was the breaking of a 56-bit RC5 encryption key (*www.distributed.net*). This effort harnessed the spare cycles of home, office, and business computers all over the world and is possibly the largest single computational problem ever solved in the history of computing outside the United States Federal government. The computation lasted over 200 days and evaluated 34 quadrillion potential keys. The average performance of the computation was equivalent to over 16,000 Pentium Pro 200 processors.

enter the high performance computing market. It's possible to utilize the idle cycles of workstations late at night or to stack 64 vintage computers up on shelves connected by a network. Generally it's harder to get peak performance from these systems because of the slow communications, but because the hardware cost is so low, the extra programming effort may be warranted for some organizations.

Tightly Coupled Distributed-Memory Processors

A tightly coupled distributed-memory MIMD system is the combination of a high performance interconnect with a large number of processing nodes. It is almost always easier to simply port and support a message-passing subroutine library compared to supporting shared memory in hardware.

Much as the proponents of noncached shared memory argue that caching is an unnecessary luxury, the message-passing proponents would argue that shared memory is an unnecessary luxury.* The most powerful computer in the world as of the writing of this book is a distributed-memory system manufactured by Intel. It uses a two-dimensional mesh interconnect and contains 9152 Pentium processors. It's installed at Sandia National Labs and performs some of the largest physical simulations on the planet. It was installed as part of the Advanced Scientific Computing Initiative (ASCI) effort. It is capable of over a trillion floating-point operations per second.

Although Intel is not currently marketing their high performance computers, for many years they pioneered the deployment of fast wormhole-routed two-dimensional meshes in their Paragon and Delta computing systems.

The IBM SP series of scalable computers is very popular for a wide variety of high performance computing applications. One unique approach of the IBM SP series is the fact that it relies on workstation hardware components. The SP uses a multi-stage interconnection network. There is a card that can be installed in any IBM RS-6000 computer that attaches the computer to the interconnect. This way IBM can improve the performance of the processors and memory independent of the interconnect performance. Over the years, IBM has continuously installed higher performance processors in their systems, going from "thin" nodes to "wide" nodes, and now even adding multiprocessor "high" nodes to the SP family.

One of the shortcomings of many scalable computing systems is that it takes too long to deploy a newer, faster version of a processor because the nodes need to be completely reengineered from scratch each time. IBM's approach allows them

---

* The great thing about the computer field is that, given the proper set of assumptions, everybody is right.

to take the latest and greatest processors off the shelf and immediately improve the performance (and prices) of an IBM SP system.

The Connection Machine company developed the first widely used SIMD machine in the CM-2. The follow-on product was a distributed-memory MIMD machine called the CM-5. The CM-5 nodes used SPARC and Fujitsu vector processors. It used an interconnection network called a "Fat-Tree." Users programmed it in a data-parallel fashion much like SIMD systems. The CM-5 had a unique synchronization network in addition to its data network that provided low-latency synchronization capabilities. The CM-5 was capable of supporting 16,384 processors.

nCUBE entered high performance computing with several products based on the hypercube interconnect. More recently with the nCUBE3 computer systems they are focusing on the on-demand, media-delivery, high performance database and data-mining markets. nCUBE systems are based on their own proprietary CPU which is optimized for data-transfer operations over their interconnect.

One way of building a low-cost high performance system is to use the interconnect technology from Myricom, Inc. Myricom offers the first example of a high-bandwidth interconnect that is available separately. A user can assemble his own MPP system using the Myrinet interconnect and expansion cards for PCI or SBUS (Sun Microsystems). The network implements an irregular interconnection topology.

Single Instruction, Multiple Data

A SIMD (pronounced *symdee*) machine is a collection of processors, usually thousands, that all perform the same operation at exactly the same time as every other, yet on different data. Each processor has a little bit of local memory and some communications paths to its neighbors. They don't share any memory, so if you want more than one processor to see the same value of a particular variable, you have to transfer it across a communications path.

The array of small processors is connected to a frontend that broadcasts each instruction to all the processors. The frontend sits on a network like any other machine. You log into it to get access to the parallel machine. Typically the frontend itself is responsible for the nonparallel part of the computations. The frontend can exchange data with the array of processors. Other peripherals, such as disk drives, input devices, or data switches, may hang off the frontend or the array of processors as shown in Figure 12-15. At first glance, this seems like a peculiar idea. But think about a do-loop. If each iteration is independent of the rest, then you are free to execute them all at the same time. Furthermore, the math for each iteration is the same (or nearly so). The only difference is that you are working with a different value of index variable: I=n in one case, and I=m in another:

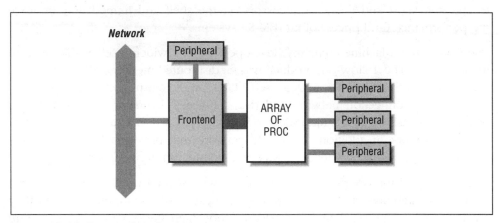

Figure 12-15: Frontend and processor array

```
DO I=1,N
  A(I) = B(I) + D(J) * ....
ENDDO
```

Same instructions, different data—this matches the concept of a SIMD machine very well. Iterations can be spread across the available processors and executed all at once. If there are more iterations than processors, they can be doubled up so that each processor handles several calculations. Communications between processors can be done simultaneously as well. Each cell can generally communicate with its neighbor to the north, south, east, and west in lock step with the rest.

Keeping communications to a minimum is key. If you are adding a vector A to a vector B, for example, and corresponding elements exist in each processor's local memory, then the addition is very fast. That is, if `A(I)` lives on the same processor as `B(I)`, and the loop says `A(I)=A(I)+ B(I)`, there won't be any interprocessor transfer of data.

However, if the loop says something else, for example, `A(I)=A(I)+ B(I+1)`, then each processor has to send its value of `B(I+1)` to the neighbor performing the addition. The communications take place in parallel, so they aren't show-stopping, but they have an effect. You can see that the layout of data among the processors matters. In the first case, no data needed to be transferred. In the second, all the `B(I+1)`'s did.

Other constructs contain greater potential communications overhead. These constructs cause problems in other architectures as well: strided references, permutations, etc. These require communications between processors; there is no way to lay out the data so that only local memory is used. With a permutation, for instance, a node may need to talk to its next-door neighbor or one all the way across the machine. Generally, there isn't a regular pattern to the communications.

Reductions, such as **MAX**, **MIN**, dot products, etc., need special treatment on SIMD machines. Each requires that all processors cooperate in coalescing a single value from many. For instance, if you are looking for the largest value **A(N)** from **A**, eventually all values **A(I)** have to be compared. Handcrafting such operations is possible, but SIMD machines generally come with very efficiently implemented reductions, transpose functions, matrix multiplies, etc.

When all the processors are executing the same instruction simultaneously, it would seem that **IF** statements would be difficult. These operations are accomplished by allowing processors to ignore certain instructions based on a flag stored in each processor. For example, look at the following code:

```
DO I=1,N
  IF ( A(I) .NE. 0 ) THEN
    B(I) = 1.0 / A(I)
  ELSE
    B(I) = 0.0
  ENDIF
ENDDO
```

To keep the example simple, we assume that there are **N** processors, and each processor has the appropriate **A(I)** and **B(I)** values stored locally. This loop takes three instructions. First, each processor tests its value for **A(I)** and sets its flag value accordingly. The next instruction is "If your flag is TRUE, divide 1.0 by **A(I)** and store the result in **B(I)**." The next instruction is "If your flag is FALSE, set **B(I)** to 0." This way, all the processors are executing the same instruction, and the flag is used to cause a subset of the processors to ignore the instructions.

While this is a clever approach that allows SIMD systems to process **IF** statements, it reduces the efficiency of SIMD systems. SIMD systems effectively execute both sides of every branch. This can be a significant problem if one branch of the **IF** is seldom executed, but takes a long time when it is executed. There could be a long code segment with one processor executing the instructions and the other 16,000 or so processors ignoring the instructions.

Another disadvantage of the SIMD approach is the fact that they don't use commodity RISC processors. Because of this, each generation of processor must be engineered by the system manufacturer. It's doubtful that there is a sufficiently large market to support enough research effort to keep SIMD systems competitive with other forms of scalable computing.

Two companies have developed SIMD computers. Connection Machine, Inc. developed the CM-2. The CM-2 supported up to 65,535 processing elements and was programmed in a SIMD fashion. Interestingly, while the CM-2 was programmed as a two-dimensional mesh, its interconnect was actually an hypercube. MasPar, Inc. also marketed a SIMD computer for some time. The MasPar could support up to 16,384 processors, each of which was somewhat more powerful than those in the CM-2.

The individual processors of SIMD machines are not particularly fast or powerful, but there are usually thousands of them, which makes the whole machine, taken together, quite powerful. Interestingly, while the SIMD computers are not the most popular given the current high performance computing market, they are in many ways the most scalable systems. Because they never have to synchronize across processors (synchronization is implicit), they eliminate a great deal of communication required on the other architectures.

Closing Notes

In many ways, this chapter should raise more questions than provide answers. Over the short 15-year history of scalable computing systems there have been many instances of wonderful technology. Unfortunately, there has never been enough demand in the marketplace for 500-processor systems to support the research needed to develop widely available, low-cost, high performance, easy-to-use products.

For many years, the fact that scalable computing was viewed as strategic by the federal government kept funds flowing into the area. However, as the political climate has changed, the federal government has been less willing to fund companies who were not a success in the general marketplace. This has caused an unfortunate shakeout and the loss of a number of promising technologies.

However, after a lull in activity, the demand for scalable computing is again on the rise, this time fueled by the needs of business and the ever-increasing demand for the ability to deliver online information across high performance networks. The continued development of low-cost scalable systems means that high performance computing users will have even better choices in the future.

It's difficult to predict exactly which architectures and vendors will be successful. It's not always the best technology that wins in the end. The successful high performance computing vendors of the future will have developed a product that satisfies both the needs of the general-purpose computing environment and the high performance computing environment. That way, the research and development investments benefit both groups of users.

Exercises

1. Go to the Top 500 site (*http://www.netlib.org/benchmark/top500.html*), and look at the most current data. Are there any new trends or continuations of the existing trends?

13

Language Support
for Performance

This chapter discusses the programming languages that are used on the largest parallel processing systems. Usually when you are faced with porting and tuning your code on a new scalable architecture architecture, you have to sit back and think about your application for a moment. Sometimes fundamental changes to your algorithm are needed before you can begin to work on the new architecture. Don't be surprised if you need to rewrite all or portions of the application in one of these languages. Modifications on one system may not give a performance benefit on another system. But if the application is important enough, it's worth the effort to improve its performance.

In this chapter, we cover:

- FORTRAN 90

- HPF: High Performance FORTRAN

These languages are designed for use on high-end computing systems. We will follow a simple program through each of these languages, using a simple finite-difference computation that roughly models heat flow. It's a classic problem that contains a great deal of parallelism and is easily solved on a wide variety of parallel architectures.

We introduce and discuss the concept of single program multiple data (SPMD) in that we treat MIMD computers as SIMD computers. We write our applications as if a large SIMD system were going to solve the problem. Instead of actually using a SIMD system, the resulting application is compiled for a MIMD system. The implicit synchronization of the SIMD systems is replaced by explicit synchronization at runtime on the MIMD systems.

Data-Parallel Problem: Heat Flow

A classic problem that explores scalable parallel processing is the heat flow problem. The physics behind this problem lie in partial differential equations.

We will start with a one-dimensional metal plate (also known as a rod), and move to a two-dimensional plate in later examples. We start with a rod that is at zero degrees celsius. Then we place one end in 100 degree steam and the other end in zero degree ice. We want to simulate how the heat flows from one end to another. And the resulting temperatures along points on the metal rod after the temperature has stabilized.

To do this we break the rod into 10 segments and track the temperature over time for each segment. Intuitively, within a time step, the next temperature of a portion of the plate is an average of the surrounding temperatures. Given fixed temperatures at some points in the rod, the temperatures eventually converge to a steady state after sufficient time steps. Figure 13-1 shows the setup at the beginning of the simulation.

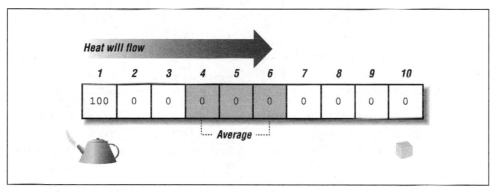

Figure 13-1: Heat flow in a rod

A simplistic implementation of this is as follows:

```
PROGRAM HEATROD
PARAMETER (MAXTIME=200)
INTEGER TICKS,I,MAXTIME
REAL*4 ROD(10)
ROD(1) = 100.0
DO I=2,9
  ROD(I) = 0.0
ENDDO
ROD(10) = 0.0
```

```
          DO TICKS=1,MAXTIME
            IF ( MOD(TICKS,20) .EQ. 1 ) PRINT 100,TICKS,(ROD(I),I=1,10)
            DO I=2,9
              ROD(I) = (ROD(I-1) + ROD(I+1) ) / 2
            ENDDO
          ENDDO
    100   FORMAT(I4,10F7.2)
          END
```

The output of this program is as follows:

```
% f77 heatrod.f
heatrod.f:
 MAIN heatrod:
% a.out
    1 100.00    0.00    0.00    0.00    0.00    0.00    0.00    0.00    0.00    0.00
   21 100.00   87.04   74.52   62.54   51.15   40.30   29.91   19.83    9.92    0.00
   41 100.00   88.74   77.51   66.32   55.19   44.10   33.05   22.02   11.01    0.00
   61 100.00   88.88   77.76   66.64   55.53   44.42   33.31   22.21   11.10    0.00
   81 100.00   88.89   77.78   66.66   55.55   44.44   33.33   22.22   11.11    0.00
  101 100.00   88.89   77.78   66.67   55.56   44.44   33.33   22.22   11.11    0.00
  121 100.00   88.89   77.78   66.67   55.56   44.44   33.33   22.22   11.11    0.00
  141 100.00   88.89   77.78   66.67   55.56   44.44   33.33   22.22   11.11    0.00
  161 100.00   88.89   77.78   66.67   55.56   44.44   33.33   22.22   11.11    0.00
  181 100.00   88.89   77.78   66.67   55.56   44.44   33.33   22.22   11.11    0.00
%
```

Clearly, by Time step 101, the simulation has converged to two decimal places of accuracy as the numbers have stopped changing. This should be the steady-state approximation of the temperature at the center of each segment of the bar.

Now, at this point, astute readers are saying to themselves, "Um, don't look now, but that loop has a flow dependency." You would also claim that this won't even parallelize a little bit. It is so bad you can't even unroll the loop for a little instruction-level parallelism!

A person familiar with the theory of heat flow will also point out that the above loop doesn't *exactly* implement the heat flow model. The problem is that the values on the right side of the assignment in the ROD loop are supposed to be from the previous time step, and that the value on the left side is the next time step. Because of the way the loop is written, the ROD(I-1) value is from the next time step, as shown in Figure 13-2.

This can be solved using a technique called *red-black*, where we alternate between two arrays. Figure 13-3 shows how the red-black version of the computation operates. This kills two birds with one stone! Now the mathematics is precisely correct, *and* there is no recurrence. Sounds like a real win-win situation.

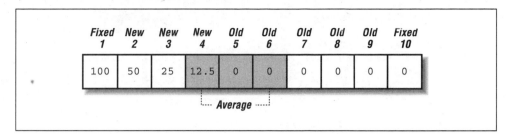

Figure 13-2: Computing the new value for a cell

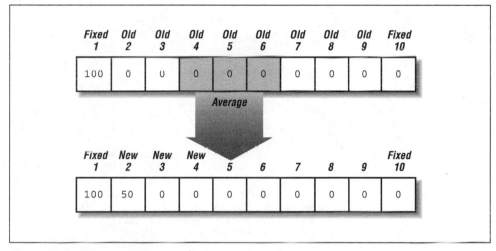

Figure 13-3: Using two arrays to eliminate a dependency

The only downside to this approach is that it takes twice the memory storage and twice the memory bandwidth.* The modified code is as follows:

```
PROGRAM HEATRED
PARAMETER(MAXTIME=200)
INTEGER TICKS,I,MAXTIME
REAL*4 RED(10),BLACK(10)

RED(1) = 100.0
BLACK(1) = 100.0
DO I=2,9
  RED(I) = 0.0
ENDDO
```

---

* There is another red-black approach that computes first the even elements and then the odd elements of the rod in two passes. This approach has no data dependencies within each pass. The ROD array never has all the values from the same time step. Either the odd or even values are one time step ahead of the other. It ends up with a stride of two and doubles the bandwidth but does not double the memory storage required to solve the problem.

```
        RED(10) = 0.0
        BLACK(10) = 0.0

        DO TICKS=1,MAXTIME,2
          IF ( MOD(TICKS,20) .EQ. 1 ) PRINT 100,TICKS,(RED(I),I=1,10)
          DO I=2,9
            BLACK(I) = (RED(I-1) + RED(I+1) ) / 2
          ENDDO
          DO I=2,9
            RED(I) = (BLACK(I-1) + BLACK(I+1) ) / 2
          ENDDO
        ENDDO
100     FORMAT(I4,10F7.2)
        END
```

The output for the modified program is:

```
% f77 heatred.f
heatred.f:
 MAIN heatred:
% a.out
   1 100.00    0.00    0.00    0.00    0.00    0.00    0.00    0.00    0.00    0.00
  21 100.00   82.38   66.34   50.30   38.18   26.06   18.20   10.35    5.18    0.00
  41 100.00   87.04   74.52   61.99   50.56   39.13   28.94   18.75    9.38    0.00
  61 100.00   88.36   76.84   65.32   54.12   42.91   32.07   21.22   10.61    0.00
  81 100.00   88.74   77.51   66.28   55.14   44.00   32.97   21.93   10.97    0.00
 101 100.00   88.84   77.70   66.55   55.44   44.32   33.23   22.14   11.07    0.00
 121 100.00   88.88   77.76   66.63   55.52   44.41   33.30   22.20   11.10    0.00
 141 100.00   88.89   77.77   66.66   55.55   44.43   33.32   22.22   11.11    0.00
 161 100.00   88.89   77.78   66.66   55.55   44.44   33.33   22.22   11.11    0.00
 181 100.00   88.89   77.78   66.67   55.55   44.44   33.33   22.22   11.11    0.00
%
```

Interestingly, the modified program takes longer to converge than the first version. It converges at Time step 181 rather than 101. If you look at the first version, because of the recurrence, the heat ended up flowing up faster from left to right because the left element of each average was the next-time-step value. It may seem nifty, but it's wrong.* Generally, in this problem, either approach converges to the same eventual values within the limits of floating-point representation.

This heat flow problem is extremely simple, and in its red-black form, it's inherently very parallel with very simple data interactions. It's a good model for a wide range of problems where we are discretizing two-dimensional or three-dimensional space and performing some simple simulations in that space.

---

* There are other algorithmic approaches to solving partial differential equations, such as the "fast multipole method" that accelerates convergence "legally." Don't assume that the brute force approach used here is the only method to solve this particular problem. Programmers should always look for the best available algorithm (parallel or not) before trying to scale up the "wrong" algorithm. For folks other than computer scientists, time to solution is more important than linear speed-up.

This problem can usually be scaled up by making a finer grid. Often, the benefit of scalable processors is to allow a finer grid rather than a faster time to solution. For example, you might be able to to a worldwide weather simulation using a 200-mile grid in four hours on one processor. Using 100 processors, you may be able to do the simulation using a 20-mile grid in four hours with much more accurate results. Or, using 400 processors, you can do the finer grid simulation in one hour.

Explicitly Parallel Languages

As we've seen throughout this book, one of biggest tuning challenges is getting the compiler to recognize that a particular code segment can be parallelized. This is particularly true for numerical codes, where the potential payback is greatest. Think about this: if you know that something is parallel, why should there be any difficulty getting the compiler to recognize it? Why can't you just write it down, and have the compiler say "Yes, this is to be done in parallel."

The problem is that the most commonly used languages don't offer any constructs for expressing parallel computations. You are forced to express yourself in primitive terms, as if you were a caveman with a grand thought but no vocabulary to voice it. This is particularly true of FORTRAN and C. They do not support a notion of parallel computations, which means that programmers must reduce calculations to sequential steps. That sounds cumbersome, but most programmers do it so naturally that they don't even realize how good they are at it.

For example, let's say we want to add two vectors, A and B. How would we do it? We would probably write a little loop without a moment's thought:

```
DO I=1,N
  C(I) = A(I) + B(I)
END DO
```

This seems reasonable, but look what happened. We imposed an order on the calculations! Wouldn't it be enough to say "C gets A plus B"? That would free the compiler to add the vectors using any hardware at its disposal, using any method it likes. This is what parallel languages are about. They seek to supply primitives suitable for expressing parallel computations.

New parallel languages aren't being proposed as rapidly as they were in the mid-1980s. Developers have realized that you can come up with a wonderful scheme, but if it isn't compatible with FORTRAN or C, few people will care about it. The reason is simple: there are billions of lines of C and FORTRAN code, but only a few lines of *Fizgibbet*, or whatever it is you call your new parallel language. Because of the predominance of C and FORTRAN, the most significant parallel language activities today seek to extend those languages, thus protecting the 20 or

30 years of investment in programs already written.* It is too tempting for the developers of a new language to test their language on the eight-queens problem and the game of life, get good results, then declare it ready for prime time and begin waiting for the hordes of programmers converting to their particular language.

FORTRAN 90

The previous American National Standards Institute (ANSI) FORTRAN standard release, FORTRAN 77 (X3.9-1978), was written to promote portability of FORTRAN programs between different platforms. It didn't invent new language components, but instead incorporated good features that were already available in production compilers. Unlike FORTRAN 77, FORTRAN 90 (ANSI X3.198-1992) brings *new* extensions and features to the language. Some of these just bring FORTRAN up to date with newer languages like C (dynamic memory allocation, scoping rules) and C++ (generic function interfaces). But some of the new features are unique to FORTRAN (array operations). Interestingly, while the FORTRAN 90 specification was being developed, the dominant high performance computer architectures were scalable SIMD systems such as the Connection Machine and shared-memory vector-parallel processor systems from companies like Cray Research.

FORTRAN 90 does a surprisingly good job of meeting the needs of these very different architectures. Its features also map reasonably well onto the new shared uniform memory multiprocessors. However, as we will see later, FORTRAN 90 alone is not yet sufficient to meet the needs of the scalable distributed and nonuniform access memory systems that are becoming dominant at the high end of computing.

The FORTRAN 90 extensions to FORTRAN 77 include:

- Array constructs
- Dynamic memory allocation and automatic variables
- Pointers
- New data types, structures
- New intrinsic functions, including many that operate on vectors or matrices

---

* One of the more significant efforts in the area of completely new languages is *Streams and Iteration in a Single Assignment Language* (SISAL). It's a data flow language that can easily integrate FORTRAN and C modules. The most interesting aspects of SISAL are the number of large computational codes that were ported to SISAL and the fact that the SISAL proponents generally compared their performance to the FORTRAN and C performance of the same applications.

- New control structures, such as a `WHERE` statement
- Enhanced procedure interfaces

FORTRAN 90 Array Constructs

With FORTRAN 90 array constructs, you can specify whole arrays or array sections as the participants in unary and binary operations. These constructs arc a key feature for "unserializing" applications so that they are better suited to vector computers and parallel processors. For example, say you wish to add two vectors, A and B. In FORTRAN 90, you can express this as a simple addition operation, rather than a traditional loop. That is, you can write:

```
A = A + B
```

instead of the traditional FORTRAN 77 loop:

```
DO I=1,N
   A(I) = A(I) + B(I)
ENDDO
```

The code generated by the compiler on your workstation may not look any different, but for some of the parallel machines available now and workstations just around the corner, the difference are significant. The FORTRAN 90 version states explicitly that the computations can be performed in any order, including all in parallel at the same time.

One important effect of this is that if the FORTRAN 90 version experienced a floating-point fault adding element 17, and you were to look at the memory in a debugger, it would bc perfectly legal for element 27 to be already computed.

You are not limited to one-dimensional arrays. For instance, the element-wise addition of two two-dimensional arrays could be stated like this:*

```
A = A + B
```

in lieu of:

```
DO J=1,M
   DO I=1,N
      A(I,J) = A(I,J) + B(I,J)
   END DO
END DO
```

Naturally, when you want to combine two arrays in an operation, their shapes have to be compatible. Adding a seven-element vector to an eight-element vector doesn't make sense. Neither would multiplying a 2×4 array by a 3×4 array. When

---

* Just in case you are wondering, `A*B` gives you an element-wise multiplication of array members—not matrix multiplication. That is covered by a FORTRAN 90 intrinsic function.

the two arrays have compatible shapes, relative to the operation being performed upon them, we say they are in *shape conformance*, as in the following code:

```
DOUBLE PRECISION A(8), B(8)
   ...
A = A + B
```

Scalars are always considered to be in shape conformance with arrays (and other scalars). In a binary operation with an array, a scalar is treated as an array of the same size with a single element duplicated throughout.

Still, we are limited. When you reference a particular array, A, for example, you reference the whole thing, from the first element to the last. You can imagine cases where you might be interested in specifying a subset of an array. This could be either a group of consecutive elements or something like "every eighth element" (i.e., a non-unit stride through the array). Parts of arrays, possibly noncontiguous, are called *array sections*.

FORTRAN 90 array sections can be specified by replacing traditional subscripts with triplets of the form `a:b:c`, meaning "elements a through b, taken with an increment of c." You can omit parts of the triplet, provided the meaning remains clear. For example, `a:b` means "elements a through b;" `a:` means "elements from a to the upper bound with an increment of 1." Remember that a triplet replaces a single subscript, so an *n*-dimension array can have *n* triplets.

You can use triplets in expressions, again making sure that the parts of the expression are in conformance. Consider these statements:

```
REAL X(10,10), Y(100)
   ...
X(10,1:10)   = Y(91:100)
X(10,:)      = Y(91:100)
```

The first statement above assigns the last 10 elements of Y to the 10th row of X. The second statement expresses the same thing slightly differently. The lone ":" tells the compiler that the whole range (1 through 10) is implied.

FORTRAN 90 Intrinsics

FORTRAN 90 extends the functionality of FORTRAN 77 intrinsics, and adds many new ones as well, including some intrinsic subroutines. Most can be *array-valued*: they can return arrays sections or scalars, depending on how they are invoked. For example, here's a new, array-valued use of the SIN intrinsic:

```
REAL A(100,10,2)
  ...
A = SIN(A)
```

Each element of array A is replaced with its sine. FORTRAN 90 intrinsics work with array sections too, as long as the variable receiving the result is in shape conformance with the one passed:

```
REAL A(100,10,2)
REAL B(10,10,100)
  ...
B(:,:,1) = COS(A(1:100:10,:,1))
```

Other intrinsics, such as **SQRT**, **LOG**, etc., have been extended as well. Among the new intrinsics are:

Reductions

FORTRAN 90 has vector reductions such as **MAXVAL**, **MINVAL**, and **SUM**. For higher-order arrays (anything more than a vector) these functions can perform a reduction along a particular dimension. Additionally, there is a **DOT_PRODUCT** function for the vectors.

Matrix manipulation

Intrinsics **MATMUL** and **TRANSPOSE** can manipulate whole matrices.

Constructing or reshaping arrays

RESHAPE allows you to create a new array from elements of an old one with a different shape. **SPREAD** replicates an array along a new dimension. **MERGE** copies portions of one array into another under control of a mask. **CSHIFT** allows an array to be shifted in one or more dimensions.

Inquiry functions

SHAPE, **SIZE**, **LBOUND**, and **UBOUND** let you ask questions about how an array is constructed.

Parallel tests

Two other new reduction intrinsics, **ANY** and **ALL**, are for testing many array elements in parallel.

New Control Features

FORTRAN 90 includes some new control features, including a conditional *assignment primitive* called **WHERE**, that puts shape-conforming array assignments under control of a mask as in the following example. Here's an example of the **WHERE** primitive:

```
REAL A(2,2), B(2,2), C(2,2)
DATA B/1,2,3,4/, C/1,1,5,5/
  ...
```

```
WHERE (B .EQ. C)
  A =  1.0
  C =  B + 1.0
ELSEWHERE
  A = -1.0
ENDWHERE
```

In places where the logical expression is TRUE, A gets 1.0 and C gets B+1.0. In the ELSEWHERE clause, A gets -1.0. The result of the operation above would be arrays A and C with the elements:

```
A =  1.0   -1.0        C =  2.0    5.0
    -1.0   -1.0             1.0    5.0
```

Again, no order is implied in these conditional assignments, meaning they can be done in parallel. This lack of implied order is critical to allowing SIMD computer systems and SPMD environments to have flexibility in performing these computations.

Automatic and Allocatable Arrays

Every program needs temporary variables or work space. In the past, FORTRAN programmers have often managed their own scratch space by declaring an array large enough to handle any temporary requirements. This practice gobbles up memory (albeit virtual memory, usually), and can even have an effect on performance. With the ability to allocate memory dynamically, programmers can wait until later to decide how much scratch space to set aside. FORTRAN 90 supports dynamic memory allocation with two new language features: automatic arrays and allocatable arrays.

Like the local variables of a C program, FORTRAN 90's automatic arrays are assigned storage only for the life of the subroutine or function that contains them. This is different from traditional local storage for FORTRAN arrays, where some space was set aside at compile or link time. The size and shape of automatic arrays can be sculpted from a combination of constants and arguments. For instance, here's a declaration of an automatic array, B, using FORTRAN 90's new specification syntax:

```
SUBROUTINE RELAX(N,A)
INTEGER N
REAL, DIMENSION (N) :: A, B
```

Two arrays are declared: A, the dummy argument, and B, an automatic, explicit shape array. When the subroutine returns, B ceases to exist. Notice that the size of B is taken from one of the arguments, N.

Allocatable arrays give you the ability to choose the size of an array after examining other variables in the program. For example, you might want to determine the amount of input data before allocating the arrays. This little program asks the user for the matrix's size before allocating storage:

```
INTEGER M,N
REAL, ALLOCATABLE, DIMENSION (:,:) :: X
  ...
WRITE (*,*) 'ENTER THE DIMENSIONS OF X'
READ (*,*) M,N
ALLOCATE (X(M,N))
  ...
  do something with X
  ...
DEALLOCATE (X)
  ...
```

The **ALLOCATE** statement creates an **M×N** array that is later freed by the **DEALLO-CATE** statement. As with C programs, it's important to give back allocated memory when you are done with it; otherwise, your program might consume all the virtual storage available.

Heat Flow in FORTRAN 90

The heat flow problem is an ideal program to use to demonstrate how nicely FOR-TRAN 90 can express regular array programs:

```
      PROGRAM HEATROD
      PARAMETER(MAXTIME=200)
      INTEGER TICKS,I,MAXTIME
      REAL*4 ROD(10)
      ROD(1) = 100.0
      DO I=2,9
        ROD(I) = 0.0
      ENDDO
      ROD(10) = 0.0
      DO TICKS=1,MAXTIME
        IF ( MOD(TICKS,20) .EQ. 1 ) PRINT 100,TICKS,(ROD(I),I=1,10)
        ROD(2:9) = (ROD(1:8) + ROD(3:10) ) / 2
      ENDDO
100   FORMAT(I4,10F7.2)
      END
```

The program is identical, except the inner loop is now replaced by a single statement that computes the "new" section by averaging a strip of the "left" elements and a strip of the "right" elements.

The output of this program is as follows:

```
E6000: f90 heat90.f
E6000:a.out
   1 100.00    0.00    0.00    0.00    0.00    0.00    0.00    0.00    0.00    0.00
  21 100.00   82.38   66.34   50.30   38.18   26.06   18.20   10.35    5.18    0.00
  41 100.00   87.04   74.52   61.99   50.56   39.13   28.94   18.75    9.38    0.00
```

```
 61 100.00  88.36  76.84  65.32  54.12  42.91  32.07  21.22  10.61  0.00
 81 100.00  88.74  77.51  66.28  55.14  44.00  32.97  21.93  10.97  0.00
101 100.00  88.84  77.70  66.55  55.44  44.32  33.23  22.14  11.07  0.00
121 100.00  88.88  77.76  66.63  55.52  44.41  33.30  22.20  11.10  0.00
141 100.00  88.89  77.77  66.66  55.55  44.43  33.32  22.22  11.11  0.00
161 100.00  88.89  77.78  66.66  55.55  44.44  33.33  22.22  11.11  0.00
181 100.00  88.89  77.78  66.67  55.55  44.44  33.33  22.22  11.11  0.00
E6000:
```

If you look closely, this output is the same as the red-black implementation. That is because in FORTRAN 90:

```
ROD(2:9) = (ROD(1:8) + ROD(3:10) ) / 2
```

is a *single* assignment statement. As shown in Figure 13-4, the right side is completely evaluated before the resulting array section is assigned into ROD(2:9). For a moment, that might seem unnatural, but consider the following statement:

```
I = I + 1
```

We know that if I starts with 5, it's incremented up to six by this statement. That happens because the right side (5+1) is evaluated before the assignment of 6 into I is performed. In FORTRAN 90, a variable can be an entire array. So, this *is* a red-black operation. There is an "old" ROD on the right side and a "new" ROD on the left side!

To really "think" FORTRAN 90, it's good to pretend you are on an SIMD system with millions of little CPUs. First we carefully align the data, sliding it around, and then—wham—in a single instruction, we add all the aligned values in an instant. Figure 13-4 shows graphically this act of "aligning" the values and then adding them. The data flow graph is extremely simple. The top two rows are read-only, and the data flows from top to bottom. Using the temporary space eliminates the seeming dependency. This approach of "thinking SIMD" is one of the ways to force ourselves to focus our thoughts on the data rather than the control. SIMD may not be a good architecture for your problem but if you can express it so that SIMD could work, a good SPMD environment can take advantage of the data parallelism that you have identified.

The above example actually highlights one of the challenges in producing an efficient implementation of FORTRAN 90. If these arrays contained 10 million elements, and the compiler used a simple approach, it would need 30 million elements for the old "left" values, the old "right" values, and for the new values. Data flow optimization is needed to determine just how much extra data must be maintained to give the proper results. If the compiler is clever, the extra memory can be quite small:

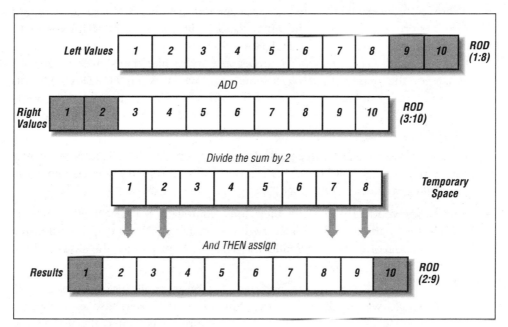

Figure 13-4: Data alignment and computations

```
SAVE1 = ROD(1)
DO I=2,9
   SAVE2 = ROD(I)
   ROD(I) = (SAVE1 + ROD(I+1) ) / 2
   SAVE1 = SAVE2
ENDDO
```

This does not have the parallelism that the full red-black implementation has, but it does produce the correct results with only two extra data elements. The trick is to save the old "left" value just before you wipe it out. A good FORTRAN 90 compiler uses data flow analysis, looking at a template of how the computation moves across the data to see if it can save a few elements for a short period of time to alleviate the need for a complete extra copy of the data.

The advantage of the FORTRAN 90 language is that it's up to the compiler whether it uses a complete copy of the array or a few data elements to insure that the program executes properly. Most importantly, it can change its approach as you move from one architecture to another.

FORTRAN 90 Versus FORTRAN 77

Interestingly, FORTRAN 90 has never been fully embraced by the high performance community. There are a few reasons why:

- There is a concern that the use of pointers and dynamic data structures would ruin performance and lose the optimization advantages of FORTRAN over C. Some people would say that FORTRAN 90 is trying to be a better C than C. Others would say, "who wants to become more like the slower language!" Whatever the reason, there was some controversy when FORTRAN 90 was implemented, leading to some reluctance in adoption by programmers. Some vendors said, "You can use FORTRAN 90, but FORTRAN 77 will always be faster."

- Because vendors often implemented different subsets of FORTRAN 90, it was not as portable as FORTRAN 77. Because of this, users who needed maximum portability stuck with FORTRAN 77.

- Sometimes vendors purchased their fully compliant FORTRAN 90 compilers from a third party who demanded high license fees. So, you could get the free (and faster according to the vendor) FORTRAN 77 or pay for the slower (wink wink) FORTRAN 90 compiler.

- Because of these factors, the number of serious applications developed in FORTRAN 90 was small. So the benchmarks used to purchase new systems were almost exclusively FORTRAN 77. This further motivated the vendors to improve their FORTRAN 77 compilers instead of their FORTRAN 90 compilers.

- As the FORTRAN 77 compilers became more sophisticated using data flow analysis, it became relatively easy to write portable "parallel" code in FOR-TRAN 77, using the techniques we have discussed in this book.

- One of the greatest potential benefits to FORTRAN 90 was portability between SIMD and the parallel/vector supercomputers. As both of these architectures were replaced with the shared uniform memory multiprocessors, FORTRAN 77 became the language that afforded the maximum portability across the computers typically used by high performance computing programmers.

- The FORTRAN 77 compilers supported directives that allowed programmers to fine-tune the performance of their applications by taking full control of the parallelism. Certain dialects of FORTRAN 77 essentially became parallel programming "assembly language." Even highly tuned versions of these codes were relatively portable across the different vendor shared uniform memory multiprocessors.

So, events conspired against FORTRAN 90 in the short run. However, FORTRAN 77 is not well suited for the distributed memory systems because it does not lend itself well to data layout directives. As we need to partition and distribute the data carefully on these new systems, we must give the compiler *lots* of flexibility. FOR-TRAN 90 is the language best suited to this purpose.

FORTRAN 90 Summary

Well, that's the whirlwind tour of FORTRAN 90. We have probably done the language a disservice by covering it so briefly, but we wanted to give you a feel for it. There are many features that were not discussed. If you would like to learn more, we recommend *FORTRAN 90 Explained*, by Michael Metcalf and John Reid (Oxford University Press).

FORTRAN 90 by itself is not sufficient to give us scalable performance on distributed memory systems. So far, compilers are not yet capable of performing enough data flow analysis to decide where to store the data and when to retrieve the memory. So, for now, we programmers must get involved with the data layout. We must decompose the problem into parallel chunks that can be individually processed. We have several options. We can use High Performance FORTRAN and leave some of the details to the compiler, or we can use explicit message-passing and take care of *all* of the details ourselves.

Problem Decomposition

There are three main approaches to dividing or decomposing work for distribution among multiple CPUs:

Decomposing computations

> We have already discussed this technique. When the decomposition is done based on computations, we come up with some mechanism to divide the computations (such as the iterations of a loop) evenly among our processors. The location of the data is generally ignored, and the primary issues are iteration duration and uniformity. This is the preferred technique for the shared uniform memory systems because the data can be equally accessed by any processor.

Decomposing data

> When memory access is nonuniform, the tendency is to focus on the distribution of the data rather than computations. The assumption is that retrieving "remote" data is costly and should be minimized. The data is distributed among the memories. The processor that contains the data performs the computations on that data after retrieving any other data necessary to perform the computation.

Decomposing tasks

> When the operations that must be performed are very independent, and take some time, a task decomposition can be performed. In this approach a master process/thread maintains a queue of work units. When a processor has available resources, it retrieves the next "task" from the queue and begins

processing. This is a very attractive approach for embarrassingly parallel computations.*

In some sense, the rest of this chapter is primarily about data decomposition. In a distributed memory system, the communication costs usually are the dominant performance factor. If your problem is so embarrassingly parallel that it can be distributed as tasks, then nearly any technique will work. *Data-parallel* problems occur in many disciplines. They vary from those that are extremely parallel to those that are just sort of parallel. For example, fractal calculations are extremely parallel; each point is derived independently of the rest. It's simple to divide fractal calculations among processors. Because the calculations are independent, the processors don't have to coordinate or share data.

Our heat flow problem when expressed in its red-black (or FORTRAN 90) form is extremely parallel but requires some sharing of data. A gravitational model of a galaxy is another kind of parallel program. Each point exerts an influence on every other. Therefore, unlike the fractal calculations, the processors do have to share data.

In either case, you want to arrange calculations so that processors can say to one another, "you go over there and work on that, and I'll work on this, and we'll get together when we are finished."

Problems that offer less independence between regions are still very good candidates for domain decomposition. Finite difference problems, short-range particle interaction simulations, and columns of matrices can be treated similarly. If you can divide the domain evenly between the processors, they each do approximately the same amount of work on their way to a solution.

Other physical systems are not so regular or involve long-range interactions. The nodes of an unstructured grid may not be allocated in direct correspondence to their physical locations, for instance. Or perhaps the model involves long-range forces, such as particle attractions. These problems, though more difficult, can be structured for parallel machines as well. Sometimes various simplifications, or "lumping" of intermediate effects, are needed. For instance, the influence of a group of distant particles upon another may be treated as if there were one composite particle acting at a distance. This is done to spare the communications that would be required if every processor had to talk to every other regarding each detail. In other cases, the parallel architecture offers opportunities to express a physical system in different and clever ways that make sense in the context of the

---

* The distributed RC5 key-cracking effort was coordinated in this fashion. Each processor would check out a block of keys and begin testing those keys. At some point, if the processor was not fast enough or had crashed, the central system would reissue the block to another processor. This allowed the system to recover from problems on individual computers.

machine. For instance, each particle could be assigned to its own processor, and these could slide past one another, summing interactions and updating a time step.

Depending on the architecture of the parallel computer and problem, a choice for either dividing or replicating (portions of) the domain may add unacceptable overhead or cost to the whole project.

For a large problem, the dollar value of main memory may make keeping separate local copies of the same data out of the question. In fact, a need for more memory is often what drives people to parallel machines; the problem they need to solve can't fit in the memory of a conventional computer.

By investing some effort, you could allow the domain partitioning to evolve as the program runs, in response to an uneven load distribution. That way, if there were a lot of requests for As, then several processors could dynamically get a copy of the A piece of the domain. Or the A piece could be spread out across several processors, each handling a different subset of the A definitions. You could also migrate unique copies of data from place to place, changing their home as needed.

When the data domain is irregular, or changes over time, the parallel program encounters a load-balancing problem. Such a problem becomes especially apparent when one portion of the parallel computations takes much longer to complete than the others. A real-world example might be an engineering analysis on an adaptive grid. As the program runs, the grid becomes more refined in those areas showing the most activity. If the work isn't reapportioned from time to time, the section of the computer with responsibility for the most highly refined portion of the grid falls farther and farther behind the performance of the rest of the machine.

High Performance FORTRAN (HPF)

In March 1992, the High Performance Fortran Forum (HPFF) began meeting to discuss and define a set of additions to FORTRAN 90 to make it more practical for use in a scalable computing environment. The plan was to develop a specification within the calendar year so that vendors could quickly begin to implement the standard. The scope of the effort included the following:

- Identify scalars and arrays that will be distributed across a parallel machine.

- Say how they will be distributed. Will they be strips, blocks, or something else?

- Specify how these variables will be aligned with respect to one another.

- Redistribute and realign data structures at runtime.

- Add a `FORALL` control construct for parallel assignments that are difficult or impossible to construct using FORTRAN 90's array syntax.

- Make improvements to the FORTRAN 90 `WHERE` control construct.

- Add intrinsic functions for common parallel operations.

There were several sources of inspiration for the HPF effort. Layout directives were already part of the FORTRAN 90 programming environment for some SIMD computers (i.e., the CM-2). Also, PVM, the first portable message-passing environment, had been released a year earlier, and users had a year of experience trying to decompose by hand programs. They had developed some basic usable techniques for data decomposition that worked very well but required far too much bookkeeping.*

The HPF effort brought together a diverse set of interests from all the major high performance computing vendors. Vendors representing all the major architectures were represented. As a result HPF was designed to be implemented on nearly all types of architectures.

There is an effort underway to produce the next FORTRAN standard: FORTRAN 95. FORTRAN 95 is expected to adopt some but not all of the HPF modifications.

Programming in HPF

At its core, HPF includes FORTRAN 90. If a FORTRAN 90 program were run through an HPF compiler, it must produce the same results as if it were run through a FORTRAN 90 compiler. Assuming an HPF program only uses FORTRAN 90 constructs and HPF directives, a FORTRAN 90 compiler could ignore the directives, and it should produce the same results as an HPF compiler.

As the user adds directives to the program, the semantics of the program are not changed. If the user completely misunderstands the application and inserts extremely ill-conceived directives, the program produces correct results very slowly. An HPF compiler doesn't try to "improve on" the user's directives. It assumes the programmer is omniscient.†

Once the user has determined how the data will be distributed across the processors, the HPF compiler attempts to use the minimum communication necessary and overlaps communication with computation whenever possible. HPF generally uses an "owner computes" rule for the placement of the computations. A particular element in an array is computed on the processor that stores that array element.

---

* As we shall soon see.

† Always a safe assumption.

All the necessary data to perform the computation is gathered from remote processors, if necessary, to perform the computation. If the programmer is clever in decomposition and alignment, much of the data needed will be from the local memory rather then a remote memory. The HPF compiler is also responsible for allocating any temporary data structures needed to support communications at runtime.

In general, the HPF compiler is not magic—it simply does a very good job with the communication details when the programmer can design a good data decomposition. At the same time, it retains portability with the single CPU and shared uniform memory systems using FORTRAN 90.

HPF data layout directives

Perhaps the most important contributions of HPF are its data layout directives. Using these directives, the programmer can control how data is laid out based on the programmer's knowledge of the data interactions. An example directive is as follows:

```
      REAL*4 ROD(10)
!HPF$ DISTRIBUTE ROD(BLOCK)
```

The !HPF$ prefix would be a comment to a non-HPF compiler and can safely be ignored by a straight FORTRAN 90 compiler. The DISTRIBUTE directive indicates that the ROD array is to be distributed across multiple processors. If this directive is not used, the ROD array is allocated on one processor and communicated to the other processors as necessary. There are several distributions that can be done in each dimension:

```
      REAL*4 BOB(100,100,100),RICH(100,100,100)
!HPF$ DISTRIBUTE BOB(BLOCK,CYCLIC,*)
!HPF$ DISTRIBUTE RICH(CYCLIC(10))
```

These distributions operate as follows:

BLOCK
> The array is distributed across the processors using contiguous blocks of the index value. The blocks are made as large as possible.

CYCLIC
> The array is distributed across the processors, mapping each successive element to the "next" processor, and when the last processor is reached, allocation starts again on the first processor.

CYCLIC(n)
> The array is distributed the same as CYCLIC except that n successive elements are placed on each processor before moving on to the next processor.

*   All the elements in that dimension are placed on the same processor. This is
most useful for multidimensional arrays.

Figure 13-5 shows how the elements of a simple array would be mapped onto
three processors with different directives.

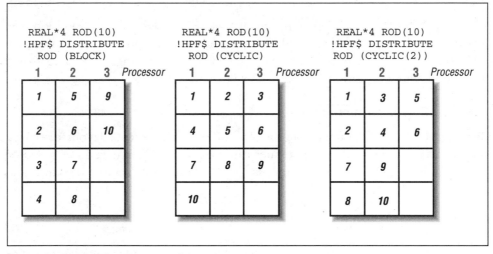

Figure 13-5: Distributing array elements to processors

It must allocate four elements to Processors 1 and 2 because there is no Processor
4 available for the leftover element if it allocated three elements to Processors 1
and 2. In Figure 13-5, the elements are allocated on successive processors, wrap-
ping around to Processor 1 after the last processor. In Figure 13-5, using a chunk
size with CYCLIC is a compromise between pure BLOCK and pure CYCLIC.

To explore the use of the *, we can look at a simple two-dimensional array
mapped onto four processors. In Figure 13-6, we show the array layout and each
cell indicates which processor will hold the data for that cell in the two-dimensional array. In Figure 13-6, the directive decomposes in both dimensions simultaneously. This approach results in roughly square patches in the array. However,
this may not be the best approach. In the following example, we use the * to indicate that we want all the elements of a particular column to be allocated on the
same processor. So, the column values equally distribute the columns across the
processors. Then, all the rows in each column follow where the column has been
placed. This allows unit stride for the on-processor portions of the computation
and is beneficial in some applications. The * syntax is also called *on-processor* distribution.

When dealing with more than one data structure to perform a computation, you
can either separately distribute them or use the ALIGN directive to ensure that

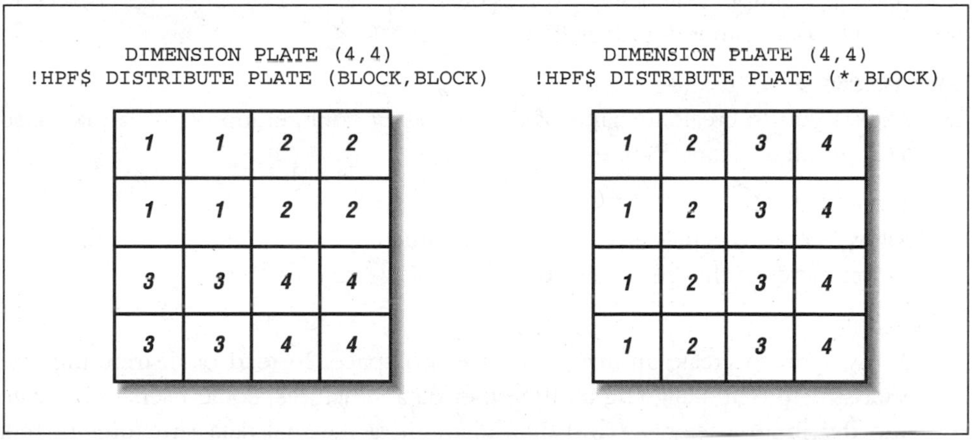

```
           DIMENSION PLATE (4,4)              DIMENSION PLATE (4,4)
   !HPF$ DISTRIBUTE PLATE (BLOCK,BLOCK)   !HPF$ DISTRIBUTE PLATE (*,BLOCK)
```

1	1	2	2
1	1	2	2
3	3	4	4
3	3	4	4

1	2	3	4
1	2	3	4
1	2	3	4
1	2	3	4

Figure 13-6: Two-dimensional distributions

corresponding elements of the two data structures are to be allocated together. In the following example, we have a plate array and a scaling factor that must be applied to each column of the plate during the computation:

```
       DIMENSION PLATE(200,200),SCALE(200)
!HPF$ DISTRIBUTE PLATE(*,BLOCK)
!HPF$ ALIGN SCALE(I) WITH PLATE(J,I)
```

Or:

```
       DIMENSION PLATE(200,200),SCALE(200)
!HPF$ DISTRIBUTE PLATE(*,BLOCK)
!HPF$ ALIGN SCALE(:) WITH PLATE(*,:)
```

In both examples, the **PLATE** and the **SCALE** variables are allocated to the same processors as the corresponding columns of **PLATE**. The * and : syntax communicate the same information. When * is used, that dimension is collapsed, and it doesn't participate in the distribution. When the : is used, it means that dimension follows the corresponding dimension in the variable that has already been distributed.

You could also specify the layout of the **SCALE** variable and have the **PLATE** variable "follow" the layout of the **SCALE** variable:

```
       DIMENSION PLATE(200,200),SCALE(200)
!HPF$ DISTRIBUTE SCALE(BLOCK)
!HPF$ ALIGN PLATE(J,I) WITH SCALE(I)
```

You can put simple arithmetic expressions into the `ALIGN` directive subject to some limitations. Other directives include:

PROCESSORS

> Allows you to create a shape of the processor configuration that can be used to align other data structures.

REDISTRIBUTE and REALIGN

> Allow you to dynamically reshape data structures at runtime as the communication patterns change during the course of the run.

TEMPLATE

> Allows you to create an array that uses no space. Instead of distributing one data structure and aligning all the other data structures, some users will create and distribute a template and then align all of the real data structures to that template.

The use of directives can range from very simple to very complex. In some situations, you distribute the one large shared structure, align a few related structures and you are done. In other situations, programmers attempt to optimize communications based on the topology of the interconnection network (hypercube, multistage interconnection network, mesh, or toroid) using very detailed directives. They also might carefully redistribute the data at the various phases of the computation.

Hopefully your application will yield good performance without too much effort.

HPF control structures

While the HPF designers were in the midst of defining a new language, they set about improving on what they saw as limitations in FORTRAN 90. Interestingly, these modifications are what is being considered as part of the new FORTRAN 95 standard.

The `FORALL` statement allows the user to express simple iterative operations that apply to the entire array without resorting to a do-loop (remember, do-loops force order). For example:

```
FORALL (I=1:100, J=1:100) A(I,J) = I + J
```

This can be expressed in native FORTRAN 90 but it is rather ugly, counterintuitive, and prone to error.

Another control structure is the ability to declare a function as "PURE." A PURE function has no side effects other than through its parameters. The programmer is guaranteeing that a PURE function can execute simultaneously on many processors with no ill effects. This allows HPF to assume that it will only operate on local data and does not need any data communication during the duration of the function execution. The programmer can also declare which parameters of the function are input parameters, output parameters, and input-output parameters.

HPF intrinsics

The companies who marketed SIMD computers needed to come up with significant tools to allow efficient collective operations across all the processors. A perfect example of this is the SUM operation. To SUM the value of an array spread across N processors, the simplistic approach takes N steps. However, it is possible to accomplish it in log(N) steps using a technique called *parallel-prefix-sum*. By the time HPF was in development, a number of these operations had been identified and implemented. HPF took the opportunity to define standardized syntax for these operations.

A sample of these operations includes:

SUM_PREFIX
  Performs various types of parallel-prefix summations.

ALL_SCATTER
  Distributes a single value to a set of processors.

GRADE_DOWN
  Sorts into decreasing order.

IANY
  Computes the logical OR of a set of values.

While there are a large number of these intrinsic functions, most applications use only a few of the operations.

HPF extrinsics

In order to allow the vendors with diverse architectures to provide their particular advantage, HPF included the capability to link "extrinsic" functions. These functions didn't need to be written in FORTRAN 90/HPF and performed a number of vendor-supported capabilities. This capability allowed users to perform such tasks as the creation of hybrid applications with some HPF and some message passing.

High performance computing programmers always like the ability to do things their own way in order to eke out that last drop of performance.

Heat Flow in HPF

To port our heat flow application to HPF, there is really only a single line of code that needs to be added. In the example below, we've changed to a larger two-dimensional array:

```
        INTEGER PLATESIZ,MAXTIME
        PARAMETER(PLATESIZ=2000,MAXTIME=200)
!HPF$   DISTRIBUTE PLATE(*,BLOCK)
        REAL*4 PLATE(PLATESIZ,PLATESIZ)
        INTEGER TICK
        PLATE = 0.0

* Add Boundaries
        PLATE(1,:) = 100.0
        PLATE(PLATESIZ,:) = -40.0
        PLATE(:,PLATESIZ) = 35.23
        PLATE(:,1) = 4.5

        DO TICK = 1,MAXTIME
          PLATE(2:PLATESIZ-1,2:PLATESIZ-1) = (
     +       PLATE(1:PLATESIZ-2,2:PLATESIZ-1) +
     +       PLATE(3:PLATESIZ-0,2:PLATESIZ-1) +
     +       PLATE(2:PLATESIZ-1,1:PLATESIZ-2) +
     +       PLATE(2:PLATESIZ-1,3:PLATESIZ-0) ) / 4.0
          PRINT 1000,TICK, PLATE(2,2)
1000      FORMAT('TICK = ',I5, F13.8)
        ENDDO
*
        END
```

You will notice that the HPF directive distributes the array columns using the BLOCK approach, keeping all the elements within a column on a single processor. At first glance, it might appear that (BLOCK,BLOCK) is the better distribution. However, there are two advantages to a (*,BLOCK) distribution. First, striding down a column is a unit-stride operation and so you might just as well process an entire column. The more significant aspect of the distribution is that a (BLOCK,BLOCK) distribution forces each processor to communicate with up to eight other processors to get its neighboring values. Using the (*,BLOCK) distribution, each processor will have to exchange data with at most two processors each time step.

When we look at PVM, we will look at this same program implemented in a SPMD-style message-passing fashion. In that example, you will see some of the details that HPF must handle to properly execute this code. After reviewing that code, you will probably choose to implement all of your future heat flow applications in HPF!

HPF Summary

In some ways, HPF has been good for FORTRAN 90. Companies such as IBM with its SP-1 needed to provide some high-level language for those users who didn't want to write message-passing codes. Because of this, IBM has invested a great deal of effort in implementing and optimizing HPF. Interestingly, much of this effort will directly benefit the ability to develop more sophisticated FORTRAN 90 compilers. The extensive data flow analysis required to minimize communications and manage the dynamic data structures will carry over into FORTRAN 90 compilers even without using the HPF directives.

Time will tell if the HPF data distribution directives will no longer be needed and compilers will be capable of performing sufficient analysis of straight FORTRAN 90 code to optimize data placement and movement.

In its current form, HPF is an excellent vehicle for expressing the highly data-parallel, grid-based applications. Its weaknesses are irregular communications and dynamic load balancing. A new effort to develop the next version of HPF is underway to address some of these issues. Unfortunately, it is more difficult to solve these runtime problems while maintaining good performance across a wide range of architectures.

Closing Notes

In this chapter, we have covered some of the efforts in the area of languages that have been developed to allow programs to be written for scalable computing. There is a tension between pure FORTRAN 77, FORTRAN 90, HPF, and message passing as to which will be the ultimate tools for scalable, high performance computing.

Certainly, there have been examples of great successes for both FORTRAN 90 (Thinking Machines CM-5) and HPF (IBM SP and others) as languages that can make excellent use of scalable computing systems. One of the problems of a high-level language approach is that sometimes using an abstract high-level language actually *reduces* effective portability.

The languages are designed to be portable, but if the vendor of your particular scalable computer doesn't support the language variant in which you have chosen to write your application, then it isn't portable. Even if the vendor has your language available, it may not be tuned to generate the best code for their architecture.

One solution is to purchase your compilers from a third-party company such as Pacific Sierra or Kuck and Associates. These vendors sell one compiler that runs across a wide range of systems. For users who can afford these options, these compilers afford a higher level of portability.

One of the fundamental issues is the chicken-and-egg problem. If users don't use a language, vendors won't improve the language. If all the influential users (with all the money) use message passing, then the existence of an excellent HPF compiler is of no real value to those users.

The good news is that both FORTRAN 90 and HPF provide one road map to portable scalable computing that doesn't require explicit message passing. The only question is which road we users will choose.

14

Message-Passing Environments

A message-passing interface is a set of function and subroutine calls for C or FOR-TRAN that give you a way to split an application for parallel execution. Data is divided and passed out to other processors as messages. The receiving processors unpack them, do some work, and send the results back or pass them along to other processors in the parallel computer.

In some ways, message passing is the "assembly language" of parallel processing. You get ultimate responsibility, and if you are talented (and your problem cooperates), you get ultimate performance. If you have a nice scalable problem and are not satisfied with the resulting performance, you pretty much have yourself to blame. The compiler is completely unaware of the parallel aspects of the program.

The two most popular message-passing environments are *parallel virtual machine* (PVM) and *message-passing interface* (MPI). Most of the important features are available in either environment. Once you have mastered message passing, moving from PVM to MPI won't cause you much trouble. You may also operate on a system that provides only a vendor-specific message-passing interface. However, once you understand message passing concepts and have properly decomposed your application, usually it's not that much more effort to move from one message-passing library to another.*

---

* Notice I said "not that much *more* effort."

Parallel Virtual Machine (PVM)

The idea behind PVM is to assemble a diverse set of network-connected resources into a "virtual machine." A user could marshal the resources of 35 idle workstations on the Internet and have their own personal scalable processing system. The work on PVM started in the early 1990s at Oak Ridge National Labs. PVM was pretty much an instant success among computer scientists. It provided a rough framework in which to experiment with using a network of workstations as a parallel processor.

In PVM Version 3, your virtual machine can consist of single processors, shared-memory multiprocessors, and scalable multiprocessors. PVM attempts to knit all of these resources into a single, consistent, execution environment.

To run PVM, you simply need a login account on a set of network computers that have the PVM software installed. You can even install it in your home directory. To create your own personal virtual machine, you would create a list of these computers in a file:

```
% cat hostfile
frodo.egr.msu.edu
gollum.egr.msu.edu
mordor.egr.msu.edu
%
```

After some nontrivial machinations with paths and environment variables, you can start the PVM console:

```
% pvm hostfile
pvmd already running.
pvm> conf
1 host, 1 data format
                    HOST      DTID     ARCH     SPEED
                   frodo     40000   SUN4SOL2   1000
                   gollum    40001   SUN4SOL2   1000
                   mordor    40002   SUN4SOL2   1000
pvm> ps
                   HOST       TID    FLAG 0x COMMAND
                    frodo    40042      6/c,f pvmgs
pvm> reset
pvm> ps
                   HOST       TID    FLAG 0x COMMAND
pvm>
```

Many different users can be running virtual machines using the same pool of resources. Each user has their own view of an empty machine. The only way you might detect other virtual machines using your resources is in the percentage of the time your applications get the CPU.

There is a wide range of commands you can issue at the PVM console. The *ps* command shows the running processes in your virtual machine. It's quite possible to have more processes than computer systems. Each process is time-shared on a system along with all the other load on the system. The *reset* command performs a soft reboot on your virtual machine. You are the virtual system administrator of the virtual machine you have assembled.

To execute programs on your virtual computer, you must compile and link your programs with the PVM library routines:*

```
% aimk mast slav
making in SUN4SOL2/ for SUN4SOL2
cc -O -I/opt/pvm3/include -DSYSVBFUNC -DSYSVSTR -DNOGETDTBLSIZ
    -DSYSVSIGNAL -DNOWAIT3 -DNOUNIXDOM -o mast
    ../mast.c -L/opt/pvm3/lib/SUN4SOL2 -lpvm3 -lnsl -lsocket
mv mast ~crs/pvm3/bin/SUN4SOL2
cc  O -I/opt/pvm3/include -DSYSVBFUNC -DSYSVSTR -DNOGETDTBLSIZ
    -DSYSVSIGNAL -DNOWAIT3 -DNOUNIXDOM -o slav
    ../slav.c -L/opt/pvm3/lib/SUN4SOL2 -lpvm3 -lnsl -lsocket
mv slav ~crs/pvm3/bin/SUN4SOL2
%
```

When the first PVM call is encountered, the application contacts your virtual machine and enrolls itself in the virtual machine. At that point it should show up in the output of the *ps* command issued at the PVM console.

From that point on, your application issues PVM calls to create more processes and interact with those processes. PVM takes the responsibility for distributing the processes on the different systems in the virtual machine, based on the load and your assessment of each system's relative performance. Messages are moved across the network using *user datagram protocol* (UDP) and delivered to the appropriate process.

Typically, the PVM application starts up some additional PVM processes. These can be additional copies of the same program or each PVM process can run a different PVM application. Then the work is distributed among the processes, and results are gathered as necessary.

There are several basic models of computing that are typically used when working with PVM:

Master/Slave

When operating in this mode, one process (usually the initial process) is designated as the master that spawns some number of worker processes. Work units are sent to each worker process, and the results are returned to the master. Often the master maintains a queue of work to be done and as a slave

---

* Note: the exact compilation may be different on your system.

finishes, the master delivers a new work item to the slave. This approach works well when there is little data interaction and each work unit is independent. This approach has the advantage that the overall problem is naturally load-balanced even when there is some variation in the execution time of individual processes.

Broadcast/Gather

This type of application is typically characterized by the fact that the shared data structure is relatively small and can be easily copied into every processor's node. At the beginning of the time step, all the global data structures are broadcast from the master process to all of the processes. Each process then operates on their portion of the data. Each process produces a partial result that is sent back and gathered by the master process. This pattern is repeated for each time step.

SPMD/Data decomposition

When the overall data structure is too large to have a copy stored in every process, it must be decomposed across multiple processes. Generally, at the beginning of a time step, all processes must exchange some data with each of their neighboring processes. Then with their local data augmented by the necessary subset of the remote data, they perform their computations. At the end of the time step, necessary data is again exchanged between neighboring processes, and the process is restarted.

The most complicated applications have nonuniform data flows and data that migrates around the system as the application changes and the load changes on the system.

In this section, we have two example programs: one is a master-slave operation, and the other is a data decomposition-style solution to the heat flow problem.

Queue of Tasks

In this example, one process (`mast`) creates five slave processes (`slav`) and doles out 20 work units (add one to a number). As a slave process responds, it's given new work or told that all of the work units have been exhausted:

```
% cat mast.c
#include <stdio.h>
#include "pvm3.h"

#define MAXPROC 5
#define JOBS 20

main()
{
  int mytid,info;
```

```
    int tids[MAXPROC];
    int tid,input,output,answers,work;

    mytid = pvm_mytid();
    info=pvm_spawn("slav", (char**)0, 0, "", MAXPROC, tids);

/* Send out the first work */
    for(work=0;work<MAXPROC;work++) {
      pvm_initsend(PvmDataDefault);
      pvm_pkint(&work, 1, 1 ) ;
      pvm_send(tids[work],1) ;      /* 1 = msgtype */
    }

/* Send out the rest of the work requests */
    work = MAXPROC;
    for(answers=0; answers < JOBS ; answers++) {
        pvm_recv( -1, 2 );  /* -1 = any task 2 = msgtype */
        pvm_upkint( &tid, 1, 1 );
        pvm_upkint( &input, 1, 1 );
        pvm_upkint( &output, 1, 1 );
        printf("Thanks to %d 2*%d=%d\n",tid,input,output);
        pvm_initsend(PvmDataDefault);
        if ( work < JOBS ) {
           pvm_pkint(&work, 1, 1 ) ;
           work++;
        } else {
           input = -1;
           pvm_pkint(&input, 1, 1 ) ; /* Tell them to stop */
        }
        pvm_send(tid,1) ;
    }

    pvm_exit();
}
%
```

One of the interesting aspects of the PVM interface is the separation of calls to prepare a new message, pack data into the message, and send the message. This is done for several reasons. PVM has the capability to convert between different floating-point formats, byte orderings, and character formats. This also allows a single message to have multiple data items with different types.

The purpose of the message type in each PVM send or receive is to allow the sender to wait for a particular type of message. In this example, we use two message types. Type one is a message from the master to the slave, and type two is the response.

When performing a receive, a process can either wait for a message from a specific process or a message from any process.

In the second phase of the computation, the master waits for a response from any slave, prints the response, and then doles out another work unit to the slave or tells the slave to terminate by sending a message with a value of -1.

The slave code is quite simple—it waits for a message, unpacks it, checks to see if it is a termination message, returns a response, and repeats:

```
% cat slav.c
#include <stdio.h>
#include "pvm3.h"

/* A simple program to double integers */
main()
{
  int mytid;
  int input,output;
  mytid = pvm_mytid();

  while(1) {
    pvm_recv( -1, 1 );   /* -1 = any task 1=msgtype */
    pvm_upkint(&input, 1, 1);
    if ( input == -1 ) break; /* All done */

    output = input * 2;
    pvm_initsend( PvmDataDefault );
    pvm_pkint( &mytid, 1, 1 );
    pvm_pkint( &input, 1, 1 );
    pvm_pkint( &output, 1, 1 );
    pvm_send( pvm_parent(), 2 );
  }
  pvm_exit();
}
%
```

When the master program is executed, it produces the following output:

```
% pheat
Thanks to 262204 2*0=0
Thanks to 262205 2*1=2
Thanks to 262206 2*2=4
Thanks to 262207 2*3=6
Thanks to 262204 2*5=10
Thanks to 262205 2*6=12
Thanks to 262206 2*7=14
Thanks to 262207 2*8=16
Thanks to 262204 2*9=18
Thanks to 262205 2*10=20
Thanks to 262206 2*11=22
Thanks to 262207 2*12=24
Thanks to 262205 2*14=28
Thanks to 262207 2*16=32
Thanks to 262205 2*17=34
Thanks to 262207 2*18=36
```

```
Thanks to 262204 2*13=26
Thanks to 262205 2*19=38
Thanks to 262206 2*15=30
Thanks to 262208 2*4=8
%
```

Clearly the processes are operating in parallel, and the order of execution is some-what random. This code is an excellent skeleton for handling a wide range of computations. In the next example, we perform an SPMD-style computation to solve the heat flow problem using PVM.

Heat Flow in PVM

This next example is a rather complicated application that implements the heat flow problem in PVM. In many ways, it gives some insight into the work that is performed by the HPF environment. We will solve a heat flow in a two-dimensional plate with four heat sources and the edges in zero-degree water, as shown in Figure 14-1.

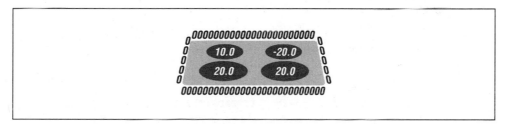

Figure 14-1: A two-dimensional plate with four constant heat sources

The data will be spread across all of the processes using a (*, BLOCK) distribution. Columns are distributed to processes in contiguous blocks, and all the row elements in a column are stored on the same process. As with HPF, the process that "owns" a data cell performs the computations for that cell after retrieving any data necessary to perform the computation.

We use a red-black approach but for simplicity, we copy the data back at the end of each iteration. For a true red-black, you would perform the computation in the opposite direction every other time step.

Note that instead of spawning slave process, the parent process spawns additional copies of itself. This is typical of SPMD-style programs. Once the additional processes have been spawned, all the processes wait at a barrier before they look for the process numbers of the members of the group. Once the processes have arrived at the barrier, they all retrieve a list of the different process numbers:

```
% cat pheat.f
      PROGRAM PHEAT
      INCLUDE '../include/fpvm3.h'
      INTEGER NPROC,ROWS,COLS,TOTCOLS,OFFSET
      PARAMETER(NPROC=4,MAXTIME=200)
      PARAMETER(ROWS=200,TOTCOLS=200)
      PARAMETER(COLS=(TOTCOLS/NPROC)+3)
      REAL*8 RED(0:ROWS+1,0:COLS+1),BLACK(0:ROWS+1,0:COLS+1)
      LOGICAL IAMFIRST,IAMLAST
      INTEGER INUM,INFO,TIDS(0:NPROC-1),IERR
      INTEGER I,R,C
      INTEGER TICK,MAXTIME
      CHARACTER*30 FNAME

*     Get the SPMD thing going - Join the pheat group
      CALL PVMFJOINGROUP('pheat', INUM)

* If we are the first in the pheat group, make some helpers
      IF ( INUM.EQ.0 ) THEN
        DO I=1,NPROC-1
          CALL PVMFSPAWN('pheat', 0, 'anywhere', 1, TIDS(I), IERR)
        ENDDO
      ENDIF

*     Barrier to make sure we are all here so we can look them up
      CALL PVMFBARRIER( 'pheat', NPROC, INFO )

* Find my pals and get their TIDs - TIDS are necessary for sending
      DO I=0,NPROC-1
        CALL PVMFGETTID('pheat', I, TIDS(I))
      ENDDO
```

At this point in the code, we have **NPROC** processes executing in an SPMD mode. The next step is to determine which subset of the array each process will compute. This is driven by the **INUM** variable, which ranges from 0 to 3 and uniquely identifies these processes.

We decompose the data and store only one quarter of the data on each process. Using the **INUM** variable, we choose our continuous set of columns to store and compute. The **OFFSET** variable maps between a "global" column in the entire array and a local column in our local subset of the array. Figure 14-2 shows a map that indicates which processors store which data elements. The values marked with a **B** are boundary values and won't change during the simulation. They are all set to 0. This code is often rather tricky to figure out. Performing a (**BLOCK,BLOCK**) distribution requires a two-dimensional decomposition and exchanging data with the neighbors above and below, in addition to the neighbors to the left and right:

```
* Compute my geometry - What subset do I process? (INUM=0 values)
* Actual Column = OFFSET + Column (OFFSET = 0)
*     Column 0 = neighbors from left
```

	0	1		50	51		100	101		150	151		200	201
0	B	B B	...	B	B	B B	...	B	B	B B	...	B	B	B B	...	B	B	B
1	B	0 0	...	0	0	1 1	...	1	1	2 2	...	2	2	3 3	...	3	3	B
	B	0 0	...	0	0	1 1	...	1	1	2 2	...	2	2	3 3	...	3	3	B
...	B	0 0	...	0	0	1 1	...	1	1	2 2	...	2	2	3 3	...	3	3	B
	B	0 0	...	0	0	1 1	...	1	1	2 2	...	2	2	3 3	...	3	3	B
200	B	0 0	...	0	0	1 1	...	1	1	2 2	...	2	2	3 3	...	3	3	B
201	B	B B	...	B	B	B B	...	B	B	B B	...	B	B	B B	...	B	B	B

Figure 14-2: Assigning grid elements to processors

```
*       Column 1 = send to left
*       Columns 1..mylen My cells to compute
*       Column mylen = Send to right  (mylen=50)
*       Column mylen+1 = Neighbors from Right (Column 51)

        IAMFIRST = (INUM .EQ. 0)
        IAMLAST = (INUM .EQ. NPROC-1)
        OFFSET = (ROWS/NPROC * INUM )
        MYLEN = ROWS/NPROC
        IF ( IAMLAST ) MYLEN = TOTCOLS - OFFSET
        PRINT *,'INUM:',INUM,' Local',1,MYLEN,
     +                    ' Global',OFFSET+1,OFFSET+MYLEN

* Start Cold
        DO C=0,COLS+1
          DO R=0,ROWS+1
            BLACK(R,C) = 0.0
          ENDDO
        ENDDO
```

Now we run the time steps. The first act in each time step is to reset the heat sources. In this simulation, we have four heat sources placed near the middle of the plate. We must restore all the values each time through the simulation as they are modified in the main loop:

```
* Begin running the time steps
        DO TICK=1,MAXTIME

* Set the heat persistent sources
        CALL STORE(BLACK,ROWS,COLS,OFFSET,MYLEN,
     +      ROWS/3,TOTCOLS/3,10.0,INUM)
        CALL STORE(BLACK,ROWS,COLS,OFFSET,MYLEN,
     +      2*ROWS/3,TOTCOLS/3,20.0,INUM)
        CALL STORE(BLACK,ROWS,COLS,OFFSET,MYLEN,
     +      ROWS/3,2*TOTCOLS/3,-20.0,INUM)
        CALL STORE(BLACK,ROWS,COLS,OFFSET,MYLEN,
     +      2*ROWS/3,2*TOTCOLS/3,20.0,INUM)
```

Now we perform the exchange of the "ghost values" with our neighboring processes. For example, Process 0 contains the elements for global column 50. To compute the next time step values for column 50, we need column 51, which is stored in Process 1. Similarly, before Process 1 can compute the new values for column 51, it needs Process 0's values for column 50.

Figure 14-3 shows how the data is transferred between processors. Each process sends its leftmost column to the left and its rightmost column to the right. Because the first and last processes border unchanging boundary values on the left and right respectively, this is not necessary for columns one and 200. If all is done properly, each process can receive its ghost values from their left and right neighbors.

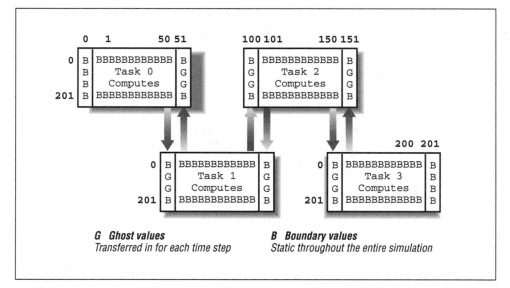

Figure 14-3: Pattern of communication for ghost values

The net result of all of the transfers is that for each space that must be computed, it's surrounded by one layer of either boundary values or ghost values from the right or left neighbors:

```
* Send left and right
        IF ( .NOT. IAMFIRST ) THEN
          CALL PVMFINITSEND(PVMDEFAULT,TRUE)
          CALL PVMFPACK( REAL8, BLACK(1,1), ROWS, 1, INFO )
          CALL PVMFSEND( TIDS(INUM-1), 1, INFO )
        ENDIF
        IF ( .NOT. IAMLAST ) THEN
          CALL PVMFINITSEND(PVMDEFAULT,TRUE)
          CALL PVMFPACK( REAL8, BLACK(1,MYLEN), ROWS, 1, INFO )
          CALL PVMFSEND( TIDS(INUM+1), 2, INFO )
```

```
         ENDIF
* Receive right, then left
         IF ( .NOT. IAMLAST ) THEN
            CALL PVMFRECV( TIDS(INUM+1), 1, BUFID )
            CALL PVMFUNPACK ( REAL8, BLACK(1,MYLEN+1), ROWS, 1, INFO)
         ENDIF
         IF ( .NOT. IAMFIRST ) THEN
            CALL PVMFRECV( TIDS(INUM-1), 2, BUFID )
            CALL PVMFUNPACK ( REAL8, BLACK(1,0), ROWS, 1, INFO)
         ENDIF
```

This next segment is the easy part. All the appropriate ghost values are in place, so we must simply perform the computation in our subspace. At the end, we copy back from the RED to the BLACK array; in a real simulation, we would perform two time steps, one from BLACK to RED and the other from RED to BLACK, to save this extra copy:

```
* Perform the flow
         DO C=1,MYLEN
           DO R=1,ROWS
             RED(R,C) = ( BLACK(R,C) +
     +                      BLACK(R,C-1) + BLACK(R-1,C) +
     +                      BLACK(R+1,C) + BLACK(R,C+1) ) / 5.0
           ENDDO
         ENDDO

* Copy back - Normally we would do a red and black version of the loop
         DO C=1,MYLEN
           DO R=1,ROWS
             BLACK(R,C) = RED(R,C)
           ENDDO
         ENDDO
      ENDDO
```

Now we find the center cell and send to the master process (if necessary) so it can be printed out. We also dump out the data into files for debugging or later visualization of the results. Each file is made unique by appending the instance number to the filename. Then the program terminates:

```
         CALL SENDCELL(RED,ROWS,COLS,OFFSET,MYLEN,INUM,TIDS(0),
     +          ROWS/2,TOTCOLS/2)

* Dump out data for verification
         IF ( ROWS .LE. 20 ) THEN
           FNAME = '/tmp/pheatout.' // CHAR(ICHAR('0')+INUM)
           OPEN(UNIT=9,NAME=FNAME,FORM='formatted')
           DO C=1,MYLEN
             WRITE(9,100)(BLACK(R,C),R=1,ROWS)
100          FORMAT(20F12.6)
           ENDDO
           CLOSE(UNIT=9)
         ENDIF
```

```
* Lets all go together
      CALL PVMFBARRIER( 'pheat', NPROC, INFO )
      CALL PVMFEXIT( INFO )

      END
```

The SENDCELL routine finds a particular cell and prints it out on the master process. This routine is called in an SPMD style: all the processes enter this routine although all not at precisely the same time. Depending on the INUM and the cell that we are looking for, each process may do something different.

If the cell in question is in the master process, and we are the master process, print it out. All other processes do nothing. If the cell in question is stored in another process, the process with the cell sends it to the master processes. The master process receives the value and prints it out. All the other processes do nothing.

This is a simple example of the typical style of SPMD code. All the processes execute the code at roughly the same time, but, based on information local to each process, the actions performed by different processes may be quite different:

```
      SUBROUTINE SENDCELL(RED,ROWS,COLS,OFFSET,MYLEN,INUM,PTID,R,C)
      INCLUDE '../include/fpvm3.h'
      INTEGER ROWS,COLS,OFFSET,MYLEN,INUM,PTID,R,C
      REAL*8 RED(0:ROWS+1,0:COLS+1)
      REAL*8 CENTER

* Compute local row number to determine if it is ours
      I = C - OFFSET
      IF ( I .GE. 1 .AND. I.LE. MYLEN ) THEN
        IF ( INUM .EQ. 0 ) THEN
          PRINT *,'Master has', RED(R,I), R, C, I
        ELSE
          CALL PVMFINITSEND(PVMDEFAULT,TRUE)
          CALL PVMFPACK( REAL8, RED(R,I), 1, 1, INFO )
          PRINT *, 'INUM:',INUM,' Returning',R,C,RED(R,I),I
          CALL PVMFSEND( PTID, 3, INFO )
        ENDIF
      ELSE
        IF ( INUM .EQ. 0 ) THEN
          CALL PVMFRECV( -1 , 3, BUFID )
          CALL PVMFUNPACK ( REAL8, CENTER, 1, 1, INFO)
          PRINT *, 'Master Received',R,C,CENTER
        ENDIF
      ENDIF
      RETURN
      END
```

Like the previous routine, the STORE routine is executed on all processes. The idea is to store a value into a *global* row and column position. First, we must determine if the cell is even in our process. If the cell is in our process, we must compute the local column (I) in our subset of the overall matrix and then store the value:

```
SUBROUTINE STORE(RED,ROWS,COLS,OFFSET,MYLEN,R,C,VALUE,INUM)
REAL*8 RED(0:ROWS+1,0:COLS+1)
REAL VALUE
INTEGER ROWS,COLS,OFFSET,MYLEN,R,C,I,INUM
I = C - OFFSET
IF ( I .LT. 1 .OR. I .GT. MYLEN ) RETURN
RED(R,I) = VALUE
RETURN
END
```

When this program executes, it has the following output:

```
% pheat
 INUM:  0 Local  1  50 Global  1  50
 Master Received  100  100    3.4722390023541D-07
%
```

We see two lines of print. The first line indicates the values that Process 0 used in its geometry computation. The second line is the output from the master process of the temperature at cell (100,100) after 200 time steps.

One interesting technique that is useful for debugging this type of program is to change the number of processes that are created. If the program is not quite moving its data properly, you usually get different results when different numbers of processes are used. If you look closely, the above code performs correctly with one process or 30 processes.

Notice that there is no barrier operation at the end of each time step. This is in contrast to the way parallel loops operate on shared uniform memory multiprocessors that force a barrier at the end of each loop. Because we have used an "owner computes" rule, and nothing is computed until all the required ghost data is received, there is no need for a barrier. The receipt of the messages with the proper ghost values allows a process to begin computing immediately without regard to what the other processes are currently doing.

This example can be used either as a framework for developing other grid-based computations, or as a good excuse to use HPF and appreciate the hard work that the HPF compiler developers have done. A well-done HPF implementation of this simulation should outperform the PVM implementation because HPF can make tighter optimizations. Unlike us, the HPF compiler doesn't have to keep its generated code readable.

PVM Summary

PVM is a widely used tool because it affords portability across every architecture other than SIMD. Once the effort has been invested in making a code message passing, it tends to run well on many architectures.

The primary complaints about PVM include:

- The need for a pack step separate from the send step

- The fact that it is designed to work in a heterogeneous environment that may incur some overhead

- It doesn't automate common tasks such as geometry computations

But all in all, for a certain set of programmers, PVM is the tool to use. If you would like to learn more about PVM see *PVM—A User's Guide and Tutorial for Networked Parallel Computing*, by Al Geist, Adam Beguelin, Jack Dongarra, Weicheng Jiang, Robert Manchek, and Vaidy Sunderam (MIT Press). Information is also available at *www.netlib.org/pvm3/*.

Message-Passing Interface (MPI)

The Message-Passing Interface (MPI) was designed to be an industrial-strength message-passing environment that is portable across a wide range of hardware environments.

Much like High Performance FORTRAN, MPI was developed by a group of computer vendors, application developers, and computer scientists. The idea was to come up with a specification that would take the strengths of many of the existing proprietary message passing environments on a wide variety of architectures and come up with a specification that could be implemented on architectures ranging from SIMD systems with thousands of small processors to MIMD networks of workstations and everything in between.

Interestingly, the MPI effort was completed a year *after* the High Performance FORTRAN (HPF) effort was completed. Some viewed MPI as a portable message-passing interface that could support a good HPF compiler. Having MPI makes the compiler more portable. Also having the compiler use MPI as its message-passing environment insures that MPI is heavily tested and that sufficient resources are invested into the MPI implementation.

PVM Versus MPI

While many of the folks involved in PVM participated in the MPI effort, MPI is not simply a follow-on to PVM. PVM was developed in a university/research lab environment and evolved over time as new features were needed. For example, the group capability was not designed into PVM at a fundamental level. Some of the underlying assumptions of PVM were based "on a network of workstations connected via Ethernet" model and didn't export well to scalable computers.* In some ways, MPI is more robust than PVM, and in other ways, MPI is simpler than PVM. MPI doesn't specify the system management details as in PVM; MPI doesn't specify how a virtual machine is to be created, operated, and used.

MPI Features

MPI has a number of useful features beyond the basic send and receive capabilities. These include:

Communicators

> A communicator is a subset of the active processes that can be treated as a group for collective operations such as broadcast, reduction, barriers, sending, or receiving. Within each communicator, a process has a *rank* that ranges from zero to the size of the group. A process may be a member of more than one communicator and have a different rank within each communicator. There is a default communicator that refers to all the MPI processes that is called `MPI_COMM_WORLD`.

Topologies

> A communicator can have a topology associated with it. This arranges the processes that belong to a communicator into some layout. The most common layout is a Cartesian decomposition. For example, 12 processes may be arranged into a 3×4 grid.† Once these topologies are defined, they can be queried to find the neighboring processes in the topology. In addition to the Cartesian (grid) topology, MPI also supports a graph-based topology.

Communication modes

> MPI supports multiple styles of communication, including blocking and non-blocking. Users can also choose to use explicit buffers for sending or allow MPI to manage the buffers. The nonblocking capabilities allow the overlap of communication and computation. MPI can support a model in which there is no available memory space for buffers and the data must be copied directly

---

* One should not diminish the positive contributions of PVM, however. PVM was the first widely available portable message-passing environment. PVM pioneered the idea of heterogeneous distributed computing with built-in format conversion.

† Sounds a little like HPF, no?

from the address space of the sending process to the memory space of the receiving process. MPI also supports a single call to perform a send and receive that is quite useful when processes need to exchange data.

Single-call collective operations

Some of the calls in MPI automate collective operations in a single call. For example, the broadcast operation sends values from the master to the slaves and receives the values on the slaves in the same operation. The net result is that the values are updated on all processes. Similarly, there is a single call to sum a value across all of the processes to a single value. By bundling all this functionality into a single call, systems that have support for collective operations in hardware can make best use of this hardware. Also, when MPI is operating on a shared-memory environment, the broadcast can be simplified as all the slaves simply make a local copy of a shared variable.

Clearly, the developers of the MPI specification had significant experience with developing message-passing applications and added many widely used features to the message-passing library. Without these features, each programmer needed to use more primitive operations to construct their own versions of the higher-level operations.

Heat Flow in MPI

In this example, we implement our heat flow problem in MPI using a similar decomposition to the PVM example. There are several ways to approach the problem. We could almost translate PVM calls to corresponding MPI calls using the `MPI_COMM_WORLD` communicator. However, to showcase some of the MPI features, we create a Cartesian communicator:

```
      PROGRAM MHEATC
      INCLUDE 'mpif.h'
      INCLUDE 'mpef.h'
      INTEGER ROWS,COLS,TOTCOLS
      PARAMETER(MAXTIME=200)
* This simulation can be run on MINPROC or greater processes.
* It is OK to set MINPROC to 1 for testing purposes
* For a large number of rows and columns, it is best to set MINPROC
* to the actual number of runtime processes
      PARAMETER(MINPROC=2)
      PARAMETER(ROWS=200,TOTCOLS=200,COLS=TOTCOLS/MINPROC)
      DOUBLE PRECISION RED(0:ROWS+1,0:COLS+1),BLACK(0:ROWS+1,0:COLS+1)
      INTEGER S,E,MYLEN,R,C
      INTEGER TICK,MAXTIME
      CHARACTER*30 FNAME
```

The basic data structures are much the same as in the PVM example. We allocate a subset of the heat arrays in each process. In this example, the amount of space allocated in each process is set by the compile-time variable `MINPROC`. The simulation can execute on more than `MINPROC` processes (wasting some space in each process), but it can't execute on less than `MINPROC` processes, or there won't be sufficient total space across all of the processes to hold the array:

```
INTEGER COMM1D,INUM,NPROC,IERR
INTEGER DIMS(1),COORDS(1)
LOGICAL PERIODS(1)
LOGICAL REORDER
INTEGER NDIM
INTEGER STATUS(MPI_STATUS_SIZE)
INTEGER RIGHTPROC, LEFTPROC
```

These data structures are used for our interaction with MPI. As we will be doing a one-dimensional Cartesian decomposition, our arrays are dimensioned to one. If you were to do a two-dimensional decomposition, these arrays would need two elements:

```
PRINT *,'Calling MPI_INIT'
CALL MPI_INIT( IERR )
PRINT *,'Back from MPI_INIT'
CALL MPI_COMM_SIZE( MPI_COMM_WORLD, NPROC, IERR )
```

The call to `MPI_INIT` creates the appropriate number of processes. Note that in the output, the PRINT statement before the call only appears once, but the second PRINT appears once for each process. We call `MPI_COMM_SIZE` to determine the size of the global communicator `MPI_COMM_WORLD`. We use this value to set up our Cartesian topology:

```
* Create new communicator that has a Cartesian topology associated
* with it - MPI_CART_CREATE returns COMM1D - A communicator descriptor

      DIMS(1) = NPROC
      PERIODS(1) = .FALSE.
      REORDER = .TRUE.
      NDIM = 1

      CALL MPI_CART_CREATE(MPI_COMM_WORLD, NDIM, DIMS, PERIODS,
     +     REORDER, COMM1D, IERR)
```

Now we create a one-dimensional (`NDIM=1`) arrangement of all of our processes (`MPI_COMM_WORLD`). All of the parameters on this call are input values except for `COMM1D` and `IERR`. `COMM1D` is an integer "communicator handle." If you print it out, it will be a value such as 134. It is not actually data, it is merely a handle that is used in other calls. It is quite similar to a file descriptor or unit number used when performing input-output to and from files.

The topology we use is a one-dimensional decomposition that isn't periodic. If we specified that we wanted a periodic decomposition, the far-left and far-right processes would be neighbors in a wrapped-around fashion making a ring. Given that it isn't periodic, the far-left and far-right processes have no neighbors.

In our PVM example above, we declared that Process 0 was the far-right process, Process NPROC-1 was the far-left process, and the other processes were arranged linearly between those two. If we set REORDER to .FALSE., MPI also chooses this arrangement. However, if we set REORDER to .TRUE., MPI may choose to arrange the processes in some other fashion to achieve better performance, assuming that you are communicating with close neighbors.

Once the communicator is set up, we use it in all of our communication operations:

```
* Get my rank in the new communicator

  CALL MPI_COMM_RANK( COMM1D, INUM, IERR)
```

Within each communicator, each process has a rank from zero to the size of the communicator minus 1. The MPI_COMM_RANK tells each process its rank within the communicator. A process may have a different rank in the COMM1D communicator than in the MPI_COMM_WORLD communicator because of some reordering.

Given a Cartesian topology communicator,* we can extract information from the communicator using the MPI_CART_GET routine:

```
* Given a communicator handle COMM1D, get the topology, and my position
* in the topology

  CALL MPI_CART_GET(COMM1D, NDIM, DIMS, PERIODS, COORDS, IERR)
```

In this call, all of the parameters are output values rather than input values as in the MPI_CART_CREATE call. The COORDS variable tells us our coordinates within the the communicator. This is not so useful in our one-dimensional example, but in a two-dimensional process decomposition, it would tell our current position in that two-dimensional grid:

```
* Returns the left and right neighbors 1 unit away in the zeroth dimension
* of our Cartesian map - since we are not periodic, our neighbors may
* not always exist - MPI_CART_SHIFT handles this for us

      CALL MPI_CART_SHIFT(COMM1D, 0, 1, LEFTPROC, RIGHTPROC, IERR)
      CALL MPE_DECOMP1D(TOTCOLS, NPROC, INUM, S, E)
      MYLEN = ( E - S ) + 1
      IF ( MYLEN.GT.COLS ) THEN
        PRINT *,'Not enough space, need',MYLEN,' have ',COLS
        PRINT *,TOTCOLS,NPROC,INUM,S,E
        STOP
      ENDIF
      PRINT *,INUM,NPROC,COORDS(1),LEFTPROC,RIGHTPROC, S, E
```

---

* Remember, each communicator may have a topology associated with it. A topology can be grid, graph, or none. Interestingly, the MPI_COMM_WORLD communicator has no topology associated with it.

We can use `MPI_CART_SHIFT` to determine the rank number of our left and right neighbors, so we can exchange our common points with these neighbors. This is necessary because we can't simply send to `INUM-1` and `INUM+1` if MPI has chosen to reorder our Cartesian decomposition. If we are the far-left or far-right process, the neighbor that doesn't exist is set to `MPI_PROC_NULL`, which indicates that we have no neighbor. Later when we are performing message sending, it checks this value and sends messages only to real processes. By not sending the message to the "null process," MPI has saved us an IF test.

To determine which strip of the global array we store and compute in this process, we call a utility routine called `MPE_DECOMP1D` that simply does several calculations to evenly split our 200 columns among our processes in contiguous strips. In the PVM version, we need to perform this computation by hand.

The `MPE_DECOMP1D` routine is an example of an extended MPI library call (hence the MPE prefix). These extensions include graphics support and logging tools in addition to some general utilities. The MPE library consists of routines that were useful enough to standardize but not required to be supported by all MPI implementations. You will find the MPE routines supported on most MPI implementations.

Now that we have our communicator group set up, and we know which strip each process will handle, we begin the computation:

```
* Start Cold

      DO C=0,COLS+1
        DO R=0,ROWS+1
          BLACK(R,C) = 0.0
        ENDDO
      ENDDO
```

As in the PVM example, we set the plate (including boundary values) to zero.

All processes begin the time step loop. Interestingly, like in PVM, there is no need for any synchronization. The messages implicitly synchronize our loops.

The first step is to store the permanent heat sources. We need to use a routine because we must make the store operations relative to our strip of the global array:

```
* Begin running the time steps
      DO TICK=1,MAXTIME

* Set the persistent heat sources
        CALL STORE(BLACK,ROWS,COLS,S,E,ROWS/3,TOTCOLS/3,10.0,INUM)
        CALL STORE(BLACK,ROWS,COLS,S,E,2*ROWS/3,TOTCOLS/3,20.0,INUM)
        CALL STORE(BLACK,ROWS,COLS,S,E,ROWS/3,2*TOTCOLS/3,-20.0,INUM)
        CALL STORE(BLACK,ROWS,COLS,S,E,2*ROWS/3,2*TOTCOLS/3,20.0,INUM)
```

All of the processes set these values independently depending on which process has which strip of the overall array.

Now we exchange the data with our neighbors as determined by the Cartesian communicator. Note that we don't need an IF test to determine if we are the far-left or far-right process. If we are at the edge, our neighbor setting is MPI_PROC_NULL and the MPI_SEND and MPI_RECV calls do nothing when given this as a source or destination value, thus saving us an IF test.

Note that we specify the communicator COMM1D because the rank values we are using in these calls are relative to that communicator:

```
* Send left and receive right
      CALL MPI_SEND(BLACK(1,1),ROWS,MPI_DOUBLE_PRECISION,
    +              LEFTPROC,1,COMM1D,IERR)
      CALL MPI_RECV(BLACK(1,MYLEN+1),ROWS,MPI_DOUBLE_PRECISION,
    +              RIGHTPROC,1,COMM1D,STATUS,IERR)

* Send Right and Receive left in a single statement
      CALL MPI_SENDRECV(
    +     BLACK(1,MYLEN),ROWS,COMM1D,RIGHTPROC,2,
    +     BLACK(1,0),    ROWS,COMM1D,LEFTPROC, 2,
    +     MPI_COMM_WORLD, STATUS, IERR)
```

Just to show off, we use both the separate send and receive, and the combined send and receive. When given a choice, it's probably a good idea to use the combined operations to give the runtime environment more flexibility in terms of buffering. One downside to this that occurs on a network of workstations (or any other high-latency interconnect) is that you can't do both send operations first and then do both receive operations to overlap some of the communication delay.

Once we have all of our ghost points from our neighbors, we can perform the algorithm on our subset of the space:

```
* Perform the flow
      DO C=1,MYLEN
        DO R=1,ROWS
          RED(R,C) = ( BLACK(R,C) +
    +                  BLACK(R,C-1) + BLACK(R-1,C) +
    +                  BLACK(R+1,C) + BLACK(R,C+1) ) / 5.0
        ENDDO
      ENDDO

* Copy back - Normally we would do a red and black version of the loop
      DO C=1,MYLEN
        DO R=1,ROWS
          BLACK(R,C) = RED(R,C)
        ENDDO
      ENDDO
      ENDDO
```

Again, for simplicity, we don't do the complete red-black computation.* We have no synchronization at the bottom of the loop because the messages implicitly synchronize the processes at the top of the next loop.

Again, we dump out the data for verification. As in the PVM example, one good test of basic correctness is to make sure you get exactly the same results for varying numbers of processes:

```
* Dump out data for verification
      IF ( ROWS .LE. 20 ) THEN
        FNAME = '/tmp/mheatcout.' // CHAR(ICHAR('0')+INUM)
        OPEN(UNIT=9,NAME=FNAME,FORM='formatted')
        DO C=1,MYLEN
          WRITE(9,100)(BLACK(R,C),R=1,ROWS)
100       FORMAT(20F12.6)
        ENDDO
        CLOSE(UNIT=9)
      ENDIF
```

To terminate the program, we call `MPI_FINALIZE`:

```
* Lets all go together
      CALL MPI_FINALIZE(IERR)
      END
```

As in the PVM example, we need a routine to store a value into the proper strip of the global array. This routine simply checks to see if a particular global element is in this process and if so, computes the proper location within its strip for the value. If the global element is not in this process, this routine simply returns doing nothing:

```
      SUBROUTINE STORE(RED,ROWS,COLS,S,E,R,C,VALUE,INUM)
      REAL*8 RED(0:ROWS+1,0:COLS+1)
      REAL VALUE
      INTEGER ROWS,COLS,S,E,R,C,I,INUM
      IF ( C .LT. S .OR. C .GT. E ) RETURN
      I = ( C - S ) + 1
*     PRINT *,'STORE, INUM,R,C,S,E,R,I',INUM,R,C,S,E,R,I,VALUE
      RED(R,I) = VALUE
      RETURN
      END
```

When this program is executed, it has the following output:

```
% mpif77 -c mheatc.f mheatc.f:
MAIN mheatc:
store:
% mpif77 -o mheatc mheatc.o -lmpe
% mheatc -np 4
```

---

* Note that you could do two time steps (one black-red-black iteration) if you exchanged two ghost columns at the top of the loop.

```
Calling MPI_INIT
Back from MPI_INIT
Back from MPI_INIT
Back from MPI_INIT
Back from MPI_INIT
 0  4  0  -1  1   1    50
 2  4  2   1  3  101  150
 3  4  3   2 -1  151  200
 1  4  1   0  2  51  100
%
```

As you can see, we call **MPI_INIT** to activate the four processes. The PRINT statement immediately after the **MPI_INIT** call appears four times, once for each of the activated processes. Then each process prints out the strip of the array it will process. We can also see the neighbors of each process including -1 when a process has no neighbor to the left or right. Notice that Process 0 has no left neighbor, and Process 3 has no right neighbor. MPI has provided us the utilities to simplify message-passing code that we need to add to implement this type of grid-based application.

When you compare this example with a PVM implementation of the same problem, you can see some of the contrasts between the two approaches. Programmers who wrote the same six lines of code over and over in PVM combined them into a single call in MPI. In MPI, you can think "data parallel" and express your program in a more data-parallel fashion.

In some ways, MPI feels less like assembly language than PVM. However, MPI does take a little getting used to when compared to PVM. The concept of a Cartesian communicator may seem foreign at first, but with understanding, it becomes a flexible and powerful tool.

Heat in MPI Using Broadcast/Gather

One style of parallel programming that we have not yet seen is the *broadcast/gather* style. Not all applications can be naturally solved using this style of programming. However, if an application can use this approach effectively, the amount of modification that is required to make a code run in a message-passing environment is minimal.

Applications that most benefit from this approach generally do a lot of computation using some small amount of shared information. One requirement is that one complete copy of the "shared" information must fit in each of the processes.

If we keep our grid size small enough, we can actually program our heat flow application using this approach. This is almost certainly a less efficient implementation than any of the earlier implementations of this problem because the core computation is so simple. However, if the core computations were more complex and needed access to values farther than one unit away, this might be a good approach.

The data structures are simpler for this approach and, actually, are no different than the single-process FORTRAN 90 or HPF versions. We will allocate a complete RED and BLACK array in every process:

```
PROGRAM MHEAT
INCLUDE 'mpif.h'
INCLUDE 'mpef.h'
INTEGER ROWS,COLS
PARAMETER(MAXTIME=200)
PARAMETER(ROWS=200,COLS=200)
DOUBLE PRECISION RED(0:ROWS+1,0:COLS+1),BLACK(0:ROWS+1,0:COLS+1)
```

We need fewer variables for the MPI calls because we aren't creating a communicator. We simply use the default communicator MPI_COMM_WORLD. We start up our processes, and find the size and rank of our process group:

```
INTEGER INUM,NPROC,IERR,SRC,DEST,TAG
INTEGER S,E,LS,LE,MYLEN
INTEGER STATUS(MPI_STATUS_SIZE)
INTEGER I,R,C
INTEGER TICK,MAXTIME
CHARACTER*30 FNAME

PRINT *,'Calling MPI_INIT'
CALL MPI_INIT( IERR )
CALL MPI_COMM_SIZE( MPI_COMM_WORLD, NPROC, IERR )
CALL MPI_COMM_RANK( MPI_COMM_WORLD, INUM, IERR)
CALL MPE_DECOMP1D(COLS, NPROC, INUM, S, E, IERR)
PRINT *,'My Share ', INUM, NPROC, S, E
```

Since we are broadcasting initial values to all of the processes, we only have to set things up on the master process:

```
* Start Cold

      IF ( INUM.EQ.0 ) THEN
        DO C=0,COLS+1
          DO R=0,ROWS+1
            BLACK(R,C) = 0.0
          ENDDO
        ENDDO
      ENDIF
```

As we run the time steps (again with no synchronization), we set the persistent heat sources directly. Since the shape of the data structure is the same in the master and all other processes, we can use the real array coordinates rather than mapping them as with the previous examples. We could skip the persistent settings on the nonmaster processes, but it doesn't hurt to do it on all processes:

```
* Begin running the time steps
      DO TICK=1,MAXTIME

* Set the heat sources
         BLACK(ROWS/3,    COLS/3)   = 10.0
         BLACK(2*ROWS/3, COLS/3)   = 20.0
         BLACK(ROWS/3,    2*COLS/3) = -20.0
         BLACK(2*ROWS/3, 2*COLS/3) = 20.0
```

Now we broadcast the entire array from process rank zero to all of the other processes in the MPI_COMM_WORLD communicator. Note that this call does the sending on rank zero process and receiving on the other processes. The net result of this call is that all the processes have the values formerly in the master process in a single call:

```
* Broadcast the array
      CALL MPI_BCAST(BLACK,(ROWS+2)*(COLS+2),MPI_DOUBLE_PRECISION,
     +                0,MPI_COMM_WORLD,IERR)
```

Now we perform the subset computation on each process. Note that we are using global coordinates because the array has the same shape on each of the processes. All we need to do is make sure we set up our particular strip of columns according to S and E:

```
* Perform the flow on our subset

      DO C=S,E
        DO R=1,ROWS
          RED(R,C) = ( BLACK(R,C) +
     +                  BLACK(R,C-1) + BLACK(R-1,C) +
     +                  BLACK(R+1,C) + BLACK(R,C+1) ) / 5.0
        ENDDO
      ENDDO
```

Now we need to gather the appropriate strips from the processes into the appropriate strip in the master array for rebroadcast in the next time step. We could change the loop in the master to receive the messages in any order and check the STATUS variable to see which strip it received:

```
* Gather back up into the BLACK array in master (INUM = 0)
      IF ( INUM .EQ. 0 ) THEN
        DO C=S,E
          DO R=1,ROWS
            BLACK(R,C) = RED(R,C)
          ENDDO
        ENDDO
        DO I=1,NPROC-1
          CALL MPE_DECOMP1D(COLS, NPROC, I, LS, LE, IERR)
          MYLEN = ( LE - LS ) + 1
          SRC = I
          TAG = 0
          CALL MPI_RECV(BLACK(0,LS),MYLEN*(ROWS+2),
```

```
    +                                    MPI_DOUBLE_PRECISION, SRC, TAG,
    +                                    MPI_COMM_WORLD, STATUS, IERR)
*              Print *,'Recv',I,MYLEN
          ENDDO
        ELSE
          MYLEN = ( E - S ) + 1
          DEST = 0
          TAG = 0
          CALL MPI_SEND(RED(0,S),MYLEN*(ROWS+2),MPI_DOUBLE_PRECISION,
    +                     DEST, TAG, MPI_COMM_WORLD, IERR)
*              Print *,'Send',INUM,MYLEN
        ENDIF
      ENDDO
```

We use `MPE_DECOMP1D` to determine which strip we're receiving from each process.

In some applications, the value that must be gathered is a sum or another single value. To accomplish this, you can use one of the MPI reduction routines that coalesce a set of distributed values into a single value using a single call.

Again at the end, we dump out the data for testing. However, since it has all been gathered back onto the master process, we only need to dump it on one process:

```
* Dump out data for verification
      IF ( INUM .EQ.0 .AND.  ROWS .LE. 20 ) THEN
        FNAME = '/tmp/mheatout'
        OPEN(UNIT=9,NAME=FNAME,FORM='formatted')
        DO C=1,COLS
          WRITE(9,100)(BLACK(R,C),R=1,ROWS)
100       FORMAT(20F12.6)
        ENDDO
        CLOSE(UNIT=9)
      ENDIF

      CALL MPI_FINALIZE(IERR)
      END
```

When this program executes with four processes, it produces the following output:

```
% mpif77 -c mheat.f
mheat.f:
MAIN mheat:
% mpif77 -o mheat mheat.o -lmpe
% mheat -np 4
Calling MPI_INIT
My Share   1  4  51  100
My Share   0  4  1  50
My Share   3  4  151  200
My Share   2  4  101  150
%
```

The ranks of the processes and the subsets of the computations for each process are shown in the output.

So that is a somewhat contrived example of the broadcast/gather approach to parallelizing an application. If the data structures are the right size and the amount of computation relative to communication is appropriate, this can be a very effective approach that may require the smallest number of code modifications compared to a single-processor version of the code.

MPI Summary

Whether you chose PVM or MPI depends on which library the vendor of your system prefers. Sometimes MPI is the better choice because it contains the newest features, such as support for hardware-supported multicast or broadcast, that can significantly improve the overall performance of a scatter-gather application.

A good text on MPI is *Using MPI—Portable Parallel Programming with the Message-Passing Interface*, by William Gropp, Ewing Lusk, and Anthony Skjellum (MIT Press). You may also want to retrieve and print the MPI specification from *http://www.netlib.org/mpi/*.

Closing Notes

In this chapter we have looked at the "assembly language" of parallel programming. While it can seem daunting to rethink your application, there are often some simple changes you can make to port your code to message passing. Depending on the application, a master-slave, broadcast-gather, or decomposed data approach might be most appropriate.

It's important to realize that some applications just don't decompose into message passing very well. You may be working with just such an application. Once you have some experience with message passing, it becomes easier to identify the critical points where data must be communicated between processes.

While HPF, PVM, and MPI are all mature and popular technologies, it's not clear whether any of these technologies will be the long-term solution that we will use 10 years from now. One possibility is that we will use FORTRAN 90 (or FORTRAN 95) without any data layout directives or that the directives will be optional. Another interesting possibility is simply to keep using FORTRAN 77. As scalable, cache-coherent, non-uniform memory systems become more popular, they will evolve their own data allocation primitives. For example, the HP/Exemplar supports the following data storage attributes: shared, node-private, and thread-private. As dynamic data structures are allocated, they can be placed in any one of these classes. Node-private memory is shared across all the threads on a single node but not shared beyond those threads. Perhaps we will only have to declare the storage class of the data but not the data layout for these new machines.

PVM and MPI still need the capability of supporting a fault-tolerant style of computing that allows an application to complete as resources fail or otherwise become available. The amount of compute power that will be available to applications that can tolerate some unreliability in the resources will be very large. There have been a number of moderately successful attempts in this area such as Condor, but none have really caught on in the mainstream.

To run the most powerful computers in the world at their absolute maximum performance levels, the need to be portable is somewhat reduced. Making your particular application go ever faster and scale to ever higher numbers of processors is a fascinating activity. May the FLOPS be with you!

V

Benchmarking

Using Published Benchmarks

Now that you are excited about making your code go really fast, you want to buy your very own high performance computer. How do you go about deciding which one? You will be spending somewhere between $10,000 and $30 million; you should make sure you get what you pay for. One approach is to just get more of the computers you already have. Another way is to get the marketing literature from each vendor and choose the best one. You could get one of each and let your users decide which they prefer after a year or so. You could call in the salespeople, have them give a presentation, and based on the quality of the graphics in the presentation, decide which computer to purchase.*

None of these approaches suffices for any engineer worth half their salt. We like to poke, prod, kick the tires, and take a test spin. In Chapter 16, *Running Your Own Benchmarks*, we discuss how to test drive one of these systems. However, you can't test drive every computer system on the planet. Often, we use published benchmark data to help guide us toward the right computer. We can use the published benchmark information to help narrow the focus, and, after doing our own performance testing, we can use published benchmarks to verify that our results are not completely out of line.

There are three sources of benchmarks:

* Vendor-specific benchmarks such as the iCOMP

* User organizations who share their benchmarks, such as Linpack, NAS, or SPLASH

---

* Don't laugh too hard. Some of these actually happen more often than you think.

- Industry organizations such as SPEC

It's important to know the value of each of these types of benchmarks so they can be appropriately used when making a decision.

There are many different types of benchmarks, ranging from very simple (30 lines of code) to very complex (100,000+ lines of code). A benchmark often summarizes a system's performance in a single number. For example, a $100,000 system might rate a 10.7, and a $150,000 system might be rated at 23.6. Which one is better? The second system, which is rated more than twice as high, but only costs 50% more, sounds like getting something for nothing. Unfortunately, the only thing that matters after you buy the system is how well the system runs your (or your users') applications under operating conditions that you expect in production.

A large challenge is to find a benchmark (or a few benchmarks) that roughly models your workload. This is why we need to understand that different benchmarks measure different things. However, before we go off and learn all about the different benchmarks, we need a little terminology.

MIPS: Millions of Instructions Per Second

The execution rate of a computer system is one way one could estimate the performance on a particular user application. However, it's one of the worst possible metrics to use. MIPS (millions of instructions per second) is typically related closely to the clock rate of the processor. And while it is pretty safe to assume that a 100-MIPS processor would be better than a 3-MIPS processor, a 50-MIPS processor could easily outperform a 100-MIPS processor.

Thankfully, few vendors still quote MIPS when comparing their computer performance to another vendor. Unfortunately, using MIPS is really comparing apples to oranges. The only reliable definition of MIPS today is, "meaningless indicator of processor speed."

Using MIPS as a tool to determine relative performance of different computers is flawed in two basic ways. First, a million instructions on one processor architecture does not accomplish the same work as a million instructions on another.* For example, if one processor does floating-point in software and takes 100 integer instructions to do a floating-point operation, your 100-MIPS processor becomes one million *useful instructions* per second. Also, especially in CISC processors, different instructions can take different amounts of time, so MIPS must be some type of weighted average of the number of instructions per second. Were your "million" instructions all NO-OPs (do-nothing instructions) or 32-bit loads from memory?

---

* It's like determining the winner of a foot race by counting who used fewer steps.

The second problem with using MIPS is that some vendors have redefined "MIP" as their own internal metric to compare different models of their own computers. For example, for a long time, folks viewed the DEC VAX 11/780, introduced in 1978, as the standard "1 MIP" machine. The funny thing is that the 11/780 isn't a 1 MIP machine at all—at least not in a pure sense. DEC published figures stating that for a reasonable job mix, the 11/780 executes at a rate of 470 thousand instructions/second—less than half of 1 MIP. So if somebody says that they have a 10-MIPS machine, by comparison with the 11/780, their computer is 10 times the speed of an 11/780, or less than 5 MIPS. You sometimes hear the expressions "VAX MIPS" or "VUPs" (VAX units of processing) to make the comparison clear.

All this taken together means that MIPS is only useful for comparisons between two processors from the same vendor that support the same instruction set with the same compilers. Intel has this type of benchmark, but they call it the iCOMP rating to emphasize that it is just an *Intel* benchmark that can be used to compare the relative performance of Intel processors.

What Are Mflops?

Floating-point benchmarks sit at the other end of the spectrum from MIPS. Floating-point performance is often measured in terms of millions of floating-point operations per second, called *megaflops* or *MFLOPS* for short. By the least controversial definition, a *floating-point operation* is one that executes on floating-point hardware. This definition includes floating-point additions, multiplies, comparisons, format conversions (between integer and floating-point form, for example), and perhaps divides and square roots, if they too are implemented in hardware. Unless otherwise stated, most megaflops figures report the rate at which the hardware can perform some mix of additions and multiplies. Square roots and divides take longer to execute, are less common in most codes, and often can't be pipelined to the same extent as additions and multiplies (they might even be software functions), which makes them less valuable in predicting general performance.

Just like MIPS, megaflops are sometimes reported in terms of machine peak speeds and sometimes in terms of benchmark speeds. However, while it is considered misleading to talk about peak MIPS ratings, vendors regularly quote peak megaflops rates. Peak megaflops for current processors are usually an integral multiple of the clock rate (usually 1, 2, or 4). The megaflops rate can be doubled because at the heart of many new machines' instruction sets is a floating-point multiply-add operation that can perform two "flops" in the space of one (under optimal conditions). The multiply-add is perfect for accumulating a running sum of vector elements, as in a dot product. On a four-way superscalar with two fully pipelined multiply-add units, a processor can produce four Mflops per cycle. As we add functional units, the peak Mflops become less and less useful. The bigger issue will be how quickly data can be moved into and out of the processor.

User Benchmarks

Consider a benchmark story. You could stay up late tonight and create a benchmark called the "zmark." It could test a few things, check the time, average things out and declare the system being tested as "12 zmarks." Then you could run it on lots of different computers, put them in a table, register the *www.zmark.org* domain and publish your ranked list of the performance of the computers you have tested. Chances are good that you would probably be ignored.

However, *if* word got out that your benchmark was the best available indicator of system performance, users might start buying their computers only after looking at your rating. Then, vendors would be banging on your door to make sure their newest computers were properly ranked in your list. They would give you time on their computers or even give you a computer to use. Now your list of performance results begins to become very complete, and the vendors begin to quote your results in their marketing literature.

Because of added attention, users put even more stock in your zmark rating. At some point, the best engineers at the vendor companies would examine your code and figure out where their compilers were generating less-than-ideal code. Then they might fix up their compilers to do their best on your code. One vendor realizes that by doubling the cache size they can improve their zmark rating by a factor of five, so they add the cache and sell lots of systems. At some point, the users who are purchasing their computers based on your zmark rating begin to realize that their applications run much faster on a computer with a lower zmark rating. Then word gets around that the zmark benchmark has been broken. Pretty soon users stop relying on your zmark to make their purchases.

For a brief moment in time you created a user benchmark. There have been many influential user benchmarks that measured high performance computing. As a matter of fact, before high performance computing became mainstream, user benchmarks were the primary source of performance information for high performance systems.

Linpack

The mother of all benchmarks is the *Linpack benchmark*, written by Jack Dongarra, formerly of Argonne National Laboratory, but now at the Oak Ridge National Laboratory in Tennessee. You hear "Linpack" so often, it's easy to believe it's the name of the benchmark. The goal of the Linpack was not to develop a benchmark, but instead to develop a set of high performance library routines for linear algebra.* As the Linpack developers gathered performance information about their library, they began to publish their results. The Linpack benchmark uses a handful of those routines to measure the time it takes to solve a dense system of linear equations using Gaussian elimination. The benchmark reports average megaflop rates by dividing the total number of floating-point operations by time.

It turned out that the Linpack 100×100 program stressed both the floating-point performance and the memory performance of the computer systems of the 1980s and early 1990s. Because of the nature of the computation, there were no "tricks" available to speed it up. Also because scientists "understood" Gaussian elimination, they could relate the Linpack results to their own applications. In some ways, Linpack was viewed as a very hard problem for a high performance computer to solve. In a sense, users felt that if a computer could do 300 Mflops on Linpack, then it would probably do 300 Mflops (or better) on their applications.

There are several versions of the Linpack benchmark, differing in size, numerical precision, and ground rules. The most useful number was the the 100×100 matrix double-precision results under strictly compiled FORTRAN—no hand optimizations. You are allowed to use whatever compiler optimizations you have at your disposal, like automatic loop unrolling, but you can't modify the code itself.

In addition to the 100×100 benchmark, there is also a 1000×1000 "anything goes" Linpack benchmark. Vendors are allowed to solve the system of equations using any method they choose, as long there isn't an appreciable loss of precision over the original. The larger Linpack is an important metric because it predicts the achievable peak performance on the largest computing systems for highly optimized applications. While there were no tricks for the 100×100 benchmark, when the problem was scaled up to 1000×1000 there were a wide range of performance improvements available.†

The heart of the 100×100 Linpack benchmark is a routine called *daxpy*. Daxpy scales a vector by a constant and adds it to another vector:

```
DO I = 1,N
  DY(I) = DY(I) + DA*DX(I)
END DO
```

Looking closely at the loop, you can count two floating-point operations (a multiply and an addition) and three memory operations (two loads and a store).

---

* The "Linpack" benchmark is such a classic that the library routines upon which it was based have now been rewritten. The new linear algebra library is called "LAPACK—Linear Algebra PACKage," available at *http://www.netlib.org/lapack/*. LAPACK and SCALAPAK focus on solving linear equations on scalable parallel processors in addition to parallel/vector supercomputers.

† See the blocking discussion in Chapter 8, *Loop Optimizations*.

Memory operations limit this loop's performance on most architectures, though it's the perfect mix for some vector supercomputers.

The Linpack 100×100 ceased to be a useful benchmark when it could be easily held in the cache of a microprocessor. The data structures for the benchmark are only 320 KB. In 1989, Linpack clearly tested the main memory performance. However, today, 250 KB is a relatively small size for a second-level cache on a home computer. Some top-end RISC processors support 2 MB or larger first-level caches. Unfortunately, you can't simply scale up the Linpack benchmark. If you increase the size to, say, 16 MB, the data structures can be accessed in a blocked fashion, again making good use of cache.

So, the Linpack 100×100 benchmark went from the most dominant single number benchmark in history to relative obscurity in about two years as one vendor after another had a sufficiently large cache to hold the entire data structure for the duration of the benchmark run.

However, the Linpack benchmark continues on as the basis for the *Top 500 Report*, which lists the 500 most powerful computers in the world.*

Linpack Highly Parallel Computing Benchmark

The Linpack Highly Parallel Computing (or table 3) benchmark is designed to explore the scalability of parallel systems. In this benchmark, the vendor is allowed to pick the size of the matrix (N), and hence the amount of work done by each processor. The available physical memory in the system under test provides a rough upper bound on the value for N. Information collected with the benchmark includes:

R_{peak}
    The system peak Gflops.

N_{max}
    The matrix size (N) that gives the highest Gflops for some number of CPUs. It could be the point beyond which making the matrix any larger does not give appreciable increase in Mflops, so it may not be the absolute highest Mflops possible; it could also be an upper bound based on memory limitations in a configuration.

$N_{1/2}$
    The matrix size that achieves half the rated R_{max} Gflops (R_{max} corresponding to N_{max} matrix size).

---

* See Chapter 12, *Large-Scale Parallel Computing*, and *http://parallel.rz.uni-mannheim.de/top500.html*.

R_{max}

> The Gflops achieved for the N_{max} size matrix.

The smaller the matrix size for a given number of CPUs, the better, because it implies that the system can achieve its highest performance on smaller problems.

Table 15-1 shows information extracted from the Oct 12, 1996 report.*

Table 15-1: Highly Parallel Computing Benchmark Results

System	CPUs	R_{max} Gflops	N_{max} Gflops	$N_{1/2}$	R_{peak}
T3E (300 MHz)	16	6.3	19968	2208	9.6
HP Exemplar S-Class	16	7.8	13320	1044	11.5
Fujitsu VPP500/16,10ns	16	23.6	21120	3360	26.0
Cray C90 (240 MHz)	16	20.7	13312	700	15.0

In these cases, 16 CPUs are used. The R_{max} Gflops, i.e., the performance reached for the given matrix size (N_{max}) is similar between pairs of systems, but the problem size needed to achieve these results is almost 50% higher on the T3E and Fujitsu systems. In addition, to achieve one-half the R_{max} Gflops, the problem size ($N_{1/2}$) varies significantly. This indicates that, if you plotted performance versus problem size for both systems, the T3E and Fujitsu takes appreciably "longer" to reach their maximum performance. For a user, high values for N_{max} and $N_{1/2}$ indicate that these systems are better suited to very scalable problems.

SPLASH

The Stanford Parallel Applications for Shared Memory (SPLASH) is a very common benchmark suite for shared-memory parallel processors. SPLASH was developed in association with the FLASH (FLexible Architecture for SHared memory) hardware architecture project at Stanford University. The FLASH system is a scalable non-uniform memory access (NUMA) system. The SPLASH benchmark consists of four kernel[†] benchmarks and eight scientific applications. One unique aspect of the applications is that they are already parallelized using a portable parallel processing macro library.

---

* Note that the C90 is using the Strassen algorithm, which accounts for the higher R_{max} than R_{peak}. This is because the Gflops calculation is based on Gaussian Elimination, and Strassen has a lower operation count. This points to a potential problem with the Linpack benchmark in situations where vendors are free to choose the algorithm to solve the problem (which is the case for N=1000 and N×N). If C90 used the standard solution method, it would have an R_{max} no larger than R_{peak} (15 Gflops). And it might also affect the problem sizes for N_{max} and $N_{1/2}$.

† A *kernel* benchmark is one where some computationally intensive subset of a large application has been extracted. The small portion of the program is augmented with data and driver routines so that it is self-contained. Using the kernel approach keeps benchmark codes smaller and more manageable.

The developers of the programs have identified the areas of memory that can be shared and the portions of the computations that can be done in parallel using multiple threads. The data areas have been carefully decomposed by hand, and the developers have even identified some areas in the code where it might be beneficial to migrate data from remote memory to local memory.

The advantage of eliminating the need for a sophisticated compiler is that it is quite convenient to test hardware parallel processing capability before the compiler is available. In a sense, the SPLASH results are a good predictor of how fast these applications might run when a good compiler would be available.

If a vendor quotes SPLASH results as their only benchmark, it might lead you to believe that their compiler was a bit weak. However, vendors do not typically quote performance results for SPLASH. Usually these codes are used in a research setting to test the newest emerging hardware.

The SPLASH web address is *http://www-flash.stanford.edu/apps/SPLASH/* and the address to download the codes is *ftp://www-flash.stanford.edu/pub/*.

NAS

The NAS benchmark suite is a set of codes developed by NASA. The primary idea of the NAS benchmark is to test large, fast, scalable parallel computer systems. There are three benchmark sets that make up the NAS parallel benchmarks:

NPB 1

> This benchmark is unique in that it is specified without using any source code. NAS publishes a report describing the mathematics and the computations to be performed. The vendors are free to choose any language to solve the problem. The goal is to have a benchmark that truly allows architectures to be shown in their best light and eliminate any architecture or compiler bias that might be present if the benchmark were expressed in source code. The downside of this benchmark from the user perspective is that you don't really know how hard the vendor had to work to make the benchmark run so fast. Perhaps it was a lazy afternoon or perhaps it took 20 of the company's top engineers a year and a half. Because the NPB-1 benchmark is part of NASA's production workload, one benefit is that NASA ends up with the modified versions of the code.

NPB 2

> This benchmark is a more traditional benchmark with two kernel codes and three application codes. It's distributed with MPI message- passing calls in place. As in the SPLASH benchmark, this benchmark developer has already identified the parallelism, the data decomposition, and the communication pat-

tern. For this reason, it's a better test of the hardware and architecture performance rather than the compiler performance.

NPB 2-serial

This benchmark is a "deparallelized" version of the NPB 2 benchmark. The idea is to allow smaller single processor and multiprocessor shared-memory systems to execute the same codes for comparison purposes. These can test compiler ability by comparing the hand-tuned parallel version to the compiler-automatic parallel version.

The NAS codes are useful to categorize the performance of the larger advanced-architecture computers. You will also see the NAS benchmarks used in research settings. You can get more information about the NAS benchmarks at *http://science.nas.nasa.gov/Software/NPB/*.

STREAM: Memory Bandwidth Benchmark

Many benchmarks measure some "overall" performance metric that attempts to determine how well the system performs in a "typical" environment. This simplification reduces many factors, including compiler, CPU architecture, and memory architecture, to one number.

The STREAM benchmark looks at user-sustainable memory bandwidth (which can be completely unrelated to peak theoretical memory bandwidth), and at the relative costs of memory accesses and floating-point arithmetic. STREAM is intended to complement LINPACK 1000 and LINPACK N×N, which provide an excellent approximation to the peak sustainable floating-point performance. While looking at the STREAM performance of your potential computer is probably not enough information to make a good decision, these numbers can be very useful.

The STREAM code executes and times several very long loops with a simple body, as shown in Table 15-2.

Table 15-2: STREAM Benchmark Components

Name	Kernel	Bytes/iter	flops/iter
COPY:	$a(i) = b(i)$	16	0
SCALE:	$a(i) = q*b(i)$	16	1
SUM:	$a(i) = b(i) + c(i)$	24	1
TRIAD:	$a(i) = b(i) + q*c(i)$	24	2

The loops access sufficiently large data structures that the data can't fit in the cache. Memory is accessed using unit stride. The effective memory bandwidth and flops are computed for each loop.

While these values are interesting and useful, another number called *machine balance* is computed. Machine balance captures the relative performance of the floating-point computations versus the memory bandwidth. Table 15-3 features information extracted from some of the STREAM results. Balance is peak Mflops (as determined by Linpack 1000×1000) divided by triad bandwidth in megawords (8 bytes per word in these figures) per second. The computer vendor names have been removed from these results. The lower the machine balance number, the faster memory is relative to the CPU.

Table 15-3: Selected STREAM Results

NCPUs	Peak Mflops	BW (MW/s)	Machine Balance
1	200.	159.4	1.3
512	76800.	14015.8	5.5
1	266.	11.8	22.5
63	31500.	1263.4	24.9
1	500.	32.9	15.2
1	20.	8.9	2.2
24	1440.	96.8	14.9
2	50.	42.1	1.2
1	25.	22.6	1.1
32	57600.	44908.8	1.3
8	7680.	7903.7	1.0
4	3840.	4380.5	0.9
1	200.	167.2	1.2
1	133.	59.6	2.2
56	49280.	770.2	64.0
8	5600.	141.5	39.6
1	866.	42.7	20.3

As you can see, there is a wide range of performance values for both the arithmetic and the memory bandwidth. However, when you examine the ratio, we see quite dramatic effects of the memory hierarchy implementations. The values range from 0.9 to 64. The computer that has a balance factor of 0.9 probably doesn't need a cache. The computer with the balance factor of 64 had better be hitting its cache 99%+ of the time.

While the STREAM benchmark can't tell you exactly how well your computer will perform on your code, it can tell you some basic performance strengths and weaknesses to help you design your benchmarks to test those strengths and weaknesses more accurately. Computer vendors often use the STREAM benchmark in their own internal testing, and it is increasingly being quoted by computer vendors in their external documentation.

The STREAM benchmark was developed by John McCalpin while at the University of Delaware. The STREAM benchmark information is maintained at *http://www.cs.virginia.edu/stream/*.

HINT

Another memory-oriented benchmark is the HINT (Hierarchical INTegration) benchmark. HINT was developed at NASA Ames Lab and Iowa State University by John Gustafson and others. HINT is reported in a graphical representation and captures floating-point performance, integer performance, memory hierarchy, unit stride memory performance, numerical accuracy, and non-unit-stride memory performance.

HINT doesn't fix the problem size, number of iterations, or the running time. HINT executes a computation and produces a speed measure called *quality improvement per second* (QUIPS). To determine the QUIPS, HINT performs a computation to determine the area bounded by $f(x)=(1-x)/(1+x)$ for $0<=x<=1$. As the program progresses, it hierarchically decomposes $0<=x<=1$ into regions and performs the computation. As long as memory, time, and computational accuracy are available, HINT continuously refines its decomposition, yielding a more accurate result. The computation benefits both from increased memory and increased computation. The measure is how quickly the accuracy of the computed integral can be improved per second, hence the term "quality improvement per second."

HINT results can either be viewed graphically, plotting the execution time versus QUIPS, or you can integrate the area under that curve to produce a single value called MQUIPS. A precursor to the HINT benchmark was the SLALOM benchmark, which measured how much useful work that can be completed in a fixed amount of time. You can get more information regarding HINT at *http://www.scl.ames-lab.gov/Projects/HINT/*.

Industry Benchmarks

With the pressure that is placed on an influential benchmark and the financial incentive to gain an advantage in the benchmark area, one of the best sources of reliable information is industry benchmarks.

Industry benchmarks are usually developed by an independent organization that sets the policies for benchmarks, distributes and updates the benchmarks, and then publishes their results. Vendors and users generally pay a fee to make use of the benchmarks. Two examples of industry benchmarks are the Systems Performance Evaluation Cooperative (SPEC) and the Transaction Processing Council (TPC).

These organizations have a strong incentive to keep their benchmarks impartial and to keep the benchmarks from becoming obsolete. While vendors would all love to gain some slight advantage for their particular rating according to one of these benchmarks, they also know that if users are to trust a benchmark result, the organization must maintain high integrity. The need for integrity keeps the games to a minimum, and if one vendor cheats a bit when reporting the results, the other vendors won't hesitate to complain loudly. The result is a self-policed environment. If a benchmark turns out to be particularly easy to get better results using questionable methods, the benchmark code or the rules for execution are generally changed by the benchmark organization to rectify the problem.

The net result is that the best benchmarks change over time as technology and user workload change over time.

The SPEC Benchmarks

In the late 1980s, a group called the Systems Performance Evaluation Cooperative (SPEC) formed to "establish, maintain and endorse a standardized set of relevant benchmarks that can be applied to the newest generation of high performance computers." Benchmarks submitted by member computer companies were assembled into the first SPEC suite of codes.* You have probably heard of *SPECmarks*— measurements of how well computers performed on the benchmark suite. These are cumulative numbers for the performance of the suite as a whole.

The first SPEC benchmark suite was called *SPEC89*. This suite was revised in 1992 and 1995, and a new version is planned for 1998. By releasing new versions, the SPEC organization can keep their benchmarks relevant to current hardware and software trends. Computer vendors can't become too skilled at tuning the codes. SPEC supplies a number of different benchmarks that test performance outside the realm of the CPU and memory. I will describe some of the SPEC benchmarks. For more detail, consult the *http://www.spec.org* web site.

SPEC89

This was the original SPECmark benchmark. It consisted of the the *geometric mean†* of the runtimes for 10 programs in the suite. This benchmark did not differentiate between integer and floating-point performance. The single, original SPECmark number was a preemptive attempt by SPEC to prevent the vendor

---

* As you can imagine, computer companies would be inclined to submit benchmarks that they do best on, and that the competition does worst on.

† The geometric mean is the *n*th root of the product of *n* numbers. A geometric mean is affected by the worst benchmarks in the suite, more than an average would be.

community from accumulating the 10 benchmark numbers into their own, possibly biased, summary result.

Interestingly, in the late 1980s the SPECmark was not a particularly important benchmark in the minds of computer buyers. The different competing computer architectures of the time (CISC, RISC, and vector) had such different performance characteristics that no benchmark could effectively relate all of their performances. In the high performance field, the dominant benchmark was the Linpack 100×100 code which measures floating-point performance and memory bandwidth. RISC and CISC microprocessors performed so poorly on the Linpack benchmark that there was really no comparison.

SPEC92

The SPEC92 benchmarks are a significant improvement over the SPEC89 benchmarks. There are 20 benchmarks in the SPEC92 CPU benchmark suite, up from 10 in SPEC89. SPEC92 includes six integer and 14 floating-point codes. SPEC92 is reported in two summary figures: floating-point (SPECfp92) and integer (SPECint92). The reason that the overall SPECmark figure has been eliminated is that it cloaked the differences between integer and floating-point performance. For instance, a machine with good floating-point performance and mediocre integer performance could come up with a similar SPECmark as a machine with the reverse situation. By having two numbers, the distinction between floating and integer performance are clearer.

Around 1992, the floating-point performance of high-end RISC processors began to creep toward that of low-end supercomputers, and cache sizes began to grow quickly. As the difference between supercomputers and RISC-based systems began to blur, the SPECfp92 benchmark became more interesting to high performance computing users. As the Linpack 100×100 benchmark was losing its title as *the* high performance computing benchmark, SPECfp92 became the battleground for the upcoming RISC processors. Vendors invested a great deal of time tuning their hardware and software for SPEC92 performance. At some point around 1994, the increasing cache sizes and clever compilers cracked the SPECfp92 benchmark. Luckily the SPECfp95 benchmark was just around the corner.

SPEC95

By the time the SPECint95 and SPECfp95 benchmarks were released, it became the only remaining single-number CPU benchmark in wide use. Improvements from the SPEC92 benchmark include the following:

- Benchmarks no longer fit into on-chip caches.

- Benchmarks run much longer.

- The codes are more like large user applications, and the loops contain more code.

- The SPEC95 suite includes all the tools and scripts necessary to run the codes and prepare the performance report for return to SPEC. This standardized the execution environment and reduced the vendor's ability to tune the benchmark environment for maximum performance (which weren't representative of how users would actually use their computers).

The SPEC organization has effectively assumed that all benchmarks have a half-life. Once they release one benchmark, they begin work designing the next benchmark. SPEC invites users (and compensates them) to submit codes for the next benchmark suite. The next set of CPU benchmarks is scheduled to be released in 1998 and is tentatively labeled SPEC98.

The integer benchmarks in SPEC95 include an artificial intelligence game, a simulation of a chip circuitry, a C compiler, a LISP interpreter, an image-manipulation program, a Perl interpreter, the UNIX compress command, and an in-memory object-oriented database.

The floating-point benchmarks in SPEC95 include mesh generation, a shallow water simulation, partial differential equations, a Monte-Carlo computation, fluid-dynamics computation, a multigrid solver in a three-dimensional potential field, turbulence modeling, weather prediction, quantum chemistry, and Maxwell's equations.

In addition to the SPECint95 and the SPECfp95 numbers, there are several related benchmark results:

SPECint_base95

Measures the performance under a restrictive set of rules including:

- All the codes must use the same compiler flags.

- There may be no more than four compiler flags.

- There can be no "assertion" flags.

- There can be no feedback-directed optimization (i.e., the compiler cannot use a profile from a previous run).

The idea is that the base rate more accurately represents the typical "mileage" the user will experience. The more widely reported SPECint95 results can have more aggressive optimization options and can use different optimizations on different codes. There is also a SPECfp_base95 value. Interestingly, looking at a subset of the SPEC95 data, there was between 0 and 10% improvement from the base to the aggressive results. Not all vendors report base rate figures.

SPECint_rate95

Measures the throughput of an entire (possibly multiprocessor) system. The vendor can run as many concurrent copies of the SPECint95 benchmarks as necessary to maximize the SPECint_rate95 value. SPECint_rate95 is computed as the highest achievable aggregate SPECint95 throughput across the entire system. There is a similar SPECfp_rate95 result.

The SPEC95 (and presumably the SPEC98) benchmark has gained the respect of the vendors and the users as a single number that can compare a wide variety of computers. By continuously improving their benchmarks, SPEC provides an excellent service to both the users and the vendors. In addition to the CPU rates, SPEC has several other benchmarks.

SPEChpc96

The SPEChpc96 is a new SPEC benchmark. This is somewhat of a follow-on effort to the Perfect Club benchmark that tried to focus attention on larger, more realistic application performance. In SPEChpc96, the set of programs is targeted directly at the top end of the high performance computing spectrum including a wide range of architectures. The two applications that are included are a seismic code and a chemistry code. Users can execute problems of different sizes based on the overall capabilities of their systems.

The applications are complete codes and make use of FORTRAN, C, and C++; they also are available in PVM. These applications also include input and output as part of the applications. Unlike the other SPEC CPU results, each application result is reported separately. The goal is to simulate as closely as possible the real high performance computing environment. Vendors are allowed to make certain modifications based on the assumption that users purchasing a $5 million computer would be willing to make reasonable modifications to their applications to achieve peak performance.

Other SPEC benchmarks

The SPEC organization is increasing its array of benchmarks beyond the traditional memory, CPU, and application program areas. Other benchmarks include:

- SPECweb96: A web server benchmark
- SPECsfs: A benchmark for a shared filesystem over a network aimed primarily at the Network File System (NFS)
- Multimedia performance: The initial code will be based on MPEG-2
- Graphics performance

- OpenGL benchmark

- X Windows System performance

The SPEC organization has established its credibility in the area of benchmarks and it is quite natural for them to expand into these new and emerging areas of benchmarking.

Transaction Processing Benchmarks

For some applications, you are more interested in the interactive response than raw compute power. Interactive applications often demand that the computer and operating system be tuned to respond quickly to outside events, and be able to handle a large number of active processes simultaneously. An appropriate model might be a banking application, or an office environment, where there can be many people sharing time and I/O bandwidth of a single computer. Each interactive request and response can be considered a transaction.

Just as there are CPU benchmarks, there are also *transaction processing benchmarks*. Transaction processing is the term generally used to refer to high- volume database applications such as those found in the banking and airline reservation industries. It is important to be able to accurately measure the performance of computing systems for these applications. The number of different computer architectures used in database processing is as varied as the architectures using in high performance computing.

The Transaction Processing Council (*http://www.tpc.org*) is an industry-based organization representing 40 computer system and database vendors. TPC provides a framework in which to benchmark these high- end database systems. The TPC results are highly respected in the database field. Vendors even publish the dollars per TPC figures for their systems when comparing their products against other vendors.

Like SPEC, TPC has had to evolve their benchmarks over time as technologies and user needs change. Originally, the TPC-A and TPC-B were the mainstream benchmarks for this field. Today, the TPC-C and TPC-D benchmarks are the main benchmarks in use by these vendors.

In these benchmarks, users are simulated by another program or another computer* that makes transactions, filling the role of many people signed on to the machine. Performance is measured by the amount of time it takes the computer to complete transactions under various loads.

---

* This is called a *remote terminal emulation benchmark*, when one computer drives another through the terminal ports, or across the network. See Chapter 16.

TPC-A

TPC-A is a benchmark of credit-debit transactions being performed by a second computer simulating bank tellers, each issuing one request every 10 seconds. To obtain a 1-TPS rating, 10 tellers issuing one request every 10 seconds must see transaction completion within 2 seconds 90% of the time. There are also some requirements on how the data is distributed throughout the database.

TPC-B

TPC-B is the same as TPC-A, except that the transactions are generated by other processes on the same computer(s), rather than being initiated across a network. This makes TPC-B less of a terminal I/O test and more of a database stress test. TPC-B numbers will always be higher than TPC-A numbers.

TPC-C

TPC-C is a newer, more complex simulation, modeling the transactions of a company that sells a product or service. Transactions are orders, payments, inquiries, and even (intentional) mistakes that need correction.

TPC-D

The TPC-D benchmark is focused on a decision-support environment where the data is being slowly modified online at some level while other processes are performing large queries, joins, and scans. The idea is to model the environment in which many central corporate databases operate.

Closing Notes

When deciding which computer to purchase, you are bombarded with many different benchmark numbers. You see them in tables, bar graphs, line charts, flip charts, and pie charts. While wading through benchmark reports can seem intimidating, someone who has a basic understanding of which benchmarks measure which aspects of performance can learn a great deal from these presentations.

Often you can learn as much from which benchmarks they don't feature as you can from the benchmarks they do. While it's dangerous to purchase a computer system based solely on the published benchmark results, careful analysis of these results can significantly improve your analysis and understanding of the performance of the system.

Use them as a performance barometer, but remember: there is nothing like benchmarking your own code. Chapter 16 discusses how to do this so that you will have faith and reproducibility in your results.

A good general web site that deals with benchmarks is *http://www.netlib.org/ benchmark/* if you want to learn about other benchmarks not covered in this chapter.

Exercises

1. Download some of the published benchmarks mentioned in this chapter and attempt to reproduce the published results for your system.

2. Find two computers with different performance levels. Using a stopwatch, measure the time it takes to perform some common task on both computers. Compare the relative performance of the systems using your informal measure to the relative performance as predicted by a common benchmark such as SPEC95. Is SPEC95 a good indicator of the performance on the task you selected? Why or why not?

16

Running Your Own Benchmarks

You can read all the magazine reviews you want when looking for a new car, but there is no substitute for the test drive. Sometimes you need to just take it out for a spin and see how well it accelerates. Actually, if you are spending all that money (on a computer *or* a car), you should have a little fun before you plop down your cash. There are some real benefits to test driving a high performance computer:

- Your application may exercise some feature of the compiler or hardware that wasn't revealed in the industry benchmarks.

- Your code may be "large," whereas some industry benchmarks are "small."

- Your program may require some support in the form of libraries or language features that aren't present on the machine.

- Your application might run (unexpectedly) slowly.

- Your program may expose a horrible bug.

Besides, no benchmark we know of measures how well the keyboard is laid out, how forgiving the compiler is, or how far the vendor deviates from what you expect. You are only going to learn these things by sitting in front of the machine.

This chapter is about benchmarking. It won't be so much a discussion of the mechanics of benchmarking, such as using the timing facilities—most of that was covered in Chapter 6, *Timing and Profiling*. Instead, we discuss benchmark preparation and policies that will give you confidence in your results.

Choosing What to Benchmark

We have seen groups scoop together a fairly random collection of programs and pass them out to vendors as a "benchmark suite." This usually happens when they're pressured to justify their choice for a computer and helps to satisfy the purchasing department's requirement for a fair and honest evaluation. The trouble is that although these suites may provide general insight into a machine's performance, they don't say much about whether the machine will be good for its ultimate purpose. By picking user benchmarks that reflect what you do every day, or intend to do in the future, you can steer the purchasing justification in favor of the right machine.

Some orthogonality in your choices is a good idea. To take an example, say that you do structural analysis for a living. It might be wise to pick problems that represent different types of analyses, rather than several different examples of the same thing. For instance, a suite consisting of one dynamic, one static, and one modal analysis would tell you how the machine (and perhaps a third-party software package) performs in three areas. If you do more of one thing than another, that's OK. Estimate the relative importance of each as a percentage of the work you do and use it as a weighting factor when it comes time to tally the benchmark results. This way, the most important things you do influence the outcome to the greatest extent.

Benchmark Runtime

Of course, you don't know how long benchmarks are going to run if you haven't run them yet. Even so, it's worth trying to project the runtime so that you can keep the total for the collection to a reasonable level. Each code should execute for more than a few minutes, but less than 15 or so. All told, it should take less than an hour to do the whole thing, if for no other reason than that you are going to end up running it over and over. If benchmarks are too short, performance may get buried in the startup and termination overhead. If benchmarks are too long, you'll get bored.

How do you estimate the runtime? Use a published benchmark such as SPECfp95. If your last machine was rated at 3 SPECfp95, and the system you are looking at today is rated at 60 SPECfp95, then everything should run 20 times faster, right? (Well, let's just hope so). Notice that this will take a significant 20-minute job and turn it into an insignificant one-minute benchmark, which brings up a good point. You need to choose benchmarks that are representative of what you are going to do in the future, when you get the new machine. This is not only true for runtime, but for memory requirements (and I/O) as well. After all, if the old machine was adequate, you wouldn't be looking for a new one.

Benchmark Memory Size

Benchmark memory size is one of the most important areas to consider when pulling a suite together. New caches and memory systems are much bigger and faster than those of machines a few years ago. But as we saw in Chapter 2, *High Performance Microprocessors*, the relative gap in memory system performance versus CPU performance has widened. This means that one program, running two different size problems, can test two completely different things:

- CPU performance for small problems
- Memory system performance for large problems

For this reason, it's a good idea to size the benchmarks realistically or make them representative of the kinds of problems you will be running down the road. Your own benchmarks are probably one of the few places you will get to see figures for the performance of large problems anyway.

Be careful, of course, that the machines have sufficient memory for whatever benchmarks you plan to run. Otherwise, your programs will page (or swap), giving you useless performance data. (You should never plan to page or swap on purpose.) If you need help determining the memory sizes of your programs, see Chapter 6.

Kernels and Sanitized Benchmarks

In some cases, the sheer bulk of an application makes it unsuitable as a benchmark. There may be hundreds of thousands of lines of code, or it may require data or resources that are difficult to port. Still, if the application is an important example of the work you do, you might want to construct a *kernel*—a subset of the code that represents the computations where the time is spent. Figure 16-1 shows the relationship between a kernel benchmark and the original application. Usually you would extract the central routines and give them their own main or *driver* routine. Data can be included in the source or read into the program at startup.

There are also cases where code is sensitive or proprietary and needs to be *sanitized* before it can be released or reviewed by others. Again, the idea is to extract the essence of the computations while leaving out the peripheral work, including setup, interaction, and output. Comments can be removed with an editor, and variable names can be disguised if necessary. As with a kernel, a sanitized benchmark can have its data included as part of the source code. A word of warning: when setting up the data for a kernel, make an extra effort to be sure you haven't left the code open to over-optimization by a clever compiler. Initialize values from a file, a separately compiled block of data or externals; hide the ultimate fate of variables from the compiler by placing some of the results in common or external

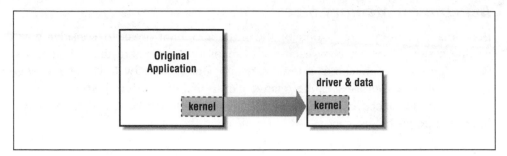

Figure 16-1: Kernel benchmark

variables; or print out the values at the end. These steps help guard against dead code removal or constant propagation that wouldn't have occurred in the original application. If one vendor's compiler recognizes an opportunity to remove unnecessary code, and another doesn't, you are no longer running the same benchmark across machines.

One common technique in kernel codes is to execute the kernel loop multiple times to get a large enough time to be meaningful:

```
PARAMETER(MAXREPS=50)

CALL HPCTIM(WTIME,CTIME)
DO IREPS = 1, MAXREPS
  DO I=1,N
    A(I) = ...
  ENDDO
ENDDO
CALL HPCTIM(WTIME,CTIME)
```

Depending on the computation, the compiler could quickly determine that the kernel loop was computing the exact same results for all of the MAXREPS iterations and only run the last iteration! Or it might interchange the loops. The way to stop this from happening is to add a call to an external routine that is compiled separately. This stops the inquisitive compiler from performing data flow analysis into the routine and is forced to execute all of the MAXREPS iterations in the order you specify:

```
PARAMETER(MAXREPS=50)

CALL HPCTIM(WTIME,CTIME)
DO IREPS = 1, MAXREPS
  CALL NOOPT(A)
  DO I=1,N
    A(I) = ...
  ENDDO
ENDDO
CALL HPCTIM(WTIME,CTIME)
```

If the compiler can detect that the NOOPT routine has no effect on the variables participating in the kernel loop, it can ignore the call and potentially remove dead code that you think you are timing. The solution to this problem is to either put the variables into the call to NOOPT as parameters or place them all in a FORTRAN common block.

Clever compilers are wonderful tools when we want our program to run fast and produce the right results. However, they can make a kernel benchmark writer's life painful at times.

Another problem with kernel codes is the effect of cache. If you must run the kernel several thousand times to make your time meaningful, then you have to be aware that it may run all but the first iteration from the cache. If the application does not normally run from cache, then you may be erroneously reporting a much faster execution time than you will see on the real application. To solve this problem, you can increase the size of the data structure so that it can't remain in the cache between iterations. Another approach is to perform some calculation to clear out the cache between successive iterations.

With all the trouble it takes to create kernel codes, they play a very important role in the decision-making process. Remember that the industry and users benchmarks generally had a few kernels and a few large codes. Each provides us with potentially different information. The large codes tell us how well the new system run applications. The kernels can often help explain why the applications run so well or so poorly. A kernel might tell you that System A does division 21 times faster than System B, while addition takes about the same amount of time. So if one of your users uses lots of division, they might want to know that information before the final decision is made.

Benchmarking Third-Party Codes

With third-party codes, you have little control over the performance on different hardware platforms. The company that owns the code ported, tested, and perhaps tuned it slightly (though not always), and shipped it out in executable form. You may have some control over the amount of memory used (which can affect the performance), but beyond that, there is usually little you can do if it runs slowly.

You might expect that the application's speed on various machines would roughly track SPEC, MIPS, and mflops, but it may not! To understand why, consider the potential problems a small- to medium-sized third-party software developer may face. Each new release incorporates bug fixes from previous releases and perhaps some enhancements—sometimes major enhancements. Developers get into real trouble if they start maintaining separate versions of the code for different platforms, so they work with one and periodically distribute the changes.

Assume that you are Mr. Software Developer. You have 10 Brand X computers, one (old) Brand Y, and know where you can borrow time on a Brand Z. On which platform will you develop? Brand X, naturally, because that's what you own.

Now say that you have finished a release for Brand X—it passed 98% of the QA suite (and the other 2% are declared features rather than bugs)—and now you are migrating the code to Brands Y and Z. It gets through the QA suite with results in the neighborhood of 92% correct. You find that by shutting off optimizations that you can bump it up to 96%. "Hmmm . . . ," you say, "I have to get this release out on time. I'll ask Mr. Computer Vendor to look into this problem later." And you ship the code with compiler optimizations reduced or shut off altogether! By sacrificing performance, you saved yourself development time.

Assuming the scenario is true (and even if it's not in your case), there is an extra step you want to take when planning a platform for third-party codes: ask the people who own the code what platform they use to develop the application. The brand(s) used for development get the earliest software releases and perhaps the best relative performance. See if the company has opinions about particular brands, and whether they have run benchmarks between them.

You won't typically find a performance report from the actual vendor of the software. For example, it would be nice if SAS (a statistical package) would publish a "SASmarc" rating for each of the computer systems. You seldom see such a rating published; if SAS were to publish such a rating, it would damage their relationship with hardware vendors. Eventually all the hardware vendors would hate them. Even if a company was happy that they had the best SASmarc performance one quarter, the next quarter another company would take over the top spot making the first company angry. Eventually there would be no company that would be willing to sell SAS on their hardware.

Because you can't depend on the software developers to "rat" on the hardware manufacturers, you might have to contact other users with experience across several platforms. They may even say "Gee, we bought a Brand W and a Brand Z. But every one runs their code on Brand Z, because it is so much faster. We turned the Brand W computer into a web server."

As ever, you will want to run your own benchmarks on various platforms, if possible. It gets a little tricky here because now you have to arrange with both the hardware vendor and the supplier of the third-party package. In the case of well-known applications, try convincing the hardware vendor to borrow the software for you. They may already have it, or they may have someone in the company who is responsible for the communication with the software supplier. For less popular packages, you probably will have to approach the software vendor yourself.

Benchmark the Compiler, Development Environment, and Operating System

Often, the quality of the compiler and development environment can have a significant impact on how well you can use the system. If the only areas you test are compute speed and memory bandwidth, you will be missing this very important aspect. Other features you may want to look for are parallel debuggers, performance tuning tools, batch queuing systems and system administration tools.

If the system will be used for some interactive activity while it chugs away at the batch jobs, make sure to test how it performs with a mix of activity. Sometime systems are turned to favor one type of activity at the expense of another.

This is a good reason to schedule a visit to the company and run the benchmarks yourself rather than sending the vendor the benchmark source and having them send back results a month later.

Benchmark the Company

Once you have purchased the computer, and the company has cashed the check, hopefully your relationship with the company will continue. You will need help and support in a wide range of areas from hardware to software, tuning and system administration. A good company can provide excellent resources to help you deploy the best possible service for you and your users. Before purchasing a system, you should test the service and support, and make sure it's satisfactory.

Types of Benchmarks

There are two components to every benchmark: the system under test, and the quantity for which you are measuring. In this book we've talked primarily about CPU/memory system performance. Accordingly, the benchmark techniques we describe are aimed at CPU performance, though you can borrow some of them for I/O and graphics tests, too. On the outside, the tests are simple: measure the time it takes to do something.

The way the benchmarks are conducted should mimic the way the machine ultimately will be used. Will you be running one job at a time, or will there be many? Are you more interested in interactive response than CPU performance? How will you compare your measurements between platforms? These are some of the questions you need to ask when planning a benchmark.

Single Stream Benchmarks

In the simplest kind of benchmark, *single stream*, you measure how long it takes the computer to execute a collection of programs, one at a time. Usually the machine is booted "multiuser," running the normal selection of daemons and background processes, but without any other demanding jobs to do, aside from your benchmark as shown in Figure 16-2. Generally, two important sets of numbers result:

- The elapsed time for the whole collection

- The elapsed time for each individual piece

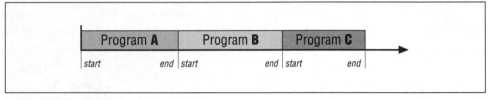

Figure 16-2: Single stream benchmarks

Often the pieces are contributed by different groups within your organization, meaning that there are going to be people who are just as interested in how their portion ran, as how things went overall. To make an objective measurement, you are going to have to gather estimates of the importance of each piece, and use those estimates as weighting factors for tallying the results as shown in Figure 16-3. Also, you will want to normalize the results because the time it takes to run a particular program may not correspond to its importance.

To illustrate, say that you got the results shown in Table 16-1 from running programs A, B, and C on brands X, Y, and Z (in seconds).

Table 16-1: Raw Time Results

	Brand X	Brand Y	Brand Z
Program A	322	369	310
Program B	694	801	714
Program C	440	484	441

Taking the same table and normalizing the times in each row by the best time obtained, we get the results (in seconds) shown in Table 16-2.

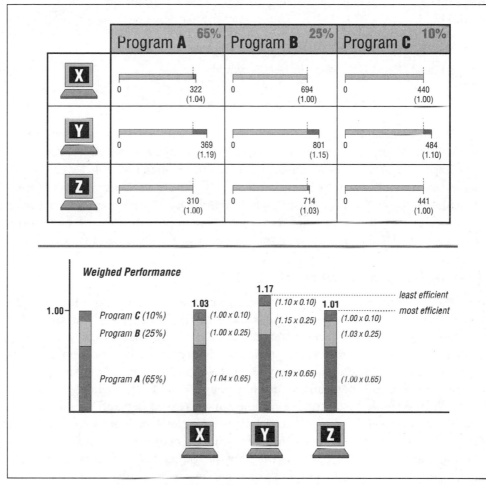

Figure 16-3: Computing an overall benchmark score

Table 16-2: Normalized Time Results

	Brand X	Brand Y	Brand Z
Program A	1.04	1.19	1.00
Program B	1.00	1.15	1.03
Program C	1.00	1.10	1.00

Now we need to apply weighting factors. Using whatever yardstick is appropriate, rate the applications by their relative importance. For example, if you run Program A most of the time, you might say that it should contribute 65% of its normalized runtime to the answer. Likewise, Programs B and C might contribute 25% and 10%,

respectively. This means that, taking Brand X, the accumulated benchmark time
would be:

```
1.04 X .65 + 1.00 X .25 + 1.00 X .10 = 1.03        Brand X
```

Brand Y and Brand Z benchmark results would be:

```
1.19 X .65 + 1.15 X .25 + 1.10 X .10 = 1.17        Brand Y
1.00 X .65 + 1.03 X .25 + 1.00 X .10 = 1.01        Brand Z
```

Brand Z wins (though not by much)! This outcome isn't immediately obvious from
the raw data. Brand X won two out of the three benchmarks, but Brand Z won the
most important of them. How much of a difference is significant? If I were buying
the system, I wouldn't let 2% or even 10% or 20% be the deciding factor. There are
other things to be concerned with, like cost and ease of use. However, a performance difference of 30% or more starts to become important. Still, the hardest part
of choosing is deciding the value of the unquantifiable features of a system.

Throughput Benchmarks

If you are shopping for a server on which you expect to run several jobs at once,
you will want to select a mix of codes to be benchmarked all at the same time.
This shows you how the machine handles a heavy load, with a higher number of
context switches and greater demands on memory and I/O. For a multitasking
multiprocessor, this is the only way you are going to be able to compare between
brands; single stream benchmarks use just one CPU at a time, whereas you need
to see them exercised all at once (including an increased demand on the memory
system). Again, you need to be conscious of your total memory requirements. If
the programs don't fit altogether in memory, the benchmark may become a disk-
bashing test (because of paging). Different programs take different amounts of
time to run. If you start them all at once, the last benchmark to finish will have
spent some time executing all by itself, as Figure 16-4 illustrates.

This is not what you want from a throughput benchmark; you want to see each
application run against a steady background load. One way to do this is to construct a "stone wall" of programs as in Figure 16-5. When one of the programs
completes it is immediately restarted, making for a (nearly) continuous contribution to the load. After a little while, you have gathered one or more times for each
benchmark, depending on how long you let them run. Average these together, if
appropriate, and add the runtimes for A+B+C+D+E . . . to get a throughput figure for collection. Be sure to discard any contributions that aren't run against the
full background load. The proportionate runtime for the different pieces will vary
between machines, so again, you may want to normalize the times for A, B, etc.,
before adding them together.

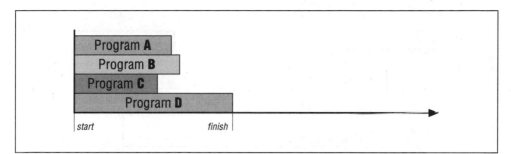

Figure 16-4: Wrong way to run a throughput benchmark

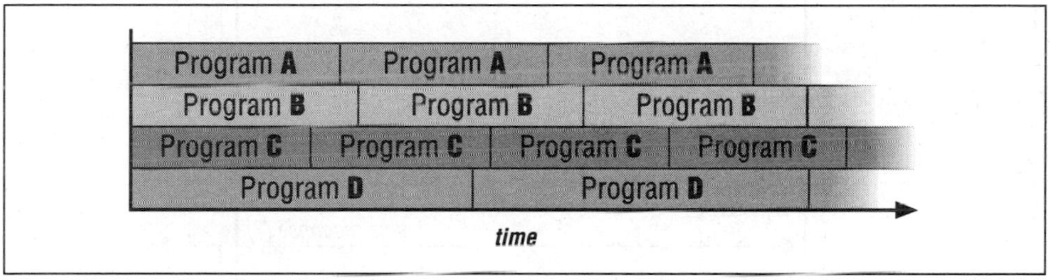

Figure 16-5: Benchmark stone wall

Interactive Benchmarks

If you are interested in more than crunching—if you are interested in knowing how a group of programmers playing Hunt the Wumpus will slow down a computer—you are going to want to run interactive benchmarks. Interactive response involves components of a computer—I/O system, operating system, networks—that are outside the scope of this book. Nonetheless, interactive response benchmarks may be important for your application. Figure 16-6 shows how an interactive benchmark is constructed. You need two systems: one plays the part of users running interactive programs (shells, editors, word processors, etc.), while the other (the one being benchmarked) provides the services. As far as the system under test is concerned, there *are* real users on the machine; they log in through the network or serial ports and hammer away. By "playing" more and more users, you can see how performance drops off as interactive demands increase. Usually you measure this as the fraction of a second it takes to get response from a command.

Constructing an interactive benchmark (often called a *remote terminal emulation* or RTE benchmark) is more challenging than constructing a CPU benchmark. Development of the simulator portion is a big project by itself. One tool that is available is called "Expect." Using Expect, you program the commands that are sent and the expected responses to those commands. Expect operates like a user:

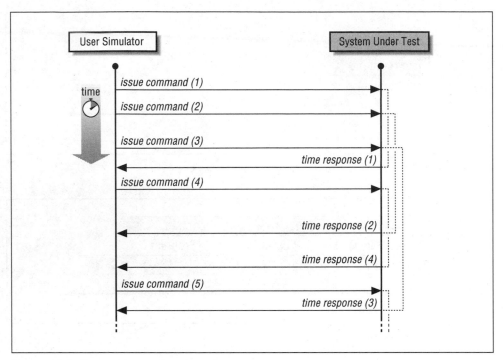

Figure 16-6: Interactive use benchmark

it waits for a prompt and then executes a command. You program Expect by writing expect scripts, which consist of prompts and responses. Another approach is to write code in Perl or Tcl/Tk that makes the connections and interacts with the systems. There are others as well.

Preparing the Code

Nothing fouls up a benchmarking effort more than discovering part way through that something is wrong with one or more of the benchmarks, and that they have to be tossed out. The time to look into portability is before you start. You will also want to package your benchmarks into a little kit so that anybody who runs them will get the same results; you don't want misunderstandings about how the code is to be handled to affect the answers.

Portability

Portability is important in a benchmark because it helps ensure that the same thing is being run on each system. Just as importantly, it frees you (and anyone else) from having to go into the code and hack it up as it migrates from platform to platform. A small mistake here or there, and suddenly it's a new benchmark. To give yourself a good feeling that the results are reproducible, you have to be able to move benchmarks from machine to machine without modifications.

The best way to check for portability in a benchmark is to port it. If you have the luxury of extended access to the machines you want to benchmark, you should make a preliminary pass through each with the same code, tweaking it for portability as you go. That way, when you get to the end, you will (most likely) have programs that compile and run on all the platforms. Then you can start the benchmark.

If, on the other hand, you don't have ready access to the machines being benchmarked, then port the code to anything! Porting exposes a fair portion of the portability problems anyway (i.e., namelist support is needed, you can't assign Hollerith strings to reals, alarm(3) behaves differently, etc.). It's going to take you longer to port the code than to benchmark it anyway, and you certainly don't want the code to be modified as the benchmarks proceed, so porting ahead of time is important.

Aside from shoehorning the code through the compiler, you also have to think about how properties of the algorithm will affect the runtime. For example, say that your program characterizes the properties of an airfoil by starting out with some initial conditions and iterating until reaching a steady state. How are you going to account for numerical differences that actually affect the number of iterations? One machine may finish in 400 time steps whereas another may execute 420 time steps. You have to decide whether you think that the 420 time steps is a bug, or whether it is acceptable, and exactly how you want to measure performance. As an alternative, you might plan to measure time per iteration, rather than total time.

Another thing to think about is data files. Does your program require unformatted data as input? If so, you are going to need to create some auxiliary programs to port the data, too; you can't assume that the unformatted files will be good on every machine. And what about interaction with the user? You will want to "hardwire" any dialog so that time spent waiting for keyboard input doesn't figure into the benchmark time. Basically, you want your benchmarks to run without help from you.

Making a Benchmark Kit

As we said at the start of this chapter, it's important to have confidence in your benchmarks. Chances are that a lot of money is going to be spent, partly on the basis of benchmarks. It would be good to feel that the benchmark results are reliable and reproducible. Furthermore, you want them to be as self-documenting as possible. We'll say more about increasing benchmark reliability in a little while.

Right now let's talk about making the results reproducible.

The best way to make a benchmark reproducible is to put a wrapper around it so that it compiles and runs with a single command. Any compiler options used and the exact measurements taken are part of the wrapper, making it easy for anyone to understand where your results came from. You probably need separate wrappers for each machine—compiler invocations, options, etc., may differ. The wrapper itself can be a *script* (command file) or a *makefile*. Once you have prepared the benchmark—wrapper, code, and data files—you want to save it into a *tar* (tape archive) file and stash it away. To run the benchmark on a Brand X computer, you should only need to unpack the archive and type:

```
%make brandx >& brandx.out.
```

Arrange the makefile so that when the benchmark runs, everything written to *stdout*—compiler messages, and timing numbers—is recorded into a file. This file should be tucked away for reference, in case you want to go over the raw data again in the future. If a vendor runs your benchmark, ask for a copy of the output. Place some commands in your script or makefile that list all the files with their respective sizes so that if something has changed (if someone hacked the code), you will know about it.

We'd be willing almost to guarantee that you are going to have to run the benchmarks again, down the road. New platforms will come out, and people in your organization will want to compare them with the ones you purchased. Also, keep in mind that compilers are constantly improving. Benchmark times can improve significantly over the life of a system, perhaps as much as 30%. If you have a nice benchmark kit, you can resurrect it and update it without giving up too much of your time.

Benchmarking Checklist

Just so we both sleep a little better, we've written down a list of steps to remember. These will help make your benchmark results better indicators of performance. Some of these may appear obvious to you, but perhaps one or two will have slipped your mind.

Compile with optimizations turned on

Don't forget to turn on compiler optimizations. The performance difference between optimized and unoptimized code can be great—often more than a factor of two. You will find that there are usually several optimization levels to choose from; however, without a degree of care, the highest ones can cause your program to run slower. And you don't necessarily want to go with the default, -O, flag. Check the manuals and ask the vendor representative to determine the best optimization level for your kind of program. Perhaps you will want to experiment with other optimization flags as well.

These experiments can lead to a good set of suggested optimizations for your users once you have purchased the system.

Check the memory size

Be sure the machine has enough memory to run your job. With too little memory, your program will page or swap, reducing the performance by as much as 20 times.

Check for other processes

There will always be a bubbling sea of daemons running in the background, but they don't generally take much time. What you are on the lookout for is other processes soaking up lots of cycles in competition with yours. Sometimes they are other "real" programs, but they can also be hung processes consuming resources.

Scrutinize the timing output

It is particularly important to pay attention to both CPU time and elapsed time. If they are not close, then look for an explanation. Perhaps your program is performing a lot of I/O. Could there be a memory problem? You would find evidence in the number of page faults.

Check the answers!

The last step is to check the results. You should be especially scrutinizing of the output when a program completes unreasonably quickly or slowly. It would be convenient if you could automatically *diff* the output from different machines, but this generally doesn't work. The problem is that vendors round numbers differently, represent them with different internal precisions and take liberties at compile time. Of course the fact that most of the computers you will be testing support the IEEE floating-point format reduces this problem somewhat.

The output formats may vary slightly; the result may be `1.0e-6` rather than `0.10E-5`. Although these are the same number, a tool like *diff* doesn't know this. If the answers are just plain wrong, or the program seems to be producing correct results, but at a snail's pace, you might want to check for bugs introduced because of nonportable code.

Check for IEEE traps

Sometimes one particular application executes much slower relative to the others for no apparent reason. One possible explanation is that there is an excessive number of IEEE exception traps. Some computers support gradual underflow in hardware and other trap to software to compute these values. If you have a computation that deals with numbers very close to zero, it can underflow regularly under normal conditions. Whatever the case, it's a good idea to see if the IEEE exception handlers were called. Some vendors have a message that tells you that this has happened at the end of each job.

Many compilers allow an option to flush denormalized numbers to zero. If you have a code* that regularly underflows, it probably makes sense to turn on flush to zero to make the benchmark fair.

Remember to benchmark your own computer

We're not suggesting that you buy another of the brand you already own, but applying the same procedure to your present machine can be revealing. You may find that you are not using the machine correctly, or that the runtime isn't as long as you thought it was. At any rate, you want a standard time to compare against.

Set the rules for the benchmark

It's important to set some rules for the benchmark unless you will be running all of the benchmarks yourself. Are modifications allowed? What type of modifications? Can they add directives or change code? Can they only change for portability, or can they rewrite algorithms? Do they have to report a baseline and modified performance figure? How many and what type of compiler options are allowed? Can they turn on the "unsafe optimization flag" for all the codes? Must the outputs of the program match your baseline results? Exactly or within some factor?

If you are unsure, the best rule is not to allow any modifications unless absolutely necessary to get the code to work. If you want to have more lenient rules we suggest you look at the rules for the industry and user benchmarks at the sites discussed in Chapter 15.

To avoid rule battles with your vendors, it's a good idea to add some rules *about* the rules:

- You have the final say in determining how the benchmarks are to be interpreted.

- You can suspend or alter the rules as you see fit.

- You make the final decision as to whether a modification or compiler option is necessary or undesired hacking on the part of the benchmarker.

---

* Try running the heat flow programs in Chapter 13, *Language Support for Performance*, with REAL*4.

If your purchasing rules permit it, it's good to provide a contact for benchmark questions. The last thing you need is to wait for four months and get completely meaningless results from the vendor. When you tell them, "Oh, I didn't mean that!," they won't be too amused regarding the time they wasted in the benchmark and may not be willing to rerun the codes with a tiny change so that it is just the way you want.

Closing Notes

You must always remember the purpose of benchmarks. Benchmarks are tools that insure you are getting the most effective possible system for the money you are spending. If done properly, they can be a good learning experience for both you and your vendors. On large system purchases, the vendors take your codes very seriously. If you permit it, they may want to keep some of the codes to add to their compiler qualification suite. If you are willing to let the decision to buy a $5 million computer rest on the performance of a particular code, then it must be pretty important.

One excellent test that is often overlooked is to travel to the company for a visit so you can run the codes yourself. You would be surprised at how much more you learn at the company headquarters compared to what you learn from the salesperson sitting in your office.* If you are dropping $2 million on a new computer, a few thousand in travel expenses up front is a small price to pay to be absolutely sure you are getting the right computer. A visit to a conference such as Supercomputing (*http://www.computer.org*) can also be a worthwhile investment. It gives an excellent opportunity for you to interact with all of the major high performance computing vendors all at one place. They often have technical personnel and equipment on-site for you to consult.†

Profit margins on high performance systems have dropped significantly. Analyst/ sales teams are being encouraged to reduce the cost of selling. This means that they are going to be less interested in helping you run a benchmark for the sale of a small or even medium-sized system than they would have been five years ago. That's not to say they don't want to sell them to you, but where benchmarks are concerned, they just can't afford to get too involved. You will probably have to (and want to) run them yourself, perhaps at their office or over the Internet, with

---

* More benchmark stories: at one company, while we were running benchmark tests, the computer locked up, and, in about 30 seconds, it caught fire. The salesman got pretty nervous. At another company, the system ran great until someone started up the *vi* editor. At that point, context switching absolutely killed performance of the running benchmark. It was OK, as long as you didn't plan to edit files on the system.

† Don't go expecting to run benchmarks on the show floor. Only one vendor has allowed me to actually run some tests on the equipment at the show. The vendors generally don't want you breaking their stuff for the rest of the show.

consulting access to the analyst.

If you are buying a large system, on the other hand, they just might be able to give you some dedicated benchmarking assistance. Perhaps they will want to drag your code down a hole and hack at it for a while. Inevitably, the process ends with the analyst presenting fabulous results on overheads to a small crowd in a darkened room. The salesperson will be a well-dressed shadow with words of good will and support to put the kabosh on any technical questions. Be careful with the numbers they give you.

One more thing: keep good notes. A month after the benchmark has been completed, someone will almost always ask you for some detail that you forgot to write down, and that turns out to be the most important detail.

VI

Appendixes

A

Processor Architectures

In this appendix, we summarize a number of different processor architectures. The study of how processor designers have approached getting the best performance out of a processor is fascinating as economic and technical constraints change over time. We don't intend to cover every processor in existence, nor do we intend to be the most thorough document on the processors that are described here. After all, it is rather difficult to capture all the detail of thousands of pages of vendor documentation in a few short paragraphs. This appendix assumes that you have read Chapter 2, *High Performance Microprocessors*, and Chapter 3, *Memory*.

We progress from one processor type to another in a roughly historical sequence. We cover CISC processors, vector processors, several generations of RISC processors, and some other architectures as well. In each processor, we focus on some of the more interesting aspects of the architecture, using the particular architecture as a motivating example.

CISC Processors

We look at the Motorola MC68000 series of processors: an example of a CISC architecture family. The MC68000 architecture is actually a number of processors, ranging from the MC68000 through the MC68060. There are many variants of each processor for applications ranging from workstations to embedded applications with built-in RAM and ROM.

Motorola MC68000 Family

The MC68000 was designed at a time when there was a significant limitation on the number of transistors that could be manufactured on a single chip. So it was important to make the best use of all of the available hardware on the processor. The MC68000 is a family of architectures with each succeeding generation of processor backwards-compatible with the previous one:

MC68000

> The first member of the family. The MC68000 supports seven 32-bit data registers and seven 32-bit address registers. This processor did not support virtual memory or any cache on the chip.

MC68020

> This was much more sophisticated than the MC68000. The MC68020 supported a 4 GB virtual memory space, had an on-chip instruction cache of 256 bytes, a three-stage instruction pipeline, and a wide variety of addressing modes. The MC68020 ran at speeds up to 33 MHz.

MC68030

> This member of the family added a 256-byte data cache in addition to the instruction cache, moved the virtual memory support on-chip and could run at up to 50 MHz.

MC68040

> This processor upped the data and instruction caches to 4 KB each and moved the MC68881/MC68882 floating-point coprocessor on-chip. The MC68040 could run at up to 40 MHz.

MC68060

> This processor increased the on-chip data caches to 8 KB. This processor also implements branch prediction and operates as a three-way superscalar processor. The MC68060 can execute at up to 66 MHz.

The MC68000 family shows how a design can change over time, adding capabilities and maintaining upwards compatibility. One should probably not expect to see a MC68080 processor anytime soon. In the general purpose market, Motorola is focusing on the PowerPC, which is a new family of processors based on a RISC instruction set. The MC68000 processor series continues in the embedded processor market with specialized processors such as the MC68302 integrated multiprotocol processor and the MC68356 signal processing communication engine (SPCE).

Complex Instructions

To look at a classic *complex instruction set* implemented by the MC68020 and later processors, let's examine the MOVE instruction, which loads and stores data. There are 18 different addressing modes used for this instruction. We look at several of these addressing modes here:

```
move.l    #43,d0              ! Move constant 43 to d0
move.l    ADDR,d0             ! Direct from memory address
move.l    d1,d0               ! From data register d1
move.l    a0,d0               ! From address register a0
move.l    (a0),d0             ! Use contents of a0 as an address
move.l    (a0)+,d0            ! Add 4 (length of a long) to a0 after use
move.l    -(a0),d0            ! Subtract 4 from a0 before use
move.l    (12,a0),d0          ! Add 12 to a0 and use that value as address
move.l    (12,a0,d1.w),d0     ! Use 12 + a0 + bottom 16 bits of d1
move.l    (12,a0,d1.l),d0     ! Use 12 + a0 + all 32 bits of d1
move.l    (12,a0,d1.l*4),d0   ! Multiply d1 by 4 before adding it
move.l    ([12,a0],d1.l*4,24),d0   ! See text and diagram below
```

Different assemblers use different notation to represent each instruction, so if you look at MC68000 assembly language, it might not look exactly like these examples. In Figure A-1, we diagram the last (and most complicated) of the addressing mode examples; In that example, 12 is added to a0, then the 32-bit value at that location is loaded, and d1 multiplied by 4 and 24 are added to that value to compute the effective address of the load into d0. The machine code for the last instruction can take up to five words depending on the length of the offset constants. We also need some temporary registers to store the values for these calculations because the value of a0 is not supposed to be changed except in the preindex and postindex instructions.

A much clearer way to express the last example is using pseudo-code. Assume we have two 32-bit scratch registers called Effective Address (EA) and Memory Data Register (MDR). We can express the last instruction by the following sequence of pseudo-code:

```
EA = a0
EA = EA + 14
MOVE (EA),MDR
EA = SHIFT(d1,2)        ! Remember multiply by 4 is a 2-bit shift
EA = EA + MDR
EA = EA + 24
MOVE (EA),MDR
a0 = MDR
```

This is an excellent way of capturing the exact process that needed to occur to handle the particular instruction. As we shall see shortly, this list of steps needed to accomplish the instruction was captured in the processor microcode.

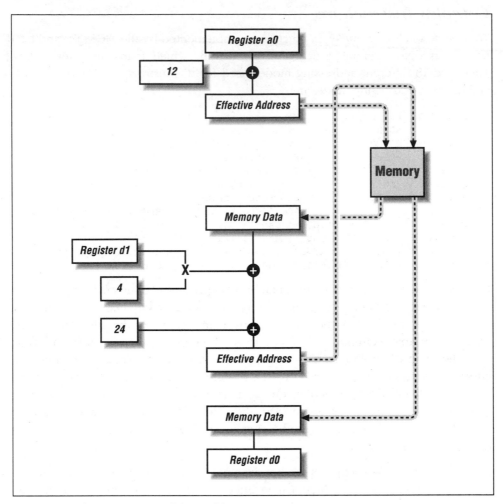

Figure A-1: The steps in a MC68020 address computation

Adding these steps added time on these processors. For example, the following table shows the number of cycles that each of the address translations added to the base instruction time for the MC68020 and MC68060 (not including memory access time).

Table A-1: Performance of Different Addressing Modes

Addressing Mode	MC68020	MC68060
d1	0	0
a0	0	0
(a0)	3	0
(a0)+	4	0
–(a0)	3	0
(12,a0)	3	0
(12,a0,d1.w)	4	0
(12,a0,d1.l)	6–10	0
(12,a0,d1.l*4)	6–10	0–1
([12,a0],d1.l*4,24)	17	3

Interestingly, the MC68020 operated at up to 33 MHz and the MC68060 operates at 66 MHz. Even though the clock rate is faster, the MC68060 can do more complex addressing modes at no apparent additional cost. A MC68060 processor might have been quite a competitor for an early RISC processor running at 66 MHz— especially if compiler writers spent some time to figure out exactly when to use these addressing modes.

A RISC proponent would look at this table and reach a very different conclusion. If the MC68060 has so much time during a 66-MHz clock cycle to throw in three extra 32-bit additions, then perhaps an equivalent RISC processor would run four times faster, or 264 MHz! Of course, as with all great arguments, neither perspective is completely correct.

Microcode

You might guess that a machine such as the MC68060, which features a range of sophisticated addressing modes and instructions, could be very complicated. Say, for instance, that a processor provides 200 different instructions, 100 of which can address memory. Of the instructions that can address memory, say each can choose from 18 different addressing modes. That means there are (100×18)+100=1900 legal instruction/address combinations. Additionally, as we have seen, some of them could be very involved, requiring several memory accesses. The length of the instruction might vary too, depending on the complexity or the number of auxiliary fields included. This is going to make the whole processor very complicated, especially the portion that decodes instructions and sequences the machine.

To get a feel for what a CPU designer is up against, picture the inside of the processor as a collection of black box components (adders, shifters, and registers) connected together by *data paths* (wiring). And on early processors, you never had enough space to throw a few extra adders on the chip. To make it all work like a computer, you have to be able to selectively allow the black boxes to share data.

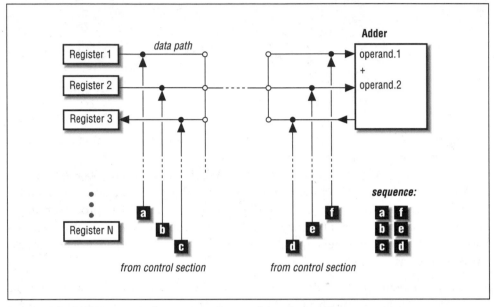

Figure A-2: Registers, a single common data path, and an adder

Figure A-2 depicts a simple machine and how it might execute a simple operation: adding the contents of two registers and returning the sum to a third. This takes three steps; in each step, the processor activates a pair of control points to move information across the data path. First it activates control points a and f, moving the contents of register 1; then b and e; then finally c and d, to move the result back to Register 3. If we had two more data paths, we could perform the addition in a single step; the operands and result could be transferred almost simultaneously.

The choreography needed to activate the control points in the proper order comes from the CPU's *control section*. On a hardwired design, the control section is a tangle of dedicated sequential and combinatorial logic gates that converts the instructions from your program into control signals. For instance, an instruction that says "add Register 1 to Register 2 and leave the result in Register 3" is logically reduced to electrical signals that activate control points. Although the above example is trivial, it helps illustrate how much logic is involved in building the control section for our hypothetical machine with 1900 instruction/address combinations. On many older machines, the control section, like the rest of the computer, was designed completely by hand. This was a difficult task in the first place, and was no easier to update and debug. In the early 1950s, the British scientist Maurice V.

Wilkes introduced an easier method for controlling the machine: *microcoding*. He demonstrated that you could replace the hardwired control section with a set of *microinstructions* and a simple sequencer to dish them out, turning data paths and functional units on and off in the proper order. Each machine instruction—the lowest level you would normally be able to see—was represented by a yet finer level of instructions called a *microprogram*. The sequencer was like a machine within a machine, interpreting your instructions with microcode and giving the computer its personality.

The immediate benefit of microcoding versus hardwiring the control section was that it made it easier to build and maintain the instruction set; essentially, the instructions were being simulated, rather than being acted upon directly in hardware.* Microcoding also had two more powerful, secondary effects. Now nearly any instruction set could be emulated by any machine with a microcoded control section. Furthermore, extremely complicated operations—more complicated than anything you would want to hardwire—could be thrown into the instruction repertoire without additional hardware.

For the sake of argument, say that you want your instruction set to include an operation that converts lowercase letters to uppercase; you give the computer an "a" and the appropriate opcode, and out pops an "A." If you were implementing a non-microcoded design, you would have to build custom hardware to recognize the instruction and sequence the machine. If, on the other hand, your architecture was microcoded, the steps for converting lowercase letters to uppercase could be written into the microcode. Either way, it would appear to the user that there was a conversion instruction, but in the second case, it would be considerably easier for you to implement; you would essentially write a routine to do it.

Since microcode allowed any machine to be emulated, it became possible to create an *architecture family*: a whole range of computers sharing a common instruction set. The first such architecture family was the S/360 series, introduced by IBM in 1964. From the programmer's point of view, the hardware looked the same for each machine in the family. Executable modules were portable between computers even though the processors might be based on completely different underlying hardware. The tremendous benefit (and marketing value) of the common instruction set architecture quickly became apparent. Incompatible computers, non-existent upgrade paths, recompilations, and recoding are discomforts people just don't

---

* The design and maintenance of hardwired processors is not as big a problem as it once was. Computers now take a big part in creating other computers. Silicon compilers, and more recently logic synthesis and VHDL—methods that turn design specifications into semiconductor layouts—have made it possible to hardwire fairly complex designs, yet retain the ability to debug or change them if necessary. They don't make the problem of complexity in hardwired designs disappear, but they go a long way to making it manageable. (VHDL stands for *V*ery *H*igh *S*peed *I*ntegrated *C*ircuit *H*ardware *D*esign *L*anguage.)

want to deal with. A single microcoded architecture, on the other hand, can survive long enough to grow a large base of software and customers.

Microcode During Instruction Execution

In some ways, microcode is like a simple RISC instruction set. You can almost think of microcode as a RISC "subroutine" call that is invoked when a particular CISC instruction is executed. For example:

```
move.l     (a0)+,d0
                                EA = A0
                                EA = EA + 4    ! 4 byte longs
                                MOVE (EA),MDR
                                D0 = MDR
                                A0 = EA
move.l     (12,a0,d1.1),d0
                                EA = A0
                                EA = EA + 12
                                EA = EA + D1
                                MOVE (EA),MDR
                                D0 = MDR
```

Using this microcode technique is a good way to reuse hardware such as an adder while supporting a wide range of addressing modes.

Microcode summary

Microcode started as an engineering convenience, but microcode (actually, complex instructions) also served to reduce traffic between the CPU and the memory system. An arbitrarily complex instruction could trigger a control sequence that would have taken a long time had it been written in more primitive steps and retrieved from memory in pieces. Furthermore, complex instructions freed up the (only) route between memory and the CPU so that data could move across it.

In short, by accomplishing multiple operations in a single instruction, microprogramming diminished traffic between the main memory system and the processor. Developments in semiconductors, compilers, and computer architecture created alternatives to microcode. High-speed caches, described in Chapter 3, pipelined instruction processing. Advanced compiler technology made it easier to replace the microcode with a compiler-generated sequence of simple instructions.*

With clock speeds increasing by leaps and bounds, it was hard for users and designers to notice the creeping overhead of a microcoded architecture and ever-more-complex instruction sets. More complex computers went faster anyway, just by virtue of increased hardware performance. Eventually, what was once added

---

* Not to imply that you can't use caches and microcode together . . .

value became a liability: all of these architectures—the VAX, the Intel 80×86 in PCs, the 680×0 family of processors, IBM's mainframes—have accumulated the baggage of many years of very complex and specialized instructions. It's not easy for microcoded CISC implementations to retain support for old instructions, yet stay competitive with RISC in terms of performance.

There was a time during the late 1980s when there was intense competition between large CISC mainframes and minicomputers, and RISC servers. Companies like DEC, Hewlett-Packard, and IBM were losing a great deal of business to RISC processors. These companies survived that period by developing their own competitive RISC processors. Companies such as Control Data, Prime, Wang, and Burroughs lost significant market share during the CISC-to-RISC transition.

Vector Processors

During the late 1970s through the mid-1980s, powerful, single-chip microprocessors were CISC designs due to the limitation of the number of transistors that could be placed on a chip. Processors such as the Intel 8086 (1978) and 80386 (1985), and Motorola's MC68000 (1979) and MC68020 (1984), were the mainstream microprocessors. The integer and floating-point processing of these processors was very slow. Their primary application was in the area of personal computers doing tasks like word processing and spreadsheets.

During this time, the unchallenged high performance computers were the vector processors produced by companies such as Control Data, Cray Research, Cray Computers, NEC, Fujitsu, IBM, and Convex.

The first successful vector supercomputer was the Cray-1S, introduced in 1975. It featured a 12.5-ns (80-MHz) clock and was fully pipelined to produce a floating-point result every cycle. While this seems slow compared to today's microprocessors, one of its competitors at the time was the Intel 8008* processor. Even now, while the current generation of RISC microprocessors is catching up quickly, vector-processor computers still have the absolute fastest processors and memory interconnect in the world.

Given the nature of scientific computing codes, a well-balanced high-performance scientific processor should be able to load two 64-bit words from any location in memory, perform a floating-point computation, and store a 64-bit result to any location in memory every cycle. Once achieved, the goal was to do more than one

---

* The Intel 8008 was introduced in 1972, had a clock rate of 108 KHz, and could address 16K of memory. It might have been capable of 100 floating-point operations per second on a good day with a tailwind. See *http://www.intel.com/intel/museum/25anniv/* for other interesting tidbits.

of each per cycle. In the 1970s and 1980s, given technology constraints, a vector processor was the only architecture that could achieve this level of performance.

There is one other aspect of the vector processors that make them very different from any of the past or present microprocessors. The vector computer companies were specifically high performance computer companies. Instead of selling millions of $100 processors in a mass market, their goal was often to sell between 5 and 20 systems per year at a cost of $30–100 million dollars per system. In this market, these vendors could deploy exotic technology such as liquid cooling, the fastest available logic, a large main memory based on static RAM, or the use of gold connectors throughout. Often these vendors would make a technological breakthrough in design or manufacturing just to finish their first system.

The fundamental extensions that make a vector processor unique are its vector registers, memory pipelines, and vector instructions.

Vector Registers

A typical vector processor has normal 64-bit address and data registers. However, it also has vector registers, each of which is made up of multiple elements. Vector registers range in length from 128 to 512 elements per register. Figure A-3 shows the available registers in a typical vector processor.

These vector registers are accessed using special vector instructions that operate on a subset of the elements stored in a vector register in a single instruction. For example:

```
VADD.W      V1,V2,V3
```

This vector add instruction can add each of the 128 elements in Vector Register V1 to the corresponding element of Vector Register V2 and store the result in the corresponding element in Vector Register V3. If V1, V2, and V3 were FORTRAN arrays, this single machine-language instruction essentially is the same as saying:

```
DO I=1,128
  V3(I) = V1(I) + V2(I)
ENDDO
```

or (for those who like FORTRAN 90):

```
V3(1:128) = V1(1:128) + V2(1:128)
```

This loop operation was implemented either directly in a hardware sequencer or by using a loop implemented in microcode.

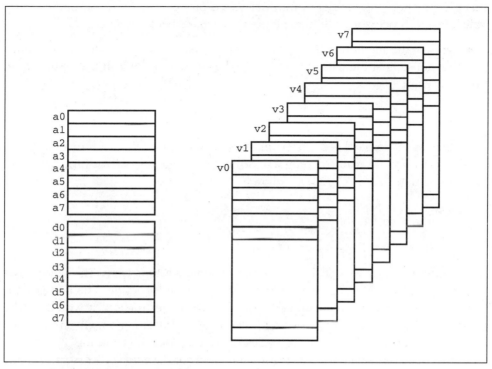

Figure A-3: Vector processor registers

Vector Processor Memory Systems

With clock rates starting at 12.5 ns and moving below 2 ns, it's important for a memory subsystem to be able to retrieve and store data at a sufficient rate so as not to stall the computation pipelines. Even if you were to create a large memory made completely of static RAM, it wouldn't be fast enough. Memory operations must be pipelined as described in Chapter 3 to support the data transfer rates needed by these processors.

When you look at the architectural specifications for vector systems, the number of memory pipelines is an important metric for the system's overall performance. The CDC Star-205* has up to four memory pipelines. The peak performance of a Star system was directly related to the number of installed memory pipelines.

A memory pipeline is hardware that's in the CPU, memory interconnect, and memory subsystem. In a sense, the CPU tells the pipeline, "get me these 128 words," and then waits. The pipeline begins the process of accessing the memory banks and, as the memory values come back, sends them to the processor. The goal is

---

* So-named because it looked somewhat like the Starship Enterprise when viewed from above.

that after a (hopefully short) startup delay, the pipeline will provide one or more values every processor cycle until all the values have been retrieved.

You can ask the memory pipeline to retrieve unit-stride data (it generally likes this best) or non-unit-stride data, or tell it to gather data according to the values in an address vector.

Vector Instructions

Now that we have pipelined vector registers, floating-point units, and memory systems, we should be ready to program. So we write our first vector program to do A(1:128) = B(1:128) + C(1:128) as follows:

```
VLOAD.W    B,V1
VLOAD.W    C,V2
VADD.W     V1,V2,V3
VSTORE.W   V3,A
```

We are quite happy except for one thing: pipeline startup delay. The good news about pipelines is that once they start, we get results every cycle. The bad news is the time it takes to get them started. For each vector instruction, it would not be outrageous to see a 10–15 cycle start-up delay for each instruction. Given that each instruction executes for up to 128 cycles once the pipeline starts, this is an unacceptable waste of resources. Some instructions on some vector processors can take over a hundred cycles to get started.

There is a technique called *chaining* that helps reduce this latency problem. Chaining allows a later instruction to get started before an earlier instruction completes. Chaining also allows values to be used out of a vector register before all of the values in the register have been computed.

This example also demonstrates why it's a good idea to have more than one memory pipeline available. Using multiple memory pipelines and chained computations, we can create multi-instruction pipelines and avoid incurring extra startup latency for each vector instruction.

First, the load from B into Register V1 begins and is delegated to one of the memory load pipelines. Then, in the next cycle, assuming that we have a pipeline available, we initiate the load of C into Register V2. As the elements of V1 and V2 begin arriving, we can chain the vector add into Register V3. If we have sufficient capability, we can even chain the store into C from Register V3 as the elements exit the addition pipeline.

Once we have started all the operations, these four instructions work together as a single pipeline to move data from memory through the CPU, and the results get moved back to memory with minimum latency as shown in Figure A-4. The achievable performance of a particular vector processor was often dependent on

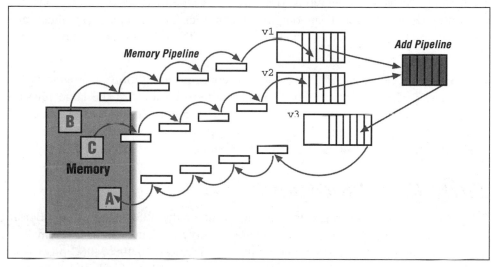

Figure A-4: A vector processor at work

the number of available memory pipelines and the degree to which one operation could be chained to another. Vector processors that simply executed vector instructions serially often had great difficulty achieving their rated peak performance.

The designers of the CDC Star-100 and ETA-10 series of computers saw this pattern of load-compute-store and decided to completely eliminate the registers and connect the compute pipeline directly to two read pipes and one write pipe. This gave outstanding performance on long unit-stride memory-to-memory operations. Unfortunately for these systems, there are many applications that can make good use of registers, either by eliminating memory accesses in store-reload patterns or load-load patterns. In these applications, a register-based architecture outperforms a pure memory architecture.

Hardware Implications

These vector systems are physically quite large. Some were six feet tall and six feet in diameter. Given the limitations of the speed of light,* it's not possible for data to travel across the entire cabinet in a single cycle. If one register were several feet from another register, it might take four or five cycles to copy data between those two registers. This makes the layout of the components within the cabinet an important part of the overall design of these large vector systems.

---

* Light and electricity are very fast, but they travel less than a foot in a nanosecond. With a clock rate of two nanoseconds, the farthest a signal could travel was two feet!

By limiting the vector operations to a carefully predefined set of instructions, the computer designers could lay out the vector registers, compute pipelines, and memory pipelines so that they could all interact without incurring any unnecessary delay.

In a sense, we can think of the vector registers as an early form of programmable data cache in a refrigerator-sized computer system. Because of the large physical size of the processor, it wasn't practical to provide a generic data cache that could be accessed using any pattern. Vector processors instead access their data cache in well-defined patterns that can be naturally pipelined.

Early RISC Processors

The year 1986 was an important turning point in the RISC architecture. Before 1986, most of the RISC microprocessors were simply too underpowered to make a significant impact on mainstream computer architectures. In 1986, RISC processors under development at Berkeley (RISC-1) and Stanford (MIPS) made their commercial debut as the SPARC V7 and MIPS-I processors, respectively. The HP PA-RISC family was also introduced in 1986. Other major RISC processor families were introduced later: Motorola 88100 (1988), IBM Power1 (1990), DEC Alpha (1992), IBM Power2 (1993), and IBM/Motorola PowerPC (1993).

In this section, we look at the two processors that are often credited with causing the RISC revolution.

MIPS R2000 and R3000

The MIPS architecture is a family of processors that has evolved over time as technology constraints have changed. The original MIPS processor was the MIPS R2000 and its follow-on, the R3000. These chips have 32 32-bit integer registers and 16 64-bit floating-point registers. Floating-point operations are supported using a coprocessor, and the cache is off-chip. The pipeline depth is five. The MIPS R3000 supported a clock rate of up to 40 MHz.

SPARC-1 Processor

The early SPARC processors were very straightforward with a pipeline depth of four (fetch, decode, execute, and write). The floating-point processor was a separate coprocessor. The unique SPARC feature was the concept of *register windows*.

Register windows pass parameters from a calling routine to a subroutine without forcing parameters to be placed in memory on a stack. The idea was to improve the performance of subroutine calls and interrupt processing. SPARC processors appear to have 32 32-bit registers, numbered from zero to 31. These registers are partitioned into four groups: global, input, local, and output. When a subroutine is entered, its first act is to rotate the register window.* The caller's out registers become the callee's in registers. The caller's local and in registers are saved to memory if the processor is out of free registers. This is called a *spill*. While it's executing, the callee can operate on its local and output registers. Its input registers and global registers are shared with the callee and the entire program, respectively. When the callee completes, it restores the caller's registers before returning to the caller.

At first blush, this seems no different than a call stack. Functionally, it operates the same as a stack. Values are saved upon entry and restored upon exit. Some values are shared between the callee and caller. Register windows are intended to be implemented completely as registers on the chip. Many implementations of the SPARC have 130 or more physical registers that save and restore the local and in registers upon each call and return. The number of physical registers are limited. If the code makes too many nested subroutine calls, the registers must be stored on a stack structure in memory.

The SPARC researchers did a careful study of existing code and determined a reasonable number of physical registers to save and restore the register windows without spilling to memory unnecessarily. In a sense, register windows are a cache of the top of a call stack supported in hardware.

Architectural Experiments

Throughout the 1980s, the computer architecture field was diverse. There was a certain restlessness with the aging CISC processors. Computer researchers (some at universities and others at new small start-up companies) were exploring the space between the CISC processors with their serial instruction streams and the high-end parallel/vector supercomputers. There have been a number of architectures that have been proposed and implemented that explore different design approaches. These architectures are not even close to successful when compared to the current RISC processors. However, these architectures bear some study because each has some strong features that may reappear in the future in a somewhat modified form.

The architectures we briefly explore in this section include:

Intel i860

> An early long instruction word RISC processor that was a precursor to superscalar RISC processors.

---

* Unless it's a "leaf" procedure.

Multiflow Trace
> A very long instruction word processor that could execute 7, 14, or 28 instructions per cycle in parallel.

Data flow processors
> Data flow processors have always had the potential to find and exploit the maximum amount of parallelism present in an application. However, while this architecture has enticing potential, it has been difficult to solve some of the technical issues for this architecture.

While it's doubtful that any of these architectures will stage a dramatic comeback, current and upcoming processors often take some of the best ideas from these architectures and use them to one degree or another.

Intel i860

The Intel i860, an early superscalar processor, was capable of executing more than one instruction side by side per clock cycle. The i860 depended on the compiler to determine when to execute multiple instructions. Later superscalar processors can dynamically find parallelism in an instruction stream at runtime. In some respects, the sophisticated instruction hardware that's not yet in the i860 is being simulated by the compiler (which makes for slow compilers, by the way).

Each parallel instruction is actually two or more regular RISC instructions cemented together into a single long instruction word. Every clock tick, one of these long instructions is fetched and fed into separate pipelines controlling different parts of the processor.

The Intel i860 has two operating modes. The first, *single instruction mode*, makes the processor look very much like a classic RISC machine. There is pipelined instruction overlap, but only one new operation can be initiated with each clock cycle.

The other, *dual mode*, starts two instructions per clock cycle—one floating-point and one of a choice of fixed point instruction, memory reference, or branch (a "core" operation, in Intel parlance).* You can switch the processor from one mode to the other during operation, and perhaps frequently within a given program. Figure A-5 shows how the i860 switches between these modes.

---

* Think of the dual-mode instructions for the Intel i860 like a wedding party making its way up the aisle: the order and relationship of the participants is fixed and determined well ahead of time.

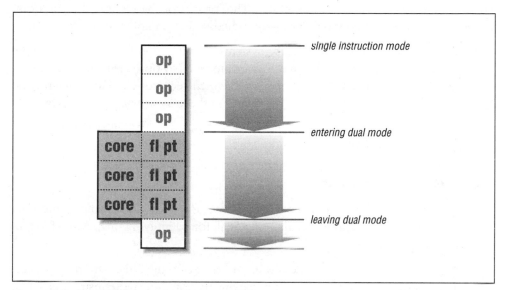

Figure A-5: Intel i860 transition between modes

Multiflow Trace

If one continues along the path of creating ganged parallel execution units that depend on the compiler to identify parallelism, one arrives at the *very long instruction word* (VLIW) architecture. VLIW machines are superscalar processors with "wider" instructions (even more operations per clock). There might be several floating-point, integer, branch, and memory operations initiated each clock cycle. The potential for VLIW processors is great, but they require very sophisticated compilers; the instruction stream decomposition that happens at runtime in a superscalar machine has to be done off-line for a VLIW. You might guess that this would make things easier because it gives the processor less to worry about at runtime.

However, everything that might go wrong has to be accounted for when compiling—conflicting memory references, instructions that depend on the results of previous instructions, out-of-order execution, etc. Instruction scheduling problems that might be self-correcting on a superscalar processor have to be carefully prepared in advance by a VLIW compiler. This limits the optimization that can be performed on these systems.

The most successful company to develop and market a VLIW system was Multiflow, which developed its Trace-7, Trace-14, and Trace-28 systems that could execute 7, 14, and 28 instructions per cycle in parallel. When plodding through "dusty deck" or legacy code, Multiflow's compiler could only schedule three or four instructions at a time, but for numerically intensive codes it was not uncommon to achieve tens of instructions per clock. The processor had eight floating-point pipelines and four memory pipelines—all scheduled at compiletime.

The great weakness of the pure VLIW systems is that if you can only do a single instruction in a cycle, you still have to execute N-1 No-op instructions. The very long instruction word can be 1024 bits long, which requires significant instruction fetch bandwidth. Programs can be quite large on these systems.

Multiflow has since gone out of business, but we'd hate to let that fact water down our endorsement of VLIW: it was a nifty idea.

Data Flow Processors

Another architecture that has been experimental for quite some time is the data flow architecture. Data flow has the potential for identifying maximal of parallelism in an application.

A traditional (non-data flow) processor has a sense of which instruction(s) are currently executing. Unless there is a branch instruction, the next instructions that execute are those instructions that immediately follow the current instructions. There is a program counter that tells us where we are currently executing and where we will execute next.

Data flow dispenses with any notion of sequential program order or program counter. Instructions are placed into a run queue. Each instruction in the queue is ready to execute or is waiting for some input operands. Once an instruction receives its operands, it can begin executing immediately.

Data flow memory semantics

The memory in a data flow processor is what makes it possible to determine which instructions have received their input values. On a traditional processor, memory locations contain a value. By executing an assignment statement, that value can be changed. In data flow, a variable can either contain a value or be *undefined.* Each variable can only be assigned a value once; this called a *single assignment* architecture:

```
X = 5
X = X + 1
```

These two instructions make perfect sense on a traditional processor. First X is set to 5, and the next instruction sets it to 6. On a data flow processor, the second instruction isn't legal because X already has a value.

To handle looping structures, data flow processors add a tag to a variable that differentiates these values of X as different variables:

```
X{0} = 5
X{1} = X{0} + 1
X{2} = X{1} + 1
```

These are not exactly the same as arrays. It is better to think of this as X at time 0, X at time 1, and X at time 2. Once no more instructions are waiting for X{0}, that value can be discarded to reclaim space.

Data flow instructions

A data flow machine language instruction consists of an operator, input operands, and output operands. For example:

```
A = 5
B = 7
C = A + B
D = C + 2
```

In data flow, the order of these instructions does not matter. For example, the following would be equivalent to the previous code:

```
D = C + 2
B = 7
C = A + B
A = 5
```

The order of execution is determined by the availability of the input operands. In the previous two examples, when the code starts, all of the variables are undefined. Instead of executing the "first" instruction, a data flow processor looks for any instruction that has all of its input operands. In the first example, the A=5 and B=7 statements are ready to execute. They can execute in any order or even at the same time. Once they execute, they define the values for A and B, making the C=A+B instruction ready to execute. Once this instruction executes, C becomes defined, making the D=C+2 instruction ready to execute.

While this may seem a bit alien to the typical procedural programmer, data flow has many advantages. For the right application, we can keep adding functional units to enhance our performance without changing the code at all. The additional functional units simply take more "ready" instructions and execute them, defining new values. The functional units don't even have to operate on the same clock cycle. Figure A-6 shows a set of data flow instructions being processed by a data flow processor.

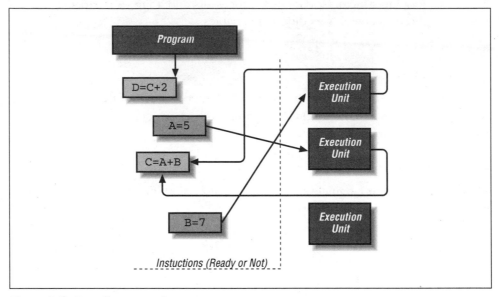

Figure A-6: Data flow execution

While data flow processors have apparent advantages, they have challenges that have not yet been solved:

- Determining which instruction (out of potentially millions) is ready to execute is a compute-intensive task. There are heuristics that work in some instances, but they don't work as a general high performance solution.

- Existing mass-market memory systems don't support the concept of an "undefined" memory location. All memory locations have a value. A data flow processor needs to find the "defined" memory locations quickly using hardware support.

- The dynamic nature of data flow processors using tagged memory leads to the creation and deletion of many instructions. Processors must be careful to do proper garbage collection so as not to run out of space.

- It's difficult to express simple looping constructs using arrays of values in primitive data flow operations.

For this reason, many of the data flow efforts are working on "hybrid" processors that combine attributes of traditional processors with elements of data flow processors. Interestingly, the post-RISC architecture, in some ways, makes use of data flow in a limited fashion.

Second-Generation RISC Processors

In this section, we see the RISC processor families move from conservative to exotic. As the chip space increased, the minimal RISC designs began to add a number of features and capabilities to improve their competitive position against one another.

MIPS R4000/R4400

The R4000 introduced the concept of the superpipelined RISC processor. By increasing the number of pipeline stages to eight, the overall clock rate could be significantly increased. The processor ran at a clock rate internally that was double its external clock rate. The R4400 can operate at up to 250 MHz (internal rate). The R4400 integrated the memory management unit, floating-point support and cache on the processor. The MIPS R4400MC had specialized support for multiprocessor cache coherency. It had an instruction that caused an updated value to be broadcast to all of the caches connected to the memory bus.

MIPS R8000

The R8000 processor was the first RISC microprocessor to specifically target high performance scientific computing. It was a four-way superscalar processor operating at 75 MHz. This processor could load two 64-bit values and perform two 64-bit floating-point computations (four if they were multiply-adds) every cycle. Through a combination of hardware and compiler support, the R8000 supported a feature called *software pipelining* that allowed the R8000 to sustain a memory-to-memory computation at a rate of two computations per 75-MHz cycle. This is similar to the hardware memory pipelines of the vector processors. The MIPS R8000 also supported conditional execution and a reciprocal instruction to speed up divides (at some loss of accuracy). The floating-point processor was on a separate chip.

An interesting feature of the R8000 is that floating-point loads and stores bypass the primary cache and go straight from the secondary cache to the registers. This is what enables the system to maintain nearly 100% of theoretical speed on vector operations in the large streaming cache. Software pipelining helps expose enough parallelism to make this possible, but the bypass of the L1 cache is crucial to getting peak efficiency on those transfers. Integer loads and stores still go to the L1 cache on the R8000, just like a normal chip.

MIPS R4300i

This processor was specifically designed to maximize performance at a very low cost per processor; it powers the Nintendo-64 video game. It was once said that the most concentrated compute power on the planet is the Nintendo warehouse. The specifications of the Nintendo-64 read like a supercomputer of a few years ago: MIPS R4300 at 94 MHz and 4 MB RAMBUS-based RAM, with a transfer rate of 600 MB/sec. The difference is that the Nintendo-64 price is only $150 and it fits nicely next to your television set.

You may also find a MIPS RISC processor in your satellite video-decoding equipment, WebTV box, or handheld computer.

DEC Alpha 21164

The DEC 21164 is a four-way superscalar RISC processor. The Alpha competes based on its extremely fast clock rate. At any point in time, DEC is typically shipping processors that have a clock rate twice as fast as the other CPU vendors. Although some of the parallelism is lost, the cost is less significant when each cycle is so quick. Keeping the architecture clean and the clock rate high is one of the primary tenets of the RISC and DEC 21164 philosophy.

The Alpha's pipeline has five stages. Every stage takes a single cycle except, in some cases, the execution unit takes more than one. The fetch and decode stages are similar to nonsuperscalar processors. A slot stage within the fetch/decode unit takes the next four decoded instructions. As resources become available, instructions are issued in order from this group of four until all have been issued.

The Alpha has an 8-K first-level instruction cache, an 8-K first-level data cache, and a 96-K second-level cache on chip. The first-level cache is relatively small compared to the other modern processors' 16-K to 32-K first-level caches, but its small size allows single-cycle access even with the Alpha's fast clock. It also has a prefetch buffer containing four blocks of 32-bit instructions. According to DEC, having a two level on-chip cache gives better overall performance than a larger, but slower, first-level cache on chip. Since the 8-K cache is less than a page and uses the virtual address as a tag, it has the further advantage of allowing partial overlap of the cache lookup and virtual memory address lookups using the translate lookaside buffer. This also means that the L1 cache needs to be flushed on each context switch.

The Alpha also supports an optional off-chip third-level cache, which is pipelined in the sense that the address on the address bus can change before the data bus is read by the processor. This feature essentially allows the third-level cache to fetch multiple words at the same time. The effect is quite similar to using pipelines to increase the rate of instruction execution.

The Alpha 21164 will not issue instructions out of order, nor will it issue instructions from different four-instruction blocks. So, if all instructions but one are issued, then, in the next clock tick, only that one instruction is issued. Although instructions are issued in order, multicycle instructions can complete out of order. Allowing out-of-order completion provides a low-latency, simple, and fast pipeline, but doesn't provide precise interrupts.

Because of the strict in-order issue, this architecture relies heavily on the compilers to schedule instructions to best utilize their functional units and prevent data dependencies from stalling the pipeline.

SUN UltraSPARC

The UltraSPARC-1 architecture is a four-way superscalar processor. It doesn't issue instructions out of order, but it does have many advanced features to improve performance. Instructions are retrieved from memory, predecoded, and placed in the I-cache. Both branch history and flow history are also stored in the I-cache. Because the SPARC architecture uses a branch delay slot, four instructions can never have more than two branches. In each four instruction segment in the I-cache, there are two branch history entries (2 bits) and one "Next Field" entry. This last entry points to the next group of four instructions to be fetched from the I-cache so the instruction fetch operation can easily be pipelined without needing to consult a branch prediction table.

Between the instruction fetch and dispatch units, the UltraSPARC has a 12-instruction queue. This queue allows fetching to continue while the execution pipeline is stalled due to a dependency or cache miss. Conversely, the execution units can continue to work even when the instruction fetch has a cache miss. Thus, the UltraSPARC's pipeline can be thought of as two connected pipelines with a buffer between them. If either pipeline stalls, the other can exploit the buffer.

Instructions are issued in order and retired in order except for several multicycle instructions (such as floating-point divide, load/store, and instructions issued to the multiple cycle integer unit). These long-latency instructions are retired out of order.

The UltraSPARC has two integer units and five floating-point units. Any combination of two integer and two floating-point instructions can be issued each cycle. Loads, stores, and branches are executed by an integer unit but outstanding loads are tracked by the load/store unit. The load/store unit has a nine-entry load buffer and an eight-entry store buffer. These buffers allow overlapping of load and store operations reducing the apparent memory latency.

Post-RISC Processors

The current crop of processors that support out-of-order and speculative execution are beginning to stray quite far from their minimalist RISC beginnings. Often the processor is smarter at runtime than the compiler. The processor can derive more optimal instruction schedules than the compiler.

If you are unfamiliar with some of the terminology used in this section, see Chapter 2 for an overview of the post-RISC architecture.

DEC Alpha 21264

While the DEC Alpha 21164 processor pursues 600-MHz performance and beyond, DEC is also developing the Alpha 21264 with out-of-order execution. While this processor was not available until 1998, it demonstrates that out-of-order execution does not necessarily imply low clock speeds. The target clock speed of the 21264 is 500 MHz. Like most of the post-RISC processors, the 21264 is a four-way superscalar processor with out-of-order execution. While the 21164 had simple branch prediction, the 21264 adds a *next fetch predictor* (flow prediction) in each cache line. To allow for register renaming, the processor implements 80 integer and 72 floating-point rename registers.

The 21264 can have 20 integer instructions and 15 floating-point instructions in queues. Up to four integer and two floating-point instructions can be issued per cycle. The floating-point add and multiply units are fully pipelined with a four-cycle latency. Up to 32 load/store instructions can be active at one time. Of those memory operations, up to eight off-chip reads and eight off-chip writes can be active at one time.

While the 21264 (500 MHz) is not available, the estimates of its floating-point performance are at 50 SpecFP95. As a comparison, both the Alpha 21164 (500 MHz) and HP PA-8000 (200 MHz) have around 20.0 SpecFP95. This is a factor of 2.5 increase in floating-point performance at the same clock rate when compared to the Alpha 21164.

HAL SPARC64

The HAL SPARC64 processor implements the SPARCV9 architecture with out-of-order execution. The SPARC64 can have up to 64 instructions active at any time. There are ten execution units. Any combination of four fixed-point, two floating-point, two load/store, or one branch instruction can be issued in one cycle. Up to 12 load/store instructions can be active simultaneously. Branch prediction is done using a standard two-bit counter mechanism.

IBM PowerPC 604

The PowerPC 604 and other members of the PowerPC family incorporate most features of a post-RISC CPU. The PPC 604 is four-way superscalar, and instructions are fetched from an on-chip cache in four-instruction segments. Instructions are predecoded as they are loaded into the cache. During the fetch stage, instruction flow prediction is performed using a 256-entry branch target address cache (BTAC).

Fetched instructions go into an eight-instruction queue where they are decoded and then dispatched. In one cycle, up to four instructions can be fetched into the queue and up to four can be dispatched from the queue. Branch prediction is handled in the dispatch stage using a two-bit prediction scheme. The bits are stored in the 512-entry branch history table (BHT).

The dispatch unit forwards instructions to the appropriate functional units from the instruction queue. The reorder buffer of the PowerPC is unique in that it is distributed across the six functional units, each having its own two-entry "reservation station." Instructions in the reservation stations can be issued in any order as resources become available. When an instruction is dispatched, a logical rename register is allocated for the result of the operation. The PPC 604 has eight rename registers for floating-point and twelve for general-purpose registers. In addition, four loads and six stores can be buffered, further increasing the number of instructions issued out of order. Results are moved into the appropriate architected register when the instruction has completed, i.e., is no longer speculative. Upon dispatch, the dispatch unit also allocates an entry in the completed instruction buffer in the completion unit. The completion unit provides in-order retirement of instructions for the PowerPC.

A unique feature of the PowerPC architecture is the "branch-on-counter" instruction, which efficiently implements counter-based loops. The Count Register is part of branch prediction, thus branch-on-counter instructions are effectively unconditional branches from the perspective of the execution stage.

MIPS R10000

The MIPS R10000 is an excellent example of the post-RISC architecture. Targeted toward high-end graphics processing and fast floating-point operation, the MIPS R10000 aggressively executes instructions out of order, while guaranteeing in-order completion and precise interrupts.

The R10000 is a fully four-way superscalar architecture containing a 64-K split two-way set-associative cache on-chip. It can fetch, decode (with branch prediction), and schedule up to four instructions per cycle. Each instruction is predecoded as it's loaded into the I-cache. During the decode, branches are predicted (although only one branch may be predicted per cycle), output dependencies are identified, and rename registers are allocated.

After being decoded, the instruction is placed into one of three 16-entry instruction queues (integer/branch, floating point, or address) for scheduling. These queues supply instructions for five execution pipelines. Instructions may execute from these queues in any order. An instruction is dispatched from the queue when the required inputs and execution units are available.

Note that the R10000 doesn't implement flow prediction but instead relies on a branch resume cache for mispredicted branches. Branch prediction uses the two-bit scheme, and the branch prediction bits are stored in the I-cache. Each branch is followed by a delay slot, so no more than two branches can be fetched in one cycle. Only one branch can be issued per cycle.

HP PA-8000

The heart of the PA-8000 is an out-of-order execution core with a 56-entry instruction reorder buffer (IRB). This buffer is divided into a 28-entry buffer for arithmetic instructions and a 28-entry buffer for memory instructions. Instructions are fetched from a large off-chip synchronous SRAM cache. Moving the cache off chip allows the cache to be quite large. Some PA-8000 processors have 2 MB or larger L1 caches. Access to the I-cache takes two cycles, so the PA-8000 uses flow prediction to pipeline the fetches. This flow prediction implementation uses a 32-entry, fully associative branch target address cache (BTAC).

Each cycle, up to four instructions can be inserted into either the arithmetic/logic unit buffer or the memory instruction buffer. Branch instructions go into both IRBs to help recover from mispredicted branches. The PA 8000 places four instructions into the IRBs on every cycle, but branches count as two instructions, since they go into both IRBs. Branches are predicted at this point using a 256-entry branch history table.

Instructions in the IRB arbitrate for the execution units. Availability of input operands is the first priority. The second priority is to choose the "oldest" instruction. The arbitration is a set-associative operation; there is no sequential search of the IRB to determine the appropriate instruction. During each cycle, at most two arithmetic and two memory instructions can be dispatched simultaneously.

There are two units that perform address computations associated with loads and stores. Once an address is computed, it is stored in the 28-entry address reorder buffer. This buffer allows the memory control to track up to 28 loads, stores, and prefetches simultaneously, and these memory operations can be completed in any order from the off-chip data cache or from main memory. Up to 10 off-chip data cache misses can be outstanding at one time.

Intel Pentium Pro

The Intel Pentium Pro is an interesting blend of architectures. It still executes the x86 CISC instruction set, but the internal implementation is a high performance post-RISC CPU. The Pentium Pro has an execution core that supports out-of-order execution. The most dramatic aspect of the Pentium Pro architecture is that the execution core is not executing Intel x86 instructions. The actual instructions are called *uops* or micro-operations. Each Intel x86 instruction is decoded and translated into a one or more uops that are executed by the out-of-order core.

Instructions go through the Pentium Pro in three stages: First, the instruction is fetched, decoded, and converted into a uop. Second, the uops are executed in the out-of-order core. The final stage retires the uops in original program order. The overall pipeline length has 14 stages.*

Fetching and decoding in the Pentium Pro is more complex than in other processors. Some x86 instructions are very complex and can decode into hundreds of uops, although the number is usually less than three. Also, the x86 instruction set has instructions with varying lengths. The logic that converts from x86 to uops performs a similar function to microcode in earlier CISC machines.

The heart of the out-of-order core is the reservation station (RS). The Pentium Pro has a register allocation table that maps the architected registers onto a larger set of physical registers located in the reorder buffer.

The RS holds up to 20 uops until they are ready for execution. The RS is the buffer between the first and second stages. If an instruction's operands are ready, and an appropriate execution unit is available, the instruction is dispatched. The Pentium Pro has five execution units: two integer arithmetic/logic units, two load/store units, and one floating-point unit.

The final pipeline stages retire instructions. When the uops complete, they wait in the reorder buffer until all of the instructions that came before them (in program order) have been retired. Once that has happened, that instruction may retire.

The most impressive aspect of this architecture is that the Pentium Pro maintains x86 compatibility. The designers handle a number of archaic (early 1980s) architectural characteristics, such as self-modifying code, which didn't concern other designers. Nonetheless, the Pentium Pro performance is competitive with other processors in the post-RISC generation.

---

* Given that the eight-stage pipeline of the MIPS R4000 was called "superpipeline," what do we call a 14-stage pipeline? Megapipeline? Ultrapipeline? Hyperpipeline?

Summary

We have looked at many different processors from different time periods. We have seen how some architectures were designed from the ground up to be high performance processors, and other processors have backed into the role of high performance computing.

One thing that history has shown is that the best high performance systems are developed when a company sets out to produce high performance systems. The system designers must completely understand and address the compute and memory demands of high performance computing when building their systems.

If you would like more detail on processor architecture, two good books on the subject are *Computer Architecture: A Quantitative Approach* by David A. Patterson and John L. Hennessy (Morgan Kaufman), and *Advanced Computer Architecture* by Kai Hwang (McGraw Hill).

At this point, it would be great to write about what the architecture of the future will look like. Will vector processors become extinct? Will our home video games be so fast and fun to play that we forget about high performance computing and just wander around in virtual reality?

While we won't predict what the future will bring in terms of architecture, there are some trends that appear to be quite clear. First, the money is going into commodity processors for now. The market is driving research and development. So it's a good guess that no significant new processors will be developed other than RISC processors aimed at the personal computer market. High performance computers for the medium term will use those processors to their best advantage.

The September 1997 issue of *IEEE Computer* offers a good look at the potential future of microprocessors. The issue looks at the uses and challenges of the billion-transistor chip.

B

Looking at Assembly Language

In this appendix, we take a look at the assembly language produced by a number of different compilers on a number of different architectures. In this survey we revisit some of the issues of CISC versus RISC, and the strengths and weaknesses of different architectures.

For this survey, two roughly identical segments of code were used. The code was a relatively long loop adding two arrays and storing the result in a third array. The loops were written both in FORTRAN and C.

The FORTRAN loop was as follows:

```
SUBROUTINE ADDEM(A,B,C,N)
REAL A(10000),B(10000),C(10000)
INTEGER N,I
DO 10 I=1,N
   A(I) = B(I) + C(I)
ENDDO
END
```

The C version was:

```
for(i=0;i<n;i++) a[i] = b[i] + c[i];
```

We have gathered these examples over the years from a number of different compilers, and the results are not particularly scientific. This is not intended to review a particular architecture or compiler version, but rather just to show an example of the kinds of things you can learn from looking at the output of the compiler.

Intel 8088

The Intel 8088 processor used in the original IBM Personal Computer is a very traditional CISC processing system with features severely limited by its transistor
count. It has very few registers, and the registers generally have rather specific
functions. To support a large memory model, it must set its segment register leading up to each memory operation. This limitation means that every memory access
takes a minimum of three instructions. Interestingly, a similar pattern occurs on
RISC processors.

You notice that at one point, the code moves a value from the **ax** register to the
bx register because it needs to perform another computation that can only be
done in the **ax** register. Note that this is only an integer computation, as the Intel
8088 doesn't support hardware floating-point operations:

```
            mov     word ptr -2[bp],0          # bp is I
    $11:
            mov     ax,word ptr -2[bp]         # Load I
            cmp     ax,word ptr 18[bp]         # Check I>=N
            bge     $10
            shl     ax,1                       # Multiply I by 2
            mov     bx,ax                      # Done - now move to bx
            add     bx,word ptr 10[bp]         # bx = Address of B + Offset
            mov     es,word ptr 12[bp]         # Top part of address
            mov     ax,es: word ptr  [bx]      # Load B(i)
            mov     bx,word ptr -2[bp]         # Load I
            shl     bx,1                       # Multiply I by 2
            add     bx,word ptr 14[bp]         # bx = Address of C + Offset
            mov     es,word ptr 16[bp]         # Top part of address
            add     ax,es: word ptr  [bx]      # Load C(I)
            mov     bx,word ptr -2[bp]         # Load I
            shl     bx,1                       # Multiply I by 2
            add     bx,word ptr 6[bp]          # bx = Address of A + Offset
            mov     es,word ptr 8[bp]          # Top part of address
            mov     es: word ptr  [bx],ax      # Store
    $9:
            inc     word ptr -2[bp]            # Increment I in memory
            jmp $11
    $10:
```

Because there are so few registers, the variable I is kept in memory and loaded
several times throughout the loop. The `inc` instruction at the end of the loop
actually updates the value in memory. Interestingly, at the top of the loop, the
value is then reloaded from memory.

In this type of architecture, the available registers put such a strain on the flexibility of the compiler, there is often not much optimization that is practical.

Motorola MC68020

In this section, we examine another classic CISC processor, the Motorola MC68020, which was used to build Macintosh computers and Sun workstations. We happened to run this code on a BBN GP-1000 Butterfly parallel processing system made up of 96 MC68020 processors.

The Motorola architecture is relatively easy to program in assembly language. It has plenty of 32-bit registers, and they are relatively easy to use. It has a CISC instruction set that keeps assembly language programming quite simple. Many instructions can perform multiple operations in a single instruction.

We use this example to show a progression of optimization levels, using a f77 compiler on a floating-point version of the loop. Our first example is with no optimization:

```
                                          ! Note d0 contains the value I
     L5:
            movl    d0,L13               ! Store I to memory if loop ends
            lea     a1@(-4),a0           ! a1 = address of B
            fmoves  a0@(0,d0:1:4),fp0    ! Load of B(I)
            lea     a3@(-4),a0           ! a3 = address of C
            fadds   a0@(0,d0:1:4),fp0    ! Load of C(I) (And Add)
            lea     a2@(-4),a0           ! a2 = address of A
            fmoves  fp0,a0@(0,d0:1:4)    ! Store of A(I)
            addql   #1,d0                ! Increment I
            subql   #1,d1                ! Decrement "N"
            tstl    d1
            bnes    L5
```

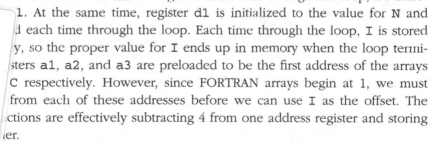

The value for I is stored in the d0 register. Each time through the loop, it's incre-
~~~~~~~~~1. At the same time, register d1 is initialized to the value for N and
~~~~~~d each time through the loop. Each time through the loop, I is stored
~~~y, so the proper value for I ends up in memory when the loop termi-
~~~sters a1, a2, and a3 are preloaded to be the first address of the arrays
~~~C respectively. However, since FORTRAN arrays begin at 1, we must
~~~ from each of these addresses before we can use I as the offset. The
~~~ctions are effectively subtracting 4 from one address register and storing
~~~ier.

~~~~~~wing instruction performs an address computation that is almost a one-to-one translation of an array reference:

```
    fmoves  a0@(0,d0:1:4),fp0      ! Load of B(I)
```

This instruction retrieves a floating-point value from the memory. The address is computed by first multiplying d0 by 4 (because these are 32-bit floating-point numbers) and adding that value to a0. As a matter of fact, the lea and fmoves instructions could have been combined as follows:

```
fmoves  a1@(-4,d0:1:4),fp0        ! Load of B(I)
```

To compute its memory address, this instruction multiplies d0 by 4, adds the contents of a1, and then subtracts 4. The resulting address is used to load 4 bytes into floating-point register fp0. This is almost a literal translation of fetching B(I). You can see how the assembly is set up to track high-level constructs.

It is almost as if the compiler were "trying" to show off and make use of the nifty assembly language instructions.

Like the Intel, this is not a load-store architecture. The fadds instruction adds a value from memory to a value in a register (fp0) and leaves the result of the addition in the register. Unlike the Intel 8088, we have enough registers to store quite a few of the values used throughout the loop (I, N, the address of A, B, and C) in registers to save memory operations.

C on the MC68020

In the next example, we compiled the C version of the loop with the normal optimization (-O) turned on. We see the C perspective on arrays in this code. C views arrays as extensions to pointers in C; the loop index advances as an offset from a pointer to the beginning of the array:

```
! d3 = I
! d1 = Address of A
! d2 = Address of B
! d0 = Address of C
! a6@(20) = N
        moveq    #0,d3                  ! Initialize I
        bras     L5                     ! Jump to End of the loop
L1:     movl     d3,a1                  ! Make copy of I
        movl     a1,d4                  ! Again
        asll     #2,d4                  ! Multiply by 4 (word size)
        movl     d4,a1                  ! Put back in an address register
        fmoves   a1@(0,d2:1),fp0        ! Load B(I)
        movl     a6@(16),d0             ! Get address of C
        fadds    a1@(0,d0:1),fp0        ! Add C(I)
        fmoves   fp0,a1@(0,d1:1)        ! Store into A(I)
        addql    #1,d3                  ! Increment I
L5:
        cmpl     a6@(20),d3
        blts     L1
```

We first see the value of I being copied into several registers and multiplied by 4 (using a left shift of 2, strength reduction). Interestingly, the value in register a1 is I multiplied by 4. Registers d0, d1, and d2 are the addresses of C, B, and A respectively. In the load, add, and store, `a1` is the base of the address computation and `d0`, `d1`, and `d2` are added as an offset to `a1` to compute each address.

This is a simplistic optimization that is primarily trying to maximize the values that are kept in registers during loop execution. Overall, it's a relatively literal translation of the C language semantics from C to assembly. In many ways, C was designed to generate relatively efficient code without requiring a highly sophisticated optimizer.

More optimization

In this example, we are back to the FORTRAN version on the MC68020. We have compiled it with the highest level of optimization (`-OLM`) available on this compiler. Now we see a much more aggressive approach to the loop:

```
! a0 = Address of C(I)
! a1 = Address of B(I)
! a2 = Address of A(I)
L3:
        fmoves   a1@,fp0            ! Load B(I)
        fadds    a0@,fp0            ! Add C(I)
        fmoves   fp0,a2@            ! Store A(I)
        addql    #4,a0             ! Advance by 4
        addql    #4,a1             ! Advance by 4
        addql    #4,a2             ! Advance by 4
        subql    #1,d0             ! Decrement I
        tstl     d0
        bnes     L3
```

First off, the compiler is smart enough to do all of its address adjustment outside the loop and store the adjusted addresses of A, B, and C in registers. We do the load, add, and store in quick succession. Then we advance the array addresses by 4 and perform the subtraction to determine when the loop is complete.

This is very tight code and bears little resemblance to the original FORTRAN code.

SPARC Architecture

These next examples were performed using a SPARC architecture system using FORTRAN. The SPARC architecture is a classic RISC processor using load-store access to memory, many registers and delayed branching. We first examine the code at the lowest optimization:

```
.L18:                               ! Top of the loop
    ld     [%fp-4],%12              ! Address of B
    sethi  %hi(GPB.addem.i),%10     ! Address of I in %10
    or     %10,%lo(GPB.addem.i),%10
    ld     [%10+0],%10              ! Load I
    sll    %10,2,%11                ! Multiply by 4
    add    %12,%11,%10              ! Figure effective address of B(I)
```

```
ld      [%10+0],%f3            ! Load B(I)
ld      [%fp-8],%12            ! Address of C
sethi   %hi(GPB.addem.i),%10   ! Address of I in %10
or      %10,%lo(GPB.addem.i),%10
ld      [%10+0],%10            ! Load I
sll     %10,2,%11              ! Multiply by 4
add     %12,%11,%10            ! Figure effective address of B(I)
ld      [%10+0],%f2            ! Load C(I)
fadds   %f3,%f2,%f2            ! Do the Floating Point Add
ld      [%fp-12],%12           ! Address of A
sethi   %hi(GPB.addem.i),%10   ! Address of i in %10
or      %10,%lo(GPB.addem.i),%10
ld      [%10+0],%10            ! Load I
sll     %10,2,%11              ! Multiply by 4
add     %12,%11,%10            ! Figure effective address of A(I)
st      %f2,[%10+0]            ! Store A(I)
sethi   %hi(GPB.addem.i),%10   ! Address of i in %10
or      %10,%lo(GPB.addem.i),%10
ld      [%10+0],%10            ! Load I
add     %10,1,%11              ! Increment I
sethi   %hi(GPB.addem.i),%10   ! Address of I in %10
or      %10,%lo(GPB.addem.i),%10
st      %11,[%10+0]            ! Store I
sethi   %hi(GPB.addem.i),%10   ! Address of I in %10
or      %10,%lo(GPB.addem.i),%10
ld      [%10+0],%11            ! Load I
ld      [%fp-20],%10           ! Load N
cmp     %11,%10               ! Compare
ble     .L18
nop                            ! Branch Delay Slot
```

This is some pretty poor code. We don't need to go through it line by line, but there are a few quick observations we can make. The value for I is loaded from memory five times in the loop. The address of I is computed six times throughout the loop (each time takes two instructions). There are no tricky memory addressing modes, so multiplying I by 4 to get a byte offset is done explicitly three times (at least they use a shift). To add insult to injury, they even put a NO-OP in the branch delay slot.

One might ask, "Why do they ever generate code this bad?" Well, it's not because the compiler isn't capable of generating efficient code, as we shall see below. One explanation is that in this optimization level, it simply does a one-to-one translation of the tuples (intermediate code) into machine language. You can almost draw lines in the above example and precisely identify which instructions came from which tuples.

One reason to generate the code using this simplistic approach is to guarantee that the program will produce the correct results. Looking at the above code, it's pretty easy to argue that it indeed does exactly what the FORTRAN code does. You can track every single assembly statement directly back to part of a FORTRAN statement.

It's pretty clear that you don't want to execute this code in a high performance production environment without some more optimization.

Moderate optimization

In this example, we enable some optimization (-O1):

```
        save    %sp,-120,%sp        ! Rotate the register window
        add     %i0,-4,%o0          ! Address of A(0)
        st      %o0,[%fp-12]        ! Store on the stack
        add     %i1,-4,%o0          ! Address of B(0)
        st      %o0,[%fp-4]         ! Store on the stack
        add     %i2,-4,%o0          ! Address of C(0)
        st      %o0,[%fp-8]         ! Store on the stack
        sethi   %hi(GPB.addem.i),%o0 ! Address of I (top portion)
        add     %o0,%lo(GPB.addem.i),%o2  ! Address of I (lower portion)
        ld      [%i3],%o0           ! %o0 = N (fourth parameter)
        or      %g0,1,%o1           ! %o1 = 1 (for addition)
        st      %o0,[%fp-20]        ! store N on the stack
        st      %o1,[%o2]           ! Set memory copy of I to 1
        ld      [%o2],%o1           ! o1 = I  (kind of redundant)
        cmp     %o1,%o0             ! Check I > N (zero-trip?)
        bg      .L12                ! Don't do loop at all
        nop                         ! Delay Slot
        ld      [%o2],%o0           ! Pre-load for Branch Delay Slot
.L900000110:                        ! Top of the loop
        ld      [%fp-4],%o1         ! o1 = Address of B(0)
        sll     %o0,2,%o0           ! Multiply I by 4
        ld      [%o1+%o0],%f2       ! f2 = B(I)
        ld      [%o2],%o0           ! Load I from memory
        ld      [%fp-8],%o1         ! o1 = Address of C(0)
        sll     %o0,2,%o0           ! Multiply I by 4
        ld      [%o1+%o0],%f3       ! f3 = C(I)
        fadds   %f2,%f3,%f2         ! Register-to-register add
        ld      [%o2],%o0           ! Load I from memory (not again!)
        ld      [%fp-12],%o1        ! o1 = Address of A(0)
        sll     %o0,2,%o0           ! Multiply I by 4 (yes, again)
        st      %f2,[%o1+%o0]       ! A(I) = f2
        ld      [%o2],%o0           ! Load I from memory
        add     %o0,1,%o0           ! Increment I in register
        st      %o0,[%o2]           ! Store I back into memory
        ld      [%o2],%o0           ! Load I back into a register
        ld      [%fp-20],%o1        ! Load N into a register
        cmp     %o0,%o1             ! I > N ??
        ble,a   .L900000110
        ld      [%o2],%o0           ! Branch Delay Slot
```

This is a significant improvement from the previous example. Some loop constant computations (subtracting 4) were hoisted out of the loop. We only loaded I 4 times during a loop iteration. Strangely, the compiler didn't choose to store the addresses of A(0), B(0), and C(0) in registers at all even though there were plenty of registers. Even more perplexing is the fact that it loaded a value from memory immediately after it had stored it from the exact same register!

But one bright spot is the branch delay slot. For the first iteration, the load was done before the loop started. For the successive iterations, the first load was done in the branch delay slot at the bottom of the loop.

Comparing this code to the moderate optimization code on the MC68020, you can begin to get a sense of why RISC was not an overnight sensation. It turned out that an unsophisticated compiler could generate much tighter code for a CISC processor than a RISC processor. RISC processors are always executing extra instructions here and there to compensate for the lack of slick features in their instruction set. If a processor has a faster clock rate but has to execute more instructions, it does not always have better performance than a slower, more efficient processor.

But as we shall soon see, this CISC advantage is about to evaporate in this particular example.

Higher optimization

We now increase the optimization to –O2. Now the compiler generates much better code. It's important you remember that this is the same compiler being used for all three examples.

At this optimization level, the compiler looked through the code sufficiently well to know it didn't even need to rotate the register windows (no save instruction). Clearly the compiler looked at the register usage of the entire routine:

```
! Note, didn't even rotate the register Window
! We just use the %o registers from the caller

! %o0 = Address of first element of A (from calling convention)
! %o1 = Address of first element of B (from calling convention)
! %o2 = Address of first element of C (from calling convention)
! %o3 = Address of N (from calling convention)

addem_:
        ld      [%o3],%g2               ! Load N
        cmp     %g2,1                   ! Check to see if it is <1
        bl      .L77000006              ! Check for zero trip loop
        or      %g0,1,%g1               ! Delay slot - Set I to 1
.L77000003:
        ld      [%o1],%f0               ! Load B(I) First time Only
.L900000109:
        ld      [%o2],%f1               ! Load C(I)
        fadds   %f0,%f1,%f0             ! Add
        add     %g1,1,%g1               ! Increment I
```

```
        add     %o1,4,%o1       ! Increment Address of B
        add     %o2,4,%o2       ! Increment Address of C
        cmp     %g1,%g2         ! Check Loop Termination
        st      %f0,[%o0]       ! Store A(I)
        add     %o0,4,%o0       ! Increment Address of A
        ble,a   .L900000109     ! Branch w/ annul
        ld      [%o1],%f0       ! Load the B(I)
.L77000006:
        retl                    ! Leaf Return (No window)
        nop                     ! Branch Delay Slot
```

This is tight code. The registers o0, o1, and o2 contain the addresses of the first elements of A, B, and C respectively. They already point to the right value for the first iteration of the loop. The value for I is never stored in memory; it is kept in global register g1. Instead of multiplying I by 4, we simply advance the three addresses by 4 bytes each iteration.

The branch delay slots are utilized for both branches. The branch at the bottom of the loop uses the annul feature to cancel the following load if the branch falls through.

The most interesting observation regarding this code is the striking similarity to the code and the code generated for the MC68020 at its top optimization level:

```
L3:
        fmoves  a1@,fp0         ! Load B(I)
        fadds   a0@,fp0         ! Add C(I)
        fmoves  fp0,a2@         ! Store A(I)
        addql   #4,a0           ! Advance by 4
        addql   #4,a1           ! Advance by 4
        addql   #4,a2           ! Advance by 4
        subql   #1,d0           ! Decrement I
        tstl    d0
        bnes    L3
```

The two code sequences are nearly identical! For the SPARC, it does an extra load because of its load-store architecture. On the SPARC, I is incremented and compared to N, while on the MC68020, I is decremented and compared to zero.

This aptly shows how the advancing compiler optimization capabilities quickly made the "nifty" features of the CISC architectures rather useless. Even on the CISC processor, the post-optimization code used the simple forms of the instructions because they produce they fastest execution time.

Note that these code sequences were generated on an MC68020. An MC68020 should be able to eliminate the three addql instructions by using post-increment, saving three instructions. Add a little loop unrolling, and you have some very tight code. Of course, the MC68060 was never a broadly deployed workstation processor, so we never really got a chance to take it for a test drive.

Convex C-240

This section shows the results of compiling on the Convex C-Series of parallel/vector supercomputers. In addition to their normal registers, vector computers have vector registers that contain up to 256 64-bit elements. These processors can perform operations on any subset of these registers with a single instruction.

It is hard to claim that these vector supercomputers are more RISC or CISC. They have simple lean instruction sets and, hence, are RISC-like. However, they have instructions that implement loops, and so they are somewhat CISC-like.

The Convex C-240 has scalar registers (s2), vector registers (v2), and address registers (a3). Each vector register has 128 elements. The vector length register controls how many of the elements of each vector register are processed by vector instructions. If vector length is above 128, the entire register is processed.

The code to implement our loop is as follows:

```
L4:     mov.w   s2,vl           ; Set the Vector length to N
        ld.w    0(a5),v0        ; Load B into Vector Register
        ld.w    0(a2),v1        ; Load C into Vector Register
        add.s   v1,v0,v2        ; Add the vector registers
        st.w    v2,0(a3)        ; Store results into A
        add.w   #-128,s2        ; Decrement "N"
        add.w   #512,a2         ; Advance address for A
        add.w   #512,a3         ; Advance address for B
        add.w   #512,a5         ; Advance address for C
        lt.w    #0,s2           ; Check to see if "N" is < 0
        jbrs.t  L4
```

Initially, the vector length register is set to N. We assume that for the first iteration, N is greater than 128. The next instruction is a vector load instruction into register v0. This loads 128 32-bit elements into this register. The next instruction also loads 128 elements, and the following instruction adds those two registers and places the results into a third vector register. Then the 128 elements in Register v2 are stored back into memory. After those elements have been processed, N is decremented by 128 (after all, we did process 128 elements). Then we add 512 to each of the addresses (4 bytes per element) and loop back up. At some point, during the last iteration, if N is not an exact multiple of 128, the vector length register is less than 128, and the vector instructions only process those remaining elements up to N.

One of the challenges of vector processors is to allow an instruction to begin executing before the previous instruction has completed. For example, once the load into Register v1 has partially completed, the processor could actually begin adding the first few elements of v0 and v1 while waiting for the rest of the elements of v1 to arrive. This approach of starting the next vector instruction before the previous vector instruction has completed is called chaining. Chaining is an important feature to get maximum performance from vector processors.

IBM RS-6000

The IBM RS-6000 is generally credited as the first RISC processor to have cracked the Linpack 100×100 benchmark. The RS-6000 is characterized by strong floating-point performance and excellent memory bandwidth among RISC workstations. The RS-6000 was the basis for IBM's scalable parallel processor: the IBM-SP1 and SP2.

When our example program is run on the RS-6000, we can see the use of a CISC-style instruction in the middle of a RISC processor. The RS-6000 supports a branch-on-count instruction that combines the decrement, test, and branch operations into a single instruction. Moreover, there is a special register (the count register) that is part of the instruction fetch unit that stores the current value of the counter. The fetch unit also has its own add unit to perform the decrements for this instruction.

These types of features creeping into RISC architectures are occuring because there is plenty of chip space for them. If a wide range of programs can run faster with this type of instruction, it's often added.

The assembly code on the RS-6000 is:

```
        ai      r3,r3,-4                # Address of A(0)
        ai      r5,r5,-4                # Address of B(0)
        ai      r4,r4,-4                # Address of C(0)
        bcr     BO_IF_NOT,CR0_GT
        mtspr   CTR,r6                  # Store in the Counter Register
__L18:
        lfsu    fp0,4(r4)               # Pre Increment Load
        lfsu    fp1,4(r5)               # Pre Increment Load
        fa      fp0,fp0,fp1
        frsp    fp0,fp0
        stfsu   fp0,4(r3)               # Pre-increment Store
        bc      BO_dCTR_NZERO,CR0_LT,__L18   # Branch on Counter
```

The RS-6000 also supports a memory addressing mode that can add a value to its address register before using the address register. Interestingly, these two features (branch on count and pre-increment load) eliminate several instructions when compared to the more "pure" SPARC processor. The SPARC processor has 10 instructions in the body of its loop, while the RS-6000 has 6 instructions.

The advantage of the RS-6000 in this particular loop may be less significant if both processors were two-way superscalar. The instructions were eliminated on the RS-6000 were integer instructions. On a two-way superscalar processor, those integer instructions may simply execute on the integer units while the floating-point units are busy performing the floating-point computations.

Conclusion

In this section, we have attempted to give you some understanding of the variety of assembly language that is produced by compilers at different optimization levels and on different computer architectures. At some point during the tuning of your code, it can be quite instructive to take a look at the generated assembly language to be sure that the compiler is not doing something really stupid that is slowing you down.

Please don't be tempted to rewrite portions in assembly language. Usually any problems can be solved by cleaning up and streamlining your high-level source code and setting the proper compiler flags.

It is interesting that very few people actually learn assembly language any more. Most folks find that the compiler is the best teacher of assembly language. By adding the appropriate option (often -S), the compiler starts giving you lessons. I suggest that you don't print out all of the code. There are many pages of useless variable declarations, etc. For these examples, I cut out all of that useless information. It is best to view the assembly in an editor and only print out the portion that pertains to the particular loop you are tuning.

C

Future Trends:
Intel IA-64

by Dr. Richard Enbody

As of the writing of this book, yet another evolutionary step in the instruction set of microprocessors is on the way. The Intel/HP joint effort, termed "Merced," is taking the next step in architecture.

The primary, outstanding speed impediments facing post-RISC processors are memory latency, the number of branch mispredictions, and the limited ability to keep multiple execution units busy (parallelism). The principle behind IA-64 is to attack latency and mispredictions using increased memory bandwidth, and to attack parallelism with EPIC.

Let us begin by defining terms. EPIC stands for *explicitly parallel instruction computing*, which defines a means for a compiler to explicitly pass information about parallelism to the hardware. EPIC was developed by Intel and Hewlett-Packard. Intel-Architecture-64 (IA-64) is a newly defined 64-bit instruction set architecture (ISA) that was defined by Intel and Hewlett-Packard. IA-64 incorporates EPIC, so it can be thought of as an implementation of EPIC. Merced is Intel's first microprocessor to implement the IA-64 ISA. In other words, Merced is an implementation of IA-64, which is an implementation of EPIC.* Starting at the highest level in Figure C-1, let us examine how EPIC allows a compiler to pass information about parallelism to hardware. The principle behind EPIC begins with the fact that current optimizing compilers consider data dependencies in constructing a set of instructions to run on hardware. However, that knowledge is currently not shared with the hardware. In fact, current out-of-order microprocessors go to great lengths to rediscover and work around dependencies in code. EPIC defines a

---

* To compare these new terms, EPIC is a design approach like RISC or CISC, IA-64 is an instruction set architecture like x86 or PA-RISC, and Merced is a particular implementation of an ISA like Pentium Pro or 8086.

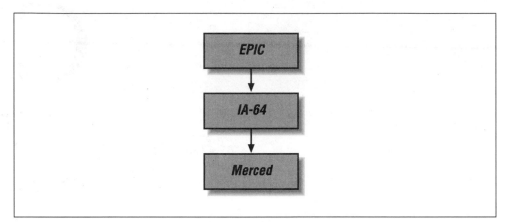

Figure C-1: Relationship between EIPC, IA-64, and Merced

means for the dependence knowledge determined by the compiler to be explicitly passed to the hardware, as shown in Figure C-2.

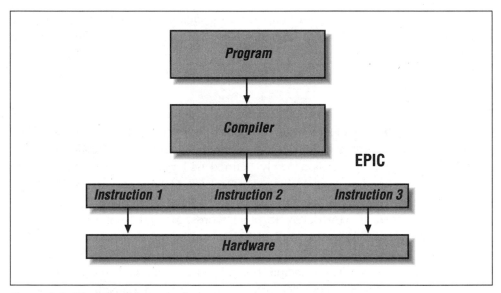

Figure C-2: The role of the compiler

The mechanism EPIC chose for communication is to use "template" bits. These bits indicate groups of instructions that are independent of each other so they need not be executed in sequence. In IA-64, instructions are bundled into groups of three with template bits indicating whether one, two, or all three instructions are independent. The IA-64 instruction format is shown in Figure C-3. With the knowledge from the compiler that groups of instructions can be executed in parallel, the

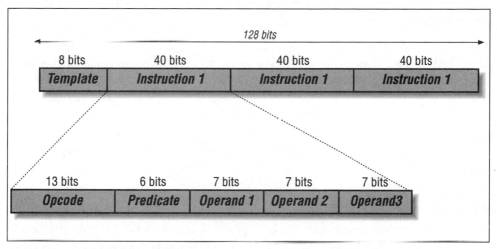

Figure C-3: IA-64 instruction format

scheduling hardware is greatly simplified over existing out-of-order processors. Instructions marked as independent can be issued directly to execution units (assuming their operands are available). Simplified hardware scheduling saves the transistor budget for other uses and provides an opportunity for a faster clock.

If all that EPIC supplied was simplified scheduling, it would not provide much performance improvement. The greater potential of EPIC is to discover and pass on knowledge of parallelism at a higher level than the instruction level. Since compilers work off-line, they have the luxury of exploring high-level structures of programs and the time to examine rearrangements of code for maximum parallelism. This higher-level examination promises to provide greater *instruction-level parallelism* (ILP) to the hardware. The combination of greater ILP together with the ability to inform hardware of the parallelism is the promise of EPIC.

IA-64 is much more than simply an implementation of EPIC, but the other ISA enhancements are more evolutionary than revolutionary. They are, nevertheless, important advances in commercial instruction sets. The three most significant enhancements announced to date are predicated instructions, speculative loads, and the three-instruction-bundled words. They are not totally new concepts, but they have not been implemented in a commodity microprocessor. Other important enhancements are an enormous increase in registers and the new-to-Intel fixed-length instruction.

The three most significant enhancements require an increase in bandwidth to be most effective. Predicated instructions and speculative loads have the potential to add bandwidth related to instructions whose results will never be used. However, increased bandwidth could be a fair trade for the potential benefits that these instructions can provide.

Predicated instructions are well-known enough to appear in popular architecture textbooks. In fact, the conditional-move instruction that exists in modern commodity microprocessors is a restricted type of predicated instruction. A conditional-move instruction moves a value from one register to another register based on some conditional value, possibly in a third register. IA-64 extends this concept to most instructions and conditions instructions using 64 one-bit predicate registers. Predicated instructions complete their execution based on the associated one-bit predicate register.

For example, consider an if-then statement based on a condition, X. If X is true, the instructions in the if clause are executed. Conversely, if X is false, the instructions in the then clause are executed. Normally, branches would be inserted at the entry and exit of the if-clause instructions to control the conditional flow. Predicating all the instructions in both the if and then clauses on the X-condition allows the branches to be removed. All instructions in both clauses are issued to execution units, but their results are not committed until the condition X has been evaluated. Those instructions whose predicate evaluates to TRUE will complete; those whose predicate is FALSE won't.

As shown in Figure C-4, the result is that instructions down both paths (if and then) are issued. With 64 predicate registers, many branches can be followed at the same time. However, not all branches can be replaced by predicated instructions. Some branches won't be replaced, and branch prediction is used in those cases.

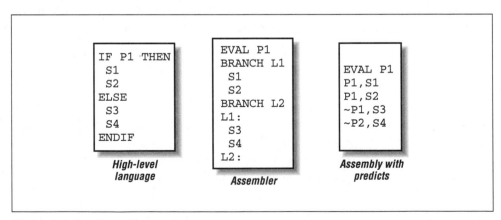

Figure C-4: Predicated instructions

Two benefits accrue from the use of the predicated instructions. One is that the conditional completion of the instruction is delayed, allowing time to calculate the condition before it is needed. Also, without guessing (branch prediction), the correct code is executed. Of course, the incorrect code is also executed (not to completion), but the cost is primarily bandwidth that may be affordable. In particular, the cost of the extra bandwidth must be measured against the cost of mispredicting a branch. The misprediction stalls may be offset by the execution of code that isn't used, but the premise is that some useful code will be accomplished during the cycles which would have been stalls. Also many sequences of if-then-else code are very short.

Research published at the 1995 International Conference on Computer Architecture by Mahlke, et al., showed that with an eight-wide machine, predicated instructions removed half of the branches in a set of benchmarks examined. Of particular note is that the removed branches represented 40% of the mispredicted branches. That is, predicated instructions tended to remove branches that were difficult to predict. Given the Intel claim that "It is not unusual for some of today's highly pipelined machines to have penalties of 20% to 30% of their performance going to branch mispredicts," the potential benefits are enormous.

Note how well predicated branches work with the EPIC concept. Instructions that follow different branch outcomes are naturally independent of each other and can be executed in parallel.

Speculative loads also promise to provide significant improvements. The problem with loads is that the memory hierarchy has been getting slower with respect to processor speeds, so memory access penalties have been growing (latency). If one can start a load well before its result is to be used, the latency of satisfying that load can be hidden by executing other unrelated instructions. However, moving loads earlier in the instruction stream can be difficult. Loads tend to be the first in a dependency chain of instructions: load, load, load, compute, store. In addition, loads tend to come at the beginning of a basic block whose predecessor was terminated by a branch. In order to move (hoist) the load earlier in the instruction stream, the load must be moved before the branch, but whether the load is actually executed depends on the whether the branch was taken. A simple example is "if a pointer is valid, use the pointer." One would not want to use the pointer before determining if it is valid. Another potential problem with moving the load occurs if the instruction were to cause an exception. Imagine speculatively executing a load that causes a page fault; the penalty incurred for such an unused load is significant.

The IA-64 solution is a speculative load that splits a load into two parts. The first is an initiation of the load that can be hoisted earlier in the instruction stream. Before the results of the load can be used, a check instruction is executed to ensure that the load should be executed, that is, the correct path was taken, and to check that the load has completed successfully. If the speculative load generates an exception, flag it (using a "token") and continue. The exception will be handled at the check time. Figure C-5 shows how the IA-64 might split a load into two parts.

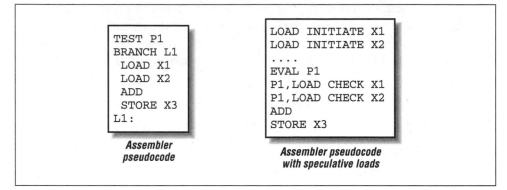

```
          TEST P1                    LOAD INITIATE X1
          BRANCH L1                  LOAD INITIATE X2
           LOAD X1                   ....
           LOAD X2                   EVAL P1
           ADD                       P1,LOAD CHECK X1
            STORE X3                 P1,LOAD CHECK X2
          L1:                        ADD
                                     STORE X3
```

**Assembler   Assembler pseudocode
pseudocode   with speculative loads**

Figure C-5: Speculative loads

The potential performance gain is significant. Access to main memory can cost a hundred clock cycles, and the penalty increases as processors speed up. Even a second-level cache miss can cost a couple of dozen cycles. Hoisting loads earlier in the instruction stream allows loads to move data from higher up the memory hierarchy onto the processor chip in time for the data to be used without delay. Given that basic blocks are frequently only six instructions long, the ability to hoist loads beyond the basic block can be significant. Since these speculative loads can be hoisted above multiple branches, the potential performance gain is even greater.

As with predicated instructions, the penalty with speculative loads is wasted band-width. That is, loads may be initiated (data moved onto the chip) that are never used. One must weigh the cost of the extra bandwidth against the cost of the elim-inated load stalls.

The IA-64 instruction format is a 128-bit instruction word that bundles three instructions together with predicate bits for each instruction. EPIC template bits are included that indicate the independence of the three instructions in the word and the independence of subsequent bundles. Part of the EPIC compiler's job is to select appropriate groups of three instructions to be bundled into each word. Ear-lier VLIW instruction sets required instructions bundled into the same word to be independent.

IA-64's template bits allow combinations of dependent and independent instruc-tions to be bundled together. This feature eliminates the need for the abundance of NOPs in earlier VLIW implementations, and allows easier compatibility across different word sizes, a serious problem for earlier implementations.

The final IA-64 announced feature is the enormous increase in registers. There are now 128 general-purpose registers and 128 floating-point registers. This increase in registers increases the register-management task of the compiler, but significantly reduces the false dependencies smaller register sets can impose on code. With this expansion of registers, the renaming capability common in the current microprocessors isn't needed.

Taken together, predicated instructions and speculative loads dramatically increase the ability of a compiler to rearrange code to achieve high levels of parallelism while eliminating the stalls of mispredicted branches and cache misses. The increased register set reduces stalls from false data dependencies that further increases available parallelism. The EPIC template bits combined with the long instruction word allows the compiler to explicitly pass on this discovered parallelism to the hardware. The restructured code with explicit dependency information allows the execution units to be highly utilized, which should result in fast execution.

The EPIC concept, combined with the IA-64 ISA, has the potential to provide significant performance improvement over current microprocessor architectures.

D

How FORTRAN Manages Threads at Runtime

In FORTRAN, an application executes with a single thread, and when the application encounters a parallel loop, it utilizes more than one thread to improve its performance. This section describes how FORTRAN manages those threads at runtime and explores some performance impacts of having too many threads. This material suppliments the material in Chapter 10, *Shared-Memory Multiprocessors* and Chapter 11, *Programming Shared-Memory Multiprocessors*.

One simple approach would be to invoke the operating system to create the necessary threads at the beginning of each parallel loop and destroy the threads at the end of the loop. Unfortunately, calling the operating system at the beginning of each loop incurs excessive overhead. In addition to the operating system overhead, the arrival times of these newly created threads to enter the parallel computation are often skewed significantly. To avoid this overhead and late thread arrival, the FORTRAN runtime library typically creates its threads once at the beginning of execution and then manages those threads in user space.

This approach, which creates a fixed number of threads at the beginning of execution and uses them throughout the duration of the application, is referred to as *fixed thread scheduling* (FTS) throughout this section. The choice of the name "fixed" emphasizes the fact that the number of threads doesn't change once the application begins execution.

In the next section, we examine how these threads are managed by the runtime library and the performance of this approach in the face of a dynamic load.

Runtime Thread Management Details

When a compiled parallel application is executed and the first parallel loop is encountered, the runtime environment starts up a number of threads. The number of threads is often the same as the number of installed processors. The number of threads is usually controlled by the user via an environment variable. These threads are scheduled by the operating system much like UNIX processes. The traditional approach is that threads are simply scheduled when there is a processor available or using some round-robin scheme designed to give threads a fair chance at using the processor. On some systems, these threads are scheduled by the operating system using *gang scheduling*. When a set of threads is gang scheduled, either all of the threads are executing or all are preempted. In Figure D-1 and Figure D-2 these approaches are graphically compared.

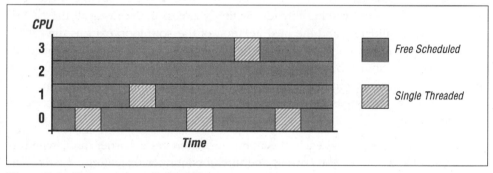

Figure D-1: Nongang thread scheduling

If gang scheduling is done in its strictest sense, a significant amount of time could be wasted when a multithreaded application is timesharing with a single-threaded application. Regardless of the way the operating system schedules the threads, when the program starts, one thread begins executing the user application while the other threads "spin," waiting for a parallel loop to be encountered. The code these waiting threads execute is as follows:

```
while ( wakeup == 0 ) ;   // "Spin loop"
goto beginning_of_loop;
```

The variable wakeup is set initially to zero. With a bus-based system, this approach might appear to cause a great deal of unnecessary memory traffic. Actually, each waiting processor ends up with a shared encached copy of the wakeup variable with the value zero. Once the caches have been filled, there is no additional memory traffic as these waiting processors execute this tight loop. Some systems have added special hardware instructions to make this wakeup from a spin loop perform even more efficiently.

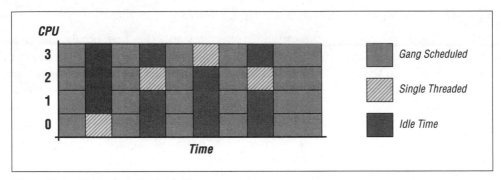

Figure D-2: Gang thread scheduling

When a parallel loop is encountered, the variable `beginning_of_loop` is set to indicate which parallel loop is about to be executed, and the variable `wakeup` is set to 1 to activate the waiting threads. Setting wakeup to 1 causes all the cached copies to be invalidated, and the next iteration of the spin loop exits as the caches reload with the new value of wakeup. The waiting threads immediately notice the change, exit the spin loop, and join the computation. Once the threads arrive at the loop, they each determine the appropriate iterations to process using the iteration-scheduling technique chosen for this particular loop and begin processing those iterations.

When the loop completes, each executing thread enters a barrier, and, when all the threads have entered the barrier, one thread continues executing in serial. The remaining threads again execute the spin loop waiting for the next parallel loop. This approach results in extremely quick thread-activation times.

To demonstrate the timing of these operations, the following FORTRAN loop was executed on the SGI Challenge:

```
IN = WALLTIME()
C$DOACROSS LOCAL(J),SHARE(MIDDLE),MP_SCHEDTYPE=SIMPLE,CHUNK=1
DO J=1,4
  MIDDLE(J) = WALLTIME()
ENDDO
OUT = WALLTIME()
```

Because the scheduling type is **SIMPLE**, the consistent mapping of a CPU to an iteration of the J loop is forced. By checking the elapsed time between the **IN** and **MIDDLE** times, we can determine the time for a thread to arrive in the parallel section of a loop (spawn time). By checking the elapsed time between the **MID-DLE** and **OUT**, the time spent processing the loop-end barrier can be determined for each thread. Once the overhead for the **WALLTIME** calls is removed, this loop does no work, and we can measure the performance of the parallel loop startup and completion. This loop measures how fast a thread can be brought into the loop from a spinning state. Later, we will measure how these timings change when a loop is executed, and there are more threads than processors.

In Figure D-3, the performance of this loop is measured on an empty system. The loop was executed a number of times, and the average values are reported in this figure.

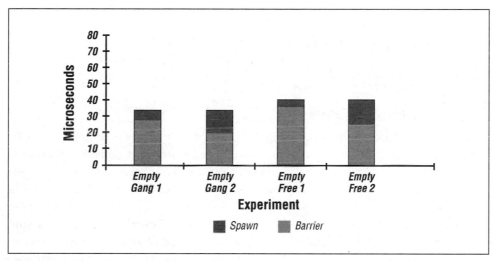

Figure D-3: Thread timing results

This figure shows the performance of the first and second threads (out of four threads) using free scheduling and gang scheduling. Using gang scheduling, the entire loop takes 36 microseconds; using free scheduling, it takes 40 microseconds. Thread 1 wakes the other threads up, so it is the first to arrive in the body of the loop. Thread 1 takes 7 microseconds to go from the serial code to the body of the loop in both cases. Thread 2 takes 16 microseconds to arrive in the body of the loop. This difference shows how quickly the "helper" threads can arrive from their spin loops. The barrier at the end of the loop takes somewhat longer in general than the spawn process. Also, since Thread 1 arrives quicker, it completes its work quicker and, as such, spends more time at the barrier waiting until Thread 2 arrives to terminate the loop. The performance for Threads 3 and 4 look identical to Thread 2.

While the spin-wakeup approach results in fast loop startup times, there is a problem because this approach assumes that all the available threads are actually executing the spin loop at all times they aren't participating in a parallel loop. There are two reasons that a thread might not be executing the spin loop when a parallel loop is encountered. The first reason is that the thread may have decided to voluntarily put itself to sleep because it has waited too long in the spin loop code at a barrier or waiting for work. The second reason is that the operating system may have pre-empted a thread involuntarily because of another unrelated load.

A spinning thread waiting for work voluntarily suspends itself to minimize wasted CPU time in case an application needs to spend a significant time running serial code. The pseudo-code for this is roughly as follows:

```
while ( wakeup == 0 ) {
  counter = 10000;
  while (counter > 0 ) {
    if ( wakeup == 0 ) break;
    counter --;
  }
  if ( counter == 0 ) release_cpu();
}
goto beginning_of_loop;
```

The `counter` value is typically controllable by the application programmer. The programmer may also be able to suppress the `release_cpu` behavior altogether. Interestingly, by suppressing the release of the CPU, the programmer gets marginally better performance for his application. Of course, the CPU time spent spinning is not accomplishing any real work and the CPU is not available for other users. Often, benchmark runs are executed with the `release_cpu` behavior suppressed. When a thread voluntarily gives up the CPU, it records this fact, so when the serial thread encounters a parallel loop, it can request that the operating system reschedule the suspended thread.

With the potential that a waiting thread might suspend itself, the pseudo-code for starting a parallel loop is as follows:

```
If any threads have put themselves to sleep, wake them up
Store starting location of parallel loop
Notify spinning threads via wakeup
Distribute iterations to threads
Process assigned iterations
Perform Barrier
One thread continues execution while others wait for the
       next parallel loop to be encountered
```

If a spinning thread has been suspended involuntarily by the operating system, the startup latency is much larger because the serial thread is not aware (and is not even allowed to awaken) the spinning thread that has been suspended. The loop startup code simply assumes the spinning threads will join in a few microseconds. The operating system must reschedule the suspended thread before the thread can execute, detect the changed wakeup variable, and join the computation. In the worst case, this latency can be on the order of an operating system time slice. Thread-arrival skew can cause a nondynamic iteration scheduling algorithm to appear to have very unbalanced load, as is shown later.

While this approach seems to waste the CPU in spin loops, a program that is well-suited to parallel processing, when properly tuned, typically runs in parallel a large part of the time. Thus, the time that processors spend spinning at the end of parallel loops should be minimized on an unloaded system.

Problems with Dynamic Load

Computer systems similar to the SGI Challenge perform very well when there is no other load on the system, and each thread has exclusive access to a CPU. Unfortunately, the performance of the SGI gets much worse when there are more threads than available processors.

There are a number of the major problems when there are more threads than processors:

- Preemption during spin-lock critical section
- Preemption of the wrong thread in a producer-consumer relationship
- Unnecessary context switch overhead
- Corruption of caches due to context switches

With the increase of CPU speed and the increasing reliance on data resident in cache, the context switch corrupting cache has had an increasing impact on performance.

Loop performance under load

In this section, we look at the performance of the simple loop when a single CPU-bound job is added to the system. The same experiments are shown in Figure D-3, with the addition of load. These experiments are run with the standard SGI compiler options that use spin without `release_cpu` at the end of a loop. In Figure D-4, the spawn and barrier times are shown for a gang-scheduled and a free-scheduled application. All the experiments use fixed-thread scheduling in that four threads are used for every parallel loop. Both the first and second thread are shown in Figure D-4. The performance for the unloaded system is included for reference. When gang scheduling is used and load is added, the change in performance is effectively unmeasurable. However, when load is added to the free scheduled program, performance suffers dramatically. Figure D-5 changes the y-axis to a logarithmic scale so that the performance of the loop under free scheduling can be observed. In Figure D-4, the free thread scheduled application performs over three orders of magnitude slower. Interestingly, Thread 1 still enters the loop in 14 microseconds, although at the increased scale, it can no longer be seen. The second thread averages 10,583 microseconds (or 0.1 seconds) for its arrival. The bulk of the time is spent in the barrier for all threads, with each thread displacing the other spinning threads to spin. Further, because there are four CPUs

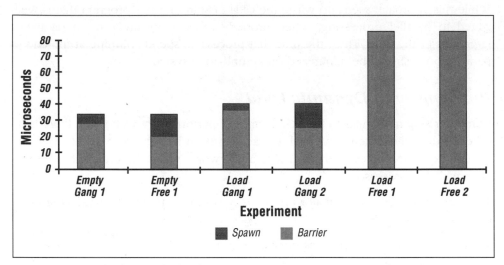

Figure D-4: Loop timing under load

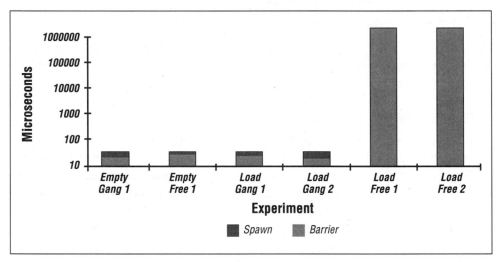

Figure D-5: Loop timing under load (log scale)

and only one single load thread, three threads are usually active in the application. These threads quickly go to the barrier and spin, waiting for the arrival of the fourth thread. Once the fourth thread arrives, it quickly completes its 15 microseconds of work and goes to the barrier.

To further understand the values that make up this average, Figure D-6 shows the performance of Thread 2 (the last bar above) for a selected number of individual iterations. The vertical axis is again logarithmic. In this figure the cost for the spawn and the barrier are shown for the second thread with free scheduling on a

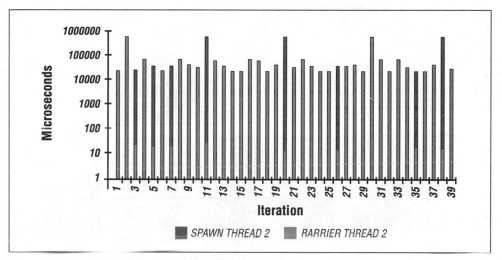

Figure D-6: Individual iteration timing: Thread 2/free (log scale)

further expanded scale. The barrier contributes the majority of the performance impact. In some iterations, the spawn time (or thread arrival time) is significant, and in a few iterations, there is a negative performance impact from both the thread arrival and barrier time.

Parallel applications and load on the SGI

The above tests focus on the potential negative impact when thread imbalance occurs. However, in a real application on the SGI, gang scheduling is available, and loops execute longer in parallel, which reduces the impact of loop startup and termination performance. In the following example, cache effect, context switch overhead, and other factors impact performance.

To test the performance impact on running applications, a simple, parallel computation is used as the benchmark application. The core loop for these tests is as follows:

```
C$DOACROSS
        DO J=1,100000
            A(I) = B(I) + C(I) * D(I)
        ENDDO
```

All of these experiments are performed on a four-processor, four-CPU SGI Challenge system. This experiment is run using the SGI compiler with gang scheduling turned on.

Figure D-7 shows the performance of the code with several compiler options and load scenarios. The first set of bars show that the application code parallelizes

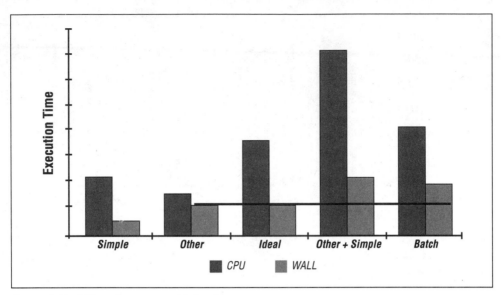

Figure D-7: SGI performance with load

automatically without any user modifications using simple iteration scheduling. The wall time is roughly one-quarter the CPU time.

The second bars represent a set of single-threaded applications with random arrival and duration. These applications don't generate enough aggregate load to completely utilize the system, which is why the wall time is not 25% of the CPU time. The wall time and CPU time shown in the chart is the aggregate for all the jobs.

The third bars show the ideal CPU and wall time for the combination of the parallel job and the set of single-threaded jobs running simultaneously, assuming perfect load balancing on four CPUs. Note that while CPU time increases additively, the wall time doesn't increase from the other bars to the ideal bars. This lack of an increase is because, on the four-CPU system, there are enough spare cycles while the other job is running for the parallel job to execute to completion. Figure D-8 shows these different combinations of runs.

The ideal performance only occurs if the parallel job can "soak up" the free cycles while the other jobs were running without adding a great deal of overhead. The next-to-last bar, `other+simple`, shows the actual performance achieved on the SGI Challenge when the jobs are run together. The system performs much worse than ideal when both jobs run simultaneously. The wall time for the combination job is 1.68 times longer than ideal, and the CPU time of the combination job is 1.76 times longer than the ideal CPU time. In fact, with the two jobs running

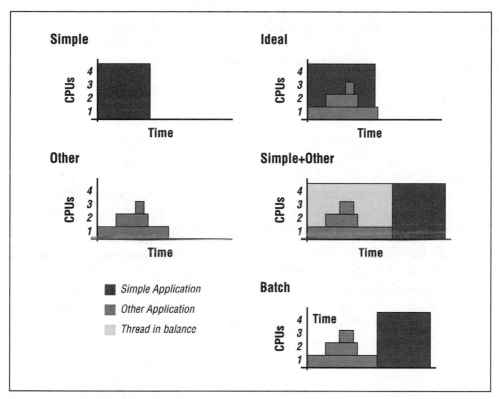

Figure D-8: Impact of thread imbalance

simultaneously, the SGI performs worse than if you ran the jobs sequentially using a batch queue, as shown by the last set of bars in the figure.

When both parallel and serial jobs are running simultaneously, the parallel application experiences poor performance and slows down the nonparallel applications as well. The problem that causes the poor performance for both jobs when they are run simultaneously is explained in Figure D-8.

When the SGI system is otherwise empty, either the parallel job or the serial jobs make good use of the resources. However, when all of the jobs are run at the same time, there can be more active threads than processors. All the threads must be timeshared across the available processors, which has a significant negative impact on both the parallel and serial jobs. The parallel job experiences a wide range of effects, as described earlier. The serial job slows due to context switches, cache loss, and the simple loss of CPU due to timesharing. The worst part of this situation is that the parallel work delays the completion of the serial work, extending the length of time the system is operating inefficiently.

The only reasonable choice on such a system is to run parallel compute jobs on an otherwise empty system. These incompatible workloads can be separated using a batch queue, a predetermined schedule for usage during different parts of the day, or some other external management policy.

Summary

There are many techniques that perform dynamic load balancing within a single application using iteration scheduling on an otherwise empty SMP parallel processor. These techniques assume that every thread has a dedicated processor. There is an excellent systemwide dynamic load-balancing solution available on expensive parallel/vector supercomputers that allows those systems to maintain 100% utilization over the long term. Unfortunately, there is no production quality solution for low-cost SMP systems that provides overall dynamic load balancing.

Supercomputers have long had the ability to mix high performance computing load with other forms of load, and maintain high efficiency and utilization. There are techniques that allow less expensive systems to have similar abilities; however, the operating systems and compilers on these computers must be aware of the problems and provide features that allow for dynamic adjustment of the threads at runtime.

E

Memory Performance

by Colin Hearne Evans

In this appendix, we examine the affects of the cache and memory hierarchy on several popular architectures using some simple benchmarks. We will look at how performance can be strongly affected by memory stride and cache usage, and we will use the benchmarks to do some simple analysis of positive and negative aspects of cach architecture. The results will illustrate programming strategies discussed in other parts of this book and give some useful methods for comparing the performance of different architectures.

The two benchmarks outlined here, `mem1d` and `mem2d`, are two FORTRAN programs that perform a large number of simple integer computations over one-dimensional and two-dimensional data structures. The benchmarks explore the effects of memory stride and variations in memory and cache speed, depending on how a data structure is accessed. Performance is measured in MOPS (millions of operations per second), a relative measure of how many millions of simple integer computations are performed per second when the data structure is accessed in a certain fashion. The results are similar to the STREAM benchmark discussed in Chapter 15, *Using Published Benchmarks*, in that they measure the bandwidth from the memory subsystems to the CPU, but the STREAM benchmark tests bandwidth from main memory, and we will look at variations in bandwidth across the whole cache and memory hierarchy.

The mem1d Benchmark

The mem1d benchmark records the time used to perform a large number of 32-bit integer additions over a one-dimensional array. The benchmark varies the amount of the array accessed over a number of tests so that the active data set for each test moves from the L1 cache to the L2 cache, and then becomes so large that it can only be contained in main memory. Memory bandwidth is consistent for data sets that fit totally in the same cache, but bandwidth drops as the data set gets too large and is pushed out into the next level of cache or into main memory. Cache performance at every level is profiled, and cache sizes can easily be determined from the results.

The core of the mem1d benchmark is the set of nested loops in the middle of the program:

```
*
* Program mem1d - Determine the performance of various loop sizes
*
        IMPLICIT NONE
*
        REAL WTIME, CTIME
        REAL*8 MOPS
        INTEGER*4 OPERATIONS, BASIS, MAX
        PARAMETER (BASIS=16, MAX= 19, OPERATIONS = (2**max) * BASIS)
        INTEGER*4 LoopSize, LoopIterations
        DIMENSION ARRAY(OPERATIONS)
        INTEGER*4 ARRAY, Iterations, Length, x
        MOPS = OPERATIONS / 1000000.0
        PRINT 110,'Len, Wall, MOPS, CPU, CPU/Wall'

* Fill the array with zeros
        Do 5 X = 1, OPERATIONS
           ARRAY(X) = 0
5       Continue
        CALL HPCTIM(WTIME, CTIME)

* Loop lengths are powers of two
        Do 10 Length = 0, max
            CALL HPCTIM(WTIME, CTIME)
            LoopSize = BASIS * (2**Length)
            LoopIterations = 2**(max - Length)
            Do 20 Iterations = 1, LoopIterations
              DO 30 X = 1, LoopSize
                ARRAY(X) = ARRAY(X) + 3
30            CONTINUE
              CALL NOOPT(ARRAY)
20          CONTINUE
            CALL HPCTIM(WTIME, CTIME)
            print 100,LoopSize*4,WTIME,MOPS/WTIME,CTIME,CTIME/WTIME
10      CONTINUE

100     FORMAT(I10, ',', 7(F10.5, ','))
110     FORMAT(A)
        END
```

The `HPCTIM` function is a timing function that returns the elapsed time from the last time the function was called. The `NOOPT` function is a placeholder function that does nothing, but prevents sneaky compilers from altering the loop structure drastically or finding other ways of subverting the benchmark.

Here is the typical output from a 143-MHz Sun UltraSPARC 1 system with a 16-KB L1 data cache and a 512-KB L2 cache:

```
     Len,       Wall,      MOPS,       CPU,  CPU/Wall
      64,    0.26762,  31.34522,   0.26665,   0.99637,
     128,    0.23364,  35.90460,   0.23358,   0.99975,
     256,    0.20930,  40.07935,   0.20912,   0.99915,
     512,    0.20170,  41.59015,   0.19998,   0.99150,
    1024,    0.19638,  42.71599,   0.19632,   0.99970,
    2048,    0.19424,  43.18660,   0.19358,   0.99662,
    4096,    0.19248,  43.58126,   0.19248,   1.00000,
    8192,    0.19209,  43.66997,   0.19195,   0.99929,
   16384,    0.19369,  43.30923,   0.19220,   0.99229,
   32768,    0.27982,  29.97848,   0.27966,   0.99943,
   65536,    0.28097,  29.85567,   0.28033,   0.99772,
  131072,    0.28051,  29.90453,   0.28035,   0.99941,
  262144,    0.28492,  29.44156,   0.28326,   0.99415,
  524288,    0.29702,  28.24304,   0.29588,   0.99617,
 1048576,    0.37726,  22.23555,   0.37538,   0.99501,
 2097152,    0.38257,  21.92676,   0.38009,   0.99351,
 4194304,    0.38122,  22.00458,   0.38019,   0.99731,
 8388608,    0.38222,  21.94689,   0.38015,   0.99459,
16777216,    0.38061,  22.03967,   0.38027,   0.99909,
33554432,    0.38119,  22.00643,   0.38006,   0.99705,
```

The output gives the array length in bytes that is used for the benchmark, the wall time and CPU time taken to complete the loops, the ratio of CPU to wall time (useful for determining if the results are invalid because of a heavy load on the system), and the MOPS bandwidth based on the wall time. The lower MOPS ratings for the very small data sets are due to missed branch prediction at the end of each loop. This dominates the execution time of the small loops due to loop overhead. Loop overhead dominates the execution time of small loops, but quickly becomes insignificant as the loops get larger. The bandwidth drops after the data set reaches sizes of 16 KB and 512 KB, consistent with the actual memory sizes of the system. The largest drop in speed on this system is from the L1 cache to the L2 cache.

Results from the Mem1d Benchmark

Figure E-1 and Figure E-2 show the results from two UltraSPARC systems running at 143 and 248 MHz, two systems with SPARC II microprocessors running at 75 and 85 MHz, and a Pentium Pro system running at 200 MHz. All systems ran Solaris. Figure E-1 illustrates raw MOPS performance and MOPS performance scaled by clock rate for the Sun systems. The points where each dataset moves from one level of memory hierarchy to the next are easily visible as large dips in the graphs. All of the systems have 16-KB L1 data caches and 1-MB L2 caches except for the 143-MHz Ultra, which has a 512-KB L2 cache.

There are large differences in the raw bandwidth performance between the 143-MHz and 248-MHz Ultra chips while the data is in the L1 or L2 caches. At peak performance, the 248-MHz chip's bandwidth performance is close to 73% greater than the 143-MHz chip, consistent with the 248-MHz chip's clock speed being 73% greater than the 143-MHz chip. In the L1 and L2 caches, there is almost a perfect speedup, where more clock cycles translate purely into more speed. But once the data set moves out to 2 MB or 4 MB, the 248-MHz chip's bandwidth is only around 22% greater than the 143-MHz chip's bandwidth. The 143-MHz UltraSPARC 1 and 248-MHz UltraSPARC 2 use the same speed memory, so the 248-MHz chips spends more time than the 143-MHz system waiting around for main memory.

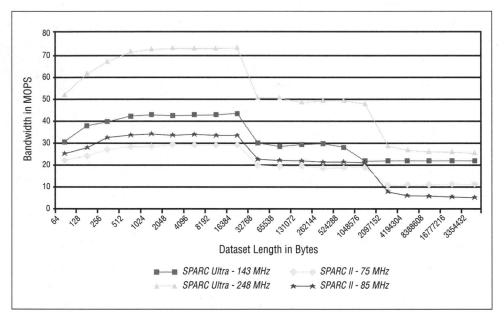

Figure E-1: Comparison of memory bandwidth between SPARC architectures

The problem of slow main memory is made plainer by the graph of bandwidth scaled by clock rates. The SPARC II systems have better performance per clock tick than the UltraSPARC systems as long as the data is in cache. However, this doesn't mean that it is a good idea to produce a 200 MHz SPARC II chip, because even between 75 MHz and 85 MHz clock rates, there is a large degradation in performance when the processors start accessing main memory. The bandwidth per clock tick goes down as clock rates rise, and, in the case of the SPARC II chips, the bandwidth drops very quickly. UltraSPARC chips have a number of features to ease access to main memory including pipelined memory accesses. These features mean that bandwidth per clock tick does not drop as quickly as earlier systems when the clock rate goes up. New trends in architecture design are primarily aimed at staving off the law of diminishing returns for clock speeds.

A comparison of the Pentium Pro 200 MHz system and two UltraSPARC1 systems shows where Intel has been successful with its newest processor. Figure E-2 depicts the Pentium Pro holding its own against the UltraSPARC chip for bandwidth performance in cache. For bandwidth from main memory though, the Pentium Pro is the slowest. In Figure E-3, it becomes more obvious that the Pentium Pro is a winner for integer bandwidth in cache, but still falls short with accessing main memory. This illustrates a difference in design philosophies, where the UltraSPARC microprocessors use extensive pipelining of loads and flow prediction in order to handle memory latency, while the Pentium Pro uses out-of-order execution. Out-of-order execution allows for loads to be started early and allows for better use of superscalar features of a chip. However, it appears from the graph that, for integer bandwidth, the superscalar scheduling is more effective than the load scheduling. These two figures suggest that the Pentium Pro systems are real contenders in the workstation market, and that future Intel chips will be worth looking at.

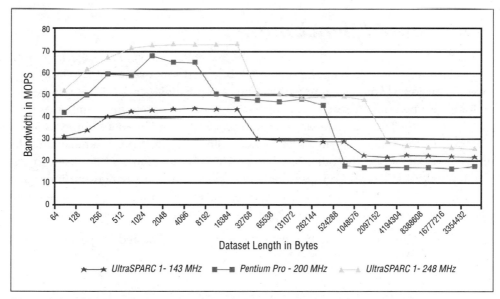

Figure E-2: UltraSPARC I versus Pentium Pro

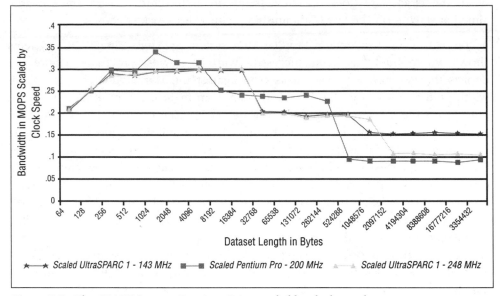

Figure E-3: UltraSPARC I versus Pentium Pro—scaled by clock speed

The mem2d Benchmark

The mem2d benchmark tests best-case and worst-case memory usage and compiler cleverness by recording the time it takes to perform a series of additions on a two-dimensional array in unit stride and against unit stride. The number of columns in the array increase over successive iterations, while the number of rows stays the same. There are two tests of non-unit stride: one uses an empty NOOPT function in the inner loop in order to keep the compiler from interchanging the inner and out loops. The other test has no NOOPT function and is meant to test the compiler's ability to find non-unit stride loops and interchange the inner and outer loops. The results compare memory bandwidth with unit stride and non-unit stride memory accesses in terms of MOPS, similar to the mem1d benchmark.

The core of the mem2d benchmark is the three sets of nested loops in this program:

```
*
* Program mem2d - Determine the performance of various loop sizes
*
       IMPLICIT NONE
*
       REAL MOPS
       REAL WTIME, CTIME
       INTEGER ROWS, COLS
       PARAMETER(ROWS = 2048, COLS = ROWS)
       INTEGER LENGTH, IREP, R, C
```

```
            INTEGER REPEAT, ADDITIONS, REPCOUNT
            INTEGER ARRAY(ROWS, COLS)

            PRINT *,'MEM2D TEST ARRAY(', ROWS, COLS, ')'
            CALL HPCTIM(WTIME, CTIME)

* Fill the array with zeros five times
            DO IREP = 1, 5
              CALL NOOPT(ARRAY)
              DO C = 1, COLS
               Do R = 1, ROWS
                  ARRAY(R, C) = 0
                ENDDO
              ENDDO
            ENDDO


* Interchangeable
            Length = 16
            PRINT *,'COLUMNS Inner (Interchangeable)...'
            PRINT 2000
10          CONTINUE
            CALL HPCTIM(WTIME, CTIME)
            REPEAT = ROWS / LENGTH
            DO REPCOUNT = 1, REPEAT
              CALL NOOPT(ARRAY)
              DO R = 1, ROWS
                DO C = 1, LENGTH
                  ARRAY(R, C) = ARRAY(R, C) + 3
                ENDDO
              ENDDO
            ENDDO
            CALL HPCTIM(WTIME, CTIME)
            ADDITIONS = COLS * (REPEAT * LENGTH)
            MOPS = (ADDITIONS / WTIME) / 1E6
            PRINT 1000, LENGTH, ADDITIONS, WTIME, MOPS
            LENGTH = LENGTH * 2
            IF (LENGTH .LE. ROWS) GOTO 10


* Rows Inner
            LENGTH = 16
            PRINT *, 'ROWS Inner...'
            PRINT 2000
20          CONTINUE
            CALL HPCTIM(WTIME, CTIME)
            REPEAT = ROWS / LENGTH
            DO REPCOUNT=1, REPEAT
              DO C=1, COLS
                CALL NOOPT(ARRAY)
                DO R=1, LENGTH
                  ARRAY(R, C)= ARRAY(R, C) + 3
                ENDDO
              ENDDO
            ENDDO
            CALL HPCTIM(WTIME, CTIME)
```

```
          ADDITIONS = COLS * (REPEAT * LENGTH)
          MOPS = (ADDITIONS / WTIME) / 1E6
          PRINT 1000, LENGTH, ADDITIONS, WTIME, MOPS
          LENGTH = LENGTH * 2
          IF (LENGTH .LE. ROWS) GOTO 20

* Columns Inner
          LENGTH = 16
          PRINT *,'Columns Inner...'
          PRINT 2000
30        CONTINUE
          CALL HPCTIM(WTIME, CTIME)
          REPEAT = ROWS / LENGTH
          DO REPCOUNT = 1, REPEAT
            DO R = 1, ROWS
              CALL NOOPT(ARRAY)
              DO C = 1, LENGTH
                ARRAY(R, C) = ARRAY(R, C) + 3
              ENDDO
            ENDDO
          ENDDO
          CALL HPCTIM(WTIME, CTIME)
          ADDITIONS = COLS * (REPEAT * LENGTH)
          MOPS = (ADDITIONS / WTIME) / 1E6
          PRINT 1000, LENGTH, ADDITIONS, WTIME, MOPS
          LENGTH = LENGTH * 2
          IF (LENGTH .LE. ROWS) GOTO 30


1000      FORMAT(I10, ',', I10, ',', 7(F10.5, ','))
2000      FORMAT(1X, 'Size, Additions, Time, MOPS')
          END
```

As in mem1d, the HPCTIM function is a timing function that returns the elapsed time from the last time the function was called. The NOOPT function is a placeholder function that does nothing, but prevents sneaky compilers from altering the loop structure drastically or finding other ways of subverting the benchmark.

Here is the typical output from a 143-MHz Sun UltraSPARC 1 system with a 16-KB L1 cache and a 512-KB L2 cache compiled with the **-depend** flag that invokes loop dependency analysis:

```
MEM2D TEST ARRAY(  2048  2048)
  COLUMNS Inner (Interchangeable)...
      Size, Additions,      Time,      MOPS
        16,  4194304,   0.14280,  29.37167,
        32,  4194304,   0.14159,  29.62393,
        64,  4194304,   0.15448,  27.15129,
       128,  4194304,   0.18877,  22.21877,
       256,  4194304,   0.19038,  22.03180,
       512,  4194304,   0.19044,  22.02428,
      1024,  4194304,   0.19177,  21.87176,
      2048,  4194304,   0.19143,  21.91084,
```

```
ROWS Inner...
     Size, Additions,       Time,        MOPS
       16,    4194304,    0.39130,    10.71890,
       32,    4194304,    0.28939,    14.49370,
       64,    4194304,    0.23864,    17.57579,
      128,    4194304,    0.21403,    19.59726,
      256,    4194304,    0.20107,    20.85961,
      512,    4194304,    0.19648,    21.34745,
     1024,    4194304,    0.19280,    21.75446,
     2048,    4194304,    0.19063,    22.00187,
Columns Inner...
     Size, Additions,       Time,        MOPS
       16,    4194304,    0.30564,    13.72289,
       32,    4194304,    0.28668,    14.63076,
       64,    4194304,    1.61858,     2.59135,
      128,    4194304,    2.60804,     1.60822,
      256,    4194304,    2.65321,     1.58084,
      512,    4194304,    2.65030,     1.58258,
     1024,    4194304,    2.66014,     1.57672,
     2048,    4194304,    2.66548,     1.57356,
```

The output gives the number of columns used with 2048 rows, the number of additions performed on the array used, the wall time, and the MOPS bandwidth. The cases with columns as the inner loop give non-unit-stride memory access, and the bandwidth drops as the amount of memory accessed in non-unit stride increases. The case with rows as the inner loop gives unit stride, and the bandwidth rises as the number of columns accessed at each row increases because the amount of memory accessed in unit stride is increasing. The -**depend** option that was given to the compiler causes the interchangeable loops to be flipped, turning a loop where every memory access is in non-unit stride into a loop where every memory access is in unit stride. As can be seen, the interchanged loops and the loops with the rows nested inside approach the same bandwidth because the loops with rows nested inside become unit-stride loops as the number of columns accessed at each row increases.

Figure E-4 depicts the results of mem2d running on a Pentium Pro at 200 MHz and an UltraSPARC 1 at 143 MHz. The SPARC system outperforms the Pentium Pro for larger datasets as in mem1d, but neither of the systems handle nonstride memory accesses well. For the larger datasets, the UltraSPARC's bandwidth with unit-stride access is faster by a factor of 13 over the non-unit-stride bandwidth. Unit-stride bandwidth on the Pentium Pro is as much as eight times faster than non-unit-stride bandwidth. These cases illustrate best-case and worst-case memory access patterns, and they show the breadth of performance on the UltraSPARC and Pentium Pro systems. Both systems are highly optimized for unit-stride access patterns, and it's important to spend time tweaking code in order to stay near the top of the performance band.

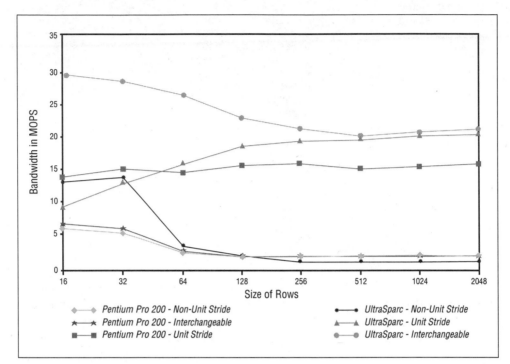

Figure E-4: Results for mem2d test

The results for the interchangeable loops show that the Sun UltraSPARC compiler was able to detect non-unit stride memory accesses and swap the inner and outer loops not held in place by data dependencies. The result was a loop that was pure unit stride accesses. The Sun compiler for the Pentium Pro was not able to identify the non-unit stride memory accesses, and this suggests that the compiler is not able to do sophisticated hardware optimizations for Pentium Pro systems. Loop swapping is only one optimization that a compiler can do, but it is a fairly fundamental optimization.

Summary

This section shows how a set of simple programs can be used to explore the performance capabilities of today's high performance computers. There are many variations that can be done using these codes. You can also compare integer and floating-point performance and explore the relative performance of single and double precision.

Index

About the Authors

Kevin Dowd is the president of Atlantic Computing Technology Corporation, located in Newington, Connecticut. He is the author of *Getting Connected: The Internet at 56K and Up*, also published by O'Reilly & Associates.

Charles Severance is the director for computing services for the College of Engineering at Michigan State University, where he is also a professor in the Computer Science Department, teaching classes on high performance computing, computer architecture, and the Internet. His current research is in the area of Internet delivery of educational material.

He has been active in IEEE standards for many years, and he edits a monthly column in the magazine *IEEE Computer* on computer standards. Charles is the co-host of a television show called "Nothin but Net," and was previously the co-host of a television show called "Internet:TCI."

Colophon

The animal featured on the cover of *High Performance Computing* is the Northern harrier (also known as the hen harrier or marsh hawk). Unlike most other hawks, this harrier likes to hunt exclusively on the wing—cruising up to 100 miles a day—and prefers roosting and nesting on the ground. Hunting forays over field and marsh consist of long, low glides powered by intermittent flaps, with an occasional pause to hover briefly. The Harrier aircraft is named for this characteristic.

This species is one of the most acrobatic and agile of the raptors. During courtship, males perform spectacular acrobatics, marked by tumbling, drifting upside down, 200-foot spiral dives, and wingovers.

Northern harriers prey on a variety of animals—predominately small mammals, birds, and reptiles—which they detect with their keen sense of hearing. (They are considered the diurnal counterpart of the short-eared owl.) An owl-like facial ruff helps reflect sound (such as squeaking mice) to the harrier's sensitive ears. This bird of prey ranges over most temperate regions of the Northern Hemisphere.

Edie Freedman and Kathleen Wilson designed the cover of this book using a 19th-century engraving from the Dover Pictorial Archive. The cover layout was produced with Quark XPress 3.32 using the ITC Garamond font.

Clairemarie Fisher O'Leary was the production editor and project manager for this book. Mary Anne Weeks Mayo copyedited the book, Kristin Barendsen proofread the book, and Madeleine Newell and John Files provided quality control reviews.

Nicole Gipson Arigo handled the final week of the production process. Seth Maislin wrote the index, and Robert Romano created the illustrations in Adobe Photoshop 4.0 and Macromedia Freehand 7.0. The inside layout was designed by Edie Freedman and modified by Nancy Priest. It was implemented in gtroff by Lenny Muellner, using ITC Garamond Light and ITC Garamond Book fonts. This colophon was written by Michael Kalantarian.

Whenever possible, our books use RepKover™, a durable and flexible lay-flat binding. If the page count exceeds RepKover's limit, perfect binding is used.

More Titles from O'Reilly

C and C++

C++: The Core Language

By Gregory Satir & Doug Brown
1st Edition October 1995
228 pages, ISBN 1-56592-116-X

C++: The Core Language is a primer for C programmers transitioning to C++, an object-oriented enhancement of the C programming language fast becoming the language of choice for serious software development. Designed to get readers up to speed quickly, this book tells you just what you need to learn first.

This book covers a subset of the features of C++. The subset consists of features without which it's just not C++, and a handful of others that make it a reasonably useful language. You can actually use this subset (using any compiler) to get familiar with the basics of the language.

C++: The Core Language includes sidebars that give overviews of all the advanced features not covered, so that readers know they exist and how they fit in. It covers features common to all C++ compilers, including those on UNIX, Windows NT, Windows, DOS, and Macs.

Practical C++ Programming

By Steve Oualline
1st Edition September 1995
584 pages, ISBN 1-56592-139-9

Practical C++ Programming is a complete introduction to the C++ language for the beginning programmer, and also for C programmers transitioning to C++. Unlike most other C++ books, this book emphasizes a practical, real-world approach, including how to debug, how to make your code understandable to others, and how to understand other people's code. Topics covered include good programming style, C++ syntax (what to use and what not to use), C++ class design, debugging and optimization, and common programming mistakes. At the end of each chapter are a number of exercises you can use to make sure you've grasped the concepts. Solutions to most are provided.

Practical C++ Programming describes standard C++ features that are supported by all UNIX C++ compilers (including *gcc*) and DOS/Windows and NT compilers (including Microsoft Visual C++).

Practical C Programming, 3rd Edition

By Steve Oualline
3rd Edition August 1997
454 pages, ISBN 1-56592-306-5

There are lots of introductory C books, but this new edition of *Practical C Programming* is the one that has the no-nonsense, practical approach that has made Nutshell Handbooks® so popular. C programming is more than just getting the syntax right. Style and debugging also play a tremendous part in creating programs that run well and are easy to maintain.

Practical C Programming teaches you not only the mechanics of programming, but also how to create programs that are easy to read, debug, and maintain. This third edition introduces popular Integrated Development Environments on Windows systems, as well as UNIX programming utilities, and features a large statistics-generating program to pull together the concepts and features in the language.

Checking C Programs with lint

By Ian F. Darwin
1st Edition October 1988
84 pages, ISBN 0-937175-30-7

The *lint* program checker has proven time and again to be one of the best tools for finding portability problems and certain types of coding errors in C programs. *lint* verifies a program or program segments against standard libraries, checks the code for common portability errors, and tests the programming against some tried and true guidelines. *linting* your code is a necessary (though not sufficient) step in writing clean, portable, effective programs. This book introduces you to *lint*, guides you through running it on your programs, and helps you interpret *lint*'s output.

Windows Programming

Developing Windows Error Messages

By Ben Ezzell
1st Edition March 1998
254 pages, Includes CD-ROM
ISBN 1-56592-356-1

This book teaches C, C++, and Visual Basic programmers how to write effective error messages that notify the user of an error, clearly explain the error, and most important, offer a solution. The book also discusses methods for preventing and trapping errors before they occur and tells how to create flexible input and response routines to keep unnecessary errors from happening.

Inside the Windows 95 File System

By Stan Mitchell
1st Edition May 1997
378 pages, Includes diskette
ISBN 1-56592-200-X

In this book, Stan Mitchell describes the Windows 95 File System, as well as the new opportunities and challenges it brings for developers. Its "hands-on" approach will help developers become better equipped to make design decisions using the new Win95 File System features. Includes a diskette containing MULTIMON, a general-purpose monitor for examining Windows internals.

Win32 Multithreaded Programming

By Aaron Cohen & Mike Woodring
1st Edition December 1997
724 pages, Includes CD-ROM
ISBN 1-56592-296-4

This book clearly explains the concepts of multithreaded programs and shows developers how to construct efficient and complex applications. An important book for any developer, it illustrates all aspects of Win32 multithreaded programming, including what has previously been undocumented or poorly explained.

Access Database Design & Programming

By Steven Roman
1st Edition June 1997
270 pages, ISBN 1-56592-297-2

This book provides experienced Access users who are novice programers with frequently overlooked concepts and techniques necessary to create effective database applications. It focuses on designing effective tables in a multi-table application; using the Access interface or Access SQL to construct queries; and programming using the Data Access Object (DAO) and Microsoft Access object models.

VB & VBA in a Nutshell: The Languages

By Paul Lomax
1st Edition October 1998 (est.)
552 pages (est.), ISBN 1-56592-358-8

For Visual Basic and VBA programmers, this book boils down the essentials of the VB and VBA languages into a single volume, including undocumented and little documented areas essential to everyday programming. The convenient alphabetical reference to all functions, procedures, statements, and keywords allows VB and VBA programmers to use this book both as a standard reference guide to the language and as a tool for troubleshooting and identifying programming problems.

Windows NT File System Internals

By Rajeev Nagar
1st Edition September 1997
794 pages, Includes diskette
ISBN 1-56592-249-2

Windows NT File System Internals presents the details of the NT I/O Manager, the Cache Manager, and the Memory Manager from the perspective of a software developer writing a file system driver or implementing a kernel-mode filter driver. The book provides numerous code examples included on diskette, as well as the source for a complete, usable filter driver.

O'REILLY™

TO ORDER: **800-998-9938** • **order@oreilly.com** • **http://www.oreilly.com/**
OUR PRODUCTS ARE AVAILABLE AT A BOOKSTORE OR SOFTWARE STORE NEAR YOU.
FOR INFORMATION: **800-998-9938** • **707-829-0515** • **info@oreilly.com**

Windows Programming

Inside the Windows 95 Registry

By Ron Petrusha
1st Edition August 1996
594 pages, Includes diskette
ISBN 1-56592-170-4

An in-depth examination of remote registry access, differences between theWin95 and NT registries, registry backup, undocumented registry services, and the role the registry plays in OLE. Shows programmers how to access the Win95 registry from Win32, Win16, and DOS programs in C and Visual Basic. VxD sample code is also included. Includes diskette.

Windows 95 in a Nutshell

By Tim O'Reilly & Troy Mott
1st Edition June 1998
528 pages, ISBN 1-56592-316-2

This book systematically unveils the Windows 95 operating system and allows the user to modify any aspect of it, using the Command Line from the DOS or Run prompt, the Explorer, the Registry, the Control Panel, or any other tool or application that exists in Windows 95.

Learning VBScript

By Paul Lomax
1st Edition July 1997
616 pages, includes CD-ROM
ISBN 1-56592-247-6

This definitive guide shows web developers how to take full advantage of client-side scripting with the VBScript language. In addition to basic language features, it covers the Internet Explorer object model and discusses techniques for client-side scripting, like adding ActiveX controls to a web page or validating data before sending it to the server. Includes CD-ROM with over 170 code samples.

UNIX Programming

UNIX Systems Programming for SVR4

By David A. Curry
1st Edition July 1996
620 pages, ISBN 1-56592-163-1

Presents a comprehensive look at the nitty gritty details on how UNIX interacts with applications. If you're writing an application from scratch, or if you're porting an application to any System V.4 platform, you need this book. It thoroughly explains all UNIX system calls and library routines related to systems programming, working with I/O, files and directories, processing multiple input streams, file and record locking, and memory-mapped files.

Programming with curses

By John Strang
1st Edition 1986
78 pages, ISBN 0-937175-02-1

curses is a UNIX library of functions for controlling a terminal's display screen from a C program. This handbook helps you make use of the curses library. Describes the original Berkeley version of curses.

Pthreads Programming

By Bradford Nichols, Dick Buttlar &
Jacqueline Proulx Farrell
1st Edition September 1996
284 pages, ISBN 1-56592-115-1

POSIX threads, or pthreads, allow multiple tasks to run concurrently within the same program. This book discusses when to use threads and how to make them efficient. It features realistic examples, a look behind the scenes at the implementation and performance issues, and special topics such as DCE and real-time extensions.

O'REILLY™

TO ORDER: **800-998-9938** • *order@oreilly.com* • *http://www.oreilly.com/*
OUR PRODUCTS ARE AVAILABLE AT A BOOKSTORE OR SOFTWARE STORE NEAR YOU.
FOR INFORMATION: **800-998-9938** • **707-829-0515** • *info@oreilly.com*

UNIX Programming

Programming Python

By Mark Lutz
1st Edition October 1996
906 pages, ISBN 1-56592-197-6

Programming Python describes how to use Python, an increasingly popular object-oriented scripting language. This book, full of running examples, is the most comprehensive user material available on Python. It's endorsed by Python creator Guido van Rossum and complements reference materials that accompany the software. Includes CD-ROM with Python software for all major UNIX platforms, as well as Windows, NT, and the Mac.

POSIX Programmer's Guide

By Donald Lewine
1st Edition April 1991
640 pages, ISBN 0-937175-73-0

Most UNIX systems today are POSIX compliant because the federal government requires it for its purchases. Given the manufacturer's documentation, however, it can be difficult to distinguish system-specific features from those features defined by POSIX. The *POSIX Programmer's Guide*, intended as an explanation of the POSIX standard and as a reference for the POSIX.1 programming library, helps you write more portable programs.

Power Programming with RPC

By John Bloomer
1st Edition February 1992
522 pages, ISBN 0-937175-77-3

RPC (Remote Procedure Calling) is the ability to distribute the execution of functions on remote computers. Written from a programmer's perspective, this book shows what you can do with RPCs, like Sun RPC, the de facto standard on UNIX systems. It covers related programming topics for Sun and other UNIX systems and teaches through examples.

POSIX.4

By Bill O. Gallmeister
1st Edition January 1995
568 pages, ISBN 1-56592-074-0

A general introduction to real-time programming and real-time issues, this book covers the POSIX.4 standard and how to use it to solve "real-world" problems. If you're at all interested in real-time applications—which include just about everything from telemetry to transaction processing—this book is for you. An essential reference.

How to stay in touch with O'Reilly

1. Visit Our Award-Winning Web Site

http://www.oreilly.com/

★ "Top 100 Sites on the Web" —*PC Magazine*
★ "Top 5% Web sites" —*Point Communications*
★ "3-Star site" —*The McKinley Group*

Our web site contains a library of comprehensive product information (including book excerpts and tables of contents), downloadable software, background articles, interviews with technology leaders, links to relevant sites, book cover art, and more. File us in your Bookmarks or Hotlist!

2. Join Our Email Mailing Lists

New Product Releases

To receive automatic email with brief descriptions of all new O'Reilly products as they are released, send email to:
listproc@online.oreilly.com
Put the following information in the first line of your message (*not* in the Subject field):
subscribe oreilly-news

O'Reilly Events

If you'd also like us to send information about trade show events, special promotions, and other O'Reilly events, send email to:
listproc@online.oreilly.com
Put the following information in the first line of your message (*not* in the Subject field):
subscribe oreilly-events

3. Get Examples from Our Books via FTP

There are two ways to access an archive of example files from our books:

Regular FTP
- ftp to:
  ftp.oreilly.com
  (login: anonymous
  password: your email address)
- Point your web browser to:
  ftp://ftp.oreilly.com/

FTPMAIL
- Send an email message to:
  ftpmail@online.oreilly.com
  (Write "help" in the message body)

4. Contact Us via Email

order@oreilly.com
To place a book or software order online. Good for North American and international customers.

subscriptions@oreilly.com
To place an order for any of our newsletters or periodicals.

books@oreilly.com
General questions about any of our books.

software@oreilly.com
For general questions and product information about our software. Check out O'Reilly Software Online at **http://software.oreilly.com/** for software and technical support information. Registered O'Reilly software users send your questions to: **website-support@oreilly.com**

cs@oreilly.com
For answers to problems regarding your order or our products.

booktech@oreilly.com
For book content technical questions or corrections.

proposals@oreilly.com
To submit new book or software proposals to our editors and product managers.

international@oreilly.com
For information about our international distributors or translation queries. For a list of our distributors outside of North America check out:
http://www.oreilly.com/www/order/country.html

O'Reilly & Associates, Inc.
101 Morris Street, Sebastopol, CA 95472 USA
TEL 707-829-0515 or 800-998-9938
     (6am to 5pm PST)
FAX 707-829-0104

International Distributors

UK, EUROPE, MIDDLE EAST AND NORTHERN AFRICA (EXCEPT FRANCE, GERMANY, SWITZERLAND, & AUSTRIA)

INQUIRIES
International Thomson Publishing Europe
Berkshire House
168-173 High Holborn
London WC1V 7AA
United Kingdom
Telephone: 44-171-497-1422
Fax: 44-171-497-1426
Email: itpint@itps.co.uk

ORDERS
International Thomson Publishing Services, Ltd.
Cheriton House, North Way
Andover, Hampshire SP10 5BE
United Kingdom
Telephone: 44-264-342-832 (UK)
Telephone: 44-264-342-806 (outside UK)
Fax: 44-264-364418 (UK)
Fax: 44-264-342761 (outside UK)
UK & Eire orders: itpuk@itps.co.uk
International orders: itpint@itps.co.uk

FRANCE

Editions Eyrolles
61 bd Saint-Germain
75240 Paris Cedex 05
France
Fax: 33-01-44-41-11-44

FRENCH LANGUAGE BOOKS
All countries except Canada
Telephone: 33-01-44-41-46-16
Email: geodif@eyrolles.com
English language books
Telephone: 33-01-44-41-11-87
Email: distribution@eyrolles.com

GERMANY, SWITZERLAND, AND AUSTRIA

INQUIRIES
O'Reilly Verlag
Balthasarstr. 81
D-50670 Köln
Germany
Telephone: 49-221-97-31-60-0
Fax: 49-221-97-31-60-8
Email: anfragen@oreilly.de

ORDERS
International Thomson Publishing
Königswinterer Straße 418
53227 Bonn, Germany
Telephone: 49-228-97024 0
Fax: 49-228-441342
Email: order@oreilly.de

JAPAN

O'Reilly Japan, Inc.
Kiyoshige Building 2F
12-Banchi, Sanei-cho
Shinjuku-ku
Tokyo 160-0008 Japan
Telephone: 81-3-3356-5227
Fax: 81-3-3356-5261
Email: kenji@oreilly.com

INDIA

Computer Bookshop (India) PVT. Ltd.
190 Dr. D.N. Road, Fort
Bombay 400 001 India
Telephone: 91-22-207-0989
Fax: 91-22-262-3551
Email: cbsbom@giasbm01.vsnl.net.in

HONG KONG

City Discount Subscription Service Ltd.
Unit D, 3rd Floor, Yan's Tower
27 Wong Chuk Hang Road
Aberdeen, Hong Kong
Telephone: 852-2580-3539
Fax: 852-2580-6463
Email: citydis@ppn.com.hk

KOREA

Hanbit Media, Inc.
Sonyoung Bldg. 202
Yeksam-dong 736-36
Kangnam-ku
Seoul, Korea
Telephone: 822-554-9610
Fax: 822-556-0363
Email: hant93@chollian.dacom.co.kr

SINGAPORE, MALAYSIA, AND THAILAND

Addison Wesley Longman Singapore PTE Ltd.
25 First Lok Yang Road
Singapore 629734
Telephone: 65-268-2666
Fax: 65-268-7023
Email: daniel@longman.com.sg

PHILIPPINES

Mutual Books, Inc.
429-D Shaw Boulevard
Mandaluyong City, Metro
Manila, Philippines
Telephone: 632-725-7538
Fax: 632-721-3056
Email: mbikikog@mnl.sequel.net

CHINA

Ron's DataCom Co., Ltd.
79 Dongwu Avenue
Dongxihu District
Wuhan 430040
China
Telephone: 86-27-83892568
Fax: 86-27-83222108
Email: hongfeng@public.wh.hb.cn

ALL OTHER ASIAN COUNTRIES

O'Reilly & Associates, Inc.
101 Morris Street
Sebastopol, CA 95472 USA
Telephone: 707-829-0515
Fax: 707-829-0104
Email: order@oreilly.com

AUSTRALIA

WoodsLane Pty. Ltd.
7/5 Vuko Place, Warriewood NSW 2102
P.O. Box 935
Mona Vale NSW 2103
Australia
Telephone: 61-2-9970-5111
Fax: 61-2-9970-5002
Email: info@woodslane.com.au

NEW ZEALAND

Woodslane New Zealand Ltd.
21 Cooks Street (P.O. Box 575)
Waganui, New Zealand
Telephone: 64-6-347-6543
Fax: 64-6-345-4840
Email: info@woodslane.com.au

THE AMERICAS

McGraw-Hill Interamericana Editores, S.A. de C.V.
Cedro No. 512
Col. Atlampa 06450
Mexico, D.F.
Telephone: 52-5-541-3155
Fax: 52-5-541-4913
Email: mcgraw-hill@infosel.net.mx

SOUTH AFRICA

International Thomson Publishing
South Africa
Building 18, Constantia Park
138 Sixteenth Road
P.O. Box 2459
Halfway House, 1685 South Africa
Telephone: 27-11-805-4819
Fax: 27-11-805-3648

O'REILLY™

TO ORDER: **800-998-9938** • **order@oreilly.com** • **http://www.oreilly.com/**
OUR PRODUCTS ARE AVAILABLE AT A BOOKSTORE OR SOFTWARE STORE NEAR YOU.
FOR INFORMATION: **800-998-9938** • **707-829-0515** • **info@oreilly.com**